Probate and the
Administration of Estates:
The Law and Practice

CALLOW PUBLISHING

Probate and the Administration of Estates: The Law and Practice

by Emma Gaudern and A K Biggs

London
Callow Publishing
2003

ISBN 1 898899 65 7

First published 2003

Printed and bound in Great Britain by MPG Books Ltd, Bodmin.

Published by Callow Publishing Limited,
4 Shillingford Street, London N1 2DP
www.callowpublishing.com

Preface

Probate continues to represent a substantial proportion of the work of many law practices. The purpose of this new book is provide practitioners with an account of the law and practice relating to non-contentious probate and the administration of estates, from the first meeting with the client to the final distribution of the estate. Thus, we have described the processes of tracing and valuing the assets; calculating and paying inheritance tax, claiming any relevant reliefs and allowances; searching for a Will and establishing its validity; entitlement on intestacy; applying for a grant of probate, letters of administration (with Will annexed) or letters of administration; collecting in the assets; taxation during the administration; paying the estate debts and legacies; and finally distributing the residue.

Also covered are interim matters such as caveats, citations and renunciations and discretionary orders; applications on summons; deeds of variation, disclaimers and claims by and against the estate.

The powers, duties and liabilities of personal representatives are dealt with; where appropriate, "executors" and "administrators" are referred as such, but where permissible the generic term of "personal representative" is used.

Appendix C contains a range of specimen forms which can be adapted for use according to the circumstances of individual cases.

We have adopted what we believe to be a practical approach to this important subject, with hints and reminders drawn from our experience.

The law is up to date to 30 April 2003.

Emma Gaudern, Manchester
A K Biggs, Winchester
April 2003

Contents

Contents

Table of Cases

Table of Legislation

Chapter 1

Making a Start

A legal adviser often first hears of a death in a telephone call from a member of the deceased's family. If the legal adviser is to act in relation to the estate, a first meeting should be arranged. The legal adviser should check whether the firm holds a Will for the deceased. If so, it should be retrieved from storage before the meeting, together with any other deeds held on behalf of the deceased. Old files of papers may also prove useful.

The First Meeting
The initial meeting between client and legal adviser varies greatly from estate to estate. Much depends on who are to be the personal representatives: if the spouse or children of the deceased are to be the personal representatives, the first meeting may well be emotionally charged, but this is less likely if the personal representatives are to be professional people.

The capacity of the client
Where a solicitor is acting in the administration of an estate, his clients are the personal representatives in their capacity as such. The expression "personal representatives" covers both executors and administrators – the people who will take out the grant of probate or letters of administration. Often, individuals may have a number of different capacities. Consider the situation where the deceased left a wife, whom he named to act as executrix of his estate, and they had a child, who received the entirety of his estate under the Will. The client is the wife in her capacity as executrix, but she is also a grieving widow, a potential claimant against the estate (because of the lack of provision made for her), and a mother concerned to act in the best interests of her child. It is the solicitor's task to help her separate out those roles and ensure that her actions as personal representative are properly carried out in that capacity.

The first meeting may not always be with the client. If professionals are instructed to deal with the estate administration, it may be productive to arrange initial discussions with the family members of the deceased, who are likely to have more information about the conduct of the deceased's affairs and about his assets.

Collation of information

There is often much information to be garnered at the first meeting. It is suggested that the most effective method of ensuring that all necessary topics have been covered is to use a questionnaire. A sample questionnaire is included at Appendix A. There is a broad range of topics that must be discussed, but these can be broken down into four main categories.

Family: All possible details of the deceased's family, including any spouse or partner, together with ex-spouses or partners; children (legitimate, illegitimate, legitimated and adopted), brothers and sisters, nieces and nephews, and parents should be obtained. A useful summary of the list of people to be discussed may be taken from the Inheritance (Provision for Family and Dependants) Act 1975, section 1(1). This lists the categories of people who may make a claim against the estate of a deceased. It is useful to establish who falls into these categories, and whether any of them may have any cause to make a claim against the estate.

All the children mentioned above – legitimate, illegitimate, legitimated and adopted – are treated as children of the deceased or of any beneficiary of his estate, under sections 1 and 19 of the Family Law Reform Act 1987, unless they are specifically excluded by the deceased's Will.

Assets: All assets which the deceased held in his name should be identified. The capacity in which he held them must also be established – for example, he may have held property as a trustee or it may belong to the deceased beneficially. Were assets held jointly with anyone else, and if so did the owners hold the assets as joint tenants or tenants-in-common? This establishes whether they pass under the Will/intestacy or by survivorship. Was the deceased a beneficiary of any trust, and if so what was his entitlement under it? Will there be any other assets or payments falling into the estate as a result of the deceased's death, to which he was not entitled during his lifetime (for example, death benefit under a work-related life assurance scheme)?

Will or intestacy: Did the deceased leave a Will, and if so is it valid on the face of it? Can the personal representatives be sure they have the last Will (see page 7 as to the checks that should be made)? Did the Will appoint executors, and are they all still alive and willing and able to act as such? If none is willing or able to act, or if there was no Will, who is to act as administrators? It is important to consider who is most suitable for this role. For example, if the deceased died leaving all his assets to his minor child by his Will, but he is also survived by a spouse who is the mother of the child, to whom he left nothing, then although the spouse would normally be the first choice to act as administratrix, to do so could prejudice her relationship with the child. In such circumstances it may be wise to seek an alternative administrator.

Other matters: There are often various miscellaneous issues, some of which can be disposed of quickly and some of which may require more thought. For example, are there any foreign issues? Was the deceased domiciled in any other country, or did he own assets there? For a more detailed discussion of such issues, see page 41.

If the deceased and his spouse or partner died together, for example in a car crash, it is important to establish the order in which they died. Section 184, Law of Property Act 1925 states that if two people die in circumstances in which the order of death cannot be ascertained, the younger is deemed to have survived the elder for the purposes of administering the estate. This is known as the principle of *commorientes*. The rule is modified in relation to inheritance tax as sections 4(2) and 54(4) Inheritance Tax Act 1984 state that for inheritance tax purposes the couple are treated as though they died at the same instant. Also, section 1(1) of the Law Reform (Succession) Act 1995 states that for a surviving spouse to take an interest under the estate of his or her deceased spouse who dies intestate, that spouse must survive the deceased by 28 days.

Urgent Steps

Often, members of the deceased's family deal with many of the immediate issues that arise upon a person's death without professional help. But where the deceased had no family, these matters may have to be overseen by the personal representatives. It should be made clear to the beneficiaries of the estate, before a professional person is instructed to take on the tasks in question, that they may be time-consuming and will increase the cost of dealing with the estate.

Registration of the death
The requirements for registering a death are contained in the Births and Deaths Registration Act 1953 and the Registration of Births and Deaths Regulations 1987 (SI 1987 No 2088) as amended. A relative often registers the death with the Registrar of Deaths. The persons responsible for registering a death are:
- those present at the death;
- the occupier of the house where the death occurred;
- any person living in the house who was aware of the death; or
- the person arranging disposal of the body (not the funeral director).

For these purposes, a "house" includes a prison, hospital and a nursing home, where the "occupier" is the governor or matron.

The death must be registered within five days of the death or of the finding of the body. This may be extended to fourteen days if the registrar, within five days, receives a written notice that a doctor has signed a certificate regarding the cause of death.

The relevant registrar is the registrar for the sub-district in which the death occurred or the body was found.

The information and papers required to register the death are:
- a certificate of death signed by a doctor; and
- the deceased's medical card (where possible); and
- the deceased's date and place of birth (obtained from his birth certificate); and
- the deceased's full name, occupation, address and marital status; and
- the widow(er)'s name and occupation.

On registration of the death, the registrar issues a certificate for burial or cremation (which will be required by the funeral director), and a Department of Social Security certificate that can be used to claim any arrears of benefits to which the deceased was entitled.

The death certificate is also produced. The registrar retains the original, and certified copies can be obtained upon payment of, currently, £3.50 per copy. Certified copies are available directly from the registrar for a period of one year, to anyone who applies, upon payment of the correct amount. After the expiry of that year, application must be made to the Superintendent Registrar at the General Register Office (see Appendix B for the address). In both cases, the information required to obtain a copy death certificate is the deceased's name, and the place and date of death.

If the deceased died abroad and the death was registered with the British Consul or the High Commissioner to the country in question, a certified copy of the death certificate can be obtained from the Overseas Registration Service of the General Register Office.

If an inquest is being held, the issue of a death certificate will be delayed until the inquest is over. To allow the body to be disposed of before the inquest, the coroner can issue a certificate allowing burial, as an alternative to the burial or cremation certificate usually issued by the registrar.

If the deceased was in the armed forces, the Ministry of Defence issues a certificate of notification of death or of presumption of death, instead of a death certificate. If he was a merchant seaman, the Registrar General of Shipping and Seamen produces a certificate or evidence of death.

If there is no death certificate, or if there is doubt about the sufficiency of the certificate, or if there is no direct evidence of the death, but there is sufficient circumstantial evidence to lead to a presumption of death, a decree of presumption of death and dissolution of marriage can be given under section 19, Matrimonial Causes Act 1973. This is not enough in itself to obtain a death certificate, but the person wishing to take out the grant may apply for leave to swear the death. The application is made on an *ex parte* basis to the probate registry (see page 125).

The funeral

The deceased's funeral must be organised. If there is a Will, it should be checked to see whether any wishes were made evident in it. There is no right of property in a body (not even in one's own), and therefore a declaration as to funeral wishes can never be binding; nor does any particular party or family member have any greater right than any other to decide how the funeral ought to be conducted.

The deceased may have purchased a pre-payment plan to cover the costs of the funeral. Reasonable funeral expenses are payable out of the deceased's estate. The Will may expressly authorise the costs of an elaborate funeral. If not, the personal representatives or other organiser of such a funeral may become personally liable for the cost unless the residuary beneficiaries of the estate specifically approve it. If the personal representatives are in any doubt, they should ask the beneficiaries for specific authorisation before any costs are incurred or paid.

If the deceased was receiving State benefits at the time of his death, and the assets in his estate are not sufficient to cover the cost of a funeral, the Department of Social Security may make a grant to pay for the funeral.

Insurance

The deceased's property and chattels must continue to be properly insured. The insurance company should be notified of the death so that it can update its records. Insurance documents should be checked for the date of expiry, which must not be overlooked. Sufficient funds may not be available at the date of renewal to meet the premiums, for example because the grant has not been received and the family is unwilling or unable to pay. It is suggested that a solicitor acting on behalf of the personal representatives should meet the premium out of office account and claim a reimbursement later, rather than leave the premium unpaid and risk a claim for negligence. Since the commencement of the Trustee Act 2000, personal representatives have been authorised under section 19 of the Trustee Act 1925 (as amended) to insure assets in an estate to their full value and against any risk. While the personal representatives (or the solicitor acting as their agent) should not have to carry out actions which it is unreasonable for them to undertake, if it is plain on the face of the insurance policy that assets are not insured to their full value, then, to avoid criticism, the personal representatives should discuss with the beneficiaries whether the insurance cover for those assets should be increased.

Particular care is needed in relation to chattels. The insurance policy may specify that certain chattels must be removed from the deceased's home if it is to remain empty. In any event, the home should be secured and the fact that it is unoccupied should be made as inconspicuous as possible, by, for example, cancelling newspaper and milk deliveries. Regular visits may have to be made to the home to check on the chattels remaining there; if no one else is willing or able to attend to these matters, the personal representatives must oversee them. The personal representatives should also be careful to secure all relevant documents or books of title.

If an item is specifically bequeathed to a beneficiary under the Will, the beneficiary must pay for storing and insuring that item. The personal representatives should liaise with him as to the best method of dealing with that asset as quickly as possible.

Duty to prevent loss

The personal representatives have a duty to ensure that no loss is caused to the estate. Thus, they must give notice of the death to the other party to any contract which the deceased made and which continues to exist, and arrange to terminate it. Examples of such contracts are tenancy agreements and contracts for digital television service. Any items rented by the deceased should be returned to the owners as soon as possible to stop rent accruing; hire purchase providers should be notified and any outstanding liability calculated. Banks and credit card companies should be made aware of the death and standing orders or direct debits should be cancelled. If the deceased was acting as guarantor in relation to another party's debt, the creditor must be informed as soon as possible. If not, the estate may be held responsible for any default by the borrower under the credit agreement.

Firearms

If the deceased was the owner of any firearms the police should be informed. They will decide how any firearm should be disposed of and set a time limit within which that must be done. Depending on the weapon, the time may be as short as twenty-four hours, so the personal representatives must be prepared to act swiftly.

Urgent grants

The personal representatives must consider whether there is any matter which can be dealt with only after the issue of a grant of representation, but which must be urgently attended to. For example, is the limitation period about to expire on any claim that could be brought by the estate, or did the deceased contract to buy or sell real property but die before completion of the transaction? The authority of an executor stems from the Will, and therefore an executor has authority to deal with the deceased's affairs from the date of death onwards. The grant of probate merely serves to confirm this authority. In some situations an executor may therefore be able to proceed and deal with some issues before a grant is issued. If the exchange of contracts for the sale of a property is urgently required the executor is able to sign the contract, but it is unlikely that the purchaser's solicitor will be willing to complete before a grant is issued. On first reading this appears to be an advantage, but executors must be wary of entering into a situation whereby they will be contractually bound to convey a property in respect of which they have no proof of title. It may be sensible to apply for an urgent grant of representation to deal with a particular matter. This is covered in more detail at page 135.

If there is no Will, if the executor named does not have the power to take a grant of probate, or if he becomes unable to do so before taking the grant, the assets in the estate vest in the Public Trustee under section 9, Administration of Estates Act 1925 until a grant is given. Afterwards, the authority is retrospective to the date of death, so that an administrator can confirm actions undertaken earlier.

Advertisements

The safeguarding of the personal representatives, and the advertisements they should place to protect themselves from personal liability to creditors, are discussed at page 256. Since two months must elapse between the advertisement and the distribution of the estate, the advertisements should be placed as soon as possible to allow the personal representatives to distribute the estate quickly.

Tracing the Last Will

A key point to establish at the outset is whether the deceased left a Will; and, if so, whether the Will in the personal representatives' possession is the last one he made. If the solicitor acting in the administration also acted for the deceased in a personal capacity in the period ending with his death, this may be easily done. If not, the deceased's professional advisers and his bankers should be approached to find out what they know. A solicitor or other professional adviser has no right of lien over a Will or codicil in respect of unpaid charges.

The deceased may have deposited his Will with the Principal Registry, so a search there should be made. Advertisements can also be placed in the Law Society's *Gazette*.

If it is believed that a person has information regarding the existence of a Will or codicil, which they are refusing to impart, an order can be obtained under rule 50 of the Non-Contentious Probate Rules 1987 (SI 1987 No 2024) (by application under section 122 or 123, Supreme Court Act 1981) for that person to be examined in court or to bring the Will or codicil to court; see page 182.

Even if the personal representatives are reasonably sure that they have the final Will, they must still consider the possibility that the testator may have executed codicil(s), and ensure they are in possession of all such documents as have not been revoked.

Non-Urgent Matters

Often, the personal representatives are under pressure from the beneficiaries of the estate to distribute assets as soon as possible. While a personal representative has a duty to act swiftly and efficiently, he should also be mindful of his duties to creditors, and the obligation to distribute the estate properly. Bearing this in mind, a personal representative should not allow himself to be persuaded to make distributions prematurely, or which may leave him with insufficient assets to discharge debts, even if further assets may fall into the estate later. For example, the deceased leaves a sum of money, a portfolio of shares and a house; the beneficiaries may request that the cash is distributed to them immediately, and that the debts of the estate are discharged once the shares and the house are sold. The values of the house and the shares cannot, however, be certain, and it is suggested that nothing should be distributed until the quantum of debts has been finalised and the two-month period mentioned above has elapsed. In addition, some or all of the shares, and the house, should be sold to cover the debts in full, and the sale proceeds received, before the cash is distributed. While a distribution could be made if urgent, with the beneficiary giving an indemnity to repay the distribution if it later becomes evident that the estate requires it, the personal representative risks becoming personally liable if the beneficiary no longer has the funds with which to repay the distribution.

Avoiding Delay

One of the main criticisms levied at personal representatives when administering an estate is that they are too slow in dealing with matters. To some extent, delay is unavoidable – it is rare that beneficiaries appreciate the delays which can arise in liaising with the Inland Revenue, or that a distribution should not be made within six months of obtaining the grant if allowance is to be made for possible claims against the estate under the Inheritance (Provision for Family and Dependants) Act 1975. These are, however, all matters that can be explained to the beneficiaries and it is wise for personal representatives to do so, so that the beneficiaries have a realistic expectation of when distributions are likely to be made.

Another major cause of delay is that many personal representatives tend to be *reactive* rather than *proactive*. Some tips on how to avoid delay are set out below.

Valuations

When seeking to establish the value of the estate, the personal representatives write to various institutions about assets held by them on behalf of the deceased. Many of these institutions are large and it is inevitable that paperwork is sometimes mislaid. It is suggested that the personal representatives should review the letters they have written every two weeks. Any organisation which has not responded should be reminded, by another letter or a telephone call. Waiting for a response to a letter that did not reach the correct destination in the first place can waste much time.

Repaying an inheritance tax loan

Delay in repaying a commercial loan taken out to pay inheritance tax can be expensive. Such loans always carry interest, and the more time that elapses before the loan is repaid, the more interest will be due. If such a loan is taken out, it is advisable for the personal representatives to prepare all the necessary forms to encash sufficient assets to repay the loan and interest in full, while the probate application is being processed. The forms should be signed by the personal representatives during that time, so that they can be sent off immediately upon receipt of the grant. In particular, if shares are to be encashed it is wise to check at the outset that all the share certificates are in the possession of the personal representatives. If any have been lost, an indemnity must be signed, and may need to be guaranteed by a bank; this should be prepared in advance where possible.

Checking the Assets

In many first meetings reams of paper are produced – receipts, old building society passbooks, correspondence regarding life assurance policies – the list is endless. While the ideal situation would be that these papers all relate to easily identifiable, current, assets, in reality this is unlikely to be the case. The personal representatives must read through all the details supplied and investigate anything that may indicate an asset exists. Particularly difficult can be old life assurance documents. Life assurance companies have merged and been taken over so many times that it may be difficult to trace whether old policies are still in force, or to identify the company with which they are now held. The Association of British Insurers (see Appendix B for the address) is usually very helpful and a call to their telephone helpline generally elicits the current identity of a company which appears no longer to exist, as well as contact details for that company.

Some Pitfalls

It is all too easy, when presented with a grieving spouse and children, to make assumptions about the family situation and to feel uneasy about asking awkward questions. But if the Will of a deceased leaves a gift to "my children", that includes illegitimate children, but not step-children (sections 1 and 19(1), Family Law Reform Act 1987) unless the Will states to the contrary. It is important to establish the exact identity and relationship to the deceased of each beneficiary.

In relation to items specifically bequeathed, a Will speaks from the date upon which it was written. If an asset is specifically gifted in a Will, the solicitor must ensure that it is the same asset as that comprised in the deceased's estate upon his death. For example, if the deceased gifted "my car" to his son, that gift is effective only if the car owned by the deceased at the time the Will was made was still his car when he died. If the gift was of "such car as I shall own at the date of my death", it takes effect as the car owned by the deceased when he died. The Will should always be read carefully for traps such as these and unclear matters must be resolved. These issues are discussed in more detail in Chapter 18.

Communicating with Beneficiaries

The beneficiaries should be kept fully informed of the progress of the administration. It is far easier to send out a letter giving a summary of the up-to-date position than to receive an irate telephone call from a beneficiary who feels he is being kept in the dark.

In addition, the beneficiaries will have to make decisions about the administration of the estate. If there is inheritance tax to be paid, the beneficiaries may wish to lend funds to the estate to pay it, rather than take out a commercial loan and incur interest charges. They should also be consulted as to whether assets should be sold or appropriated to the beneficiaries *in specie*.

By raising these issues early, and giving the beneficiaries time to consider them, the personal representatives will be able to progress the administration of the estate as swiftly as possible.

Assets for which a Grant is not Required

Some assets can be received before a grant is issued, either because they do not form part of the deceased's estate for the purposes of the grant and as such are not dealt with by the grant; or because it is possible to realise them without the production of a grant, notwithstanding that they do form part of his estate. These assets are described below.

Life assurance policies written into trust

Life assurance policies written into trust do not form part of the deceased's estate for the purposes of the grant and can be encashed by the surviving trustees. If the deceased was the sole surviving trustee his personal representatives have power to appoint new trustees, but the life assurance company may allow them to encash the policy themselves without appointing new trustees.

Death benefit payable under a pension scheme

Trustees of company pension schemes often reserve to themselves the right to decide how the death benefit payable under the scheme should pass. If this is the case, the trustees generally pay it to the persons they select without sight of a grant.

If the pension scheme is personal, or a retirement annuity contract, the death benefit usually passes automatically to the deceased's estate if it was not written into trust. In that case, a grant will have to be obtained before the benefit can be paid. But if the death benefit was written into trust, it is transferred to the trustees once they have produced evidence of the death. Having said this, though, many personal pension providers have begun to draw up policies which reserve to themselves the right to decide to whom the death benefit will be paid; if so, the death benefit should be paid without sight of a grant.

Joint assets

If the deceased owned an asset in joint names with another person the legal title to that asset always passes to the other person automatically. How the *beneficial* ownership passes depends on how the asset was held. There are two methods of holding the beneficial interest in an asset jointly – as joint tenants, or as tenants-in-common. If an asset was held as joint tenants the beneficial interest automatically passes to the co-owner upon the deceased's death. Joint tenants do not own identifiable "shares" in an asset and therefore cannot own that asset in any manner other than equally between them. tenants-in-common can own an asset in varying proportions. The portion owned by the deceased passes under his Will or intestacy, not to his surviving co-owner. See page 189 for how to transfer the beneficial ownership in a jointly held asset.

Nominated assets

Some National Savings products and building society accounts can be dealt with by a nomination rather than under the deceased's Will or intestacy. To do this, the deceased must have completed a form of nomination indicating how the asset should pass after his death.

Assets held in bare trust

If a third party held assets as nominee for the deceased, the nominee is known as a bare trustee. The assets subject to the bare trust form part of the deceased's estate and are dealt with under his Will or intestacy. As legal title to the asset was not vested in the deceased, a grant does not need to be produced for the asset to be realised.

Assets of low value

Under the Administration of Estates (Small Payments) Act 1965 any asset worth less than £5,000 can, at the discretion of the asset holder, be paid out without a grant. This is particularly useful for bank and building society accounts as well as National Savings products.

Funds valued at less than £5,000 belonging to a deceased who died intestate and which are held in court can be paid out to anyone who appears to be entitled to them, under the Civil Procedure Rules 1998 (SI 1998 No 3132), Part 36.

The outstanding salary of a public servant employed by a government department, a member of Her Majesty's Forces, merchant seamen and Members of Parliament can be paid without sight of a grant.

On the other hand, banks, and sometimes other institutions, may require the personal representatives to complete an undertaking, and possibly also to sign an indemnity, that the funds are properly payable. In this case, it may be cheaper and quicker for a grant to be extracted, particularly if this would be necessary in any event.

Chattels

Documentation confirming the ownership of chattels rarely exists, and title to them can therefore pass by delivery. If the chattels are of low value and the personal representatives are satisfied that they will not need recourse to the proceeds of their sale to pay tax or debts, they can often be passed to the beneficiaries named in the Will or entitled under the intestacy, or distributed in accordance with the wishes of the family. A practical approach is often the most sensible here – provided there appears to be no conflict, it is often wisest to allow assets not specifically bequeathed to be distributed by the deceased's family. The chattels should, though, always be valued for the purposes of the probate papers if a grant is to be sought. In addition, it should be agreed with the residuary beneficiaries whether the chattels received by them are to be taken into account when calculating the share of the estate each beneficiary has taken *in specie*.

Partnership assets

If the deceased was a partner in a business, the partnership agreement usually specifies what happens on the death of a partner. Often, this is that the assets pass to the surviving partners, and a formula is provided for calculating the compensation to be paid to the deceased's estate. The Partnership Act 1890 states that if no agreement is in existence, the partnership is deemed to dissolve on the date of the partner's death, and the assets are to be divided among all the partners (including the deceased) in accordance with the ratio in which they shared the partnership profits.

Donatio mortis causa

Prior to his death, the deceased may have made a gift under the doctrine of *donatio mortis causa*. This provides that where a gift is made by the deceased in contemplation of death, which was conditional upon his death, and title to the property gifted was capable of being passed via a *donatio mortis causa*, the gift was properly made and accordingly passes to the recipient of the gift outside of the deceased's Will.

Foreign Assets

Not all of the assets owned by a deceased but held in a foreign country necessarily pass under his UK Will. Initially, the UK Will should be checked to see whether it is capable of dealing with any foreign assets, or if it is limited to the testator's UK estate. If it does not cover the country in which the foreign assets are situated, enquiries should be made as to whether a Will exists to deal with the assets in that country. In any event, the personal representatives should check whether a later Will was made in the foreign country to deal specifically with the assets there. If there is no Will disposing of those assets, the rules of intestacy may apply to them, and it is usually advisable to instruct a foreign agent to deal with them. Which rules of intestacy – those of the UK or those of the foreign country – apply depends on whether the property is moveable or immovable (see below). Although a Will may not specifically deal with foreign assets, it may be the law of the country concerned to accept the Will as a proper document to pass title.

The meaning of the "situation" of property is important. Immovable property is treated as situated in the country in which it is physically present. Moveable property is treated as situated in the country in which it is registered. For the purposes of inheritance law, moveable property generally passes in accordance with the law of the country of domicile of the deceased, whereas immovable property must pass in accordance with the law of the country in which it is situated. Therefore, even if the deceased's Will purports to deal with his house in France, the French rules of heirship would override the Will to the extent that they differ from it. This is significant in relation to European countries, in particular as many of them have rules of forced heirship that provide, *inter alia,* for the deceased's children to take a fixed share of his estate upon his death.

Chapter 2

Assets and Liabilities: Initial Enquiries

Introduction

The first substantial task of the personal representatives is to ascertain and value the assets and liabilities of the estate. To do this, the personal representatives must provide the holder of each asset with an original certified copy death certificate, obtainable from the registrar on payment of a fee of £3.50. The Law Society has produced a protocol containing a standard letter and form for use in lieu of a certified copy death certificate; copies of the Protocol can be obtained from the Law Society. All asset holders, however, have the right to insist that an original certified copy of the death certificate is forwarded to them. In practice, very few institutions enforce this right, although life assurance companies generally do.

In view of the above, it is generally simpler to make the initial contact with the asset holders in writing, rather by telephone, requesting a valuation of the asset as at the date of death, and enclosing the certified copy death certificate. An asset holder needs to be able to identify the deceased on its records and find the relevant information; details of the deceased's name, address and account/reference number are usually sufficient.

While the value of the asset as at the date of death is the main information required, certain other questions, raised at the outset, will speed up matters later in the administration. Examples of queries which can usefully be raised in respect of each type of asset are given below.

Where it is clear that the value of the deceased's estate is below the inheritance tax nil rate band (£255,000 in respect of deaths on after 6 April 2003), or that it falls within the surviving spouse exemption from inheritance tax (see page 74), it may be tempting for the personal representatives to "guesstimate" the value of an asset, or to use an old valuation. For a number of reasons this should not be done:

- If it later becomes clear that the estate of the deceased is greater than originally thought and an Inland Revenue account must be filed, the personal representatives will have to go back and obtain proper values of assets. This will delay the administration and cost more than if the matter were dealt with properly in the first place.
- The personal representatives have a duty to produce proper and

accurate estate accounts. This duty is not complied with if the original information is not correct.

- The base cost for capital gains tax purposes of the assets in the hands of the personal representatives, or any beneficiary to whom an asset is assented, is the value at the date of the deceased's death. That value must be accurate, to save time later when proving the base cost to the Inland Revenue after a sale of the asset in question.

Tracing All the Assets

The personal representatives can never be sure that they have traced all the deceased's assets, but they must do everything they possibly can to do so. Generally, this means going through all the papers held by the deceased which may prove the existence of an asset. Every possibility, no matter how remote, must be followed through. Also, the deceased's family and professional advisors (particularly accountants) should be helpful in this regard.

Basis of Valuation

As will be seen below, most assets of the deceased, such as bank accounts and shares in public limited companies, have a clearly ascertainable value. Some assets, such as land and chattels, however, can be valued only on the basis of a professional opinion that cannot be objectively verified unless the assets are sold. Where that is the case, the asset must be appraised at its "open market value" (section 160, Inheritance Tax Act 1984). This cannot be reduced on the grounds that "… the property is to be placed on the market at one and the same time", but must instead be calculated on the assumption that a sale will be made between a willing buyer and a willing seller. It used to be the case that a "probate value" could be obtained and submitted as the value at the date of death. "Probate value" used to be understood to be the open market value less a discount of around ten per cent or more. IR Capital Taxes (formerly the Capital Taxes Office) has become much stricter, insisting that an open market value is used. Any documents submitted to IR Capital Taxes showing that a "probate valuation" has been prepared will be queried, and if the value submitted is shown to be lower than the open market value, a penalty may be payable (see page 76). "Probate value" in this book means full market value.

Banks

Questions to be addressed to the bank(s) at which the deceased held an account(s) include:

- How much was in the account at the date of death?
- How much interest had accrued on the account but was unpaid at the date of death? This is an asset of the estate for inheritance tax purposes.
- Does the bank hold any deeds, documents or safety deposit boxes for the deceased? If so, who may have access to them, and how?
- What standing orders and direct debits are in place? This information will help identify other potential assets and liabilities of the estate.
- Did the deceased hold any other accounts, either in his sole name or with another person?
- How much interest was paid on the deceased's account(s) for the period from 6 April to the date of death, and how much income tax was deducted? This information is required to complete the deceased's income tax return for the period from 6 April last to the date of death. In addition, if the deceased died shortly after 6 April, leaving his tax return for the previous year not completed and filed, the like details in respect of the previous tax year should be requested.
- Is the bank willing to release funds held by it to pay inheritance tax? Very often banks decline this request as they do not wish to release monies before a grant is issued.
- The bank should be asked to transfer any credit balances to any accounts having a debit balance to stop interest accruing on them, and then to transfer any outstanding credit balances to an interest-bearing account if they are in an account that does not bear interest. This ensures that the personal representatives do all they can to maximise the value of the estate.
- What formalities will be required for the personal representatives to open an account of their own for use during the administration of the estate?

Building Societies

The following questions may usefully be addressed to the appropriate building society/ies:

- How much was in the account at the date of death?
- How much interest had accrued on the account but was unpaid at the date of death?
- Did the deceased hold any other accounts, either in his sole name or with another person?
- Is the building society willing to release funds held by it to pay inheritance tax? Often building societies are more amenable to this than banks, although, for security purposes, the cheque will only ever

be drawn in favour of the Inland Revenue.

- The passbook, if there is one, should be sent to the building society with a request that it be brought up to date. An updated passbook usually shows the interest paid to the deceased from 6 April to the date of death, and the income tax deducted from it; if not, this information should be requested;
  - Any forms which the personal representatives must complete to close the account should be requested.

Building society "windfalls" paid to account holders on the demutualisation of a society form part of the deceased's estate for inheritance tax if the building society formally announced its plans to demutualise, by issuing a transfer document or prospectus, before the date of death. It may, though, be possible to discount the value of the windfall if there is uncertainty over whether it will be paid (as, for instance, where the members may not approve the demutualisation), or if a substantial delay before payment is expected. If the death occurs before the demutualisation has been approved, the discount available will be in the region of 25 – 35 per cent of the value of the windfall. If the approval has already been given, a discount of 10 – 17.5 per cent may be allowed (Inland Revenue Tax Bulletin, April 1998, p. 520).

Life Assurance Companies

The following questions may be addressed to life assurance companies which issued relevant policies:

- What was the policy worth at the date of death? Often, the value of a life assurance policy is based on the value of the units in the relevant fund that have been purchased with the premiums paid by the deceased, subject to a minimum amount assured. This is generally accepted by the Inland Revenue as the value of the policy as at the date of death;
- How much will be paid out under the policy as at the date of death?
- Were the policy proceeds written into trust and if so who are the trustees?
- The forms required to claim the policy proceeds, together with any necessary indemnity if the original policy document cannot be located, should be requested.
- The death of a life assured is a chargeable event in relation to all "qualifying" life assurance polices and some "non-qualifying" life assurance policies (section 540, Income and Corporation Taxes Act 1988), apart from mortgage protection policies and certain other policies specified in section 539 of that Act. The gain deemed to arise on the chargeable event is assessed to income tax on the person originally owning the policy (even if he has since assigned it to a

trust) or on his personal representatives, as stated in section 547, Income and Corporation Taxes Act 1988. The life assurance company should be asked to clarify whether the gain arising on the policy is chargeable to income tax, and if so a chargeable event certificate should be requested, showing the gain made. This can then be used when completing the estate's or the deceased's income tax return, as the case may be.

National Savings

There are many different types of National Savings investment and the correspondence addresses in relation to each also differ; many are given in Appendix B to this book. Very generally, each investment should be valued at the date of death, and the forms to encash the investments should be requested. A valuation of all the deceased's National Savings investments can be requested on form DNS904. Many National Savings investments can be transferred to the beneficiaries *in specie* and the relevant forms should be requested if this is a possibility. In addition, National Savings may be willing to issue a cheque to the Inland Revenue, from the assets held by them, to pay any inheritance tax due. This should be investigated at the earliest opportunity. National Savings often have a four-week backlog of correspondence and it may take some time for the personal representatives to receive a reply.

Interest on National Savings certificates is free of income tax but is still subject to inheritance tax within the deceased's estate. Details of interest which had accrued but was unpaid at the date of death must be requested in respect of all investments, for declaration regarding inheritance tax. In addition, confirmation of all income paid on the investment for the period from 6 April to the date of death should be sought, for declaration, if necessary, on the income tax return to the date of death.

Premium bonds may remain in the prize draw for up to a year from the date of death and the personal representatives should, in consultation with the beneficiaries of the estate, decide whether they wish this to happen, since it may delay the administration of the estate. It is a strange fact that the premium bonds of many deceased holders appear to win more in the year after death than during their owner's lifetime. In any event, consent to leave the funds in the draw is not irrevocable – the personal representatives can ask for the bonds to be encashed at any time. If the holder's card cannot be located, National Savings will require a copy of the deceased's signature to verify that the holder was the same person as the deceased. A copy of the signature page of the Will or codicil is generally sufficient.

Pensions and Annuities

The following information should be sought from relevant pension providers:

- Will any lump sum be payable as a result of the deceased's death? If the pension scheme is personal or a retirement annuity contract, was this lump sum written into trust, must it be paid to the estate, or is it payable at the discretion of the pension company? If it was a company scheme, the death benefit will probably be paid at the discretion of the scheme trustees. In the case of a scheme which allows discretion as to who will be paid the lump sum, however, guidance as to the deceased's family situation and the beneficiaries of his Will or intestacy may be needed.
- Will any pension be paid to the deceased's spouse, children or dependants? If so, the forms to be completed to claim it should be requested.
- What pension was paid to the deceased from 6 April to the date of death and what income tax was deducted?

State Pension and Benefits

The personal representatives should contact the Pensions and Overseas Directorate of the Department of Social Security (see Appendix B for the address) for details of any state retirement pension the deceased was receiving, and whether any was unpaid at the date of death. If the pension book can be found, any unused counterfoils should be sent with the initial enquiry letter.

The Disability Benefits Unit (see Appendix B for the address), or the local Benefits Agency office that dealt with the deceased, should be approached in connection with attendance allowance and all other benefits. The deceased's national insurance number will need to be given. Again, any benefits that were due to the deceased but unpaid at the date of death can be claimed by the personal representatives, but if the deceased was entitled to any benefits that he was not claiming, it is unlikely that the personal representatives will be able to submit a posthumous claim.

If any of the benefits the deceased was claiming were means-tested, the Benefits Agency may check with the probate registry the value of the estate given in the application for the grant of representation. If not fully satisfied, the Benefits Agency may investigate further, and request more information, including a summary of the estate, from the personal representatives. If this investigation shows that the deceased was over-claiming, or wrongly claiming, the estate will have to repay that which was overclaimed.

The Benefits Agency is another institution which often has a large backlog of correspondence and it is generally wise for the personal representatives to keep in close contact to ensure that matters are being dealt with and that correspondence has not become mislaid.

The personal representatives also need to know what and how much pension and benefits were received by the deceased from 6 April to the date of death, as these may need to be declared on the deceased's final income tax return.

Chattels

Where the estate of the deceased is not subject to inheritance tax and the deceased did not own any chattels which are out of the ordinary or which appear to have any significant value, the personal representatives' estimate of the value of the chattels should be sufficient. But if they are in any doubt about the value of the estate or the chattels, the personal representatives should obtain a professional valuation. This can also be useful where the entire estate falls within the surviving spouse exemption (see page 74) but the deceased appeared to own chattels of significant value, as it will confirm the base cost at which the spouse takes those chattels (i.e., the value of the chattels at the deceased's death) for capital gains tax purposes should the spouse later sell those assets and realise a gain.

If the deceased held a linked group of chattels, for example a set of china, the group must be valued as a set rather than individually.

It is suggested that, when asking for a valuation, the personal representatives should request that any items worth more than £50 are shown individually, and a global value is inserted for all other chattels. The insurance value of an item is not the same as its open market value. An insurance value relates to how much it would cost to replace the asset, whereas the open market value is how much it would sell for. Often, the insurance value is greater than the open market value.

Real Property

Any land and buildings held by the deceased must always be valued by a professional person.

Shares, Securities and Unit Trusts

Shares and securities tradable on the open market should be valued on the "quarter up" basis. This is calculated by consulting a newspaper (the *Financial Times* is generally the most helpful) published on the day after the deceased died, for the prices at which the shares were selling on the day of death. If the deceased died on a day when the shares were not traded, the figures from the previous or the next day's trading can be used, whichever are the most favourable. The newspaper will show the highest and lowest prices at which the shares were traded. The lowest price should be deducted from the highest price. One quarter of the difference should then be added to the lowest price, to find the "quarter up" price.

If any share is marked "xd" in the newspaper, it was "ex-dividend" at the date of death. The register of shareholders of a company cannot be updated every day to include new owners of shares – it is always a few weeks out of date. As a result, the person registered as the owner of shares on the date a dividend is paid may have sold those shares and so is not entitled to that dividend. To counteract any unfairness, four to six weeks before a dividend is paid, a share is declared to be "ex-dividend". This means that a purchaser of the shares will not be entitled to receive the next dividend; it will instead pass to the seller of the shares. As a result, the price of the shares in the open market is reduced. Therefore, if a shareholding is declared to be "ex-dividend" at the date of death, the value of the dividend should be included in the deceased's estate for inheritance tax purposes.

For example, Fred held 100 shares in Boots plc at the date of his death. The paper shows that the shares were marked "xd" at the date of death, and that the dividend declared was 1p per share. The lowest trading price of the shares on the date of death was £1.00 per share, and the highest was £1.40. The value of the shares at the date of death is calculated as follows:

- £1.40 - £1.00 = 40p;
- one quarter of 40p = 10p;
- £1.00 + 10p = £1.10 per share x 100 shares = £110.00;
- the dividend on the shares is 1p per share x 100 shares = £1.00;
- the total value of the shares is £110.00 + £1.00 = £111.00.

Shareholders may be entitled to new shares, or to buy new shares, either now or in the future. If any of these rights had accrued to the deceased's shares at the date of death, the value of the new shares or the right to buy them must be included as part of the capital value of his estate.

Interest-bearing securities accrue interest at a daily rate. If sold, the sale may be with the benefit of the interest, or the seller of the securities may retain the interest. Securities marked "IK" or "IM" transfer to a purchaser with the benefit of the interest accrued during the seller's ownership – those marked "IKX" or "IMX" do not. The value of the interest should therefore be deducted from, or added to, the market value of the securities at the date of death, as appropriate.

Unit trusts, investment trusts and interests in open-ended investment companies are not valued on the quarter-up basis, but on the lowest of the prices shown per unit. The manager of the relevant fund must be approached about outstanding dividends and distributions, as these are not published in the press. In any event, the fund manager's valuation may well be the most accurate, and often no charge is made for this.

If there is a number of shareholdings, or the personal representatives are not confident about preparing an accurate valuation, any stockbroker will prepare a valuation on payment of a fee. Alternatively, the London Stock Exchange Historic Price Service (see Appendix B) provides valuations upon receipt of the details of the shares and securities held by the deceased, together with confirmation of the date of death. A charge is made for this service.

Unquoted shares and securities are more difficult to value. A good starting place is the accountants to the company in question, as they are generally in the best position to provide a realistic valuation. The Memorandum and Articles of Association of the company should be considered carefully. They may restrict how the shares may pass after the death of a shareholder. While this cannot be used artificially to depress the value of the shares, it is permissible for the open market valuation to reflect that these conditions would be imposed on any purchaser of the shares and would thus affect his ability to sell them onwards. This may affect the number of purchasers, or the price they would be willing to pay.

Partnership Interests

The factors to be taken into account when valuing a partnership interest are similar to those which apply when valuing unquoted shares. Often the accountants or auditors are the best people to approach first. Any partnership agreement should be consulted as it may contain provisions applying on the death of a partner.

Assets at Lloyds

A detailed discussion of the manner in which Lloyds underwriting is conducted and the method of valuing Lloyds assets is beyond the scope of this book. Personal representatives may, however, need some understanding of what it means to be a "Lloyds Name" and the consequences for the estate. Very briefly, Lloyds carries on the business of underwriting insurance, like any other insurance company. But the method of distributing the profits and funding the losses is unique. Lloyds has various "Names", who effectively participate in the underwriting business. Each Name has links with an agency company, and with one agent within that company. The agent liaises with the Name regarding how much the Name is willing to underwrite, and the type of underwriting business the Name wishes to be involved in. The agent and the Name decide which underwriting "syndicates" the Name is to participate in, and the extent of his participation, as a percentage share. Each syndicate covers one type of underwriting business in one year. Effectively, the Name is agreeing to meet that percentage of losses of that syndicate for that year (should it make a loss), and establishing the percentage of profits he will receive if it makes a profit.

Once the extent of the Name's total involvement at Lloyds has been decided, the agent calculates the value of assets the Name must deposit with Lloyds to secure the position should the syndicates he participates in realise a loss and thus require him to make a payment to fund that loss. The Name must then deposit assets (shares, land, cash or bank guarantees are good examples of suitable assets) with Lloyds to secure his liability. Lloyds can easily liquidate these assets to fund a loss should that be necessary.

The results of each Lloyds syndicate are not quantified until three years after that syndicate has closed down (each syndicate runs for one calendar year). This means that there is always a delay between the year in which a profit or loss arises and when it is paid. If a Name dies during a year, his last year of participation is deemed to have ended on 31 December prior to his death.

The assets of a Lloyds Name include the assets held by him at Lloyds to secure his underwriting liability, and the profits and losses which arise from years that are "open"; a valuation on death includes both elements. Generally, assets held at Lloyds to secure the Name's liability qualify for business property relief from inheritance tax, although this depends to some extent on whether the Name retained at Lloyd's assets in excess of the underwriting requirement, in which case the relief may be limited.

The best method of valuing assets in connection with Lloyds is to contact the agent for the Name. He or she is often an invaluable source of information, and may deal directly with IR Capital Taxes regarding any queries raised by them.

Obviously, if the syndicates in which the deceased participated are not finalised at his death, the quantum of his likely profits or losses can only be estimated. If losses arise, they must be met by the estate, but this may greatly hinder the distribution. This may be offset somewhat if the Name took out an estate protection plan. This is basically an insurance policy under which the insurer agrees to pay the losses of a Lloyds Name accruing after his death. Like many other insurance policies, there is usually an excess, which may run to several thousand pounds. This generally means that, providing the personal representatives allow sufficient assets to remain at Lloyds to cover the payment of that excess, they can proceed to liquidate and distribute the deceased's remaining Lloyds assets without fear that they will be called upon to meet future losses. For further commentary on this see page 257. The insurer under the estate protection plan will, however, have a lien over any future profits payable to the estate of the deceased, to the extent that it has funded his losses.

Joint Assets

Assets held jointly with a third party must be valued as a whole, and the value of the deceased's share then calculated. If the asset can be easily separated into the shares held by the deceased and his co-owner (for example, a bank account in the names of the deceased and his partner), the value of the deceased's share is the proportion of the asset owned by him. But where the assets cannot be readily split down (as in the case of land), a discount is permitted, for inheritance tax purposes, on the value of the share owned by the deceased. Generally this discount is ten to fifteen per cent of the value of the asset at the date of the deceased's death, based on the asset itself and the proportion owned by the deceased. With this in mind, it may be wise for the personal representatives to claim a fifteen per cent discount; the Inland Revenue may seek to negotiate downwards, but the personal representatives are in a stronger position than if they are trying to negotiate the discount upwards.

The joint owner should be approached to discover whether the asset was held as joint tenants or tenants-in-common (for the differences between these two types of ownership see page 11). It is usual for most assets, other than land and buildings, to be held as joint tenants, although this should never be assumed. In addition, where land was held as tenants-in-common and was rented out, any bank account holding the rental income is taken to be held in a tenancy-in-common, particularly if the co-owners held unequal proportions of the land.

Even if assets were originally held by persons as joint tenants, it is possible for the joint tenancy to be severed to create a tenancy-in-common. If land is held in a tenancy-in-common, this should be noted in the land or charge certificate, but the bundle of documents containing the title deeds should be checked in case severance has already taken place but has not been noted on the certificate. If the land is unregistered, the severance may be noted on the title document itself, or, again, may be a separate document held with it.

A severance does not have to be set out explicitly in writing, which can make difficulties for personal representatives who think severance may have taken place but cannot find definitive evidence. In *Re Woolnough, Perkins v Borden* WTLR May 2002, 595, three siblings owned property as joint tenants. When the first sister died, her share in the property passed to her brother and sister as the surviving joint tenants. After that, the brother and sister both made Wills at the same time, dealing with their half shares in the property. It was held that as they both acted in the belief that they could separately dispose of their own shares in the property, they had signified their intention to sever the joint tenancy and create a tenancy-in-common.

Assets Subject to an Option to Purchase

One or more of the deceased's assets may be subject to an option to purchase, an option having been granted before death, or arising under the deceased's Will. If so, the assets must be valued on the open market and an appropriate deduction made in relation to the option. The deduction must relate to the position of the option at the date of death, and is not affected by events after death. For example, in *Re Bliss (deceased)* [2001] 1 WLR 1973 (Ch D), the deceased left A an option to purchase her home subject to the right of her husband to live there for the rest of his life. Shortly after she died, the husband had to move into a nursing home and the home was sold pursuant to the option. It was held that the husband's timely move into the nursing home could not be taken into account when valuing the option, as this was an event subsequent to the deceased's death.

Employers

The following questions may usefully be put to the deceased's employer:
- Was the deceased owed any outstanding salary or other payments at the date of death?
- Was the deceased a member of a group life assurance or pension scheme?
- The employer should be asked to provide the personal representatives with a certificate showing the income and benefits received by the deceased for the period from 6 April last to the date of death. This will be required when completing the final income tax return for the deceased.

Life Interest Trust

If the deceased was a beneficiary of a life interest trust, either as a life tenant or remainderman entitled after the death of the life tenant, his interest must be valued. The trustees of that trust should be contacted and asked for:
- their reference at IR Capital Taxes;
- a copy of the Will or other instrument which created the trust;
- details of the deceased's interest in the trust;
- the value of the trust at the date of death, together with the value of the deceased's interest in it;
- the value of any income or other sums due to the deceased from the trust at the date of death.

The trustees cannot be bound to supply the personal representatives with a copy of the trust document, as this is not strictly relevant to their needs, but they must supply all the information the personal representatives require to complete the inheritance tax forms.

Creditors

Evidence of debts offered by standing orders and direct debits paid from the deceased's bank account should all be followed up and the details ascertained. Any papers held by the deceased which indicated that he was a debtor should likewise be investigated.

The personal representatives should also place the advertisements and make the searches referred to in section 27, Trustee Act 1925 (see page 256) if they wish to be able to claim the exemption from personal liability offered by that section. This is also a matter of good practice, particularly if the personal representatives are unfamiliar with the deceased's personal affairs.

Most household bills are received quarterly and so these debts are notified (simply by being received in the post) within three months of the deceased's death. In any event, it would be unusual to find a household that did not have most of the following utilities: gas, electricity, oil, water and telephone; the personal representative should expect these bills and make appropriate enquiries if they are not received.

Any person who was a creditor of the deceased should be contacted and asked to confirm how much was owed by the deceased at the date of death, together with the rate at which interest is accruing on the debt. In relation to mortgages on properties of which the deceased was the landlord, a statement of the interest paid during the period from 6 April to the date of death should be requested, as this interest will be deductible for the purposes of income tax.

It is vital that the personal representatives do not make any promise to pay any debt. If the estate is discovered to be insolvent and such a promise has been made, the personal representatives may become personally liable to pay the debt.

Lifetime Transfers

Any lifetime chargeable transfer ("LCT") into a discretionary trust, gift, or the gift element of a transaction at an undervalue (the latter two being known as potentially exempt transfers or "PETs") made within seven years before the deceased's death may be brought back into the deceased's estate for inheritance tax purposes. In addition, LCTs made within seven years of a PET are aggregated with that gift to determine the inheritance tax payable on it. A gift made under the doctrine of *donatio mortis causa* (see page 13) qualifies as a gift made prior to death for these purposes.

The deceased's family, the beneficiaries under his Will and his professional advisers should be approached to discover whether any such gifts or transfers were made. The value of the assets gifted should be ascertained, both at the date of the gift and at the date of death. If the value at death is less than the value at the time the gift was made, the personal representatives can elect to substitute the former for the latter for inheritance tax purposes.

Income Tax and Capital Gains Tax

If the deceased employed an accountant, the accountant should be approached for a copy of the last tax return filed or completed. This will provide much useful information as to the type and level of the deceased's assets at the date of death. If the deceased did not employ an accountant, the Inland Revenue should be asked for a copy of the last return filed. Either the accountant or the Inland Revenue should be able to confirm whether any further income tax or capital gains tax, or payments on account, are or will become due, and should know whether there is any dispute about the amount. The Inland Revenue normally postpones payments of outstanding amounts until thirty days after the issue of the grant of representation, after which time interest accrues.

As mentioned above, an income tax return or claim for repayment of tax must be completed for the deceased in respect of the period from 6 April to the date of death. In addition, if the death occurred before the return for the previous tax year had been filed, that return must also be completed. If the deceased did not employ an accountant, the personal representatives may decide to complete this return themselves. It is beyond the scope of this book to explain how an individual's tax return should be completed, but if the personal representatives are unsure how to proceed they should take professional advice. In any event, the personal representatives are responsible for ensuring that all the information contained in the return is correct.

Miscellaneous Matters

Professional advisers
As outlined above, highly useful information regarding the deceased's estate can be obtained from the deceased's solicitor, accountant, stockbroker and any other professional agents employed by him during his lifetime.

Private health insurance
Inquiries should be made to ascertain whether the deceased held, or was entitled through his employment to, private health insurance; and, if so, whether any payments or reimbursements are due to the estate, or whether any other claim ought to be made.

Passport
The deceased's passport should be returned to the Passport Office for cancellation or destruction.

The Court of Protection
If the deceased was a patient of the Court of Protection, or if he was the donor of an enduring power of attorney that was registered, the Court of Protection should be notified of the death.

Checklist

At the commencement of the administration of an estate in particular, it can be very difficult to remember what assets are thought to be in the estate, who has been approached to provide a valuation and whether a response has been received. A good way to keep track of the assets in the estate is to prepare a table with seven headings as follows:

- description of asset/liability;
- date on which valuation requested;
- value obtained;
- date grant registered;
- date of sale or transfer to beneficiary;
- proceeds of sale or value at date transferred to beneficiary;
- date creditor paid.

This provides a quick guide to the progress of the estate administration and can be useful in keeping on top of matters that need to be chased up.

Chapter 3

Inheritance Tax Accounts

Calculation of the Estate

There are two separate bases upon which the value of an estate is calculated. The first is the value of the estate for the purposes of paying inheritance tax. This takes into account all the assets deemed to form part of the deceased's estate for the purposes of inheritance tax, including assets held in the deceased's sole name or jointly with other persons otherwise than as trustee; foreign assets; assets held in a life interest trust for the deceased's benefit; and assets subject to a gift with reservation of benefit.

The second calculation is that of the deceased's estate that will pass under the grant of representation. This includes only assets held in the deceased's sole name, and may not include foreign assets if they fall to be dealt with under a foreign grant.

In both situations the gross value is that of the assets only; the net value is the value remaining after any relevant liabilities have been deducted.

Excepted Estates

Once the personal representatives have ascertained the value of the deceased's gross and net estates, they need to consider whether an Inland Revenue account must be submitted to the Inland Revenue Capital Taxes (the branch of the Inland Revenue which deals with inheritance tax). A full account is not always necessary; in some cases a shortened version may be sufficient; see page 31. Alternatively, many estates are "excepted" from the requirement to complete any form of account at all.

The requirements for an excepted estate are prescribed by the Inheritance Tax (Delivery of Accounts) (Excepted Estates) Regulations 2002, SI 2002 No 1733. For deaths on or after 6 April 2002, an estate is excepted if, immediately before his death:

- the deceased was domiciled in the UK (see page 41 for a discussion of domicile);
- the value of the deceased's estate is attributable wholly to property passing under his Will or intestacy or under a nomination (see page 11) of an asset taking effect on death or under a single settlement in

which he was entitled to an interest in possession in settled property or by survivorship in a beneficial joint tenancy;
- of that property –
  - not more than £100,000 represented value attributable to property which, immediately before the deceased's death, was settled property; and
  - not more than £75,000 represented value attributable to property which, immediately before the deceased's death, was situated outside the UK;
- the deceased died without having made any chargeable transfers during the period of seven years ending with his death other than specified transfers (see below) where the aggregate value transferred did not exceed £100,000; and
- the aggregate of the gross value of the deceased's estate and of the value transferred by any specified transfers made by that person did not exceed £220,000.

An estate is also an excepted estate where:
- the deceased was never domiciled in the UK or treated as domiciled in the UK by section 267 of the Inheritance Tax Act 1984; and
- the value of that person's estate situated in the UK is wholly attributable to cash or quoted shares or securities passing under his Will or intestacy or by survivorship in a beneficial joint tenancy, the gross value of which does not exceed £100,000.

"Specified transfers" are chargeable transfers made during the period of seven years ending with the deceased's death where the value transferred is attributable to –
- cash;
- quoted shares or securities; or
- an interest in or over land (and furnishings and chattels disposed of at the same time to the same donee and intended to be enjoyed with the land), save to the extent that –
  - sections 102 and 102A(2), Finance Act 1986 (gifts with reservation of benefit) apply to that transfer; or
  - the land (or furnishings or chattels) became settled property on that transfer.

If an estate is excepted and the personal representatives are professionally represented, the application for a grant of representation may be made without submitting any forms to IR Capital Taxes.

If the personal representatives are acting in person, they should complete form IHT 205 (Short Form for Personal Applicants), and forward it, together with the application for the grant of representation, to the probate registry. All enquiries relating to tax must be made to IR Capital Taxes; the probate registries are not involved.

In either case, if IR Capital Taxes does not call for an inheritance tax account to be completed within thirty-five days of the grant of representation being issued, the personal representatives are deemed to have an automatic clearance from inheritance tax unless they failed to disclose all the facts at the time of their application to the probate registry; or property later becomes comprised in the estate, or property of which they were previously unaware comes to their attention, rendering the estate "unexcepted". In that situation, the personal representatives have six months within which to file an account with IR Capital Taxes.

Inheritance Tax Forms
The inheritance tax forms comprise the main form, IHT200, in which all the figures in relation to the deceased's estate are to be inserted, and the "D" forms in which are to be given the details of how those figures are arrived at. There are nineteen "D" forms in total. The forms are available from IR Capital Taxes stationery orderline (telephone 0845 234 1000); or may be downloaded at www.inlandrevenue.gov.uk/cto/.

The manner of completing the forms may differ slightly if the deceased died domiciled in Scotland or Northern Ireland. The text below relates to persons dying domiciled in England and Wales only.

An inheritance tax form is completed to show all the assets that fall within a deceased's estate upon his death. If the assets are exempt (either automatically or because of the identity of the beneficiary to whom they will pass) or relieved from tax (see Chapter 4), they must still be shown on the form, but the exemption or relief can also be claimed. IR Capital Taxes must be provided with the fullest information possible in order to approve or calculate the inheritance tax payable.

Reduced inheritance tax form
The personal representatives may be permitted to complete a reduced inheritance tax form if:
- the deceased died domiciled in England and Wales, Scotland or Northern Ireland;
- any assets not passing to the deceased's spouse (who is domiciled as above) or a charity, when taken together with:
  - assets held jointly passing by survivorship not to the deceased's spouse;
  - assets held in trust for the deceased not passing to an exempt beneficiary;
  - gifts with reservation of benefit made by the deceased (and those from which he ceased to take any benefit in the seven years prior to his death);

- assets held by the deceased outside the UK not passing under his UK Will or intestacy,

  after deduction of all liabilities, reliefs and exemptions, do not exceed the inheritance tax nil rate band;

- any assets not passing as above pass only to charity or to the deceased's spouse who was domiciled in England and Wales, Scotland or Northern Ireland at the date of death.

If the residue of the deceased's estate, no matter what its value, is divided between exempt and non-exempt beneficiaries, a full account must be completed. Spouses and charities are exempt beneficiaries; all other persons and institutions are non-exempt; see pages 74 and 75.

Even if the estate qualifies under the above criteria, the entire IHT200 must nevertheless be filled in, together with any relevant "D" forms. But, where assets are passing to an exempt beneficiary, an estimated value of those assets can be used and the fact that the value is an estimate need not be specified in box L3 on page 8 of IHT200. In addition, if Forms D7 to D14, D16 or D17 (see below) would otherwise have to be filled in, but the assets that would be entered on them pass to exempt beneficiaries, the forms need not be completed. Form D18 must always be completed. Again, if the personal representatives later become disentitled to complete the reduced form, they should fill in the complete form and forward it to IR Capital Taxes with a form D3 and any other documents necessary, such as any deed of variation which may have led to the disentitlement.

Full inheritance tax form

The full inheritance tax form should be filled in for all estates that are not excepted and which do not fall within the "reduced form" criteria. If in the first instance a limited grant is being applied for, in that it is intended to deal solely with certain assets, only those assets that will be subject to the grant need be shown on the form. The deceased's entire estate must, however, be taken into account when calculating the tax payable on the delivery of the form. As this requires the value of the entire estate to be ascertained, it is often simplest to complete one form covering all the assets, to avoid the risk of confusion or double counting, or of leaving assets out of the account completely.

This chapter contains an explanation of how to fill in each element of IHT200 and the D forms. As mentioned on page 15, the open market value must be entered on the form. Values given on the form should be rounded down to the nearest pound.

Form IHT200: Inland Revenue Account for Inheritance Tax

Section A
Section A of IHT200 should be completed to show the location of the probate registry dealing with the application for the grant.

Section B
Section B, headed "about the person who has died", should be completed by inserting the deceased's personal details. If there is not enough room in box B1 to insert the deceased's full title, this can be continued into B2. Boxes B8 to 10 require only a tick if the relative to which each box relates survives the deceased. The same applies to box B13 if the deceased was resident in a nursing or residential home when he died. If the deceased was resident in such a home at the date of his death, even if only for a short period, it is that address which should be given in B7, not his home address if he still retained his home. Into boxes B11 and B12 should be inserted the number of children and grandchildren surviving the deceased.

The deceased's domicile must be entered in box B14. If he was domiciled in the UK, his domicile is entered as England and Wales, Scotland or Northern Ireland (not "UK"). If the deceased was so domiciled, form IHT200 must be completed in relation to his worldwide estate. If he was not so domiciled, IHT200 should be completed only in relation to his assets situated in the UK, but the value of his worldwide estate not situated in the UK must be included in form D2, question 6 (see page 43).

Section C
Section C, "Solicitor or other person to contact", is to be completed to show the details of the personal representatives or the solicitor acting on their behalf.

Section D
Section D, "Supplementary pages", is a series of questions offering "yes" or "no" answers. If the "yes" box is ticked in reply to any question, the relevant "D" form must be completed before the rest of the IHT200 is filled in.

Section E
Section E is relevant only where the deceased was domiciled in Scotland.

Section F
Section F, "Estate in the UK where tax may not be paid by instalments", should be completed to show details of any non-instalment option property that was held in the deceased's sole name in the UK. Non-instalment option property is any property that does not qualify as instalment option property;

see page 78.

Box F1 (quoted stocks, shares and investments) should show the total from box SS1 on form D7 (see page 50), while F2 (UK Government and municipal securities), the total from box SS2 on form D7. Box F3 (unquoted stocks, shares and investments) is to be filled in to show the total value of shares shown in reply to question 3 on form D7; and F4, "Traded unquoted stocks and shares", the total in the reply to question 4. Box F5 (dividends or interest) is to show the total dividends and interest inserted in response to questions 1 to 4 on form D7.

There is no supplementary ("D") page for premium bonds, the total value of which should be inserted directly into box F6 (premium bonds) on IHT200. All the deceased's National Savings investments (apart from premium bonds and cash accounts) must be listed on form D17 (see page 59) and their total value inserted into box F7 (National Savings investments) on IHT200. All bank and building society accounts (including National Savings cash accounts) should again be detailed on form D17 and totalled in box F8 (bank and building society accounts). The information required in respect of National Savings investments and bank and building society accounts is:

- the name of the bank or building society (where relevant);
- the type of account or investment;
- the capital value at the date of the deceased's death; and
- the interest accrued on the account but unpaid at the date of death.

Box F9, "cash", must show the total of:

- cash found on the deceased when he died,
- cash held in safes and safety deposit boxes;
- cash held on account at a stockbroker;
- traveller's cheques; and
- uncashed cheques made out in favour of the deceased.

Cash held in a foreign currency (but which is not a foreign asset as it is not held abroad) should be converted to sterling using the "pound spot forward against the pound" table published in the *Financial Times* the day after the date of death; this contains the figures relevant to the date of death. If the date of death was not a trading date, the table published the preceding or subsequent day, whichever is the more favourable, may be used. If the currency in question is not shown in that table, the figures from the *Financial Times Guide to World Currencies*, published every Monday, should be used.

A separate form D8 must be completed in respect of each debt due to the deceased. The total value of all loans made by the deceased and secured by a mortgage should be inserted into box F10 (debts due to the deceased and secured by mortgage); and all other debts in box F11 (other debts due to the deceased). These include a director's loan account or other current account due to the deceased from any business or company in which he was concerned.

If the deceased was landlord of any property, any rent outstanding and due to him at death must be inserted in box F12 (rents due to the deceased). It is not compulsory to detail these rents on form D17 but it may be helpful to do so, to save further queries being raised by IR Capital Taxes.

Boxes F13 (accrued income) and F14 (apportioned income) relate to settled property of which the deceased was the life tenant. If income had been received by the trustees but not paid over to the deceased at the date of death, the amount should be inserted into box F13. Box F14 is to contain any income due to the trustees (and therefore the deceased) at death, but not paid to them at that time.

If payments under an annuity or a pension scheme continue to be made after the deceased's death, they should be shown in box IP4 on form D9 (see page 51) or PA1 on form D6 (see page 48). They should be totalled and transferred to box F15 (other income due to the deceased) on IHT200, together with any salary or DSS benefits due at death.

If the deceased was either a life assured, or the owner of a life assurance policy on someone else's life, the value of the life assurance policy/ies should be stated in boxes IP1 and IP2 on form D9 (see page 51). Monies due under mortgage protection policies should also be included here, even though they were linked to the deceased's interest in land. They are totalled in box IP3 and that figure is transferred to box F16 (life assurance policies).

If any payments under private medical insurance policies were due at the date of death but unpaid the amount should be inserted in box F17 (private health schemes). Any repayment of income tax or capital gains tax due from the Inland Revenue to the deceased should be included at box F18 (income tax or capital gains tax repayment).

Form D10 (see page 52) is used to set out details of the deceased's chattels. Most of the figures to be inserted in IHT200 are values of the deceased's assets at the date of death. If these values alter as the assets are sold after death, or if a capital gain or capital loss is realised, an application for the sale price to be taken as the value at the date of death should be made. Unusually, box HG1 on form D10 calls for the gross sale proceeds of any asset that was sold after death, instead of the value at the date of death. Presumably, this is because a chattel does not generally increase or decrease in value from day to day, so the gross proceeds of sale should be an accurate reflection of the value at death. These sale proceeds are carried to box F19 (household or personal goods, sold) on IHT200. It is the gross, not net, proceeds which should be given. This should be a true reflection of the asset's value. The value of any unsold chattels should be listed in HG2 on form D10 and included at box F20 (household and personal goods, unsold) on IHT200.

If the deceased was a beneficiary under a third party's estate, any benefit he was due to receive from the estate, but had not received at the date of death, is to be shown in box UE1 on form D11 (see page 52) and carried to box F21 (interest in another estate).

The value of an interest in expectancy should be shown in box F22. This is where the deceased would become entitled to property, but only after the interest of a third party in the property had terminated. For example, assets may have been held in trust for A for life and after her death for C. During A's lifetime, C has a reversionary interest in the property held in trust. Reversionary interests are generally excluded property under section 48, Inheritance Tax Act 1984, but details of them must nevertheless be included in the inheritance tax forms. The name of the settlor of the trust creating the reversionary interest, together with the date of trust or the date of death of the settlor (if the trust was created in his Will), and the name and age of the life tenant should be shown on form D17 (see page 59). As the reversionary interest generally "falls in" only after the death of the life tenant, the value of the interest can be arrived at only by an actuarial calculation based on the value of the trust property and the age of the life tenant.

Any other assets not falling within any of the above classes, but which were held in the deceased's sole name in the UK, and which do not qualify as instalment option property, should be detailed on form D17, and their value included in box F23 (other personal assets in the UK) on IHT 20.

Box F25 (liabilities) is to be completed to show the total liabilities of the deceased. These must be the liabilities which had been incurred by the deceased at the date of death, not those arising as a result of the death. For example, the date of a fee note for work carried out does not matter – as long as the work was undertaken prior to death and the fee is unpaid, the liability should be included in the total at F25. Thus, an accountant's outstanding charges for completing a tax return are deductible if the accountant completed the work before death; but fees for completing the final tax return to the date of death are not, because the work is carried out after death. This applies notwithstanding the fact that the deceased would, had he lived, have paid an accountant to prepare a tax return for that period in any event.

If loans and overdrafts, or debts due to friends and relatives, are to be included at F25, they must also be listed on form D16 (see page 58).

Debts due to persons not based in the UK should be deducted from foreign assets first on form D15. If the value of the debts exceeds the value of the property, the amount outstanding may be shown in F25 providing the debts do not relate to instalment option property.

Funeral costs, reasonable mourning expenses of the close family and the cost of a headstone or tombstone should be shown in F26 (funeral expenses).

If the total in box F27 (total liabilities and funeral expenses) is greater than the total assets in box F24, a minus figure should not be shown in box F28 (net total of assets less liabilities). Instead, zero should be inserted and the surplus debt carried forward to Section G (see below).

The exemptions and reliefs available are discussed in Chapter 4. Where a specific or pecuniary legacy passes to an exempt beneficiary such as a spouse, the amount of the exemption is easily ascertainable for insertion in box F29 (total exemptions and reliefs). Where the entire residue is exempt, but there are chargeable legacies, care is needed when ascertaining how much property actually qualifies for an exemption. For example, if the deceased left a legacy of £500,000 to his children and the residue of the estate to his spouse, how should the spouse exemption be apportioned between Sections F (in respect of which tax may not be paid by instalments) and G (in respect of which tax may be paid by instalments) of Form IHT200? If it has already been decided which assets will be used to satisfy the legacy, the spouse exemption can be deducted only from such of the other assets as have been identified as assets which will pass to the spouse. If, however, the personal representatives do not yet know whether they intend to assent to the children a share in the family home, or cash from the deceased's bank account, it cannot be known whether the spouse exemption will be deducted from instalment or non-instalment option property. The family would probably wish the form to be completed as though the legacy to the children is to be satisfied from the instalment option property. This would leave the spouse exemption to be deducted from non-instalment option property and thus the initial inheritance tax bill will be lower.

Probably the most accurate way of dealing with this situation would be to apportion the legacy and the spouse exemption between instalment and non-instalment option property and to explain the situation on form D17. As the administration of the estate progresses, the final position can be reported to IR Capital Taxes and the allocation of the exemption between the different types of property amended at that time.

Section G

Section G (estate in the UK where tax may be paid by instalments) is for details of all the property held by the deceased in his sole name, in the UK, upon which inheritance tax may be paid by instalments. The definition of instalment option property is given at page 78.

The first question asks whether the personal representatives wish to pay the tax arising on these assets by instalments. If the personal representatives are unsure, they should respond, "yes", to allow them maximum flexibility. If instalment option property is later sold, however, the right to pay the inheritance tax by instalments is lost and all the tax on that property becomes payable immediately. In addition, if the personal representatives subsequently assent to a beneficiary any property upon which inheritance tax is payable in instalments, they will no longer control the property but will remain liable for the inheritance tax on it. They should therefore, before they execute the assent, obtain from the beneficiary an indemnity for any outstanding tax payable.

Box G1 (deceased's residence) should be completed to show the value of the deceased's home, even if he resided in a nursing home at the time of his death, unless the home falls within certain categories. Thus, if it was rented by the deceased to a third party, its value should be inserted in box G2 (other residential property), together with any other property that was actually available to rent at the deceased's death. If the deceased owned any farm land, buildings or a farmhouse (including his home if it falls into this category), the value of that land and buildings should be given in box G3 (farms). Any timber or woodland not part of a farm should be given separately in box G5 (timber and woodland).

The value of any land or buildings from which the deceased ran a business should be inserted in box G4 (business property). The value of land or buildings not already included, such as derelict buildings, lock-ups, redundant and unused land, quarries and mines, airfields and rights over land, such as mineral rights or fishing rights, should be inserted in box G6 (other land and buildings).

Generally, a professional valuation of any land or buildings should be prepared. If this is not possible or is deemed not necessary (for example, where a reduced form IHT200 is being completed), a value can be ascertained by looking in local papers or visiting estate agents who have similar properties for sale. Factors that differentiate the deceased's land or buildings from any other, such as a particularly good or bad condition, or a better location, must be borne in mind.

Boxes G7 to G12 deal with business interests held by the deceased. G7 relates to any farming business with which the deceased was concerned. If he ran the business as a sole trader, the value goes in box G7.1, and if it was as a partnership the value is placed in box G7.2. If he was a party to more than one farming business, details of them should be set out in form D14 (see page 56) and the totals only inserted in boxes G7.1 and G7.2. The total of boxes G7.1 and G7.2 is inserted in box G7.

Boxes G8.1, G8.2 and G8 relate to any other business interests. Again, if the deceased was party to more than one business, each should be described on form D14. If the deceased was a Lloyds name, the value of his cash, shares and other assets used in his participation should be included in box G8. Shares held as security by him at Lloyds should be valued and entered on a form D7, separately from other shareholdings, but their total value should not be given in box SS1 of form D7 (to indicate that the total is not carried forward to boxes F1 to 4 of IHT200).

Any assets used by the deceased for the purposes of a business, but not included as part of the value of the business in box G7 or G8, should be included in the total at box G9 (business assets). Boxes G9.1 and G9.2

distinguish between assets used for farming and those used in any other type of business.

To ascertain the values required to complete boxes G7 to G9, either the last set of accounts can be used (providing they are still accurate), or accounts can be prepared to the date of death.

Shares in a company quoted on the London Stock Exchange, which gave the deceased control of that company (more than 50 per cent of the shares), should be valued and given at box G10 (quoted shares and securities, control holding only). The value of these shares must be included on a form D7 separately from the deceased's other shareholdings, and should not be totalled in box SS1 of D7.

The value of shares in an unquoted company which qualify as instalment option property should be included in box G11 or G12, depending on whether or not they are quoted shares. Boxes G11.1 and G11.2, and G12.1 and G12.2, also draw a distinction between a controlling and a non-controlling holding. Again, these values should be shown on a form D7, separately from that which details the non-instalment option property shares.

Boxes G14 (name and address of mortgagee) and G15 (other liabilities) are to be completed to show debts that relate to instalment option property, for example a mortgage over the deceased's home or a business loan made to him. They must be detailed on form D1 (see page 40).

Box G16 (net total of assets less liabilities) should not show a deficit. Any excess debt that cannot be set against instalment option property may be carried back and inserted in box F25 (total liabilities). Only if both Sections G and F would carry a negative figure can the outstanding debt be carried forward to form D15 (see page 57) and set off against foreign property.

Box G17 is for exemptions and reliefs; see Chapter 4. The exemptions and reliefs section in any part of the form can, at lowest, produce a zero, never a negative figure. If a negative would otherwise result, the amount of the exemption or relief is reduced; it cannot be carried to any other section of the form.

Joint, foreign, settled and gifted property (including gifts with a reservation of benefit) are not detailed anywhere in Sections F or G. They have their own separate "D" forms and are brought from those forms into the later calculation of the value of the estate in Section H.

Section H

Section H (summary of the chargeable estate) draws together the entire value of the estate, so as to arrive at an aggregate chargeable transfer. Depending on the complexity of the calculations, the personal representatives may wish to use Form IHT(WS) (inheritance tax work sheet) to calculate the liability of the estate to inheritance tax. For personal representatives acting without professional assistance, or practitioners who are less used to completing form IHT200, using the work sheet is strongly recommended. The total value of the transfer deemed to be made by the deceased at the date of death is inserted in box H15 of IHT200.

Section J

In Section J, the inheritance tax due is calculated. The total inheritance tax payable in relation to the death is calculated by completing boxes J1 to 7. The resulting tax bill is then separated down into the amount which must be paid immediately and that which may be paid by instalments, the figures being inserted in boxes J8 to J19. These boxes also deal with how much interest is payable where the tax is late, and any double taxation (or "quick succession") relief that is granted.

Section K

Section K (authority for repayment of inheritance tax) provides for the personal representatives to specify the name of the person to whom any inheritance tax repayment should be made. This is usually the firm of solicitors dealing with the administration of the estate, so that any repayment can be processed through their client account; or the name in which the personal representatives' bank account is held.

Section L

Section L contains the various declarations that must be made by the personal representatives. The type of grant sought is to be inserted in box L1. Box L2 is to be filled in to show how many supplementary pages are attached. Box L3 is extremely important. The personal representatives must insert the numbers of any boxes which give only a provisional valuation. If any provisional valuation is omitted from this box, and it later becomes evident that its value was only an estimate, IR Capital Taxes may impose penalties upon the personal representatives for failing to disclose it. See page 76.

Each personal representative must give his full name and address and sign and date the form as correct. He should also read the declarations in section L and feel comfortable that he is able to make them properly and honestly.

Form D1: The Will

Form D1 deals with the deceased's Will, if there is one. Question 1 asks "[i]s the address for the deceased as shown in the Will the same as the address on page 1 of form IHT200? If the answer is 'no', say below what happened to the property shown in the Will". If the deceased's home as at the time of making his Will has been sold, this should be indicated. If the sale proceeds were invested in a new home, the chain of home ownership should be explained. If the Will was signed before 18 March 1986 and the chain of home ownership is long, IR Capital Taxes should be satisfied if the form confirms that the home was sold and replaced. If the deceased did not own a home at the date of death, a statement of how the sale proceeds are represented in the value of the deceased's estate should be provided.

Question 2, "[a]re all items referred to in the Will, for example, legacies referring to personal possessions, stocks and shares, loans or gifts made by the deceased, included in form IHT200? If the answer is 'no', say below why these items are not included". This requires the personal representatives to confirm whether the assets specifically gifted by the deceased's Will continued to form part of his estate when he died. If not, it should be stated whether they were given away (if so, to whom, when and what were they worth at the time of the gift); or sold (and where the sale proceeds are currently shown in the estate).

If the answer to either question 1 or 2 is "no", a copy of the Will and codicil must be sent to IR Capital Taxes with the IHT200.

Question 3 asks "[d]oes the whole estate pass to beneficiaries who are chargeable to inheritance tax? If the answer is 'no', deduct the exemption on form IHT200". If the whole estate does not pass to beneficiaries chargeable to inheritance tax, the name of the deceased's spouse, the spouse's date of birth and domicile, or the identity of the charitable beneficiary, should be given.

Form D2: Domicile Outside the UK

As has already been mentioned, a person cannot be domiciled in the UK as such, but only in one of the three UK domicile "jurisdictions" – England and Wales, Scotland or Northern Ireland. The Channel Islands and the Isle of Man do not fall within England and Wales for domicile purposes – they are separate jurisdictions outside the UK.

If the domicile was outside England and Wales, Scotland or Northern Ireland, form D2 must be filled in. "Domicile" is a nebulous concept. In the UK, there is a distinction between "residence", "ordinary residence" and "domicile". In other countries, this distinction is not always made.

Under UK law, a person always has a domicile, but the concept of domicile is not defined anywhere. At birth, a person acquires his father's domicile as his domicile of origin, unless his father and mother were unmarried or do not live together, in which case he takes on his mother's domicile. Once a person is over sixteen, he can lose his domicile of origin and acquire a domicile of choice at any time. Very broadly, this is achieved by displaying a permanent intention to reside in a particular country for the rest of one's days. A person's country of domicile is often understood as the country in which he "intends to die".

A woman who married before 1 January 1974 automatically acquired her husband's domicile as her "domicile of dependence". For marriages after that date, a wife is permitted to retain her own domicile.

In addition, statute defines when a person may be deemed to be domiciled in England and Wales. Section 267, Inheritance Tax Act 1984 provides that a person is deemed to be domiciled in the UK if he was:

- domiciled in the UK at any time in the three years before his death; or
- resident in the UK for seventeen out of the last twenty tax years before his death, ending with the year of assessment within which he died.

The concept of domicile is important in UK inheritance tax law, as it governs what assets in a person's estate may be subject to inheritance tax in the UK. If a person is, or is deemed to be, domiciled in the UK, his entire worldwide estate may be subject to UK inheritance tax. If he is domiciled abroad, only his assets situated in the UK may be subject to UK inheritance tax. There is a possibility that the deceased's assets may be subject to inheritance tax in more than one country. Provisions are in place to relieve the burden of this double taxation; they are discussed in Chapter 4.

Question 1 on form D2 requires a brief life history of the deceased, and of her husband if she was a woman who married before 1 January 1974 (because of the domicile of dependence rules outlined above). Information to be included in this paragraph includes:

- the deceased's nationality;
- where he was born;
- his educational and employment history;
- the date he left the UK and moved abroad;
- the date upon which he returned to the UK, how long he stayed in the UK and the purpose of his stay;
- the reason the deceased did not intend to remain in the UK at his death.

The answers to questions 2 ("Was the deceased domiciled in the UK at any time during the 3 years up to the date of death?") and 3 ("Was the deceased resident in the UK for income tax purposes during the 4 years up to the date of death? If the answer is 'yes', give details of any periods that the deceased was treated as resident in the UK during the last 20 years") enable IR Capital Taxes to establish whether the deceased should be deemed to have been domiciled in the UK at his death (see above).

Question 4 asks "Who will benefit from the deceased's estate under the law that applies in the country of domicile?", eliciting whether the deceased's Will or the rules of intestacy apply to his foreign estate, or whether any rules of forced heirship govern the estate distribution. If the

Will applies, a copy should be sent to IR Capital Taxes.

Question 5b refers to a regime known as "community of property", asking whether such a community has been established in the relevant foreign country, and, if so, asking for details. "Community of property" does not exist in the UK. Elsewhere, it can arise automatically on marriage, or by choice on signature of a marriage contract. Very briefly, such a scheme provides for how property is held between a husband and wife during their lifetimes, and what rights over that property arise upon the death of the first spouse to die. The personal representatives should specify which country's community of property rules operate, and what rights they confer. If the rights arose under a contract, a copy of the contract should be enclosed with the IHT200.

If there is a community of property, the answer to question 5d, "Has the form IHT200 been completed on the basis of the community?" should always be "yes", as this is the basis upon which the form must be completed. If the deceased was domiciled abroad, it is almost certain that he will have left assets in another country. The rest of his worldwide estate should be totalled and inserted in answer to question 6 ("Did the deceased leave any assets of any description outside the UK? If so, give their approximate value").

If the answer to question 8 ("Is any foreign tax to be paid on assets in the UK as a result of the deceased's death?") is "yes", evidence of the tax paid should be sent to IR Capital Taxes as soon as possible.

Form D3: Gifts and Other Transfers of Value

Form D3 deals only with gifts made since 18 March 1986. "Gift" here is a generic term for a lifetime chargeable transfer ("LCT") into a discretionary trust or to a company, or a potentially exempt transfer ("PET") (any other type of gift). Questions 1a to 1d concern gifts or transfers; the creation of any trust or settlement; the payment of a life assurance premium for the benefit of someone other than the deceased's spouse; and the cessation of any right to benefit from any assets held in a trust or a settlement, within seven years before the deceased's death. If the "yes" box is ticked, further information should be given in the table on the form.

PETs that are exempt from the charge to inheritance tax, and which as a result do not need to be declared in the table, are transfers:

- of any asset, made to the deceased's spouse, if he or she was domiciled in the UK (section 18, Inheritance Tax Act 1984);
- of quoted shares or cash, to any individual, providing that the total value of gifts made in any one year (in aggregate, not per recipient) is less than £3,000 (section 19, Inheritance Tax Act 1984). In addition, if the deceased did not fully use this £3,000 annual allowance in any

year, the unused portion of the allowance can be carried forward to the next year;

- of quoted shares or cash, made to any individual, in any one year, totalling less than £250 per recipient (section 20, Inheritance Tax Act 1984);
- unconditionally, of cash or shares, made to an individual, out of the deceased's income, as part of his normal expenditure, and which left the deceased with sufficient income to maintain his usual standard of living (section 21, Inheritance Tax Act 1984). A good example is the payment by the deceased of the premiums under a life assurance policy which was written into trust for a third party.

Each of these exemptions is discussed in more detail in Chapter 4. The last two are not available to offset against PETs made by virtue of the deceased's ceasing to have any right or interest under a settlement.

If any gifts made do not fall within the above criteria, this does not necessarily mean that inheritance tax is chargeable on them; they should be listed in the table and any exemption claimed. For example, if the deceased gave a car valued at £2,000 to his granddaughter in year 1, and cash of £4,000 to his daughter in year 2, the gift to the granddaughter would have to be shown in the table because it was not of cash or shares. But the annual exemption would be deducted from the gift, so the total value given away would be reduced to nil. In addition, the gift to the daughter should be shown because it was over £3,000. Initially, the exemption left over from the previous year (£1,000) would be deducted from the value of the gift, then the annual exemption for year 2. Again, the total value gifted in year 2 would be reduced to nil.

The annual small gifts exemption of £250 cannot be combined with the annual exemption, to reduce the value of a gift of £3,250 to nil. It can be utilised only if all the gifts made to a particular person in any one year totalled less than £250.

If the personal representatives are unsure whether a gift qualifies for a certain exemption, they should declare it on the form, claim the exemption and wait and see what questions are raised by IR Capital Taxes.

In this context, a "gift" comprises not only a transfer of an asset from one person to another, but also any transaction that reduces the value of the deceased's estate (section 3, Inheritance Tax Act 1984). Thus it includes, for example:

- a sale at an undervalue;
- a grant of a lease at less than a full market rent; and
- the re-arrangement of rights attaching to shares in a company which results in a reduction in the value of the deceased's shares.

If the deceased ceased to have a right under a trust before his death, this will also have reduced the value of his estate. The gift must be declared as made by him, even though it may have been the trustees of the trust who decided to remove his rights under it, the deceased having had no control over the decision. If this is the case, the annual exemption and that relating to gifts upon marriage cannot be offset against the value of the gift unless the deceased, within six months of the date of it, gave notice to the trustees that the exemption was available.

The value of any gift is always taken at the date upon which it is made and this is the value for inheritance tax purposes. Section 131, Inheritance Tax Act 1984 allows the personal representatives to substitute a lower value for the gift than the original value in the following limited circumstances:

- inheritance tax becomes payable on the gift upon the deceased's death; and
- the asset transferred was retained by the donee or his spouse at the date of the deceased's death; or
- the asset transferred was sold in an arm's length transaction by the transferee or his spouse before the deceased's death.

Where the asset transferred was retained by the donee or his spouse at the date of the deceased's death, the value to be substituted is that at the date of death. If the third situation applies – the asset transferred was sold in an arm's length transaction by the transferee or his spouse before the deceased's death, the substituted value is the gross sale proceeds. However, the new value should be entered only in the second column of the table, and should not be used to calculate the value of the gift made. IR Capital Taxes will then consider whether the reduction claimed should be allowed.

Once the value of all the PETs and LCTs has been ascertained, that total is the first figure to be set against the nil rate band when calculating the inheritance tax payable in relation to the estate.

Question 2 deals with gifts with reservation of benefit. These are gifts made after 18 March 1986 under which:

"(a) possession and enjoyment of the property is not *bona fide* assumed by the donee at or before the beginning of the relevant period; or

(b) at any time in the relevant period the property is not enjoyed to the entire exclusion, or virtually to the entire exclusion, of the donor ...".

(section 102, Finance Act 1986)

For the purposes of this section, "relevant period" is the period of the seven years ending with the date of death of the deceased, or the period between when the gift is made and the deceased's death, if shorter. Sections 102A, B and C provide further clarification of the meaning of a gift with reservation when the asset gifted away is land or an interest in land. Questions 2a to 2c ask, where the deceased transferred any assets during his lifetime:

- whether the person receiving the gift did not take full possession of it;
- where the gift was of land, whether the deceased or the deceased's

spouse enjoyed a significant right or interest, or was a party to a significant arrangement, in relation to the land; and
- if the gift was of any other asset, whether the deceased continued to have some right to benefit from all or part of it.

If the answer to any of these questions is "yes" a gift with reservation of benefit has taken place and the table at the foot of question 2 must be completed, giving the details.

If the deceased ceased to take any benefit from the gift with reservation at any time during the seven years prior to his death, it will have become a PET at that time (section 102(4), Finance Act 1986) and question 1 must be answered in respect of it. However, no exemption can be deducted from the value of the value of the PET if it is made in this manner.

If the deceased gave land away and ceased to take any benefit from it, but then resumed taking a benefit, that resumption does not turn the original gift into a gift with reservation of benefit, as long as:
- the resumption resulted from a change in his circumstances, which was unforeseen when the gift was first made, and which was not brought about by the deceased to receive the benefit of the exemption; and
- the resumption occurred at a time when the deceased was unable to maintain himself through old age, infirmity or otherwise; and
- the resumption represented reasonable provision by the donee of the land for the care and maintenance of the deceased; and
- the donee was a relative of the deceased or his spouse.

(paragraph 6(b), Schedule 20, Finance Act 1986)

Question 3 deals with LCTs made within seven years of a PET identified by question 1. Those earlier LCTs reduce the value of the nil rate band available to the PET when calculating the inheritance tax payable on it. The earlier LCT is not relevant when calculating the value of the PET that must be aggregated with the deceased's nil rate band.

Form D4: Joint and Nominated Assets

Form D4 deals with assets held in the joint names of the deceased and another person, and with nominated assets. Separate forms should be completed for assets held by the deceased as joint tenant, and for assets held as tenant-in-common. The form is divided between instalment and non-instalment option property, as on form IHT200.

Question 1 seeks an explanation of how much of the property belonged to the deceased beneficially. If there is anything to suggest that the proportion belonging to the deceased does not accord with the answers given to that question, an explanation will have to be provided. For example, if it is claimed that a bank account belonged 50 per cent to the deceased and 50 per cent to a third party, but the deceased took all the income arising on the account, the personal representatives will have to explain why the entire account cannot be said to have belonged to the deceased.

If the deceased held an asset as tenant-in-common such that his interest in the asset passes under his Will or intestacy rather than by survivorship, totals should not be inserted in boxes JP3 to 5 or JP8 to 10. Instead, the figures should be entered in the relevant boxes in Sections F and G of form IHT200. If the assets were held as joint tenants, the figures should be transferred onto the work sheet or directly into Section H of IHT200. But details of any land or buildings held by the deceased must still be entered on form D12 (see page 53), as this form must contain information relating to all land and buildings in which the deceased held an interest. It will be forwarded directly to the District Valuer, so must provide all the particulars the District Valuer needs.

As mentioned at page 24, between ten and fifteen per cent may be deducted from the value of the deceased's interest in the asset if the asset was jointly owned. The deduction should be entered on form D4.

The amount of any joint mortgage should be deducted at box JP7, and the proceeds of any joint life assurance policies assigned to pay off that mortgage included at box JP1. But any joint policies that do not provide for a payment on the deceased's death should be detailed on form D9 (see page 51) only.

Assets owned jointly by the deceased in partnership with another person should not be included on form D4, but on form D14 (see page 56).

Foreign property held jointly between the deceased and another party should be entered on form D15 (see page 57) only, but answers to the questions raised in relation to joint property on form D4 must be given on form D17 (see page 59).

Question 3 deals with assets that were nominated by the deceased during his lifetime. As mentioned at page 11, assets capable of nomination are largely National Savings products and some building society accounts. These should be detailed on this form, but their value must be carried forward to the relevant box in Section F of IHT200. Their value must not be included when totalling the assets in Section F to be copied to form D18, as they do not pass under the deceased's Will or intestacy.

Form D5: Assets Held in Trust (Settled Property)

Form D5 is for listing all the assets held in a trust from which the deceased was entitled to take a benefit at his death. If the deceased was a beneficiary of a trust created by a settlor who was not domiciled in the UK at the time the trust was set up, and the trust was not UK-resident at the time of the deceased's death, only question 1 (on the basic details of the trust) need be completed. In these circumstances, the assets in the trust do not form part of the deceased's estate for inheritance tax purposes (section 48(3), Inheritance Tax Act 1984).

Assets in a discretionary trust of which the deceased was a beneficiary do not need to be included on form D5, as a beneficiary of a discretionary trust has no entitlement under that trust.

Questions 2 and 3 separate out instalment and non-instalment option property, and require details of assets and liabilities, and any exemptions and reliefs claimed.

If the trustees of the trust are willing, the simplest course may be to forward them the form D5 and ask them to complete it and return it to the personal representatives. They cannot be compelled to provide a complete breakdown of the assets and liabilities of the trust, although often they are willing to do so. If not, they may choose to provide only the total assets, liabilities and exemptions and reliefs, for inclusion in boxes SP3 to 5 and SP8 to 10. If they are unwilling to provide even this information, the most practical solution is for the personal representatives to fill in the form to the best of their knowledge and give an explanation in a covering letter when the form is forwarded to IR Capital Taxes. IR Capital Taxes will be able to bring greater pressure to bear on the trustees to provide the necessary figures.

If a liability is shown in box SP2 as income due to the deceased at the date of death, this must be carried forward to box F13 or F14 (depending on whether the income had been received by the trustees at the date of death) on form IHT200 as an asset of the deceased. If the total of liabilities shown in box SP2 is greater than the total assets figure in box SP1, the excess liability may be carried over and included in SP7 and *vice versa*. It cannot be carried forward to IHT200.

If the deceased was a beneficiary of a trust of a life assurance policy, the details should be included on form D5 and a copy of the policy document forwarded to IR Capital Taxes.

Form D6: Pensions

Form D6 deals with all pension policies and retirement annuity contracts held by the deceased. For income tax purposes, a pension policy is either "approved" or "unapproved" under section 590, Income and Corporation Taxes Act 1988. The scheme documentation should confirm whether or not the scheme in question is approved. If a scheme in which the deceased participated was unapproved, details of the benefits payable under it after the deceased's death, and those taken by him during his lifetime, should be included on form D17 (see page 59), and form D6 should also be completed.

Some pensions or annuities provide that an income will continue to be paid even after the deceased's death. If that is the case, the amount of those

payments, together with the name of the person to whom they will be made, should be given in response to question 1. Other information that should be included is:
- the name of the scheme or title of the policy;
- whether the scheme is approved;
- the frequency of payments;
- the date of the final guaranteed payment; and
- any guaranteed increase in the amount payable.

If the pension or annuity continues in favour of the deceased's spouse it does not need to be listed here, as it will fall within the surviving spouse exemption from inheritance tax.

Question 2 deals with any lump sum payments to be made to the estate under a pension scheme or policy as a result of the death; and whether the personal representatives receive those payments as of right or at the discretion of the trustees of the scheme. Very broadly, any death benefits payable under a pension scheme only at the discretion of the trustees of the scheme (as under company pension schemes), or which were assigned into trust by the deceased during his lifetime (as can be done with personal pension schemes or retirement annuity contracts) are free from inheritance tax within the deceased's estate. In addition, in an attempt to allow benefits to pass free from inheritance tax, many personal pension providers are now reserving to themselves a discretion to decide who is to receive any lump sum death benefit. Again, the name or title of the scheme should be given in response to question 2, and whether it was approved, together with the name of the person who ultimately receives the payment. The amount payable should also be included unless the trustees of the scheme had discretion over its destination or it was written into trust, in which case it does not form part of the deceased's taxable estate.

Question 3 is intended to elicit whether the deceased deliberately postponed the taking of benefits from his pension scheme in the knowledge that he was ill, in an attempt to make a lump sum available, free of tax, to his intended beneficiaries. If so, the deceased may have made a PET or LCT at that time. If the personal representatives are aware of this and agree that it was a PET or LCT, the details of the gift must be inserted on form D3 (above, page 43). Thus, in response to question 3 it must be stated whether the deceased, within two years of his death:
- altered the benefits he was taking under a pension scheme;
- deferred taking benefits under a pension scheme; or
- altered how the benefits payable under the scheme would pass upon his death.

The information required is the name or title of the scheme; whether it was approved; when the benefits were altered; and in favour of whom. Evidence as to the deceased's health and life expectancy is also needed.

Form D7: Stocks and Shares

Form D7 consists of a table in which are to be inserted details of all the deceased's stocks, shares and securities. If a stockbroker has been employed to prepare a valuation of the shares, the totals shown in the formal valuation can be transferred to the form and the valuation enclosed with the IHT200; there is no need to replicate all the figures.

Question 1 relates to the deceased's stocks, shares, debentures and other securities listed on the Stock Exchange Daily Official List, together with his unit and investment trusts, Open Ended Investment Companies (OEICs), Individual Savings Accounts (ISAs), Personal Equity Plans (PEPs) and foreign shares listed on the London Stock Exchange. Cash held in a share PEP or ISA should also be shown here.

Question 2 requires details of the deceased's treasury bills, exchequer, convertible, consolidated and loan stock, savings and victory bonds, war loans, UK municipal securities and any government stock held on the Bank of England Register.

Questions 3 asks for the value of any unquoted shares and securities in limited companies, business expansion schemes and business start-up schemes.

Question 4 deals with shares quoted on the Alternative Investment Market (AIM) or traded on OFEX, which is a trading facility for unquoted shares.

Shares traded on NASDAQ (in the USA) or EASDAQ (in Europe) should be listed not on form D7, but on form D15 (see page 57) as foreign assets.

The method of valuing quoted shares and securities has been discussed above; see page 20.

Form D8: Debts Due to the Estate

Form D8 is used to set out details of the debts due to the deceased. A separate form should be completed for each debt. For the purposes of this form, insurance products based on a loan made by the original settlor of a policy of insurance, to the trustees, is a debt that must be included.

If the debt was simply a director's loan account, only questions 3 and 4 need be answered. These ask for the amount outstanding at the date of death, and for any reason why the debt should not be included as part of the deceased's estate.

If the answer to question 6, on whether there is evidence to prove the loan, is "yes", the evidence should be supplied when sending in form IHT200. If no evidence can be offered, details of the period of the loan prior to death, and when it will become repayable, should be given. If interest is charged on the loan, the rate of interest and the period over which it is charged should be stated in reply to question 7. If capital was repaid to the deceased during his lifetime, the amount and date of the repayment should be given in answer to question 8. If the capital was not repaid, but was released by the deceased during his lifetime, this must have been evidenced in a deed, to be valid. A copy of the deed of release should be attached to the form. The release will also have been a PET (or LCT if made to a company) by the deceased if it was made within the seven years prior to death, and details of it should be included on form D3.

Form D9: Life Assurance and Annuities

Form D9 must be completed if the deceased paid any premiums on any life assurance policies, or if he was the life assured under any such policy. It also deals with payments made after the deceased's death under purchased life annuities. If the life assurance policy or annuity was in the joint names of the deceased and someone else, and a payment under it falls due on the deceased's death, it should not be included on this form, but on form D4 (see page 46).

Question 1 relates to any policy owned by the deceased and not written into trust. The name of the insurance company, policy number and amount payable must be given. Question 2a deals with "joint life second death" policies and 2b with second-hand policies, or policies taken out by the deceased on someone else's life. A copy of the policy document and details of its value at the date of death should be supplied. If the deceased paid all the premiums on a policy which was on the joint lives of him and someone else, and the policy was also owned by them jointly, he may have been making a PET and details of the premiums paid should be included on form D3 (see page 43).

If the deceased purchased a life annuity under which regular payments continue to be made after his death, the details to be given in response to question 3 are:
- the name of the annuity company;
- the annual gross amount payable;
- the proportions of that payment that are classed as income and capital;
- the regularity of the payment;
- the date of the final guaranteed payment and any guaranteed increases in the remaining period; and
- the value of the right to receive the remainder of the payments.

Question 4 deals with the situation where a lump sum is payable to the estate under a purchased life annuity; the reply must contain the name of the annuity company, how the lump sum is calculated and the amount payable. If the lump sum does not fall into the estate, an explanation must be given as to whom it passes.

If the answer to question 5, "Did the deceased, within seven years of their death, pay any premium on a life insurance policy for the benefit of someone else, other than the deceased's spouse?" is "yes", this will have been a gift by the deceased, and form D3 should be completed in respect of it.

Question 6 asks whether the deceased had any right to benefit from a life insurance policy taken out on another person's life and held in trust for the benefit of the deceased and others. If the answer is "yes", the deceased will have been a beneficiary of a trust, details of which should be given on form D5 (see page 47).

Form D10: Household and Personal Goods

Form D10 concerns the deceased's chattels. Question 1 asks for information relating to any chattels that have already been sold. The gross sale price shown should be the market value at the date of death, even if chattels have been sold at an undervalue.

Question 2 relates to unsold items. If a valuation has been prepared, it should be appended to the form. If the deceased owned a car, an estimate of its value should be obtained from a professional dealer, or may be taken from *Glass's* or *Parker's* guide. For cars, boats, caravans and aeroplanes, confirmation of the make, model, year of registration and registration number should be given. A private number plate may also have a value, which should be stated separately.

Form D11: Interest in Another Estate

Form D11 relates only to a vested interest the deceased had in another estate, i.e. he was absolutely entitled to the interest at the date of his death, but the assets had not yet been passed to him from the estate. The form does not apply to interests that are contingent or conditional upon the happening of a certain criterion.

The full nature of the deceased's entitlement should be inserted in reply to question 4, and confirmation of any assets that had already been passed to him should be given in 5. Question 6 requires information about what the deceased had yet to receive from the estate. The value to be given is the value of the assets not passed to the deceased as at the date of his death, and is therefore not the same as the value of those assets for probate purposes in the predecessor's estate. It may be particularly difficult to produce a valuation if the deceased was entitled to the residue of the predecessor's estate. The debts and distributions still to be paid from the other estate must be taken into account. If the figure can be provided only as an estimate, this must be clearly marked in box L3 on form IHT200.

If inheritance tax was payable on the estate of the predecessor on the assets passing to the deceased, those assets may also be taxable in the deceased's estate. "Double tax" or "quick succession" relief from inheritance tax may be available. This is considered in more detail at page 73 *et seq.*

Form D12: Land, Buildings and Interests in Land

Form D12 must be completed for all land and buildings, or interests in land and buildings, held by the deceased, whether in his sole name or jointly with anyone else. The contact details for the personal representatives or the solicitor acting on their behalf should normally be inserted in box 1. If a professional valuer was employed, and is willing to act on the personal representatives' behalf in negotiating the value of any land or buildings with the District Valuer, his details also can be inserted here. In practice, however, it is often easier if negotiations are conducted through the personal representatives or their solicitor, to enable them to control the process.

Column B on form D12 should contain an accurate description of the property so that the District Valuer can obtain maps and plans of the area or visit it easily. If the postcode is not known and the land may be difficult to locate, it is generally helpful if the personal representatives can provide a plan to IR Capital Taxes when the form is sent in. If the deceased held the land jointly with a third party, the deceased's share should be given in this column as well. Column C elicits whether the land or property was held freehold or leasehold by the deceased, and any rent being paid. If the deceased leased the property to a third party, details of the lease should be included in column D and a copy of the agreement enclosed with the form. The information that must be provided in the lease or given in the form is:
- the date of commencement and expiry;
- the rent payable;
- whether and, if so, when, the rent may be reviewed;
- who pays the outgoings on the property; and
- the name of the tenant.

If the property was unoccupied at the date of death, this should be specified in column D.

If any of the reliefs at the head of column E (agricultural, timber or heritage) are being claimed, the value of the relief must be inserted in column E. The value of the land or buildings without deducting any relief is given in column F. If the deceased was the joint owner of the property and the value of his share has been discounted, this column should also contain an explanation of how that discount has been calculated. The total in column F must equal the values of the deceased's property carried forward to section G of form IHT200 (see page 37) and in question 2 on form D4 (see page 46).

Question 3 calls for details of any damage to any property which might affect its value. A deduction from the value is permitted only if the damage is substantial; the need for redecoration, for example, does not suffice. The Inland Revenue help sheet, form D12 (Notes), gives the example that the damage is "of the kind that is likely to be covered by insurance". If that is the case, the personal representatives must declare, on form D17 (see page 59) that they intend to make a claim, and append copies of any correspondence with the insurers.

Column H of form D12, headed "present position of sale", should be used to confirm whether the property is on the market, whether a sale has been agreed, or whether contracts have been exchanged. If contracts have been exchanged, the date of exchange must be given. The prospective or agreed selling price is to be shown in column I, and the personal representatives may state in column L whether they wish to use this as the value at the date of death. Column J is used to clarify whether or not the sale is at "arm's length".

The value submitted in relation to any property is generally the most difficult matter to be agreed with IR Capital Taxes during the course of the administration. The form D12 is automatically forwarded to the District Valuer, who will consider whether the valuation submitted is appropriate. If he considers it to be incorrect, he opens negotiations with the personal representatives as to what the correct value should be. This is based on the selling prices of other similar properties in the area and any other factors the District Valuer decides to take into account. He may also wish to visit the property in person. It is advisable for the personal representatives to co-operate with the District Valuer fully in these negotiations. Usually, a compromise can be reached. If not, the District Valuer may impose a value upon the personal representatives, although they do have the right to appeal this decision.

Form D13: Agricultural Relief
Form D13 must be completed if agricultural property relief from inheritance tax is being claimed on any of the deceased's assets. The criteria for qualifying for the relief, and the rates at which it is given, are discussed at page 68 *et seq*. A different form should be filled in for each separate property in respect of which agricultural property relief is claimed.

Questions 2a and 2b ask whether the deceased occupied the property in question for the purposes of agriculture throughout the two years before his death; and whether the whole of the property was owned by the deceased and occupied for agricultural purposes throughout the seven years up to his death. If both are answered in the negative, agricultural property relief is not usually available. The personal representatives are, however, given an opportunity, in response to question 2c, to explain why the property should nevertheless qualify. This is usually because the deceased inherited the property from someone else, or the property replaced other agricultural property.

Question 3 should be answered to say whether the land was used for arable, pastoral or mixed farming; the type of crop grown or livestock kept; the number of livestock; and, if the land was of mixed use, the number of acres used by each.

If the deceased ceased agricultural activities on the land, when and why this happened must also be given in reply to question 4. The land may qualify for agricultural property relief if it was managed under an agri-environmental or habitat scheme arrangement.

If a copy of any lease relating to the land cannot be appended as requested by question 5c, the following information must be provided:

- when the tenancy started;
- the length of the lease; and
- the rent paid.

The date of 31 August 1995 mentioned in the question is relevant, because if a tenancy started after this date the land automatically qualifies for relief at 100 per cent.

For deaths after 10 March 1992, if the deceased was able to obtain vacant possession of the land within twenty-four months of the date of death, agricultural property relief at 100 per cent is available. If vacant possession could not be obtained within that time, agricultural property relief is available at the reduced rate of 50 per cent. There is a limited circumstance in which the higher rate of relief may nevertheless be available, but the criteria for this are:

- the tenancy began before 10 March 1981; and
- the deceased owned the land before that date; and
- the land would have qualified for full agricultural property relief at that date under the then existing law; and
- the deceased did not and could not obtain vacant possession of the land between 10 March 1981 and the date of death.

If these criteria are met, a form 220 should be completed and sent to IR Capital Taxes with the IHT200.

In response to question 7, on the occupation of any farmhouse, building or cottage, the personal representatives need to give details of:

- who lived in the building(s);
- how long they had been living there;
- the type of tenancy (agricultural or assured shorthold);
- the rent payable;
- why the occupier lived there; and
- whether the building is of a character "appropriate" to the

agricultural property.

Question 8 asks whether the property, or any part of it, was subject to a binding contract for sale at the date of death. A binding contract for sale is one under which the deceased's personal representatives can be forced to convey the property. If the answer to the question is "yes", the land subject to the contract does not qualify for agricultural property relief (section 124, Inheritance Tax Act 1984), unless the majority of the consideration payable under the sale is shares in a company purchasing the property, and the shares to be made over to the deceased would give him control of the company.

Question 9 deals with gifts of agricultural property made by the deceased during his lifetime. For these purposes, the "relevant period" is the period from the date of the gift to the deceased's date of death.

Form D14: Business Relief, Business or Partnership Interests

Form D14 relates to assets upon which business property relief from inheritance tax is claimed. The availability of this exemption, and the amount of relief available, are dealt with at page 63 *et seq*. A separate form should be completed for each business (or interest in a business) in respect of which the relief is claimed.

Question 2 asks how long the deceased held the business assets in question. If they did not belong to him throughout the two years prior to his death, business property relief may not be available unless the deceased inherited the assets from someone else, or they replaced other business assets that had been disposed of.

Under section 113, Inheritance Tax Act 1984, if the assets were subject to a binding contract for sale at death, they do not qualify for business property relief. But the transaction does qualify for relief if the assets are to be purchased by a company wishing to use the assets in its own business and the consideration for the sale is shares or securities in that company; or the sale is of shares and is taking place solely to facilitate a reconstruction or amalgamation of the company. If either of these situations is relevant, an explanation should be given in reply to question 3.

If the deceased owned unquoted shares, the number and type of the shares, and name of the company, should to be listed in reply to question 4a. In addition, the company registration number, and a brief description of the company's activities, must be given. If the deceased's spouse also owned shares in the company, the number and type of shares should be listed on form D17 (see page 59). If the company was in liquidation or in the process of being wound up at the date of death, this may jeopardise the business property relief available. The date of the liquidation, or how far the process had progressed, should be inserted in box 4a.

Question 5 deals with a business in which the deceased was a sole trader or partner. A useful starting point in valuing such a business is the last set of accounts. If the business is simple, combining the value of the capital and current accounts may be sufficient. Book values of assets should not be used, as they do not necessarily represent the true open market value at the date of death. It is, however, likely that the accountants for the business will have to be approached to prepare a formal valuation. In any event, the accounts for the two years prior to the deceased's death should be forwarded to IR Capital Taxes.

The name and principal activity of the business must be shown in reply to question 5b. If the business changed its name or activity in the two years prior to death, details of its previous name and/or activities should also be supplied.

If the business was a partnership, question 5c should be answered "yes" and a copy of the partnership agreement supplied. If an agreement is not available, the personal representatives must specify when the partnership began; who provided the partnership capital and in what shares; and how the profits were shared.

Question 6 deals with assets that were owned by the deceased but used by a partnership or company in which he had an interest. The value given in reply to question 6a is transferred to box G9 on form IHT200. In response to question 6b, the personal representatives should describe the main activities of the business or company and the extent to which the deceased participated in running it.

Question 7, on claiming business relief in connection with a lifetime transfer, relates only to gifts made during the deceased's lifetime. Business property relief is generally available only if:

- the recipient of the gift still owned it at the deceased's death; and
- the assets in the hands of the recipient would have qualified for business property relief at the date of death; and
- the assets were not subject to a binding contract for sale.

Form D15: Foreign Assets

Form D15 must be completed if the deceased was domiciled (or deemed to be domiciled) in England and Wales, Scotland or Northern Ireland at the date of his death and held assets abroad. For these purposes, if a grant is being applied for in England and Wales, assets situated in Scotland and Northern Ireland are treated as foreign assets and should be listed on this form. The converse applies if the grant application is being made in Scotland or Northern Ireland.

Questions 1 and 2 of the form distinguish between instalment and non-instalment option property, calling for details of the assets outside the UK. The rules on whether an asset qualifies as instalment option property are the same in relation to foreign assets as in relation to any other asset (see page 78).

The value of assets should be given in both the relevant foreign currency and in sterling, using the conversion rate in force at the date of death. Conversion rates are dealt with at page 34.

If a share is in a foreign company but listed on the London Stock Exchange it does not qualify as a foreign asset. It should be shown on form D7 (see page 50) with the deceased's other shareholdings.

If a debt is owed to anyone resident abroad it should be shown as a liability on form D15, unless it was charged on UK property owned by the deceased, or it arose in the UK. In either of those situations it must be shown in Section F or G on IHT200. The extra cost of dealing with the asset as a result of its being situated abroad can also be treated as a liability, but only to the extent of the difference between how much the asset costs to be dealt with abroad, compared with how much it would cost to be dealt with in the UK. In any event, this extra cost is not allowed as a liability unless it is greater than five per cent of the gross value of all the deceased's foreign assets. If the net assets in box FP5 (net assets, non-instalment property) on form D15 would be a negative figure, the excess debt may be carried over to box FP10 (net assets, instalment property) and *vice versa*. Only if there is a deficit in both boxes may the surplus debt be carried over to Section F or G on IHT200, as appropriate.

Assets held abroad in joint names should be shown on this form, not on form D4. The questions raised on form D4 (see page 46) should, however, still be answered on form D17.

The figures from form D15 must be transferred onto the inheritance tax work sheet or directly into section H of the IHT200.

Form D16: Debts Owed by the Estate

Form D16 is used to give more information regarding loans made to the deceased and which the estate must repay. Question 1 deals with debts due to close friends or relatives. The name of the lender, together with the date on which the loan was made, and why it was made, should be given. An explanation of why the deceased did not use his own funds must be included. If the debt relates to money spent on behalf of the deceased by a third party the name of the lender must again be given, together with the date on which the money was spent, and why the deceased did not use his own funds to repay the loan during his lifetime.

Other loans and overdrafts are to be detailed in reply to question 2. The date a loan was made, and whether the deceased gave security for the loan, should be specified. How the value of the money lent is reflected in the deceased's estate should also be stated.

Question 3 relates to guarantee debts. These arise when one person agrees to repay a loan made to a second person if the second person defaults on the loan. The following details should be given:

- the name of the original debtor;
- the circumstances giving rise to the guarantee;
- whether the deceased has ever been called upon to fulfil the guarantee and pay part of the debt; and
- if not, why a deduction should be allowed.

Section 103, Finance Act 1986 deals with loans made to a person after 18 March 1986 where the money lent is gifted back to the person who made the loan; or the money lent is used to purchase a policy of life assurance, the proceeds of which are written into trust. Section 103 may apply even if the loan was repaid before death. If the personal representatives are claiming that such a debt falls within the deceased's estate, and it has not already been detailed in any of the previous boxes, details, similar to those set out above, should be given in reply to question 4. If the money lent was the subject of a later gift made by the deceased, that gift may also have to be declared on form D3 (see page 43). Details of the original debt must be given, if made in these circumstances, even if it was repaid prior to the deceased's death.

Form D17: Continuation Sheet for Additional Information

Form D17 is used for any extra information not contained in any of the other D forms, or as a continuation sheet if there is not enough space on any form. In particular, it should be used to give the name, date of birth and domicile of any spouse in respect of whom the spouse exemption is claimed (see page 74); and the registered charity number of any charity taking a benefit in respect of which the charity exemption has been deducted (see page 75).

Form D18: Probate Summary

Form D18 is completed so as to summarise the inheritance tax position. In due course it is endorsed as the receipt for any inheritance tax paid. It relates only to the assets passing under the grant of representation, so must not contain any figures relating to assets held as joint tenants; foreign property passing under a foreign grant; assets held in trust over which the deceased did not have a general power of appointment (or over which he did have such a power but chose not to exercise it in his Will); or nominated assets.

Form D19: Confirmation that No Inheritance Tax is Payable

Form D19 is used as a substitute clearance certificate where no inheritance tax is payable. It may be submitted with the IHT200 to IR Capital Taxes. If

IR Capital Taxes agrees that no inheritance tax is chargeable on the estate, the form is duly stamped and returned. This acts as confirmation to the personal representatives that IR Capital Taxes have no queries to raise in relation to the value of the estate, and the personal representatives can go ahead to make distributions in the knowledge that no further enquiries will be made. If, however, the estate changes in value, or new assets come to the attention of the personal representatives, the form ceases to protect the personal representatives, who must notify IR Capital Taxes of the changes.

Submitting the Completed Forms

Once form IHT200 and any supplementary D forms have been completed, if a solicitor is acting on behalf of the personal representatives, the forms are forwarded to IR Capital Taxes in Nottingham, unless the application for the grant is being made to the Newcastle Probate Registry, in which case the forms should be forwarded to IR Capital Taxes in Edinburgh. If the deceased was domiciled in Scotland or Northern Ireland, the forms should be sent to IR Capital Taxes in Edinburgh or Belfast respectively. See Appendix B for the appropriate addresses.

If there is inheritance tax to pay, the documents that must be sent are:
- form IHT200 and forms D1 to 17;
- form D18;
- supporting documents, such as leases or contracts;
- a cheque for the inheritance tax due.

IR Capital Taxes stamps form D18 as a receipt for the inheritance tax paid and returns it to the solicitor. It is then forwarded on to the probate registry with the application for the grant. If the personal representatives need the grant particularly urgently, they can ask IR Capital Taxes to return the D18 directly to the probate registry, which may save a day or two.

If there is no inheritance tax to pay, the following items should be sent to IR Capital Taxes:
- form IHT200 and forms D1 to 17;
- form D19;
- supporting documents.

Form D19 is stamped and returned by IR Capital Taxes as soon as it is in agreement that no inheritance tax is payable, or IR Capital Taxes raises queries.

If the personal representatives are acting in person, they should first submit the form D18, together with the other documents necessary to apply for the grant, to the probate registry and attend for an interview. The documents are examined at the probate registry, and, if everything is correct, D18 is returned to the personal representatives. The application for the grant is not processed at the registry until the procedure with IR Capital Taxes has been completed. IR Capital Taxes will itself calculate the inheritance tax payable, in which case a cheque for the tax need not be sent until it is requested. Only after any inheritance tax has been paid does IR Capital Taxes complete form D18 as a receipt and return it to the applicants for lodging in the probate registry, clearing the application for the grant to be processed. Alternatively a D19 certificate that no inheritance is payable allows the application for a grant to be dealt with.

Changes to the Estate Value
If, during the course of the administration, the personal representative(s) discover further assets, or for any other reason the value of any asset changes, or the initial valuation alters, IR Capital Taxes must be notified and a corrective account may need to be filed; see page 232. IR Capital Taxes should also be notified if a grant of double probate is applied for (see page 169).

Allowances against, and relief from, inheritance tax are discussed in Chapter 4. Finalising the inheritance tax position and closing matters with IR Capital Taxes is dealt with in Chapter 20.

Chapter 4

Inheritance Tax Reliefs and Allowances

The Basis for the Charge

Completing the inheritance tax forms for submission to IR Capital Taxes has been explained in Chapter 3 above, but it is important to understand how the inheritance tax regime operates.

Upon a person's death he is deemed to make a "transfer of value" of all the assets in his estate immediately before his death (section 4, Inheritance Tax Act 1984). A person's "estate" is defined in section 5 as:

"... the aggregate of all the property to which he is beneficially entitled, except that the estate of a person immediately before his death does not include excluded property".

For the purposes of this section, property over which the deceased had a general power of appointment (i.e. he was able to control its destination by his Will or codicil or other document executed by him during his lifetime) is treated as belonging to him beneficially.

Excluded Property

"Excluded property" is referred to in various sections of the Inheritance Tax Act 1984. Section 6 defines "excluded property" in a person's free estate (free estate being assets in the deceased's legal name and belonging to him beneficially) as:

- property situated outside the UK if the person to whom it beneficially belonged was not domiciled in the UK;
- UK government securities authorised as exempt, and owned by a person who was not resident or ordinarily resident in the UK when he died, and his death was after 6 April 1998;
- war savings certificates, National Savings certificates, premium bonds, deposits with the National Savings bank and certain SAYE schemes if they belonged to a person domiciled in the Channel Islands or the Isle of Man.

Occasionally, foreign currency accounts held at some high street or foreign banks qualify as excluded property – an enquiry should be raised with IR Capital Taxes if this may be the case.

Excluded property in relation to a trust is defined in section 48 as:
- a reversionary interest not acquired for money or money's worth; not belonging to the settlor or his spouse; and not arising under a lease upon which a full market rent is not payable;
- property in a trust held outside the UK where the settlor of the trust was not domiciled in the UK at the time he created the trust.

While property falling within the above definitions is not subject to inheritance tax, some assets may be partially or wholly relieved from the charge to inheritance tax. These reliefs and exemptions can operate in relation to property in the deceased's taxable estate (including any property forming part of his estate by virtue of his being entitled to it under a trust) or to gifts and transfers made by him prior to death but which are brought back into his taxable estate upon his death. There are several types of relief, explained below.

Business Property Relief

Business property relief is governed by the Inheritance Tax Act 1984, sections 103 to 114. Section 104 provides for the relief. It applies to shares in companies, interests in businesses, and assets used by them both. Section 103(3) states that a "business ... includes a business carried on in the exercise of a profession or vocation, but does not include a business carried on otherwise than for gain". To be "carried on for gain" does not mean that the business must be profitable, but it should be a "... serious undertaking earnestly pursued" (*Rael Brook Limited v Minister of Housing and Local Government* [1967] 2 QB 65, [1967] 2 WLR 604, [1967] 1 All ER 262). The business must be more than a simple hobby or leisure pastime.

Before the relief is applied, the business interests or shares are valued. If the assets are shares in a company or an interest in a partnership, a discount may be applied to the value of the business because of the lack of realisability of the asset. Generally, if the deceased owned 75 per cent or more of the shares or business, the discount is limited. If he owned 50 to 75 per cent of the business or shares, the discount is greater, the maximum applying if the deceased owned less than 50 per cent. The discount depends on the type of business or company, and how easy it would be to sell.

A separate decision is then taken as to how much of the business assets or shares qualify as "relevant business property" (see below). The relief is applied to the relevant business property, to reduce its value. Inheritance tax is charged on the reduced value.

How much qualifies?

There is no limit to the amount of property that can qualify for business property relief, but the value of a business is its net value (including goodwill), after deducting any liabilities of the business, even if they are secured on non-business assets (section 110, Inheritance Tax Act 1984). While the value of an asset qualifying for business property relief should never be artificially inflated, there is nothing to be gained (and possibly much to be lost) by understating the value of assets qualifying for the relief. If the assets are not relieved from tax in the deceased's estate, it makes no difference whether they are shown as worth £1 or £1,000,000, as long as the value is correct and can be substantiated. But there may be a substantial effect on future liability to capital gains tax. As the beneficiary taking the assets will have, as his capital gains tax base cost, the probate value of the assets in the deceased's estate, the beneficiary will naturally wish the probate value to be as high as possible.

In addition, even if an asset does not qualify for business property relief, if it can be shown that it is a business asset, the inheritance tax on it may be paid by instalments (see page 78). Thus it may be advisable for the personal representatives to seek to include as many assets as possible as business assets, even if they do not qualify for business property relief.

Relevant business property
To qualify, a business asset must be "relevant business property", as defined in section 105. This is:
1. a business or interest in a business. This includes a capital account held by a partner in a business. Once the partner retires from that business, however, he is treated as any other creditor and the account does not qualify as relevant business property (*Beckman v IRC* [2000] STC (SCD) 59);
2. unquoted securities in a company which, on their own or together with other unquoted shares and securities owned by the deceased, gave the deceased control of the company;
3. any unquoted shares in a company (this includes companies listed on AIM as unquoted);
4. quoted shares or securities in a company which, on their own or with other shares and securities owned by the deceased, gave him control of the company;
5. any land or building, machinery or plant which was used wholly or mainly for the purposes of a business in which the deceased was a partner or by a company that he controlled. If, though, this property was leased to the business or company by the deceased at a commercial rent, it may qualify as an investment property and as such fail to qualify for business property relief (see below);
6. any land, building, machinery or plant which was used wholly or mainly for the purposes of a business carried on by the deceased and which was subject to a trust in which the deceased had an interest in

possession.

The case of *Hardcastle v IRC* [2000] STC (SCD) 532 related to the estate of a Lloyds Name. It is of general application, however, in that it confirmed that ordinary commercial contracts, if they are not "assets used in a business", even if they were incurred by the business or by a person acting on behalf of a business, are not to be taken into account in valuing the business for the purposes of business property relief. In the circumstances of the case, this decision was beneficial to the estate because it meant that losses arising on open accounts (i.e., accounts under which the final profit/loss figures had not been announced before the deceased's death) that had not been declared by Lloyds before the date of the deceased's death were not deductible when valuing the business assets for the purposes of business property relief. This meant that they could instead be deducted from the deceased's estate that would otherwise have been subject to inheritance tax. The decision would, however, have led to a greater inheritance tax bill in relation to the estate if the accounts in question had generated a profit.

The case of *IRC v Mallender* [2001] STC (SCD) 514 (Ch D) also related to a Lloyds Name. The deceased's bank had guaranteed his Lloyds liabilities in return for his giving the bank an indemnity. The indemnity was secured by a mortgage granted to the bank over commercial land owned by the deceased. Upon the deceased's death, the personal representatives submitted that the value of the land itself should be taken into account as an asset used for the purposes of a business because it was used as security. The Capital Taxes Office (the forerunner of IR Capital Taxes) argued that the land was not used in the business, but was only facilitating a guarantee. They agreed that the *guarantee* should be classed as a business asset. On appeal from the decision of the Special Commissioners, it was held that the Capital Taxes Office was correct. The land itself was not used for the purposes of the business – it merely supported other assets that were.

Period of ownership

An asset must have been held during the period of two years prior to the deceased's death if it is to qualify as relevant business property (section 106), although assets which have been held for less than two years may still qualify if they have replaced other relevant business property (section 107). If the deceased inherited the assets from a third party, he is treated as having owned them from the date of that party's death. If the third party was his spouse, he is treated as having owned them throughout his spouse's period of ownership (section 108), but this applies only to assets to which the deceased became entitled on someone else's death; if he purchased the assets from that person's estate, his ownership begins on the date of purchase.

The meaning of "control"

As mentioned above, certain shares or securities qualify for business property relief only if they gave the deceased control of the company. "Control" is defined in section 269, Inheritance Tax Act 1984 as:

"the control of powers of voting on all questions affecting the company as a whole which if exercised would yield a majority of the votes capable of being exercised on them".

The definition means that control can be beneficially held only by a person who holds *more than* 50 per cent of the shares in the company. In *Walkers Executors v IRC* [2001] STC (SCD) 86, however, the Special Commissioners held that owning 50 per cent of the voting shares, together with having a casting vote as Chairman of the board of directors, meant that the shareholder had voting control of the company.

Rate of relief

The rate of relief depends on the date of death. For deaths after 6 April 1996, categories 1, 2 and 3 listed on page 64 qualify for relief at 100 per cent. Assets in categories 4, 5 and 6 qualify at 50 per cent. For deaths prior to that date, different rates applied in respect of unquoted shares in a company, depending on whether they gave a controlling holding, a substantial holding (more than 25 per cent of the voting rights), or less.

Assets which do not qualify

Assets used by a business or shares in a company do not qualify as relevant business property if the main or whole activity of the business or company is dealing in stocks, shares, land or buildings, or making or holding investments, unless the business or company is a market maker or discount house carrying on business in the UK, or is a holding company of a company whose business does not fall within one of those categories.

This means that even if the deceased owned unquoted shares in a trading company, the relief may be limited if the company held cash in excess of that which would be needed by the company either at the time the deceased died or in the foreseeable future.

Problems can arise where it is arguable whether an activity qualifies as a trade or an investment. A good example is the business of providing furnished holiday rentals. Properties that are rented out are investments, while the ownership and running of a hotel qualifies as a trade. Holiday lettings fall between these two categories. IR Capital Taxes Advanced Instruction Manual indicates, at L.99.3, that if the rental period is short (e.g. weekends or weeks) and the rental business is carried out personally by the owner, the activity should qualify as a trade. However, if the property is let on a longer lease, or if the owner takes very little active part in managing the lettings, or if the property is let only to friends and relatives, the availability of relief should be considered in more detail.

The phrase "wholly or mainly" in the definition of relevant business property means that where a business or company has both a trading and an investment operation, they may still qualify for business property relief. IR Capital Taxes generally accepts that the "wholly or mainly" criterion is satisfied if the trading operation is more than 50 per cent of the business. There are, however, many different methods of judging how much of the business is accounted for by trading activities. This has led to much case law, particularly in the field of the ownership of caravan parks, the nature of which typically includes both investment activities (the rental of caravans) and trading activities (the sale of goods to tenants, providing entertainment facilities). In 1999, it was held, in the case of *Farmer and Another v IRC* [1999] STC (SCD) 321, that a global picture of the business should be examined and that regard should be had to five factors before a decision could be made. The five factors were: the overall context of the business, the net profits produced, the time spent on each activity, the capital employed in each activity and the level of turnover generated. That case highlighted that the presentation of the business accounts is also important. If they are presented as a single composite set, the business can be seen as one business consisting of different types of activity. This may mean that if the investment activities are too great given the context of the business, business property relief will not be available on the entire value of the business. If the accounts were separated out, however, this may mean that business property relief is available for one side of the business only, and not the other.

Contracts for sale

If the relevant business property is subject to a binding contract for sale at death, business property relief will be refused under section 113, Inheritance Tax Act 1984. A binding contract for sale arises, not only if the deceased had made a contract to sell his shares but died before it could be completed, but also where a contract exists such that, upon the death of the deceased, his personal representatives must sell the assets to a third party. The personal representatives should examine any shareholders' agreement, the Memorandum and Articles of Association, any option agreement or partnership agreement, to check whether such a contract has been made. Generally, option agreements are "safe" in that they do not impose on either party an obligation to buy or sell, but tightly structured "put and call" agreements may come under scrutiny by IR Capital Taxes.

Contracts for sale do, however, qualify if the sale is of a business or an interest in a business to a company which will carry on the business, and the consideration for the sale is shares or securities in that company; or if the sale is of shares or securities in a company and the contract is made for the purposes of reconstruction or amalgamation.

Business and agricultural property

Section 114 provides that where an asset could qualify for both business property relief and agricultural property relief, agricultural property relief takes precedence.

Agricultural Property Relief

Sections 115 to 124 of the Inheritance Tax Act 1984 provide for agricultural property relief. It is awarded in respect of "agricultural property" and is dealt with in a manner similar to that relating to business property relief. The agricultural assets of the deceased are valued and the personal representatives then assess how much of that value is attributable to agricultural property. The relief appropriate is deducted from the value of the agricultural property to determine the value which is subject to the charge to inheritance tax.

The meaning of "agricultural property"

Agricultural property is defined in section 115(2) as:

"... agricultural land or pasture and includes woodland and any building used in connection with the intensive rearing of livestock or fish if the woodland or building is occupied with agricultural land or pasture and the occupation is ancillary to that of the agricultural land or pasture; and also includes such cottages, farm buildings and farmhouses, together with the land occupied with them, as are of a character appropriate to the property".

Only land in the UK, Channel Islands or the Isle of Man qualifies.

Section 115(4) specifically states that the breeding, rearing and grazing of horses on a stud farm is agriculture and any buildings used in connection with that activity are farm buildings.

Only the agricultural value of agricultural property qualifies for relief from inheritance tax. The agricultural value is the value of the property as if it were subject to a perpetual covenant prohibiting its use otherwise than as agricultural property (section 115(3)). Therefore, if land the deceased was farming at his death has an increased value because it has potential for development, only the value of the land attributable to the farming activities qualifies for relief; the increased development value does not, although it may be eligible for business property relief instead.

The meaning of "agriculture"

The inheritance tax legislation does not itself define "agriculture". The most commonly used definition is contained in section 38(1) of the Agricultural Tenancies Act 1995, which provides that it includes:

"... horticulture, fruit growing, seed growing, dairy farming and livestock breeding and keeping, the use of land as grazing land, meadow land, osier land, market gardens and nursery grounds, and the use of land for woodlands where that use is ancillary to the farming of land for other agricultural purposes."

In addition, the IR Capital Taxes Advanced Instruction Manual (paragraph L.220.1) sets out:

"Although not defined in the [inheritance tax] legislation agriculture should in practice be treated as including horticulture, fruit growing, seed growing, dairy farming, livestock breeding and keeping where the animals are for consumption or the production of food, the use of land as grazing land for such animals, osier land, market gardens and nursery grounds, and the use of land for woodlands where that use is ancillary to the farming of land for other agricultural purposes. Agricultural land is taken to mean land used for agriculture."

Further, section 154, Finance Act 1995 permits short rotation coppice to qualify as agriculture, and section 124C, Inheritance Tax Act 1984 confirms that land used in certain habitat schemes (as specified in that section) is regarded as agriculture.

Period of occupation or ownership

The legislation allows agricultural property relief where:

- the deceased himself used the land for the purposes of agriculture; or
- the deceased owned the land and allowed it to be used by another for the purposes of agriculture.

In the first situation, to qualify for relief, the deceased must have occupied the land for a minimum of two years. In the second situation, the deceased must have owned the land for seven years prior to his death and throughout that time it must have been occupied by a third party for the purposes of agriculture (section 117, Inheritance Tax Act 1984).

Section 118 provides for agricultural assets to qualify if, although they do not fulfil the above conditions, they were purchased as replacement assets for other agricultural assets, subject to certain conditions. Section 120 states that where the deceased inherited the land on the death of a third party, he is treated as having owned and occupied it (where relevant) from the date of the third party's death. As with business property relief, if the third party was his spouse, the deceased is deemed to have owned and occupied it throughout the time his spouse did so.

The meaning of "occupation"

While ownership of land is largely a question of fact, occupation can be more difficult to define. The Special Commissioners, in *Harrold v IRC* [1996] STC (SCD) 195, concluded that the levels of activity required to qualify as occupation would vary significantly, depending on what agricultural activities were carried out on the land. For example, the cultivation of hay may require relatively minimal input, whereas the keeping of dairy cattle is labour-intensive.

Section 119 of the Act confirms that if a company occupies land for the purposes of agriculture, the land is deemed to be occupied by the person controlling that company.

Agricultural buildings

To satisfy the conditions for relief, a farm house or building must be of a "character appropriate" to the agricultural property. This is a question of fact rather than law. The farm house should be the building from which the farm is run. In a letter to the magazine *Taxation* dated 15 June 2000, Peter Twiddy, the deputy director of IR Capital Taxes, indicated that the District Valuer would examine:

- whether the house is primarily a dwelling with land, or an agricultural unit incorporating an appropriate dwelling;
- local practice regarding what constitutes an appropriate farm house; and
- whether the land is capable of generating sufficient funds to maintain and run the house.

Farm buildings are generally easy to identify, but problems may be raised if farm cottages are let out, either to workers or as holiday cottages. Cottages let to farm workers generally qualify for full relief, because they are occupied for the purposes of agriculture. If they do not qualify for 100 per cent relief, a reduced rate of 50 per cent may still be available. This is dealt with in IR Capital Taxes Advanced Instruction Manual and two Extra-Statutory Concessions made in 1995. IR Capital Taxes consider such matters on a case-by-case basis.

Holiday cottages on farms do not qualify for agricultural property relief at all, although they may qualify for business property relief.

Assets which do not qualify

While the farm land and buildings qualify for agricultural property relief, assets used on the farm, including machinery and animals, do not. They should instead qualify for business property relief.

Milk quotas are no longer treated as forming part of the land to which they relate. They are a separate asset and should qualify as relevant business property.

Rate of relief

The crucial date determining the rate at which agricultural property relief is given is 10 March 1992. If the deceased died before that date, and the land was in vacant possession, or the deceased had a right to obtain vacant possession within twelve months of his death, the rate of relief is 50 per cent. If vacant possession could not be obtained within that time, the rate is reduced to 30 per cent.

If the deceased died after 10 March 1992, the rates are 100 per cent and 50 per cent respectively. In addition, if the deceased could not obtain vacant possession within twelve months because the property was let on a tenancy beginning after 1 September 1995, the rate of relief remains at 100 per cent (section 116, Inheritance Tax Act 1984).

Woodland Relief

Generally, woodland qualifies for agricultural property relief, but sections 125 to 130, Inheritance Tax Act 1984 allow for "woodland" relief in circumstances where woodland does not qualify for agricultural property relief. The deceased must have been entitled to the land during the five years prior to death, or become entitled to it without the payment of consideration. If either of those criteria is satisfied, and the person receiving the woodland so elects, the value of the underwood growing on the land (but not the land itself) can be deducted from the deceased's estate when calculating the liability to inheritance tax. This relief does not, however, operate to remove the liability to tax, only to defer it. When the underwood is later disposed of, inheritance tax must be paid on it at that time. In addition, the inheritance tax then charged is calculated on the value of the wood at the time of disposal, not at the time of the deceased's death.

Heritage Property

Relief in respect of heritage property is highly complex and it is beyond the scope of this book to cover it in any great detail. It is though, important to recognise when the heritage exemption *may* be available. It is granted by sections 30 to 35, Inheritance Tax Act 1984. Once again, this is a relief that allows deferral of the tax liability, but does not extinguish it altogether.

Eligible property

The exemption can apply to any real or personal property. IR Capital Taxes must designate that the property is:
- an object or collection of objects which are pre-eminent for their national, scientific, historic or artistic interest; or
- land which is of outstanding scenic, historic or scientific interest; or
- a building that should be preserved because of its historic or architectural interest and an area of land which is essential for its protection or an object which is historically associated with it

(section 31).

Whether an asset qualifies for the exemption is usually determined by IR Capital Taxes after taking advice from the appropriate body or council in relation to that asset, such as the National Trust. If an application for the exemption is to be made, it is often wise, before the papers are submitted, to discuss the position with the body that would be consulted by IR Capital Taxes, so that the personal representatives can decide on the best approach.

Period of ownership
In relation to assets being transferred as a result of the deceased's death, there is no minimum period of ownership by the deceased. If the deceased made a gift of the asset during his lifetime, he must have owned it for a minimum period of six years unless he obtained it on the death of a third party (section 30(3)).

Undertakings
To qualify for the exemption, the personal representatives in the first instance, and then the beneficiary entitled to the asset, must be willing to give undertakings to IR Capital Taxes regarding the retention of the asset within the UK, preserving it, and allowing the general public access to it.

Crystallisation of tax burden
Inheritance tax becomes payable under section 32 if the undertakings are breached or the asset is sold. It also becomes chargeable if the new owner of the asset dies or gives it away, although in those circumstances a new exemption may be claimed.

The tax charge is calculated by reference to the value of the asset at the time of crystallisation, not the value at the date of death.

Taper Relief
Taper relief is granted by section 7 of the Inheritance Tax Act 1984. It operates to reduce the inheritance tax payable on a PET or LCT that becomes chargeable on the subsequent death of the transferor. A popular misconception is that it reduces the value of the PET or LCT itself. This is not the case. Additionally, as a PET or LCT uses up the nil rate band of the deceased in priority to his chargeable estate (because it happened earlier in time than the deceased's death), it is often the case that the PET or LCT is not chargeable to tax at all, and so the relief is not available.

Taper relief becomes operative only if the deceased died more than three years after making the gift. If that is the case, the relief is as follows:

Number of whole calendar years between gift and death	*Percentage of tax payable*
3 – 4	80 per cent
4 – 5	60 per cent
5 – 6	40 per cent
6 – 7	20 per cent

Quick Succession Relief

Where the deceased received assets from a third party, and those assets were subject to inheritance tax upon that party's death, and the assets are also subject to inheritance tax upon the deceased's death, quick succession relief is available to reduce the inheritance tax payable upon the deceased's death, provided the two deaths occurred within five years of each other. This relief is provided for by section 141 Inheritance Tax Act 1984. The rates are:

Periods of time between deaths in calendar years	*Percentage reduction in inheritance tax payable on second death*
less than 1 year	100 per cent
1 – 2 years	80 per cent
2 – 3 years	60 per cent
3 – 4 years	40 per cent
4 – 5 years	20 per cent

Double Tax Relief

As mentioned above, where the deceased held assets abroad, or if he could be held under the laws of two countries to be domiciled in each, it is possible that a double charge to inheritance tax could arise if his assets are taxed in both jurisdictions.

There are two systems in place to alleviate this burden. The first is the double tax treaty, which is dealt with by section 158, Inheritance Tax Act 1984. Where, under the rules of two countries, a person could be domiciled in both of them, the double tax treaty governs where the person is to be treated as domiciled, and which country has the right to tax his assets. Double tax treaties also generally provide for one country (usually the country of domicile) to allow a credit in respect of the inheritance tax already paid in the country of non-domicile so that assets are not subject to a double charge to tax. Double tax treaties currently exist between the UK and Eire, South Africa, the USA, the Netherlands, Sweden, Switzerland, France, Italy, India and Pakistan.

Unilateral relief is also available under section 159. It applies where a tax (that is similar to inheritance tax) is chargeable in a foreign country on the deceased's assets, and those assets are also subject to inheritance tax in the UK. A credit is allowed in the UK in respect of the tax paid in the foreign jurisdiction, but only on the assets that are taxable in the UK. The tax paid abroad is converted at the London Selling Rate (see page 34) available on the date upon which the tax is paid there. If the currency was available only at a premium, that premium can also be deducted.

In addition to the reliefs afforded in respect of the assets listed above, the identity of the beneficiary, or the value of a transfer, may also lead to an exemption from inheritance tax. The exemptions available are given below.

Spouse Exemption

Section 18, Inheritance Tax Act 1984 provides that transfers to a spouse are exempt from inheritance tax. If the gift to the spouse takes effect only on the termination of any other interest in the asset (such as a life interest trust for the deceased's child with the interest in remainder passing to the spouse), or if the transfer is dependent on a condition that is not satisfied within twelve months of the transfer, the exemption is not available.

Subsection (4) confirms that assets transferred to be held on trust for a spouse qualify as assets passing to the spouse. This means that the creation of a life interest trust for a spouse would also be exempt if the spouse is the life tenant.

If the deceased was domiciled in the UK but the recipient spouse was not, the exemption is limited to assets to the value of £55,000.

If the deceased benefited under the Will or intestacy of his spouse who died before 13 November 1974, the capital value of the assets he received may not be brought into account when valuing his estate if estate duty was paid or treated as paid when the spouse died and the deceased was not competent to dispose of those assets at his death (because, for example, they were held in trust for his benefit).

Annual Exemption

The annual exemption allows each person to make gifts in any year to the value of £3,000, without inheritance tax becoming chargeable on them. In addition, if the deceased did not fully utilise his annual exemption in any one year, the unused part can be carried forward to the following year. The annual exemption applies by reference to the date upon which the gift was made, so that if the deceased gave £3,000 to his daughter on day 1, and a further £3,000 to his son on day 2, the gift to the daughter would be entirely exempt, and the gift to the son would be taxable.

The exemption is permitted by section 19, Inheritance Tax Act 1984 and is allowed only in relation to gifts made during the deceased's lifetime; it does not apply to any dispositions made in his Will.

Small Gifts

Section 20 of the Act allows the deceased to make gifts to as many individuals as he chooses in any year that do not exceed £250 in total per person. This exemption cannot be cumulated with the annual exemption in relation to any recipient, which means that the recipient either benefits from the £3,000 annual allowance (or part of it), or the gift made to him may fall within the small gifts exemption. The personal representatives must choose how to apply the exemptions in the most tax efficient manner.

Normal Expenditure out of Income

Where a gift was made unconditionally by the deceased out of his income, as part of his normal expenditure, and after the gift was made he still had sufficient income to maintain his normal standard of living, that gift is exempt under section 21.

The most difficult aspect of claiming this exemption is proving that the gift was made out of income and not out of capital. Evidence of the deceased's annual income and outgoings is necessary. The difference between the two is income that may be disposed of under this exemption. A client who kept accurate records of his income and expenditure in the years before his death simplifies this task greatly, although accountants can also be an invaluable source of information as to the amount of income received by the deceased.

The income gifted must also have formed part of the deceased's "normal expenditure". This is generally established by showing a regular pattern of payments. If the deceased dies after making only one or two payments, this does not necessarily preclude the exemption from applying, although it may make it more difficult to prove.

Gifts in Consideration of Marriage

A gift made on or shortly before a marriage, to either or both of the parties to that marriage (but so that only one exemption applies per marriage), may be exempt. If the deceased was a parent of one of the parties to the marriage, the amount exempt is £5,000. If either party was the grandchild or remoter issue of the deceased, the limit is £2,500; and if the party was any other person the amount allowed is £1,000 (section 22, Inheritance Tax Act 1984). The gift must be fully effective on the marriage taking place.

Gifts to Charities

Section 23 states that a gift to a charity is exempt from inheritance tax provided the gift takes full effect within twelve months of the date of transfer and is not subject to any prior interest. The deceased cannot have reserved to himself, or anyone connected with him, the right to use or reside in the asset, unless he pays a full market rent for that use or residence.

The asset may be gifted into a trust for charity, providing it can be used for charitable purposes only. If the Will is particularly restrictive of how the gifted asset may be used, this may disentitle the charity from the exemption.

Other Exemptions

There are other exemptions in sections 24 to 28, Inheritance Tax Act 1984. They are not discussed in detail here. Very briefly, they relate to:

- gifts to political parties, if two members of the party were elected to the House of Commons at the most recent general election, or one member was elected but at least 150,000 votes were cast in favour of that party's candidates (section 24);
- gifts made of land and buildings to a registered housing association (section 24A);
- gifts made for "national purposes" to various public bodies listed in Schedule 3 to the Act (sections 25 and 26A);
- gifts made into trust for the maintenance of certain heritage property (section 27);
- gifts made into trust for the benefit of employees of a certain company (section 28);
- *ex gratia* payments made to British prisoners of war held in Japan during World War II (extra-statutory concession F20).

Inland Revenue Penalties

In recent times, IR Capital Taxes has become more ready to penalise personal representatives for submitting inaccurate values in the IHT200. There are three main reasons why inaccurate values are submitted:

- The personal representatives know they are submitting an incorrect figure but wish to mislead IR Capital Taxes. Clearly this is fraud and attracts severe penalties.
- Knowingly submitting an estimated value that is later discovered to be wrong, generally with the intention of obtaining a grant as quickly as possible. If this is the case, for example because an asset is difficult to value and it will take some time for a proper market appraisal to be produced, it is acceptable for an estimate to be shown on the IHT200, but it should be clearly identified as a provisional estimate in box L3 on page 8 of the form. The personal representatives must undertake to supply a proper valuation as soon as it is available (section 216(3A), Inheritance Tax Act 1984). Even

so, IR Capital Taxes may still seek to levy a penalty if it considers the estimate to have been unreasonable.

• Mistakenly submitting an incorrect valuation. Providing the personal representatives make their mistake known to IR Capital Taxes as soon as possible and attempt to rectify it, they may escape without penalty.

These are rules of thumb and cannot be relied upon – every case is assessed on its merits. IR Capital Taxes is permitted to penalise anyone liable to pay the tax in relation to an estate for:

• late or non-delivery of an account (section 245, Inheritance Tax Act 1984);
• fraudulently or negligently delivering an incorrect account, supporting information or document (section 247, Inheritance Tax Act 1984); or
• failing within a reasonable time to rectify an error made in an account (section 248, Inheritance Tax Act 1984).

As mentioned above, these sections are strictly interpreted by IR Capital Taxes. The recent case of *Robertson v IRC (No 2)* [2002] STC (SCD) 242 demonstrates the harsh stance now being taken by IR Capital Taxes, but offers some hope to the taxpayer that it may have to relax its attitude. In that case, the solicitor acting for the personal representatives submitted estimated values for various assets in the deceased's estate, but clearly marked them as estimates upon submission of the IHT200. When the proper market values for the assets were established, and were substantially higher than the estimated values which had been submitted, he notified IR Capital Taxes immediately. IR Capital Taxes sought to penalise him on the basis that he did not make "the fullest enquiries reasonably practicable", as required by section 216(3A), Inheritance Tax Act 1984, and criticised the solicitor for his undue haste in submitting the form.

The Special Commissioners overruled the decision of IR Capital Taxes. They said that the solicitor acted in accordance with good practice and made the fullest enquiries that were reasonably practicable in the circumstances. They also awarded the solicitor his costs of the matter – an award made only where the Special Commissioners consider IR Capital Taxes to have acted unreasonably.

While this case is positive for the taxpayer, it is highly recommended that a proper valuation be obtained wherever possible before the IHT200 is completed. If such a valuation cannot be obtained, the estimate should be as accurate as possible and based upon a professional valuer's recommendations, so that the personal representatives can be seen to have acted properly.

Providing for Inheritance Tax

As mentioned on page 37, the inheritance tax payable on some assets must be paid immediately, and in respect of others it may be paid by instalments.

Instalment option property

Instalment option property is defined in sections 227 to 229 Inheritance Tax Act 1984 as "qualifying property". This is:

- land of any description, wherever situated;
- a business or an interest in a business;
- shares or securities in a company:
  - which gave the deceased control of the company (defined in section 269 as voting control, which is owning more than 50 per cent of the voting shares); or
  - which are unquoted, and 20 per cent or more of the total inheritance tax payable is attributable to them or to other property upon which the instalment option is available; or
  - which are unquoted and IR Capital Taxes is satisfied that the inheritance tax payable on them cannot be paid in one lump sum without causing undue hardship;
- shares (not securities) in a company which are valued at more than £20,000 and either the nominal value of the shares is 10 per cent or more of the nominal value of all the shares in the company, or the shares are ordinary and their nominal value is not less than 10 per cent of the nominal value of all the ordinary shares in the company. Ordinary shares are defined in section 228(4) as shares carrying a right to dividends that are not restricted to a fixed rate, or to which are attached a right to be converted into shares of this type.

In addition, inheritance tax payable on the disposal of woodlands which previously qualified for relief under section 125, Inheritance Tax Act 1984, may be paid by instalments under section 229, Inheritance Tax Act 1984.

Inheritance tax due on a failed PET or LCT can be paid by instalments only if:

- the asset gifted continued to be held by the transferee at the date of the deceased's death; or
- if it did not continue to be so held, the property disposed of has been replaced by property which also qualified for business property relief or agricultural property relief within section 113B or 124B, Inheritance Tax Act 1984; and
- in the case of unquoted shares, they remained unquoted at the date of death.

Interest

Although inheritance tax on qualifying property may be paid by instalments, interest is chargeable on those instalments from the date upon which the first instalment is due. Section 234, however, provides that interest on relevant business or agricultural property which has not qualified for relief from tax at 100 per cent will run only from the date upon which each instalment is due (i.e. interest is payable only if the tax is paid late).

Funding the Payment

Any inheritance tax due must be paid on submission of the IHT200. Once the amount has been established, the personal representatives must decide how the liability is to be discharged. They have a number of options.

Using the assets in the estate

It may be possible to secure the release of funds from the deceased's bank or building society, if the relevant institution is willing to do so. Building societies are often more responsive than banks in this regard. In April 2003, the Inland Revenue announced a new scheme to allow banks and building societies to make a direct transfer from the deceased's account to IR Capital Taxes in settlement of inheritance tax due. This should encourage the use of the deceased's funds to meet tax due and make it less likely that personal representatives need to take out a loan to pay the tax.

Alternatively, National Savings investments may be utilised. This is done by sending details of the deceased's National Savings investments to IR Capital Taxes at the same time as sending the form IHT200 to them. IR Capital Taxes then corresponds directly with National Savings to liquidate the investments and pay the tax. This can, though, be a lengthy process.

If the deceased owned shares that were held in the nominee name of a stockbroker, the shares can be sold by the nominee and the monies released by them to fund the tax bill.

Finally, if the deceased was a patient of the Court of Protection, the court may agree to pay the tax directly from funds held by it.

Life assurance policies

A life assurance policy on the deceased's life, which provides for payment on death, may have been taken out. If such a policy was taken out by the deceased and written into trust, the death benefit is automatically payable to the trustees upon proof of death. Equally, the owner of the policy may be a third party who took out a policy on the deceased's life. If this was the case and the beneficial owner of the proceeds of the policy (i.e. the trust beneficiary or third party who owned the policy) is the same person as the residuary beneficiary of the estate, that person may be willing to allow the policy proceeds to be used to pay the inheritance tax bill.

If that person is not the residuary beneficiary, or if, for example, he is one of two residuary beneficiaries, he may be willing to lend the policy proceeds to the estate on terms more favourable than a commercial loan (see below).

Raising a loan

If the personal representatives are not able to raise sufficient funds to pay the inheritance tax bill in any other manner, they may have to take out a loan. This could be a loan from an estate beneficiary or someone who has benefited from a policy of assurance on the deceased's life. If so, it is to be hoped that the terms of the loan could be favourable to the estate, although the beneficiary may wish to charge some interest.

If no such loan is possible, the personal representatives may have to take out a commercial loan from a bank. This can be quite time-consuming as banks usually require a complete breakdown of the estate, and an undertaking from the personal representatives that they will treat the loan as a first charge on the estate when repaying the deceased's debts. A bank usually charges both an arrangement fee and interest on the loan. It may be worthwhile for the personal representatives to agree a higher rate of interest and a lower arrangement fee, as interest is deductible from the income of the estate for income tax purposes, but an arrangement fee is not.

Using trust funds

If the deceased was a beneficiary of a life interest trust, and the remaindermen of the trust are the same people as the residuary beneficiaries of the estate, the trustees may agree to utilise the trust fund to pay *all* the inheritance tax due, not just the part relating to the trust assets.

Transfer of assets in satisfaction

Under sections 230 and 231, Inheritance Tax Act 1984, IR Capital Taxes may accept property transferred to it in lieu of the charge to inheritance tax and interest. The Secretary of State must agree to this. Any asset may be accepted, but in the case of chattels, they must be considered to be "pre-eminent", for example, a valuable work of art. The person making the offer can be anyone liable to pay the inheritance tax, and the asset offered does not have to be one upon which any of the inheritance tax is payable. So, for instance, a beneficiary of a person's estate can offer one of his own assets in satisfaction of the tax due in relation to the estate.

Quantum of Inheritance Tax

When the personal representatives complete the IHT200, they calculate the inheritance tax liability as at the time of submitting the form. IR Capital Taxes may, however, then raise queries with the personal representatives about the value of assets submitted, the level of reliefs claimed, or whether an asset forms part of the deceased's estate for inheritance tax purposes. The stance taken by IR Capital Taxes in relation to any of these issues may be different from that of the personal representatives and it is always advisable for the personal representatives to try and reach negotiated agreement with IR Capital Taxes. If agreement cannot be reached, the Board of the Inland Revenue issues a notice of determination in relation to the disputed matter. The personal representatives have thirty days in which to appeal. Any appeal is heard by the Special Commissioners or the Lands Tribunal, depending on the nature of the dispute, although if the personal representatives disagree with IR Capital Taxes on a point of law they can take the matter directly to the High Court (sections 222 to 225, Inheritance Tax Act 1984).

If an appeal is to be heard (whether by the Special Commissioners, the Lands Tribunal or the High Court), IR Capital Taxes can in the meantime seek to recover only the inheritance tax agreed to be due. But if the tax payer loses the appeal and wishes to appeal further, IR Capital Taxes is entitled to be paid the inheritance tax in dispute while the second appeal is waiting to be heard (section 242, Inheritance Tax Act 1984).

Liability for Inheritance Tax

Once the quantum of inheritance tax due has been established, it is important to consider who is liable to pay it. This is dealt with in sections 199 and 200 of the Inheritance Tax Act 1984.

The personal representatives are liable for all inheritance tax arising on the deceased's free estate (section 200(1)(a)). If for some reason they do not pay the tax due, IR Capital Taxes has a right of recourse against the beneficiaries of the estate or the trustees of any trust into which the deceased's assets pass. It is important to be aware that a beneficiary entitled only to the income generated by an asset is treated for these purposes as though entitled to the entire asset (section 200(1) and (3), Inheritance Tax Act 1984).

Any inheritance tax due on capital assets contained within a trust of which the deceased was life tenant is payable from that trust (section 201). Similarly, tax due on jointly held assets is payable by the person entitled to the asset after the deceased's death (section 200(1)(c)).

If inheritance tax is payable on a potentially exempt transfer or lifetime chargeable transfer made by the deceased, the donee of the transfer is liable for it (sections 199(1) and 204(6)). If that liability is not discharged within twelve months of the due date, or if the tax payable exceeds the value of the asset in the donee's hands, the personal representatives have a secondary liability to meet the tax payable (sections 199(1) and (2) and 204(8)). Unfortunately for the personal representatives, they do not have a statutory right of recovery against the donee in relation to any inheritance tax paid by them, unless the transfer was also a gift with reservation of benefit (not to a settlement) (section 211(3)).

Section 204 of the Inheritance Tax Act 1984 serves to limit the personal representatives' liability to inheritance tax, by providing that they are not liable for tax greater than the value of the assets passing into their hands, or the assets that would have passed into their hands but for their neglect or default (section 204(1)).

To secure the inheritance tax payable, IR Capital Taxes automatically imposes a charge over any property that was transferred by a chargeable transfer, unless it was personal property beneficially owned by the deceased before his death, devolving on his personal representatives and situated in the UK (section 237). In most situations, IR Capital Taxes does not seek to register this charge but that is of no effect – any disposition of the property in question is made subject to the charge, by virtue of section 237(6). The only exception is where the property is disposed of to a purchaser; here, if the charge is to continue to take effect after the purchase it must have been registered against the asset (in the case of land), or the purchaser must have had knowledge of the charge (in the case of personal property) (section 238).

Chapter 5

Questions ConcerningWills and Codicils

Tracing the Last Will
A key point to establish at the outset is whether the deceased left a Will; and, if so, whether the Will in the personal representatives' possession is the most recent. If the solicitor acting in the administration also acted for the deceased in a personal capacity in the period ending with his death, this may be easily done. If not, the deceased's professional advisers and his bankers should be approached to find out what they know. A solicitor or other professional adviser has no right of lien over a Will or codicil in respect of unpaid charges.

The deceased may have deposited his Will with the Principal Registry, (see page 278) so a search there should be made. Advertisements can also be placed in the Law Society's *Gazette*.

If it is believed that a person has information regarding the existence of a Will or codicil, which that person refuses to impart, an order can be obtained under rule 50 of the Non-Contentious Probate Rules 1987 (by application under section 122 or 123, Supreme Court Act 1981) for that person to be examined in court or to bring the Will or codicil to court; see page 182.

Even if the personal representatives are reasonably sure that they have the final Will, they must still consider the possibility that the testator may have executed codicil(s), and ensure they are in possession of all such documents as have not been revoked.

Pre-Lodgment Enquiries
Many of the queries which arise in connection with a Will may be resolved by enquiring at a probate registry. A solicitor or probate practitioner may raise any query or point relating to a non-contentious probate matter, with the registry to which it is intended that the application for a grant will be made, as a "pre-lodgment enquiry", i.e., an enquiry before applying for the grant.

The enquiry may relate not only to some aspect of a Will, but to an application for a grant or for a discretionary order; it may seek guidance as to the form of application; by whom it may be made; the documentation required; or the procedure.

The registries prefer enquiries to be made by letter or FAX, setting out the relevant facts, but simple or urgent enquiries may be made by telephone.

As a general rule, pre-lodgment enquiries are answered by a registrar, or referred to a registrar before answering. At the Principal Registry the Probate Manager deals with pre-lodgment enquiries after, where appropriate, referral to a district judge.

Evidence to Support a Will

If there is a dispute regarding the validity of a Will because, for example, there are allegations of duress or lack of capacity, then unless the dispute is resolved by agreement, it falls to be determined on application by claim in the Chancery Division.

Where there is a doubt about due execution, the form of the Will when executed, the validity of alterations to the original text, or where the condition of the Will creates doubt about possible revocation in part or in whole, the question falls to be determined by the probate registry, this being non-contentious (common form) work assigned to the Family Division. Enquiry may be made of the district judge or registrar for directions as to whether evidence is necessary and, if so, what form that evidence must take and by whom it must be given.

Where it is clear that evidence is required, however, and that evidence can be readily obtained, there need be no pre-lodgment enquiry. The evidence should be lodged with the application for the grant.

Due execution

Rule 12 of the Non-Contentious Probate Rules deals with the provision of evidence to establish due execution.

Where the Will lacks an attestation clause, or the attestation clause is defective, or where it appears to the district judge or registrar that there is doubt about due execution, an affidavit establishing due execution, from the attesting witnesses, or one of them, is required. Where the witnesses are unavailable to give evidence, or where tracing a witness would be prohibitively expensive in relation to the value of the estate, or there is other good reason why a witness cannot give evidence, an affidavit may be obtained from any other person present at the execution of the Will (see rule 12(1)).

Where evidence to establish due execution cannot be obtained from a person present when the Will was executed, the district judge or registrar may accept evidence on affidavit from any other person, showing that the testator's signature is the handwriting of the testator. Evidence may also be given on affidavit by any person who may establish due execution in some other way.

It is a matter of judicial discretion whether such evidence is acceptable. Case law generally inclines towards a presumption in favour of due execution, the courts applying the principle *omnia praesamunter rite esse acta* ("all things are presumed to have been done correctly"; see *Re Webb (deceased); Smith v Johnston* [1964] 1 WLR 509, [1964] 2 All ER 91).

A witness may be compelled, under section 122 of the Supreme Court Act 1981, to attend and given evidence about a Will; see page 182.

Circumstances in which evidence is not required

Where there is doubt about due execution of a Will, but the distribution of the estate would be unaffected by proof of the Will, the district judge or registrar may dispense with evidence to establish due execution. The distribution of the estate is unaffected if those who would benefit under the Will which is in doubt would have received the same benefit under an earlier, valid, Will or under the intestacy provisions (see rule 12(3)). A statement confirming that rule 12(3) applies may be included in the oath to lead the grant or in a letter accompanying the application.

Consents

Where it is impossible or impractical to obtain affidavit evidence to establish due execution, the district judge or registrar may admit the Will to proof provided all those prejudiced by its admission to proof consent. The persons prejudiced are those who would receive a benefit, or a greater benefit, under an earlier Will or on intestacy. Consent must be given in writing. For a form of consent, see page 304.

Will confirmed by codicil

Where a Will has not been properly executed or there is doubt about execution, but it has been confirmed by a properly executed codicil, then the Will may be admitted to proof without supporting evidence. Evidence may, however, still be required if there is no confirmation of the Will in the codicil, or if the codicil fails to refer to the Will and its date, either at all or incorrectly.

Refusal of probate

After considering the evidence, the district judge or registrar may, if satisfied that the Will is not properly executed, refuse probate of the Will. The original Will is endorsed by the district judge or registrar with the refusal and retained in the registry. Usually a Will is marked "probate refused" only when there has been an attempt to prove it.

Thereafter, application may be made in respect of an earlier Will, or on an intestacy, as appropriate.

Testator Blind or Illiterate

Where a Will has been signed by a testator who was blind or illiterate, or by another person on the direction of the testator, the district judge or registrar, before admitting the Will to proof, must be satisfied that the testator had knowledge of the contents of his Will at the time of its execution. Other apparent irregularities, such as a particularly frail signature by the testator, may also mean that the district judge or registrar needs to be satisfied that the testator had knowledge of the contents of the Will at the time of execution.

No evidence to support the admission to proof of the Will is needed if the attestation clause properly records:

- the testator's disability;
- that the Will was read or otherwise communicated to him, and by whom, before execution; and
- that the testator had knowledge of the content of the Will and approved it.

Nor is evidence required if the attestation clause reflects that the terms of the Will were communicated to the testator by sign language, and that the testator appeared to understand and approve the content. (See rule 13.)

Establishing the Date of Execution

Unless rule 12(3) applies (see above), evidence is required to establish the date of execution if (see rule 14(4)):

- the date has been omitted from the Will or codicil or only partially completed;
- the Will contains two different dates (see below);
- the date is in the body of the Will or differs from that in the endorsement;
- there are two dates and the applicant's title to the grant depends on the date, or
- the date of execution contained in the Will is clearly wrong (e.g. the 31st day of June).

The district judge or registrar has discretion to accept the Will to proof without evidence to support the date of execution if the Will contains two dates and:

- the difference between those dates is small, e.g. up to a month;
- the year has been altered and execution took place early in a new year;
- the later date appears at the end of the Will and there is no reason to doubt that this is the actual date of execution.

It is equally important to establish the date of execution of any codicil; the principles above apply.

Date of Will Misrecited in Codicil

Where a codicil wrongly gives the date of the Will to which it purports to refer, affidavit evidence is required to establish that there is no other Will of the date quoted in the codicil. Evidence may be dispensed with if it can be clearly shown there was no Will of the other date and that the reference to that date is merely a typographical error. However, if the date is indeed that of an earlier Will then, subject to the wording of the codicil, evidence may be required to show there was no intention to revive the earlier Will. The evidence would be expected to come from someone (perhaps the draftsman of the codicil) with knowledge of the facts surrounding the making of the codicil.

Condition of the Will

If, on examination of the original Will or any codicil, there appears on the document any mark of a pin, staple or clip, leading to a suspicion that another document, perhaps also testamentary, was attached to the Will or codicil, evidence to account for the mark may be necessary.

If the explanation of any mark is simple, it may be dealt with in the letter accompanying the application for the grant, e.g. the Will had been pinned to a letter from the bank which held it in safe custody.

If there is some non-testamentary document attached to the Will, it should not be removed to avoid questions. The Will should be submitted to proof with the document attached; the document will be removed in the registry.

If there is no simple explanation, however, an affidavit should be made, dealing with the condition of the Will when executed and its condition when found after the testator's death.

Where a document is or was attached and contains dispositions, it may be necessary to incorporate that document in the testamentary documents (see page 88).

Damaged Will

When dealing with a Will which has been damaged in some way, the court must decide whether the damage was caused by the testator in an attempt to revoke the Will or part of it. Clearly, if the original Will was never in the possession of the testator, any damage to it could not have been done by him and there is no question of partial or total revocation.

Where the Will has been accidentally damaged, an affidavit explaining the cause of the damage may be made by someone with knowledge of the cause of the damage. The affidavit may be filed with the application for a grant. To avoid delay in the application, however, the affidavit may be submitted to the district judge or registrar as a pre-lodgment matter, to establish whether the evidence is satisfactory. Indeed, it is usually preferable to submit a draft affidavit (see page 285 for a form) to the court for approval before it is sworn (see page 94).

If accidental damage renders the Will unsuitable for photocopying by the registry, an engrossment should be made and lodged with the original Will (which is marked with the oath) and lodged on application for the grant (see also rule 11). Alternatively, with the leave of the court, a copy may be submitted with the original.

Alterations to the Will

Section 21 of the Wills Act 1837 provides that no obliteration, interlineation or other alteration made to a Will after execution has effect unless executed in the same manner as a Will, i.e., signed by the testator in the presence of two witnesses who each sign in his presence (see also rule 14(1)).

Alterations made to a Will *at the time of execution* may be authenticated by the signature or initials of the testator and both witnesses. Alternatively they may be authenticated by a note or other reference in the attestation clause or at the end of the Will, stating that the Will was executed containing the alteration.

Alterations made after execution may be acceptable to proof only if the Will is re-executed in accordance with section 21 (see above, and see *In Re White, Barker v Gribble* [1991] Ch 1, [1990] 3 WLR 187, [1991] 3 All ER 1). If alterations made after execution cannot be validated, they are excluded from probate. The district judge or registrar usually requires an engrossment of the Will to be made, restoring it to the form and content when executed. The original Will should be marked on swearing the oath and lodged with the engrossment. The latter, when endorsed with the district judge or registrar's fiat, is copied to make the probate and record copies.

Incorporation of Other Testamentary Documents

Where it appears from the condition of the Will that there may have been some other document, perhaps testamentary, attached to it, it may be that that other document (if it exists) should be incorporated with the Will on proof. The same possibility arises where a Will refers to another document which may contain dispositions (see rule 14(3)).

Where a Will refers to another document, list or memorandum, that other item must be incorporated and proved with the Will. A doubtful case may be referred to the court for a decision before applying for a grant, because if incorporation is directed, the other document will need to be marked with the Will. The preconditions for incorporation are:

- the other document must contain (an) actual disposition(s) of estate (and not simply set out the reason why the estate has been disposed of by the testator in the way it has);
- that other document must have been in existence at the time the Will was executed or before a codicil to the Will was executed; and
- the Will must sufficiently identify the other document by reference to it so that there is no doubt the other document is that mentioned in the Will.

If the above criteria are not met in full, the other document is not incorporated.

Where incorporation is directed, the oath should refer to the deceased's last Will and testament "as contained in the paper writings marked 'A' and 'B' (*et seq*) (with a codicil)", the Will being marked "A" and any other documents being lettered in alphabetical sequence.

Privileged Wills

Any soldier or member of the Air Force on actual military service, or seaman or mariner at sea, may direct the disposal of his estate without the formalities of execution required by section 9 of the Wills Act 1837 (see section 11 of that Act).

A privileged Will may be in the form of a letter or statement, including an oral statement made to another person. If the latter, that oral statement must be transcribed into written form. All applications where the privilege is claimed must be referred to a district judge or registrar for directions as to the privilege and, if allowed, the form of the Will.

Omission of Offensive Words in a Will

Section 20 of the Administration of Justice Act 1982 allows the court to direct the insertion of words into a Will, or the exclusion of words from it, before admitting the Will to proof. Rectification is dealt with below.

Where a Will contains words which are offensive, libellous or blasphemous, the court may direct their exclusion from the probate and record copies, and from all other copies supplied after proof. Personal representatives may apply for an order that any such words be omitted.

In *Re Hall's Estate* [1943] 2 All ER 159, it was held that a testator has the right to explain the way he has disposed of his property, but may not use his Will "as a vehicle for slander".

If a Will submitted for proof contains offensive words, the district judge or registrar may refuse to grant probate until application for those words to be omitted is made. Where a disposition is contained within, or surrounded by, offensive words, the form and content of the engrossment is determined by the court.

Unopposed applications may be dealt with by a district probate registrar, but if the application is opposed, application must be made to a district judge in the Principal Registry, on summons.

Rectification

The court has, by virtue of section 20 of the Administration of Justice Act 1982, power to rectify a Will by the inclusion and/or exclusion of words. The Family Division's jurisdiction is limited to unopposed applications. "Unopposed" does not mean "by consent", but that there is no opposition to the application. If the application is opposed, the matter falls within the jurisdiction of the Chancery Division.

Pre-lodgment enquiry should be made to ascertain whether the district judge or registrar will entertain an application; this is especially important where there is some doubt whether the criteria in section 20 are met. If rectification is to be permitted, it must be shown that the Will as executed fails to carry out the testator's intention by reason of clerical error or failure by the draftsman to understand the testator's instructions.

Application may be made without enquiring in advance; see page 142 for the procedure, and page 291 for a form of affidavit.

Interpretation

Section 21 of the Administration of Justice Act 1982 gives the court power to interpret a Will in so far as:
- any part of the Will is meaningless; or
- the language used in any part of it is ambiguous on the face of it; or
- evidence, other than evidence of the testator's intention, shows that the language used in any part of it is ambiguous in the light of surrounding circumstances.

The probate registry has jurisdiction to interpret a Will only to the extent necessary to determine title to the grant. Thus, the district judge or registrar may be asked to interpret the clause appointing executors, or whether there is sufficient to constitute a gift of residue for a beneficiary taking that gift to take letters of administration (with Will annexed). The procedure for applying for a direction on interpretation is dealt with at page 144. A form of affidavit is set out at page 292.

Lost Wills

Where, after the testator's death, the original of his Will cannot be found or has been mistakenly destroyed, an application may be made for leave to prove a copy or reconstruction. Where the original Will was in the testator's possession before his death but cannot be found after it, there is a presumption of revocation by the testator in his lifetime.

Evidence to rebut the presumption of revocation is needed if the Will is to be proved. The procedure is dealt with at page 138 *et seq*. A precedent affidavit is set out at page 290.

Deceased Domiciled Outside England and Wales

The probate registry's jurisdiction is largely based on the deceased's domicile. Where the deceased died domiciled outside England and Wales, the normal order of priority contained in rules 20 and 22 of the Non-Contentious Probate Rules 1987 (see pages 149 and 161) does not apply. Where the deceased was domiciled outside the UK, it is advisable to seek the court's direction. Applications for grants in these cases are made under the provisions of rule 30:

"30. *Grants where deceased died domiciled outside England and Wales*

(1) Subject to paragraph (3) below, where the deceased died domiciled outside England and Wales, a district judge or registrar may order that a grant, limited in such way as the district judge or registrar may direct, do issue to any of the following persons –

    (a) to the person entrusted with the administration of the estate by the court having jurisdiction at the place where the deceased died domiciled; or

    (b) where there is no person so entrusted, to the person beneficially entitled to the estate by the law of the place where the deceased died domiciled or, if there is more than one person so entitled, to such of them as the district judge or registrar may direct; or

    (c) if in the opinion of the district judge or registrar the circumstances so require, to such person as the district judge or registrar may direct.

(2) A grant made under paragraph 1(a) or (b) above may be issued jointly with such person as the district judge or registrar may direct if the grant is required to be made to not less than two administrators.

(3) Without any order made under paragraph (1) above –

    (a) probate of any will which is admissible to proof may be granted –

        (i) if the will is in the English or Welsh language, to the executor named therein; or

        (ii) if the will describes the duties of a named person in terms sufficient to constitute him executor according to the tenor of the will, to that person; and

    (b) where the whole or substantially the whole of the estate in England and Wales consists of immovable property, a grant in respect of the whole state may be made in accordance with the law which would have been applicable if the deceased had died domiciled in England and Wales."

Before considering the procedure for applying for a grant, the deceased's domicile at the time of death must be determined. This is not a matter to be resolved by the probate registry. If necessary, an application to determine domicile may be made to the county court under the Domicile and Matrimonial Proceedings Act 1973.

Validity of a Will

No Will may be admitted to proof unless it meets the requirements in sections 1 and 2 of the Wills Act 1963, set out below:

"1. *General rule as to formal validity*

(1) A will shall be treated as properly executed if its execution conformed to the internal law in force in the territory where it was executed, or in the territory where, at the time of its execution or of the testator's death, he was domiciled or had his habitual residence, or in a state of which, at either of those times, he was a national.

2. *Additional rules*

(1) Without prejudice to the preceding section, the following shall be treated as properly executed –

(a) a will executed on board a vessel or aircraft of any description, if the execution of the will conformed to the internal law in force in the territory with which, having regard to its registration (if any) and other relevant circumstances, the vessel or aircraft may be taken to have been most closely connected;

(b) a will so far as it disposed of immovable property, if its execution conformed to the internal law in force in the territory where the property was situated;

(c) a will so far as it revokes a will which under this Act would be treated as properly executed or revokes a provision which under this Act would be treated as comprised in a properly executed will, if the execution of the later will conformed to any law by reference to which the revoked will or provision would be so treated;

(d) a will so far as it exercises a power of appointment, if the execution of the will conformed to the law governing the essential validity of the power.

(2) A will so far as it exercises a power of appointment shall not be treated as improperly executed by reason only that its execution was not in accordance with any formal requirements contained in the instrument creating the power."

Where a Will was executed in English form, i.e. in accordance with section 9 of the Wills Act 1837, in Northern Ireland, the Republic of Ireland, Australia, Canada or New Zealand, and the deceased was domiciled there, that Will is acceptable to proof without supporting evidence (Practice Direction, 20 November 1972, unreported).

Where it is clear that validity under the above provisions is established, the Will may be submitted for proof applying rule 30 (see page 91). Where any doubt arises, the directions of the district judge or registrar should be sought. Where evidence is required, that evidence may be:

- by production of a decree, order or grant of the court having jurisdiction at the place of domicile which states that the Will is valid or has been accepted to proof as valid;
- by notarial statement or act made by a notary practising in the country concerned, establishing validity; or
- by affidavit of law, the deponent being qualified in the law of the place of domicile, which establishes validity (see rule 19).

Scottish Wills

A will executed in Scotland in proper Scottish form is acceptable to proof in England and Wales provided the criteria in section 1 of the 1963 Act are met, and provided no confirmation has been obtained in Scotland (see also page 175).

If the deceased's domicile was Scotland, his Will should be proved there to enable the confirmation to be effective to administer estate throughout the United Kingdom. If it is unclear where the Will should be proved, enquiry should be made of the district judge or registrar.

Forfeiture of Benefit by Witnesses

By virtue of section 15 of the Wills Act 1837, any person who benefits under a Will as a specific or residuary legatee and/or devisee loses that benefit if he was a witness to the Will. The benefit is also lost if the Will was witnessed by the husband or wife of the beneficiary. It is only the gift to the beneficiary which is lost; the Will remains a validly executed Will.

If the Will was witnessed by three or more witnesses then the gift to the beneficiary witness may be saved, there being two "other" (non-beneficiary) witnesses to execution.

Two or More Wills

Where there are two or more Wills, both or all should be considered, to determine which is to be proved, or whether both or all need to be proved. For example, if the testator made two Wills, neither of which specifically states that it relates to estate in a particular country, it may be necessary to prove both Wills, they together comprising the last wishes of the testator for the disposal of his estate.

Even though one of two Wills specifically states that it is made in relation to and disposes of estate in a particular country, its effect on the other Will, which purports to be in respect of worldwide estate, must be considered. Similarly, if two or more Wills each states that it specifically deals with estate in a particular place, they must all be considered, especially in respect of revocation clauses.

It is suggested that where the deceased had executed more than one Will, copies of all testamentary dispositions be submitted to the district judge or registrar for directions.

Submitting Draft Documents

Any document required by the probate registry in a non-contentious matter may be submitted in draft form for the district judge or registrar to consider and settle or approve. Only those documents which contain incontrovertible facts may be settled. Documents which give evidence or opinion, such as affidavits of due execution or affidavits to lead discretionary orders, may be submitted for approval, the district judge or registrar approving only their form and content as sufficient to enable the court to reach a decision.

Documents which may be submitted for settling include:

- oaths to lead grants;
- renunciations;
- powers of attorney (except enduring powers of attorney);
- citations;
- nominations of co-administrators;
- subpoenas.

Documents which may be submitted for approval include:

- affidavits to support execution of a Will;
- affidavits to lead the issue of a citation or subpoena;
- affidavits of foreign law; and
- all affidavits to lead discretionary orders.

Precedents are contained in Appendix C.

Chapter 6

Intestacy

A full intestacy arises where the deceased failed to leave a valid Will. A partial intestacy arises where the Will the testator did leave did not dispose of all of the estate. In either of those situations the estate not dealt with by a Will must be administered in accordance with the intestacy rules, which are set out in the Administration of Estates Act 1925 and the Intestates Estates Act 1952.

It is essential to make a thorough search for a Will. Where no Will is found, careful enquiries must be made to ascertain whether any Will was made but might have been lost. The distribution of the estate may be very different under any Will than under the intestacy rules. (See page 141 for the position where there is thought to be a Will but no copy can be found.)

The order of entitlement under the intestacy rules is governed by the value of the deceased's estate and the family members he left. The persons entitled to the estate of a person dying intestate since 1 January 1952 are set out below. Title to apply for letters of administration follows the same order of priority (rule 22, see page 161).

Where a life or minority interest arises, there must be at least two grantees, or a trust corporation must take the grant: section 114(2), Supreme Court Act 1981. That section also provides that a district judge or registrar may, if the circumstances of the case so warrant, allow a grant to a sole grantee. A life interest arises where there is a surviving spouse but the value of the estate exceeds the statutory legacy payable to the spouse (see the tables below, and page 100). A minority interest arises where a child under eighteen is a beneficiary.

Distribution on Intestacy

Deceased died leaving husband or widow and issue
Net estate not exceeding:
- £125,000, death on or after 1 December 1993;
- £75,000, death on or after 1 June 1987 but before 1 December 1993;
- £40,000, death on or after 1 March 1981 but before 1 June 1987;

- £25,000, death after 14 March 1977 but before 1 March 1981;
- £15,000, death after 30 June 1972 but before 15 March 1977;
- £8,750, death after 31 December 1966 but before 1 July 1972;
- £5,000, death before 1 January 1967.

Distribution of estate: All to husband or widow.

Person(s) entitled to letters of administration: Husband or widow.

Deceased died leaving husband or widow without issue

Net estate not exceeding:
- £200,000, death on or after 1 December 1993;
- £125,000, death on or after 1 June 1987 but before 1 December 1993;
- £85,000, death on or after 1 March 1981 but before 1 June 1987;
- £55,000, death after 14 March 1977 but before 1 March 1981;
- £40,000, death after 30 June 1972 but before 15 March 1977;
- £30,000, death after 31 December 1966 but before 1 July 1972;
- £20,000, death before 1 January 1967.

Distribution of estate: All to husband or widow.

Person(s) entitled to letters of administration: Husband or widow.

Deceased died leaving husband or widow and issue

Net estate exceeding:
- £125,000, death on or after 1 December 1993;
- £75,000, death on or after 1 June 1987 but before 1 December 1993;
- £40,000, death on or after 1 March 1981 but before 1 June 1987;
- £25,000, death after 14 March 1977 but before 1 March 1981;
- £15,000, death after 30 June 1972 but before 15 March 1977;
- £8,750, death after 31 December 1966 but before 1 July 1972;
- £5,000, death before 1 January 1967.

Distribution of estate:

(i) Husband or widow takes:
- personal chattels,
- the "statutory legacy":
  - £125,000, death on or after 1 December 1993;
  - £75,000, death on or after 1 June 1987 but before 1 December 1993;
  - £40,000, death on or after 1 March 1981 but before 1 June 1987;
  - £25,000, death after 14 March 1977 but before 1 March 1981;
  - £15,000, death after 30 June 1972 but before 15 March 1977;
  - £8,750, death after 31 December 1966 but before 1 July 1972;
  - £5,000, death before 1 January 1967,

  free of costs and duty, with interest at the appropriate rate (currently 6 per cent); and
- a life interest in half the remainder of the estate, with reversion to the issue.

(ii) The other half to the issue absolutely.

Person(s) entitled to letters of administration: Husband or widow and a child.

Deceased died leaving husband or widow without issue

Net estate exceeding:
- £200,000, death on or after 1 December 1993;
- £125,000, death on or after 1 June 1987 but before 1 December 1993;
- £85,000, death on or after 1 March 1981 but before 1 June 1987;
- £55,000, death after 14 March 1977 but before 1 March 1981;
- £40,000, death after 30 June 1972 but before 15 March 1977;
- £30,000, death after 31 December 1966 but before 1 July 1972;
- £20,000, death before 1 January 1967.

Distribution of estate:
(i) Husband or widow takes:
- personal chattels,
- the "statutory legacy":
  - £200,000, death on or after 1 December 1993;
  - £125,000, death on or after 1 June 1987 but before 1 December 1993;
  - £85,000, death on or after 1 March 1981 but before 1 June 1987;
  - £55,000, death after 14 March 1977 but before 1 March 1981;
  - £40,000, death after 30 June 1972 but before 15 March 1977;
  - £30,000, death after 31 December 1966 but before 1 July 1972;
  - £20,000, death before 1 January 1967,

  free of costs and duty, with interest at the appropriate rate (currently 6 per cent); and
- one half of the remainder absolutely.
(ii) As to the other half of the remainder:
- where there are parents, to the parents absolutely;
- where there are no parents, to the brothers and sisters of the whole blood in equal shares, the issue of such brothers and sisters as have predeceased the intestate taking *per stirpes* the share to which their parent would have been entitled.

Person(s) entitled to letters of administration: Husband or widow.

Deceased died leaving husband or widow without issue, parent, brother or sister of the whole blood or their issue (whatever the value of the estate)

Distribution of estate: All to husband or widow.

Person(s) entitled to letters of administration: Husband or widow.

Deceased died leaving issue only

Distribution of estate: Issue who attain full age or marry under age take equally. Children, including illegitimate children when the intestate died after 4 April 1988, of predeceasing children take their parent's share *per*

stirpes.
Person(s) entitled to letters of administration: Issue.

Deceased died leaving father or mother
Distribution of estate: Father or mother.
Person(s) entitled to letters of administration: Father or mother.

Deceased died leaving father and mother
Distribution of estate: Father and mother in equal shares.
Person(s) entitled to letters of administration: Father or mother or both.

Deceased died leaving brothers and sisters of the whole blood and issue of such brothers and sisters as died in the lifetime of the intestate
Distribution of estate: Brothers and sisters of the whole blood in equal shares, the issue of such brothers and sisters as have predeceased the intestate taking their parent's share *per stirpes.*
Person(s) entitled to letters of administration: A person or persons entitled to share in the estate.

Deceased died leaving brothers and sisters of the half blood and issue of such brothers and sisters as died in the lifetime of the intestate
Distribution of estate: Brothers and sisters of the half blood in equal shares, the issue of such brothers and sisters as have predeceased the intestate taking their parent's share *per stirpes.*
Person(s) entitled to letters of administration: A person or persons entitled to share in the estate.

Deceased died leaving grandparents
Distribution of estate: The grandparents in equal shares.
Person(s) entitled to letters of administration: Grandparent (one or more).

Deceased died leaving uncles and aunts of the whole blood and issue of such uncles and aunts as died in the lifetime of the intestate
Distribution of estate: Uncles and aunts of the whole blood in equal shares, the issue of such uncles and aunts as have predeceased the intestate taking their parent's share *per stirpes.*
Person(s) entitled to letters of administration: A person or persons entitled to share in the estate.

Deceased died leaving uncles and aunts of the half blood and issue of such uncles and aunts as died in the lifetime of the intestate
Distribution of estate: Uncles and aunts of the half blood in equal shares, the issue of such uncles and aunts as have predeceased the intestate taking their parent's share *per stirpes.*
Person(s) entitled to letters of administration: A person or persons entitled to share in the estate.

Deceased died leaving no blood relation taking an interest as above
   Distribution of estate:
   • The Crown;
   • The Duchy of Lancaster;
   • The Duchy of Cornwall.
   Person(s) entitled to letters of administration:
   • The Treasury Solicitor for the use of Her Majesty;
   • The Solicitor for the Duchy of Lancaster for the use of Her Majesty;
   • The Solicitor for the affairs of the Duchy of Cornwall.

Deceased died leaving a creditor
   Person(s) entitled to letters of administration: A creditor, but only on clearing all persons with a prior entitlement as set out above.

Entitlement to Take Letters of Administration
Rule 22 of the Non-Contentious Probate Rules prescribes the order of entitlement to take letters of administration; it is the same as the order of beneficial entitlement set out above. The rule is set out in full on page 161.

Renunciation or disclaimer
A renunciation is a document, executed by a person entitled to take a grant of representation, whereby that person relinquishes the title to the grant. It does not confer a *right* to a grant of representation on any other person, that right remaining with the person beneficially entitled.

   A disclaimer is a document executed by a person entitled to benefit in an estate whereby he or she relinquishes that benefit. It does not transfer the beneficial entitlement to any other person; if the beneficiary wishes to achieve that effect, a deed of assignment (see page 160) or a deed of variation (see page 261) is the appropriate course.

   See page 118 *et seq* for renunciations, and page 265 for disclaimers.

Accretion
The renunciation of a surviving spouse entitled to the whole estate (i.e. where the net estate does not exceed the spouse's statutory legacy, currently £200,000 where there is no issue, or £125,000 if there is issue) does not convey beneficial entitlement to the assets of the estate, but does allow an application for a grant to be made by a person who would be entitled to share in the estate in the event of an accretion, i.e. if the estate increased in value so that it exceeded the spouse's statutory legacy. For example, a husband dies leaving his lawful wife and a son surviving and an estate of £100,000; on the widow's renunciation the son may apply for a grant as a person entitled on accretion. Again, where a wife dies leaving her lawful husband, no issue or parent but a brother of the whole blood and an estate of

£150,000, on the husband's renunciation, the brother may apply for the grant as a person entitled on accretion.

The Surviving Spouse

Life interest arising
It is not uncommon, where a spouse survives, for a long time to elapse between the date of death and the application for the grant, usually because the surviving spouse does not need a grant immediately, or does not realise the need for a grant. Where the estate increases in value, it is the value of the estate at the time of the application which passes under the grant. It may therefore be that, by the time a grant is applied for, a life interest arises although there was none at the time of death. Consideration must be given to the need for a second grantee or dispensation for a second grantee pursuant to section 114(2) of the Supreme Court Act 1981 (see page 123).

In these circumstances, section 46 of the Administration of Estates Act 1925 allows certain deductions to be made to bring the net estate below the statutory amount. They are:
- personal chattels,
- debts,
- inheritance tax, and
- legal expenses and court fees.

These deductions, and the amount of each to bring the estate below the statutory legacy, should be sworn to in the oath.

Redemption of spouse's life interest
A surviving spouse who has a life interest may require the deceased spouse's personal representative to redeem the life interest by payment of a capital sum (see section 47A, Administration of Estates Act 1925), so that the whole of the former matrimonial home can belong to the survivor without any trust arising over it. The capital sum is calculated in accordance with the Intestate Succession (Interest and Capitalisation) Order 1977 (SI 1977 No 1491).

Unless and until a personal representative is constituted, the surviving spouse cannot require redemption. Title to the grant is unaffected by an intention of the surviving spouse to require redemption.

Where the surviving spouse is not also the personal representative, the surviving spouse gives notice to redeem under section 47A to the personal representative. If the surviving spouse is the sole personal representative, notice to redeem is given to the Senior District Judge of the Principal Registry. In either case, notice must be in writing, within twelve months of the date of the issue of the grant. Notice may be given after that time with the leave of the court in special circumstances.

The form of notice is prescribed (Form 6 in Schedule 1 to the 1987 Rules; see page 306) and may be lodged in the Principal Registry or (in duplicate) at the registry from which the grant issued. The original grant should be lodged for notation.

Once notice has been given, it cannot be revoked without the consent of the personal representatives.

Under section 145, Inheritance Tax Act 1984 any capitalisation is read back to the date of death for the purposes of calculating the inheritance tax payable on the deceased's death. As the value of assets passing to the surviving spouse will inevitably be reduced if the life interest is capitalised, careful consideration must be given to the inheritance tax position when deciding whether to capitalise a life interest, as this could result in more inheritance tax becoming payable. See further, page 74.

The matrimonial home

A surviving spouse has the right to require the matrimonial home to be vested in him in satisfaction of the legacy passing to him under the deceased's estate (section 5 and Schedule 2, Intestates' Estate Act 1952). This right is automatic, apart from in the circumstances set out below. Again, notice of the spouse's desire to exercise the right must be given in writing to the personal representatives within twelve months of taking out the grant. If the legacy is lower in value than the deceased's share in the matrimonial home, the spouse could request that his life interest in the remainder of the deceased's estate is capitalised (as mentioned above) and the home is appropriated to him in satisfaction of that sum together with the legacy. Alternatively, if the legacy and/or the lump sum are still of smaller value than the deceased's share in the home, the spouse is permitted to make up the difference himself using his own funds and effectively buy such part of the home as cannot be appropriated to him from the estate.

The value of the home for the purposes of the appropriation is taken as the value at the date upon which the appropriation takes place, and the spouse is entitled to request that the personal representatives obtain a new valuation of the home at that time.

If the surviving spouse were also a personal representative the normal rules against self-dealing would apply to preclude this transaction. However, paragraph 5 of Schedule 2 to the Act expressly allows an exception to the rule in this circumstance.

As a result of this right being awarded to the surviving spouse, the matrimonial home cannot be sold within twelve months of taking out the grant without the consent in writing of the surviving spouse, unless the sale proceeds of the home are required for the administration of the estate and no other assets are available to meet those needs, or unless the court so orders (paragraph 4 of Schedule 2 to the Act).

As mentioned above, this right is not always automatic. If the house was leased by the deceased under a tenancy which would automatically have determined or could have been determined by notice by the landlord within two years of the date of death, the right does not exist. A court order is required before the spouse can exercise his right (paragraph 2 of Schedule 2) if:

- the house was held in conjunction with other land or buildings, such as agricultural land,
- it was also used for non-domestic purposes, or
- it was a hotel or lodging house.

The order will be granted only if the court is satisfied that the exercise of the right will not diminish the value of the assets in the residuary estate or make them more difficult to dispose of.

Death of surviving spouse before grant

Section 1 of the Law Reform (Succession) Act 1995 provides that one spouse must survive the other by twenty-eight days to attain a beneficial interest in the deceased spouse's estate. If the surviving spouse fails to survive for the requisite period those next entitled in the order of priority prescribed in rule 22 (see page 161) may apply. On application for the grant by the person(s) entitled, the oath to lead the grant should state that the husband or wife failed to survive by twenty-eight days and that section 1 of the Act therefore applies.

Where the surviving spouse survives sufficiently long to acquire a beneficial interest but then dies without taking a grant:

(a) if he was entitled to the whole estate, the grant may be taken by his personal representatives. If application is to be made by someone of lower title under the rule then the personal representative must be cleared off by renunciation or citation (see pages 119 and 115). If there is no personal representative constituted by a grant then, unless the person(s) entitled to be personal representatives renounce their title, they must be cited to accept or refuse a grant (see page 115) or application must be made to pass over their right to the grant by application under section 116 of the Supreme Court Act 1981 (see page 136); or

(b) if he was not entitled to the whole estate, the grant may be taken by any of those entitled to share in the estate.

Effect of divorce or judicial separation

A decree of divorce or nullity granted in England and Wales removes the former spouse as a person entitled to benefit under the other spouse's intestacy (except where relief is granted on application made after the issue of a grant under section 1, Inheritance (Provision for Family and Dependants) Act 1975 – see page 252).

Where the deceased was divorced, or his marriage was annulled by decree, order or pronouncement of a foreign court and such decree is recognisable under sections 46 to 49 of the Family Law Act 1986, the divorce or annulment has the same effect as an English decree on the right to benefit on a person's dying intestate and domiciled in England and Wales. Section 46(2) of the Act also provides for the recognition of a divorce effected overseas other than by court proceedings.

The oath to lead the grant should recite details of the final decree and that the deceased did not remarry.

Under section 18(2) of the Matrimonial Causes Act 1973, where, after a court has pronounced a decree of judicial separation and the separation continues, either party to the marriage dies intestate, the deceased spouse's estate devolves as if the other spouse had predeceased.

It follows that where a marriage is dissolved by a legally recognisable decree etc., or there is a continuing judicial separation, the surviving spouse has no right to benefit under an intestacy, and the estate devolves to children or other issue, including adopted children (see below). For a form of oath, see page 326.

Grant to Children or Other Issue

Where the deceased never married, or married but was divorced or judicially separated, or his spouse predeceased him, the benefit of his estate (and title to the grant) falls to his child(ren). If any child predeceased leaving issue, such issue take the share to which their parent would have been entitled if that parent had survived. If there is more than one such child, they take in equal shares.

Effect of adoption order

Under an adoption order, whether made under the Adoption Act of 1958 or 1976, or the Adoption and Children Act 2002 (when in force), or recognisable as valid by those Acts, an adopted child is treated as the lawfully born child of his adoptive parents. The child ceases to be the child of his natural parents (see section 39(2) of the 1976 Act). It follows that an adopted child is entitled to benefit from the estate of his intestate adopted parent(s) equally with a child born of those parents. Similarly, the adoptive parents benefit if their adopted child dies intestate without spouse or issue. From the date of the adoption order, the child ceases to benefit from the death intestate of his natural parents.

An adopted child is entitled to benefit as the child of his adoptive parents from any other estate under the tables set out on pages 95–99.

Illegitimate children

Since the passing of the Legitimacy Act 1926 an illegitimate child has had the right to inherit under his mother's intestacy.

The Family Law Reform Act 1969 increased an illegitimate child's rights to inherit under an intestacy. In respect of deaths after 1 January 1970, Part IV of the Administration of Estates Act 1925 (from which the tables above are extracted) is construed so that any reference to the issue of an intestate includes a reference to any illegitimate child of his and to the issue of such child, and any reference to a child or children of the intestate includes a reference to any illegitimate child or children.

With effect from 4 April 1988, the Family Law Reform Act 1987 provides that illegitimacy is not relevant in determining an illegitimate person's right to inherit or any right to inherit from an illegitimate person. This means that there is now no difference between legitimate and illegitimate children as regards their rights to inherit.

Grant to Parents

Where the deceased died leaving no surviving spouse or issue, title to benefit falls to the deceased's parents, in equal shares, or to the survivor of them, absolutely. If both parents survive, either or both may apply for the grant. "Parents" includes adoptive parents (see page 103).

Grant to Brothers or Sisters and their Issue

Where no spouse or issue (including adopted children) or parent survives, the deceased's estate passes to brothers and sisters of the whole blood or their issue; failing whom, to the brothers and sisters of the half blood (i.e. with only one parent in common). The child or remoter issue of a brother or sister who predeceased the deceased takes the share to which his parents would have been entitled if alive. Issue of a predeceased sibling of the whole blood take in preference to a sibling of the half blood.

Grant to Grandparents

Where no spouse, issue (including adopted children), parent or sibling of the whole or half blood, or their issue, survive, title falls to the deceased's grandparents, the benefit being divided equally between those who survive, and any or all survivors may take the grant.

If a grandparent survived but then died without taking a grant, his personal representative may apply, subject to the preference of a live interest (i.e. another surviving grandparent) over that of the personal representative of the now deceased grandparent. (See rule 27(5).)

Grant to Uncles and Aunts and their Issue

Where no spouse, issue (including adopted children), parent, sibling of the whole or half blood or their issue, or grandparents survive, title falls to uncles and aunts of the whole blood or their issue, failing which to uncles and aunts of the half blood or their issue.

The issue of a predeceased aunt or uncle take the share which their parent would have taken if alive, in equal shares. The children of cousins are second cousins to each other, and are outside the degrees of consanguinity entitling them to benefit on another's death intestate.

Grant to the Crown

Where there are no known kin, title to an intestate's estate passes to the Crown. If the Treasury Solicitor claims *bona vacantia* on behalf of the Crown he has title to take the grant.

Grant to a Creditor

On clearing of all kin by predecease, renunciation or citation, a creditor may apply for the grant, although if the Treasury Solicitor claims *bona vacantia* he has preference over a creditor. The procedure in *bona vacantia* cases and creditors' applications is dealt with on page 159.

Grant to an Assignee

Where all persons entitled to the estate of the deceased under an intestacy assign their interests to another or others, the assignee(s) take the place(s), in the order of priority in rule 22, of the assignor(s). See rule 24 and page 160 where the procedure for assignees to apply is dealt with.

Forfeiture

A person who unlawfully causes the death of another by murder or manslaughter is prohibited, on grounds of public policy, from benefiting from the estate of the deceased. This is subject to certain relief available under the Forfeiture Act 1982. In *Re DWS (deceased)* [2001] Ch 568, [2000] 3 WLR 1910, [2001] 1 All ER 97 (CA), it was held that the rule of public policy disqualifying a murderer did not require the court to treat the murderer as having predeceased his victim for the purposes of the distribution of his estate. The son of the murderer of the deceased persons (the grandparents) did not therefore inherit his grandparents' estates.

Where a person has been convicted of murder or manslaughter his right to the grant to the estate of his victim may be passed over by discretionary order under section 116 of the Supreme Court Act 1981 (see page 136). The certificate of conviction should be exhibited to the affidavit.

Property to which the Intestacy Rules Apply

The rules of intestacy apply only to property that could have been disposed of under the deceased's Will had he made one. They do not, therefore, operate in relation to assets held jointly by the deceased and another party, or to assets held in trust for the deceased's benefit and which pass under the terms of the trust after his death. In respect of deaths before 1 January 1996, property received under a trust settlement, or as a gift from the deceased during his lifetime, had to be brought into account when determining the value of assets passing to the children of the deceased under the intestacy rules. However, this requirement was abolished by section 1(2) of the Law Reform (Succession) Act 1995.

Chapter 7

Caveats

Purpose

A solicitor may be given instructions, not to obtain a grant of representation, but to prevent a grant issuing to another person.

Rule 6, Non-Contentious Probate Rules 1987, provides that no grant of probate may issue within seven days of the deceased's death and no grant of letters of administration within fourteen days of the death. These times may be abridged, with leave of a district judge or registrar, but their purpose is to enable a caveat to be entered to prevent a grant issuing. The client who wishes to enter a caveat ("the caveator") may wish to oppose the issue of the grant, or may need further time to make enquiries and obtain information and evidence:

- to oppose the proof of a Will;
- to obtain evidence that there is a valid Will, or that the purported last Will is not valid;
- to satisfy himself he is the nearest kin entitled on intestacy; or
- to oppose a grant issuing to the person entitled because he has doubts the grantee will properly administer the estate.

There may be other reasons to oppose the issue of a grant, but provided the reason can be justified, a caveat should be entered. A caveat must also be entered before citation proceedings are issued (see page 114).

A caveat should be entered only by a person having an interest in the estate and who wishes to oppose the issue of a grant to another person. If the purpose is to ascertain when a grant issues, to launch proceedings against the estate, or to make a claim under section 1 of the Inheritance (Provision for Family and Dependants) Act 1975, a standing search should be applied for (see page 275).

Definition

A caveat is a notice in writing, lodged in the Principal Registry, a district probate registry or probate sub-registry, to show cause against the issue of a grant to anyone other than the caveator. It requires the court not to allow a grant of representation to issue in the deceased's estate without notice to the caveator. A caveat also prevents the resealing of a colonial grant.

A caveat does not stop a grant which issues on the day the caveat is entered. All grants are deemed to be sealed immediately before 10 a.m. on the day on which the grant is dated as issuing. Clearly a caveat cannot be entered until after 10 a.m., the time at which all registries are open.

Entering a Caveat

Rule 44, Non-Contentious Probate Rules 1987, deals with the procedure for the entry of a caveat and subsequent procedures. The form of a caveat is prescribed by the Rules – Form 3 (see page 299).

A caveat is entered by lodging the caveat, in the prescribed form, personally or by post, in a registry, and paying the prescribed fee (see below). The caveat may not be entered until the correct fee is paid. The registry acknowledges the entry of the caveat by notice.

The *Probateman* computer system, which links the probate registries into the national index of applications for grants, also deals with caveats. The entry or extension of a caveat is recorded by the entering registry and updating information is automatically sent to any registry at which a grant application is pending. The Leeds District Probate Registry is notified of the entry of all caveats, since all proceedings concerning caveats are dealt with at that registry (see below).

Duration and Renewal

Once entered, a caveat remains in force for six months from the date of entry. It may be renewed by application on written notice (letter) lodged by post within the last month of the period of six months from entry. A caveat may be further extended for periods of six months until removed. The caveat remains in force until:

- a probate claim is issued in the Chancery Division; or
- an order to remove it and discontinue proceedings is made after application on summons to a district judge of the Principal Registry; or, if the order is consented to, a district probate registrar.

The commencement of a probate claim extends the caveat until the determination of the claim. It prevents any grant, save a grant of administration pending determination of the claim, issuing, until the claim is finally determined. The final order pronouncing for or against a testamentary document provides for a grant to issue to the person(s) entitled under the order; that grant issues out of the registry in which the grant application (if any) is pending.

A caveat entered as a prerequisite to citation proceedings remains in force until:

- it is removed by order of a district judge of the Principal Registry on summons;
- it is withdrawn by the caveator; or
- the citation proceedings are determined.

Grants Which May Issue While a Caveat is in Place

A grant *ad colligenda bona,* or a grant pending determination of a probate claim (formerly a "grant pending suit"), may issue notwithstanding a caveat is in place.

A grant *ad colligenda bona* is a limited grant, issued pursuant to an order of a district judge or registrar, for the administration or preservation of a particular part of the deceased's estate where there is an urgent need to administer that part of the estate, or until any dispute is resolved and a full grant may be issued.

A grant pending determination of a probate claim issues pursuant to an order of a district judge, or a master of the Chancery Division where a claim has been commenced in that Division. Again, the grant is one of administration for a specific purpose pending determination of the dispute. See pages 135 and 166, where these grants are dealt with in detail.

A fee of £15 is payable for the entry or extension of a caveat.

Warning to Caveat

The person(s) applying for the grant or wishing to apply for a grant may issue a "warning" to the caveator. The form of warning is prescribed by the Rules (Form 4, Schedule 1; see page 299). The warning may be entered only at the Leeds District Probate Registry (see Appendix B for the address).

The person warning must state in the warning his interest under a Will (giving the date of it), or intestacy, in the deceased's estate. He must also give an address for service in England and Wales.

A warning is a notice to the caveator:

- to enter an appearance within eight days of service; the warning must set out the interest of the person issuing the warning (i.e. why he disputes the Will or claim to an intestacy); or,
- if the person warning has no contrary interest but wishes to oppose the sealing of a grant, to issue a summons for directions.

There is no fee for lodging a warning to a caveat.

The warning may be served by post, DX or FAX in accordance with Rules of the Supreme Court 1965 (SI 1965 No 1776), rule 5 (these rules continuing to apply to non-contentious probate applications). The warning must be endorsed as to service.

Entering an Appearance

The caveator has eight days to enter an appearance to the warning at the Leeds District Probate Registry. The form of appearance is prescribed by the Rules (Form 5, Schedule 1; see page 300). When an appearance is entered within that time, no grant may issue, except to the caveator, without an order of a district judge or registrar.

An appearance may still be entered after the prescribed time (eight days from service of the warning) has expired, provided no affidavit of service has been filed (see below).

No fee is payable on entering an appearance.

Where the caveator does not enter an appearance within the prescribed time, and fails to issue a summons for directions (see below), the person warning may file an affidavit of service of the warning in the Leeds District Probate Registry. That registry then searches for an appearance or summons, and, if neither has been filed, re-issues the caveat. The *Probateman* computer system is noted so the grant may issue from the registry at which the application is pending. If no application for a grant has been made, it may now be made in the normal way.

Summons for Directions

A caveator having no continuing interest, but objecting to the issue of a grant, may issue a summons for directions. The summons must be issued within the eight days prescribed, but may be issued outside that time provided the person seeking removal of the caveat has not filed an affidavit of service of a warning.

The summons for directions is issued for hearing by the registrar of the registry in which the application for a grant is pending, or to which it is proposed to apply for a grant. The summons must be supported by an affidavit. The issue of a summons is recorded by the issuing registry in the *Probateman* computer system.

The district judge or registry hearing the summons may remove the caveat and direct representation be granted to the person warning, or to such other person(s), exercising the court's discretionary powers (see page 136), as the court considers appropriate. The court may make such other directions as to further proceedings, and/or the application for a grant, as may be appropriate.

Restriction on Entering Further Caveat

Unless a district judge of the Principal Registry gives leave, no further caveat may be entered by a caveator where:
- the caveat has ceased to have effect by reason of failure to enter an

appearance to the warning;
- a district judge or registrar has removed the caveat by order; or
- a decision of the court in a probate claim or citation proceedings has been made.

Withdrawal of Caveat

The caveator may withdraw his caveat at any time before he enters an appearance to the warning. Where a warning has been entered, then the caveator must give notice of his withdrawal to the person warning. The caveat must be withdrawn at the registry at which it was entered, producing the receipt for the caveat issued by that registry. The *Probateman* computer system is noted by the registry which entered the caveat, the system automatically informing the registry at which the grant application is pending, enabling the grant to issue. Unless there is any reason to doubt that the applicant still wishes to obtain the grant, the grant is issued. Where a lengthy time has elapsed from the entry of the caveat, the registry from which the grant is to issue requests confirmation that the circumstances at the time of the grant application, e.g. estate values, still apply.

No fee is payable on the withdrawal of a caveat.

Death of Caveator

A caveat which has been properly entered must be removed by order on summons if the caveator dies before other action is taken.

Chapter 8

Citations

Nature of a Citation

A citation is a direction issued by the court requiring the person cited to take certain prescribed actions, failing which the court will make an order in the terms set out in the citation. A citation may issue requiring the citee:

- to accept or refuse a grant of representation;
- to take a grant of probate; or
- to propound a Will.

A citation may issue only at the instance of a person with an interest in the deceased's estate. It must contain an address for service in England and Wales.

The order of priority to take a grant of representation is set out in rules 20 and 22 (see pages 149 and 161). Where a person has first title to the grant under the rules, but neglects or refuses to apply for the grant and does not renounce title, he may be cited to accept or refuse the grant (rule 47(1)). The citation may be issued by a person entitled to the grant in a lower capacity under the rules. For example:

- a residuary legatee or devisee may cite executor(s) to take probate;
- a child of the deceased with a beneficial interest may cite his surviving parent to take letters of administration;
- a creditor of the deceased may cite the nearest of kin entitled under an intestacy.

The citor must have a direct beneficial interest in the deceased's estate and be next entitled after the citee.

The citation serves two purposes. Firstly, it directs the person(s) with the higher entitlement to take the grant or renounce entitlement to do so. Secondly, if the citee fails to apply or renounce, it allows the court to direct that a grant issue to the citor. This allows the citor to administer the estate and acquire his benefit.

Where the deceased died testate, all executors who survive must be cited by the beneficiary citor. Similarly, all persons entitled in the same degree, for example, siblings, must be cited. Where there is no known kin entitled under an intestacy, a citation issued at the instance of a creditor must be directed to any kin and to the Treasury Solicitor, or Solicitor for the Duchies of Cornwall and Lancaster, the Crown being entitled to *bona vacantia* in the absence of kin. The "Treasury Solicitor" means the solicitor for the affairs of Her Majesty's Treasury and includes the solicitor for the affairs of the Duchy of Lancaster and the Duchy of Cornwall (see rule 2). See Appendix B for the address of the Treasury Solicitor.

Citation to Accept or Refuse a Grant

The purpose of a citation to accept or refuse a grant is to bring matters to a head, by requiring the person entitled to take the grant to do so, or by the court's directing administration be granted to the citor. This form of citation cannot be issued against an executor who has intermeddled in the estate without taking the grant. An intermeddling executor cannot renounce, i.e. refuse to take the grant, but his title may be passed over (see below, and page 136), and see in *In the Estate of Biggs* [1966] P 118, [1966] 2 WLR 536, [1965] 1 All ER 358.

For the form of citation see page 302.

Citation to Take Probate

Where an executor has intermeddled, i.e., begun to collect in and/or distribute estate, but has not obtained a grant of probate within six months of the testator's death, he may be cited to take the grant of probate. If the executor fails to comply with the citation by taking the grant, the citor may:

- apply by summons to the court for an order directing the executor to take probate within a specified time; or
- ask the court to order that a grant issue to himself or to another person named in the summons.

(See rule 47(5)(c) and (7)(c).)
For the form of citation, see page 300.

Obviously, if the validity of the Will is in dispute and proceedings to determine validity are pending, the executor cannot be cited to prove the Will.

Citation to Propound a Will

Where there is thought to be a Will, or a later Will, the validity of which may be questionable, those persons interested under the alleged Will or later Will may be cited to propound it, that is, to take the steps necessary for it to be proved.

Any person interested in an intestate estate or under a Will, whose interest is or may be adversely affected by, respectively, a Will or a later Will, may extract the citation. All persons with an interest under the alleged

Will or later Will must be cited. This may be difficult without full knowledge of the alleged Will, but rule 48(1) requires it. Where the difficulty cannot be overcome, an application for the issue of a subpoena for the lodgement of the alleged Will in a registry, under section 123 of the Supreme Court Act 1981 (see page 124), may be appropriate. Another alternative is to apply under section 122 of the Act (see page 182) for an order for the attendance of a person to be examined by the court about the alleged Will.

Where an executor believes there may be a codicil or another codicil to his testator's Will, it is for him to seek evidence to support or reject that codicil. The executor is obliged to seek to prove all testamentary documents which together contain his testator's wishes. Thus, citation proceedings by an executor in respect of an alleged codicil are inappropriate.

The Procedure

A citation may issue out of the Principal Registry or a district probate registry. The form of the citation must be settled by a district judge of the Principal Registry or a district registrar (rule 46(1)). A fee of £10 is payable for settling the citation.

The citor (or, with the permission of a district judge or registrar, the citor's solicitor) must depose to and lodge an affidavit verifying all averments made in the citation (rule 46(2)). The affidavit may be submitted in draft for the approval of a district judge or registrar before being sworn. A fee of £10 is payable.

A caveat (see page 107) *must* be entered by the citor before a citation may issue. This prevents the citee from taking a grant without the citor's being aware of his intentions and able to object. The caveat, unless withdrawn by the caveator, remains in force until the court determines the person who may take the grant and that person makes the application. On application by that person, the caveat ceases to have effect (rule 46(3)).

Every Will referred to in a citation should be lodged in the registry before the citation issues. Where, however, the Will is not in the citor's possession, and the district judge or registrar is satisfied it is impracticable to require the Will to be lodged, lodgment may be dispensed with (rule 46(5)).

Where the Will is in the possession of someone other than the citor or citee, an application may be made under rule 50 (applying section 123 of the Supreme Court Act 1981) for the issue of a subpoena for the Will to be lodged in the registry. For the procedure for issuing a subpoena, see page 124.

No fee is payable on the issue of a citation.

Service

The citation must be served personally, unless a district judge or registrar directs otherwise. Substituted service by registered post is possible if the court can be satisfied that the citee cannot be personally served. Alternatively, the court may order substituted service by advertisement. This form of service is not, however, likely to be directed unless there is good reason to suppose the advertisement will come to the notice of the citee. Where the citee's whereabouts are unknown, an application under section 116, Supreme Court Act 1981 (see page 136) may be appropriate.

Immediately after service the citation must be endorsed as to service by the server. An affidavit of service should be sworn.

Where there are no known kin, the Treasury Solicitor and the Solicitors for the Duchies of Cornwall or Lancaster are served as agents for the Crown. Service may be effected personally or, with the leave of a district judge or registrar, by post.

Citation to accept or refuse a grant

Any person cited to appear may, within eight days of service, enter an appearance in the registry from which the citation issued. Even after the eight days have elapsed, as long as the citor has taken no action, the citee may still enter an appearance. Once the appearance has been entered, a copy, sealed by the registry, is immediately served on the citor (rule 47(6)).

For a form of appearance, see page 303. No fee is payable on the entry of an appearance.

If the citee is willing to take the grant, he files an affidavit requesting the district judge or registrar to make an order for a grant to issue to him. The order usually includes a time limit for making the application, and once the order has been made, the citee then applies for the grant in the usual way (rule 46(4)).

If the citee fails to file an affidavit, or files it but then fails to apply for the grant within the time specified (or, if no time was specified, within a reasonable time), the citor should issue a summons seeking an order for a grant to issue to himself. On the hearing of the summons the district judge or registrar may make such order as he sees fit (rule 47(7)(a)).

Where the citee was an executor who had had power reserved to him on the original grant of probate and he fails to apply for probate, the citor may issue a summons seeking orders that the appearance be struck out and for the original grant to be endorsed that the citee has been cited, but failed to apply, and therefore all his right and title to act as executor ceases (rule 47(7)(b)). The citor may then apply for letters of administration (with Will *de bonis non*; see page 170) in the usual way.

If the citee fails to enter an appearance within the time limit, the citor may apply by summons for an order for a grant to issue to himself (rule

47(5)(a)). Again, if the citee was an executor who had had power reserved, the citor applies by summons for an endorsement on the original grant that the citee has not entered an appearance and that his rights as executor have ceased. The citor may apply for letters of administration (with Will annexed) *de bonis non* in the usual way (rule 47(5)(b)).

All summonses are returnable before the district judge or registrar of the registry from which the citation issued. An affidavit of facts by the citee (or, with permission, his solicitor) must be filed with the summons and a copy served with the summons.

Citation to take probate

A citee who enters an appearance may file an affidavit seeking an order for a grant to issue to him. The district judge or registrar may direct the grant be taken within a specified time.

If the citee fails to file his affidavit or to apply within the time specified (or a reasonable time, if no time limit was imposed), the citor may apply by summons for an order:
- that the citee takes probate within a specified time;
- that a grant issues to the citor; or
- that a grant issues to some other person named in the summons.

Where an order that a grant issues to some other person named in the summons is sought, the court must be satisfied that the other person named is willing to take the grant and is a fit and proper person to act as administrator (rule 47(7)(c)).

If the citee fails to enter an appearance and the time for so doing has expired, the citor may apply by summons for an order that:
- the citee takes the grant within a specified time;
- the grant issues to himself; or
- the grant issues to some other person named in the summons.

(See rule 47(5)(a).)

Citation to propound a Will

If the citee enters an appearance, he is required to propound the Will the subject of the citation with "reasonable diligence" (rule 48(2)(a)). This may be done by the issue of a probate claim in the Chancery Division for proof of the Will in solemn form. But it is now more usual (initially at least) for the Will to be lodged in the probate registry and attempts made to resolve matters there without litigation.

If the citee fails to enter an appearance and the time for so doing has expired, or if he enters an appearance but fails to proceed to propound the Will, the citor may apply by summons for an order that a grant may issue on the basis that the Will the subject of the citation is invalid (rule 48(2)(a) and (b)).

Any summons must be supported by an affidavit of facts (which must also be served on the citee) and the affidavit of service of the citation.

No fee is payable on the issue of a summons.

Alternatives to Citations

Order passing over title

A citation to accept or refuse a grant or a citation to take probate may prove effective in forcing the citee to take the grant to which he is entitled and administer the deceased's estate. The inherent danger in citing a person to take a grant, such a person having already demonstrated reluctance to act, is that that person may indeed take the grant but thereafter not proceed with due diligence to administer the estate.

Where an executor or administrator entitled to apply for a grant shows no inclination to do so within a reasonable time after the deceased's death, an application may be made for a discretionary order under section 116 of the Supreme Court Act 1981 to pass over his title and for representation to be granted to another person. The proposed grantee would be either a person next entitled, or a person whom the court would approve as a fit and proper person to act. For the procedure, see page 136.

Subpoena to bring in a Will

Where the requirement is for a Will to be produced, but not to compel any person to prove that Will, a subpoena for its production may issue.

Section 123 of the Supreme Court Act 1981 provides that where it appears a person has in his possession, custody or power any document which purports to be testamentary, a subpoena may issue requiring him to lodge the document in court. For the procedure, see page 124.

Order to attend for examination

Section 122 of the Supreme Court Act 1981 allows the court, on application, to order any person with knowledge of a document which purports to be testamentary to attend before the court to be examined about the Will. For the procedure, see page 182.

Chapter 9

Renunciations

Introduction

Any person entitled to probate or administration may abandon that right by signing a renunciation witnessed by a disinterested witness. Renunciation must be absolute, i.e., without contingency.

The only exception to the general rule is where an executor has intermeddled, i.e. commenced the administration without taking probate of his testator's Will. Such an executor cannot renounce but may be cited to take probate (see page 113) or may be passed over by application under section 116 of the Supreme Court Act 1981 (see page 136).

A renunciation takes effect from the time it is signed, but may be withdrawn at any time before it is lodged in the probate registry. Once lodged, it may be retracted only with the leave of a district judge or registrar (see page 121).

Who May Renounce

An executor may renounce probate on the death of his testator (but not before).

An executor who is also entitled to a grant in another capacity in the order prescribed by rule 20 (see page 149), i.e. as a residuary legatee and devisee, may renounce probate but take letters of administration in the lower capacity so that he breaks any chain of representation under section 7 of the Administration of Estates Act 1925 (see page 169). If the renouncing executor wishes to abandon all his right and title, he must renounce his title in all capacities.

Again, even if there is an effective appointment of an executor who survives, any person next entitled under rule 20 may renounce letters of administration (with Will annexed) and lodge the Will and his renunciation in a registry. In effect this applies to a residuary beneficiary or person entitled to the undisposed of estate. The renunciation would, like that of an executor, be recognisable only after the death of the testator and provided that any executor named had predeceased or had also renounced.

Lodging the Will

A person renounces by filing his renunciation with the original Will in the Principal Registry or any district probate registry.

If the original Will is missing, but *not* revoked, the renunciation of the executor or other person entitled may be lodged with a copy of the Will, providing the district judge or registrar accepts the explanation of why the original Will is missing.

The original Will lodged on renunciation is held in the registry in which it was filed. An entry is made in the *Probateman* computer system, the national index of probate applications. Any future application for a grant thus leads to the discovery of the Will. On application for proof of a Will, the Will must be marked with the signatures of the deponent to the oath and the commissioner. This requires attendance at the registry in which it is lodged to mark it in accordance with rule 10(1)(a), unless a district judge or registrar gives leave to mark a copy under rule 10(2). See also page 153.

Deceased Testate

It is usual for the person who is first entitled to be the personal representative but does not wish to be, to lodge a renunciation or, perhaps more accurately, to have it lodged by the person taking the grant, on the application for the grant. Provided the renunciation is effective to clear all title of the renunciant, the person next entitled under rule 20 may apply for a grant. For a form of renunciation, see page 347.

Deceased Intestate

A renunciation by the nearest of kin does not pass title to the grant to remoter kin, e.g., a spinster dying intestate without issue leaves her parents beneficially entitled to her estate and the grant. The parents remain the only persons beneficially entitled to the estate even if they renounce – title to the grant following beneficial entitlement. A sibling of the deceased has no title.

The only exception is where the deceased is survived by a spouse and the value of the estate is below the surviving spouse's statutory legacy (see page 99). Here issue, then parents (if no issue) and siblings (if no issue or parent) of the deceased may take the grant on the surviving spouse's renunciation, as persons beneficially entitled to share the estate under an accretion (i.e. if the estate increased in value so as to exceed the spouse's statutory legacy). Similarly, on the renunciation of the nearest of kin a creditor may take letters of administration (rule 22(3); page 162).

Rule 27(4) allows letters of administration to be granted to any person entitled without notice to any other person of equal entitlement, e.g. a sibling may take with notice to any other sibling. It follows that no renunciation is recognised from persons of equal entitlement.

A person who has renounced in one capacity cannot then take in a lower capacity (e.g. next of kin and creditor).

Renunciation by Attorney

An attorney acting under a registered enduring power of attorney may renounce administration for the use and benefit of the donor of the power (see rule 35(2)(c)).

An attorney may effect a renunciation on behalf of the donor – the person entitled to take letters of administration – only if the power of attorney specifically authorises him to do so. The attorney cannot renounce probate if the donor is an executor.

Renunciation by a Minor

In the unlikely event a minor is appointed executor, the minor's right to probate cannot be renounced. Application may be made for a grant of letters of administration (with Will annexed) for the use and benefit of the minor by the person entitled under rule 32(1). Alternatively, the court may be asked to exercise its discretionary power under section 116 of the Supreme Court Act 1981 (see page 136) to pass over the minor's title.

Where the minor is entitled to letters of administration his title may be renounced only by the person appointed by order of a district judge or registrar made under rule 32(2) (see page 132). The order specifically authorises the renunciation.

Mental Incapacity

Where the person first entitled to a grant is mentally incapable of managing his affairs, probate or administration may be renounced only by a person appointed specifically to do so by order of the Court of Protection. Where there is a registered enduring power of attorney, the attorney may renounce his right to the grant (see above).

Renunciation by Partners in a Firm

Where all the partners in a firm were appointed executors, those partners may renounce their title by any two of them effecting a renunciation on their behalf and with their authority (rule 37(2)(a)). For a form, see page 347.

Retraction of Renunciation

Rule 37(3) allows a renunciation of probate or administration to be retracted at any time with the leave of a district judge or registrar. Only in exceptional circumstances is an executor who has renounced probate allowed to retract his renunciation if the grant has issued to a person of lesser entitlement under rule 20.

Application for leave to retract is made *ex parte* on affidavit to the district judge or registrar of the registry in which the renunciation is filed. The affidavit must set out why the renunciant wishes to retract and now take a grant.

Chapter 10

Discretionary Orders

An application for any of a number of discretionary orders under the Non-Contentious Probate Rules 1987 may be made *ex parte* on affidavit. The Rules of the Supreme Court 1965 (SI 1965 No 1776), as in force immediately before 26 April 1999, apply to such applications by virtue of the Non-Contentious Probate (Amendment) Rules 1999 (SI 1999 No 1015). The Civil Procedure Rules 1998 (SI 1998 No 3132) do not apply.

Both the Principal Registry and the district probate registries have jurisdiction in these matters, but the application should be made to the registry at which it is proposed the application for the grant will be made.

The affidavit to lead the order should be made by the proposed grantee(s), but may be accepted if made by one of several proposed grantees. With the permission of the district judge or registrar, the solicitor or probate practitioner, or other person with knowledge of the relevant facts to support the application, may be the deponent. Permission is usually given where the solicitor or probate practitioner has conducted enquiries on behalf of the client, or where the facts relied on are completely within his own knowledge, for example, on an application to allow a copy Will to be proved, the original having been lost while in the solicitor's custody.

No separate "application" for the order is necessary, as the affidavit should conclude with a request for the order sought in precise terms.

The procedure for making enquiries before applying for a grant is discussed at pages 83–84. Such an enquiry may lead to an application for one of the discretionary orders dealt with in this chapter. It is suggested that, unless it is obvious that the facts relied on to lead the order are sufficiently clear to give the court all the relevant evidence to make its decision on the application, a draft affidavit is submitted for approval in advance; again, the procedure for this is discussed at page 94. Prior approval reduces the risk that the court may require a further affidavit, and in the long run reduces delay and expense.

Dispensing with Notice to a Non-Proving Executor
Rule 27(1) of the 1987 Rules provides that where, on an application for

probate, power is to be reserved to executors who are not proving and have not renounced, the oath must recite that notice of the application has been given to those executor(s). See page 307 for the form of notice.

Paragraph (3) of the rule allows the district judge or registrar to dispense with the giving of notice where to do so is impracticable or would cause unreasonable delay or expense. By way of exception to the general rule that applications are made by affidavit, this application may, subject to the district judge's or registrar's requirements, be made by letter. The letter must set out who is applying; who is having power reserved; and the grounds for seeking the dispensation.

If satisfied, the court directs no notice be given. The oath to lead the grant should recite that power is reserved to the non-proving executors and that the giving of notice was dispensed with by direction of the district judge or registrar, quoting the date of the direction.

Personal Representatives

Application to join co-administrator
Rule 25(1) provides that where there is a requirement for two grantees (because a life or minority interest arises; see page 95), a person entitled to the grant may apply with a person of lower capacity (i.e., lower in the order of priority set out in rules 20 and 22; see pages 149 and 161) where there is no other person of equal title who is ready and willing to apply.

Under rule 25(2), where there is no such person of a lower capacity willing to be a co-administrator, application may be made for an order for a person with no right to the grant to be joined in the application as proposed co-administrator. The affidavit should be made by the first proposed grantee, setting out the facts relied on. The consent of the proposed second grantee need not be given by separate document (although it usually is), but a statement that he agrees to act should be included in the affidavit.

No application under this rule is necessary if a minority interest arises and application is made by a person with parental responsibility, such a person being able to nominate the co-administrator under rule 32.

Application for grant to sole grantee
As an alternative to applying for joinder of a co-administrator, a direction for the grant to issue to a sole grantee may be sought. Where there is good reason, sufficient to satisfy the district judge or registrar that the estate will be properly administered by the person first entitled to the grant, and/or that there is no one prepared to act as co-administrator, the requirement for a co-administrator may be dispensed with. Section 114(2) of the 1981 Act, the provision requiring two grantees, also gives the court discretion to dispense

with the requirement if the circumstances warrant.

The affidavit should set out the circumstances of the case and why it is considered appropriate for the grant to issue to a sole grantee. If the district judge or registrar permits, application may be made less formally by letter.

Application to add a personal representative

Although any application to add a personal representative would be made after the issue of a grant, the procedure is dealt with here, as the authority to make such an order emanates from section 114 of the Act.

An application under rule 26, for a personal representative to be added, may be made where:

- after a grant has issued, a minority or life interest is discovered, but there was only one grantee; or
- there was a known minority or life interest, and the grant was issued to two grantees, but one has died.

Application is made by affidavit by the grantee, with the consent of the proposed additional personal representative. The affidavit should recite the facts relied on and the reason the additional personal representative is needed. The original grant should be lodged with the application.

The district judge or registrar, if not satisfied with the application, may impound the original grant or revoke it, directing a new application be made. On the other hand, if the district judge or registrar is satisfied that the order is appropriate, the original grant is annotated with the order and the second personal representative added.

Subpoena to Bring in a Will

Section 123 of the Supreme Court Act 1981 provides that:

"Where it appears any person has in his possession custody or power any document which is or purports to be a testamentary document, the High Court may, whether or not any legal proceedings are pending, issue a subpoena requiring him to bring in the document in such manner as the court may in the subpoena direct."

The procedure is set out in rule 50, which requires the application to be supported by an affidavit. The affidavit is usually made by the person who requires the Will to be lodged so that he may prove it or seek to have it pronounced against. Two copies of the subpoena should be lodged, one of which, sealed, will be returned to the solicitors for the applicant for service. For forms of affidavit and subpoena, see pages 296 and 348.

The subpoena may direct the testamentary document be lodged in *any* registry, but it usually directs lodgment at the registry from which the subpoena was issued. The person subpoenaed has eight days within which to lodge the document as directed. The proper officer with whom the testamentary document should be lodged is the Probate Manager (either at the Principal Registry or a district probate registry).

If the person subpoenaed does not have the testamentary document in his possession, custody or power, he must file an affidavit to that effect in the registry which issued the subpoena (rule 50(2)).

If the person subpoenaed fails to answer the subpoena by lodging the testamentary document or filing an affidavit, proceedings for committal for disobedience may be commenced against him.

Alternatively, the party issuing the subpoena may apply for an order requiring the person subpoenaed to attend before a judge to give evidence regarding the alleged testamentary document. Or it may be appropriate to apply for leave to prove a copy of the testamentary document, by application under rule 54 (see page 138).

Leave to Swear Death

Death certificates are usually issued by the Registrar of Births, Deaths and Marriages, but the Ministry of Defence (in respect of service personnel) and the Registrar General of Shipping and Seamen (in respect of merchant seamen) also issue certificates which are acceptable as proof of death.

Where there is no death certificate or other document acceptable as proof of death, then application may be made for an order giving leave to swear to the death of a presumed deceased person, as having occurred on or since the date he was last seen or known to be alive.

Where the fact of death is known but the date is uncertain, application for the grant may be made without other formality, the oath stating the deceased "was last known to be alive on [date]"; "last seen on [date] and his dead body found on [date]". If the death certificate states the deceased died "on or about [date]", the oath may simply contain a recital of the statement. Enquiry may be made of the registry for the form of words to be used, or a draft oath may be submitted for settling.

Making the application

Application for the order is made on affidavit. The affidavit should be deposed to by the person with the best knowledge of the facts – usually the proposed grantee. If the affidavit is not made by a member of the presumed deceased's immediate family, supporting evidence, on affidavit, from a member of the family should also be obtained.

The application should be made to a district judge of the Principal Registry if the application for the grant is to be made there. Otherwise, it should be made to the registrar of the district probate registry where it is proposed the application for the grant will be made.

The affidavit should contain details of the following facts:

- the reason the deponent believes the presumed deceased has died;
- when the presumed deceased was last seen or heard from;
- any insurance policies effected on the presumed deceased's life; any reports or enquiries made by the issuing companies; if there is no "report", then any views expressed in writing by the insurers. The value of any policies should also be given;
- any communication (letter, telephone call, text message) received from the presumed deceased and the date of the communication;
- any advertisement or enquiry for anyone having knowledge of the presumed deceased or his disappearance, and the result (if any) of such advertisement or enquiry;
- whether the deceased had made a Will or died intestate and the beneficiaries of his estate;
- any transactions by credit card or through a bank or building society account made after the disappearance, and the date(s) of the last of any such transactions;
- the value of the estate at the date of the presumed death and any increase or decrease since that date.

All letters, reports, replies to enquiries and statements, including bank or building society statements, should be exhibited. If the deceased died testate, a copy of his Will should be exhibited.

All reports of official bodies, such as the police or coastguard, must also be exhibited unless their evidence is contained in a supporting affidavit.

Foreign nationals

If the deceased was a foreign national or not domiciled in England and Wales, details of any enquiry made by any relevant authority (such as the police, the coastguard, or the equivalent) at the place of disappearance should be exhibited. Similarly, if the court having jurisdiction at the place of the disappearance has made a finding, any decree, pronouncement, declaration or order must be exhibited. Such evidence is corroborative but not sufficient alone.

Presumed death in a disaster

Where the death is presumed to have occurred in a disaster involving several persons, such as an aircraft accident, an enquiry should be made of the Principal Registry. The Principal Registry collates records of presumptive deaths in circumstances such as these, and of the evidence in support of applications in respect of them. An enquiry will reveal the type of evidence which has been accepted in other cases arising out of the same incident.

Divorce

A husband or wife whose spouse is missing and is presumed dead may apply to a divorce county court for a decree dissolving the marriage (see section 19, Matrimonial Causes Act 1973).

Even where a decree of divorce based on presumption of death has been granted, it is insufficient to allow a grant of representation to the presumed deceased's estate to be issued. Application for leave to swear death must still be made, and the evidence used to support the decree may be used to support the application for the order.

Multiple deaths in a disaster

Sometimes a disaster occurs in which numerous people are killed, but, because of the nature of the disaster, bodies are not found and no death certificates issued, with the result that persons are presumed to have died. It is therefore necessary to apply for leave to swear to the deaths of those presumed deceased.

The Principal Registry of the Family Division, through the Senior District Judge, maintains a record of the evidence used to support an application for leave to swear death where the presumed deceased was one of many presumed to have died in a disaster. An enquiry may be made of the Principal Registry to see whether any order giving leave to swear death has been made in another estate. If so, the form and content of evidence filed in that application may be disclosed to assist in the later application.

The application, based on the evidence disclosed, may be made to any registry. The discretion of each registrar is, however, unfettered by the outcome of a former application.

Commorientes

Entitlement to benefit under a Will or intestacy may depend on a question of survivorship. But where multiple deaths occurred in a disaster, there may well be uncertainty about who survived whom. The Senior District Judge may issue a circular listing the names of those who died in the incident in question, stating that he is satisfied on the evidence before him that there is doubt as to whom, of those known to have died, survived the others.

Section 184 of the Law of Property Act 1925 provides that a younger person is deemed to survive an older person. In respect of a husband or wife dying on or after 1 January 1996 intestate, the surviving spouse must survive by at least 28 days to acquire a beneficial interest in the deceased spouse's estate (section 1, Law Reform (Succession) Act 1995).

The Principal Registry should be contacted to ascertain whether a *commorientes* circular has been issued in respect of a particular disaster. If not, the application proceeds on evidence put before the district judge or registrar to satisfy him as to survivorship.

The order

The district judge or registrar, if satisfied on the evidence, makes an order giving leave to swear to the death having occurred on or since a specific date. The order is not served, but the registry communicates the details of it to the applicant. The oath to lead the grant recites the details of the order.

Severance of Estate

Section 113(1) of the Supreme Court Act 1981 provides that the High Court may grant representation in respect of any part of an estate, limited in any way it thinks fit. An application may be made for a temporary grant (an *ad colligenda bona defuncti* grant), or for a full grant, by order made pursuant to section 116 of the Act. Both these forms of application are dealt with later in this chapter.

Section 113(2) of the Act provides that where it is known that the estate is insolvent, it may not be severed except in respect of a trust in which the deceased held no beneficial interest.

Application for the order to sever an insolvent's estate in respect of trust property is made to a district judge or registrar of the registry at which the proposed application for the grant is to be made. The application should be made by the first entitled in priority to the grant. If the person entitled in priority cannot or will not apply, then an application under section 116 of the Act to pass over his title (see page 136) must also be made.

The affidavit must contain details of the insolvent estate and the trust property. If satisfied, the district judge makes the order, setting the limitation to be imposed in the grant. The applicant must then make and file the oath to lead the grant, reciting details of the order.

Refusal of Probate

Where an application to prove a Will has been made, and the district judge or registrar has called for evidence to support the execution of the Will, but the evidence is unsatisfactory, the district judge or registrar may refuse to grant probate. If the evidence clearly proves the Will was not properly executed, the Will is endorsed "probate refused". But if the evidence is unclear or incomplete, the district judge or registrar may refuse probate at that time, giving the applicant a further opportunity to validate the Will.

Where, before an application for a grant is made, it is clear from the Will, or from evidence supplied to the solicitor instructed, that the Will is invalid, it should not be submitted for marking that probate is refused. Instead, an application in respect of an earlier valid Will, or under the intestacy provisions, as appropriate, should be made in the usual way.

Foreign Domicile

Where the deceased died domiciled outside England and Wales, the normal order of priority to take a grant of representation in rules 20 and 22 (see pages 149 and 161) does not apply. An application must be made in accordance with rule 30 (see page 91).

The question of domicile is not a matter for the probate court; nor is domicile for tax purposes the same as domicile in respect of application to a probate registry.

The validity of the Will of a person domiciled in a foreign country must be established under the provisions of section 1 of the Wills Act 1963; see page 92. If there are different laws for particular states or territories, the evidence must relate to the relevant state or territory.

Application by person entrusted

Rule 30(1)(a) (see page 91 for the text of the rule) allows the person entrusted with the administration of the estate by the court having jurisdiction at the place of the deceased's domicile to apply for an order for a grant to himself. The grant is of letters of administration (with Will annexed) if the deceased died testate, or letters of administration if intestate. If the person entrusted is the executor, or one of the executors, named in the Will, then, once validity of the Will is established, the executor may apply for a grant without order (rule 30(3)(a)). If the person entrusted is not the executor named in the Will he may apply under this rule without giving notice to the others, by-passing the executor's right to a grant.

The entrusting document: To constitute an entrusting document sufficient for the order, the foreign court must have issued a grant, or made a pronouncement, decree or order which confers upon the administrator the same or substantially the same powers as a full grant of representation issued in England and Wales. An entrusting document conferring the appropriate powers but which is limited to particular assets, e.g. personalty, or is for a limited period of time, may be accepted as sufficient. In such a case, the district judge or registrar imposes a similar limitation on the grant in respect of the estate in England and Wales.

If there is any doubt about the sufficiency of the entrusting document or its limitation, it should be referred to a district judge or registrar for directions.

Will proved by foreign court: If the deceased died testate and the entrusting document incorporates or refers to the Will, then no separate evidence to validate the Will is necessary. The fact that the court of the place of domicile has accepted it is sufficient to establish validity under section 1 of the Wills Act 1963.

Application for the order: The application for the order may be made by lodging the original grant, decree or order, or a court-certified (official) copy of the relevant document together with (if not incorporated within it) a court-certified (official) copy of the Will. These documents are retained by the registry as part of the court record. If the grant, decree or order is not in English, an authenticated translation of it (and of the Will, if any) must be lodged. Authentication may be effected by a notarial certificate or by evidence on affidavit by the translator, which sets out his qualifications to effect the translation and exhibits the (copy) entrusting document and the translation. Details of the order must be recited in the oath (for a form of oath, see page 341).

The application may be made either before the application for the grant is submitted, or contemporaneously with it. If the latter, the documents referred to above should be lodged, and a request for the order should be made in the oath to lead the grant.

The lawfully appointed attorney of the person entrusted may make the application.

Application by person beneficially entitled

Where there is no person entrusted with the administration of the estate, an application may be made under rule 30(1)(b) by the person, or one of the persons, beneficially entitled to the estate by the law of the place of domicile.

Although the Will names beneficiaries, evidence, not only to validate the Will under section 1 of the Wills Act 1963, but also of beneficial entitlement, is necessary. The Will cannot speak for itself to establish such entitlement; under the foreign law a gift in a Will may not be permissible. Evidence in accordance with rule 19 (see page 93) may be given on affidavit by someone qualified in that law, or by notarial statement. If the Will has been proved by the court having jurisdiction at the place of domicile then no further evidence is required in respect of the Will. Where the Will has not been proved, the evidence to support validity and beneficial entitlement may be included in the same affidavit or notarial statement.

Where more than one person is beneficially entitled, the district judge or registrar has discretion to entertain an application by one or some of those persons. The usual rule that no more than four personal representatives may be appointed applies (see section 114, Supreme Court Act 1981).

The application for the order: As in the case of an application under rule 30(1)(a), an application for an order under rule 30(1)(b) may be made before the grant is issued, either by lodging the evidence, or by a request contained in the oath to lead the grant (supported by the evidence). The evidence, if not in English, must be accompanied by an authenticated translation. If the application is made before the grant has been issued, details of the order must be recited in the oath (for a form of oath, see page 341). No more than four persons beneficially entitled may apply.

The application may be made by the lawfully appointed attorney(s) of the person(s) beneficially entitled.

No person entrusted or entitled

If there is no person entrusted with the administration and no person beneficially entitled, or should such person be unable or unwilling to apply, the court may entertain an application for a discretionary order under rule 30(1)(c). It is usually wise to seek the district judge or registrar's views on such an application by way of a pre-lodgment enquiry.

The application must be made before the grant is applied for. The court has absolute and unfettered discretion to appoint any fit and proper person to take the grant.

The application is made on affidavit, usually by the proposed grantee, setting out details of:
- the deceased;
- his domicile;
- whether the deceased died testate or intestate;
- any order which has been made by the court of the place of domicile;
- who benefits from the estate;
- why the person(s) entrusted or beneficially entitled will not or cannot apply;
- the estate values;
- the person seeking the grant and why that person wishes to apply.

Any evidence of foreign law not contained in a separate affidavit or notarial statement should be exhibited, as should any Will. The affidavit should conclude with a request for the order.

The validity of any Will must be established.

The grant is issued, in due course, to the person named in the order.

Life or minority interests

In any application made under paragraphs (1)(a), (b) or (c) of rule 30, where a life or minority interest arises, there must be two applicants for the grant unless the district judge or registrar exercises his discretion to allow the grant to issue to a sole grantee, section 114 of the Supreme Court Act 1981 (see page 123) applying to foreign domicile cases.

No order required: named executor or executor according to the tenor

Rule 30(3)(a)(i) provides that probate of any Will, the validity of which has been established, may be granted to the executor named in the Will without any order. The only proviso is that the Will must be in the English or Welsh language, the meaning of "executor" being regarded as peculiar to English law. Any expression meaning "executor" in a foreign language, or translated from a foreign language as "executor", is unacceptable in this context.

Sub-paragraph (a)(ii) of the rule allows probate of a Will, again where validity has been established, to be granted to the person named in it whose duties are described sufficiently to constitute him executor according to the tenor of the will. This applies irrespective of the language in which the original Will was written. A verified translation is necessary. If there is doubt about the sufficiency of the appointment, a pre-lodgment enquiry (with the relevant documents) should be made to the district judge or registrar.

Where rule 30(3)(a)(i) or (ii), described above, applies, the application may be made by the attorney(s) of the executor or executor according to the tenor.

Immovable estate

Rule 30(3)(b) provides that where the whole, or substantially the whole, estate in England and Wales consists of immovable property the usual rules of entitlement to a grant, had the deceased died domiciled in England and Wales, apply. This in effect means the order of priority in rules 20 and 22 (see pages 149 and 161) applies. No distinction is drawn between a testacy or intestacy. If there is a Will, however, its validity must be established, but thereafter rule 20 applies.

The rules refer to the whole or substantially the whole estate consisting of immovable property (realty). No definition of "substantially" exists, but provided the real estate constitutes more than 50 per cent of the total value of the estate it can be argued that it is the substantial part of the estate.

The oath to lead the grant must contain details of the estate and the values of the real and personal estate; this is particularly important if the "substantial" test is to be applied.

Minor(s) Entitled to a Grant

Where the person entitled to a grant of letters of administration (with Will annexed) or letters of administration under an intestacy is a minor, the grant may be taken for his use and benefit by the person or body having parental responsibility for him, or his guardian, under the Children Act 1989. Rule 32(1) sets out those to whom a grant may issue without an order of the court. Paragraph (3) of the rule provides that where there is only one person qualifying under paragraph (1), that person may nominate a fit and proper person to be his co-administrator. Where there is no person with parental responsibility, or that person cannot or will not apply for the grant, an application must be made under paragraph (2) to a district judge or registrar for a person to be appointed to take the grant for the minor's use and benefit.

The application

The application for a person to be appointed is made on affidavit under rule 32(2). Although the rule refers to the appointment of "a person" it is usual for the application to be for the appointment of two persons, rather than one who then has to nominate a co-administrator. The affidavit should recite:

- details of the deceased;
- whether he died testate or intestate;
- the name of the minor and his age;
- the person who has parental responsibility for him or has been appointed his guardian and why that person cannot or will not take the grant, or that there is no person with parental responsibility or guardian;
- where and with whom the minor resides;
- the relationship (if any) of the applicant to the minor;
- whether there are, or are contemplated, any proceedings under the Children Act 1989, and any order made in any such proceedings;
- whether the minor is a ward of court;
- the value of the estate; and
- any other relevant facts.

The affidavit should conclude with a request for the order.

If the minor has been made a ward of court and the wardship order subsists, the application may be referred to the district judge to whom the wardship is assigned.

The deponents to the affidavit are the proposed grantees, or one of them, provided it is clear on the evidence that the other proposed grantee agrees to act. See page 293 for a form of affidavit.

A draft of the affidavit may be submitted for the district judge or registrar's approval before swearing.

When sworn, the affidavit should be lodged in the registry to which the application for the grant is to be made. If satisfied, the district judge or registrar makes the order, and a copy is sent to those representing the applicants. No fee is payable on the application.

The oath to lead the grant must recite the details of the order, and the limitation imposed by it as it is to appear in the grant.

Mental Incapacity

Rule 35 deals with applications on behalf of persons who are entitled to a grant but who are mentally incapable of managing their affairs.

Paragraph (1) provides that a capable person entitled to a grant in the same degree as an incapable person must be "cleared off" (see page 157) before an application on behalf of the incapable person may be made.

Paragraph (2) provides the order of priority to apply. Applications under paragraph (2) are dealt with at page 158. Where there is no one entitled in the order of priority under paragraph (2) or such a person cannot or will not act, an application for a discretionary order – to appoint someone to take the grant – must be made under paragraph (4).

The affidavit is usually deposed to by the proposed grantee, but may, subject to a district judge's or registrar's discretion, be made by the solicitor instructed if the relevant facts are within his knowledge. The affidavit should contain details of:

- the deceased and whether he died testate or intestate;
- if testate, whether it is the executor who is incapable of managing his affairs, or, if not the executor, why the executor cannot act (e.g., because he has predeceased, or has renounced probate); and if it is not the executor who is incapable of managing his affairs, details of the residuary beneficiary;
- evidence to support the incapacity. If the incapable person is in an institution, the evidence may comprise a certificate from a responsible medical officer of the institution, in the following form:

    (Name of Institution)

    (Name of patient)

    I certify that:

    The above-named patient, who is now residing in this Institution, is in my opinion by reason of mental disorder incapable of managing his property and affairs.

    In my opinion the above-named patient is unlikely to be fit to manage and administer his property and affairs within a period of three months.

    Date:

    Signed: .... Responsible Medical Officer;

    If the person resides outside an institution, a letter or certificate from his general practitioner would be appropriate;
- whether any receiver has been appointed by the Court of Protection under a First General Order, or whether any application to that court is pending or contemplated;
- the relationship (if any) of the proposed grantee to the incapable person;
- any other relevant information to support the application.

The affidavit should conclude with a request for the order.

The medical evidence from the responsible medical officer or general practitioner should be exhibited, as should a copy of the Will or other testamentary document.

Notice must be given to the Court of Protection under rule 35(5) to ensure that no application for authority to act, or the registration of an enduring power of attorney, is pending. The acknowledgement of the notice should be lodged with the affidavit.

A draft of the affidavit may be submitted to the district judge or registrar of the registry to which it is proposed to apply for the grant, for his approval before it is sworn (fee £10). For a form of affidavit, see page 293.

The sworn affidavit should be lodged with the exhibits. No fee is payable on the application.

A copy of the order, when made, is sent to those instructed. Details of the order giving title to apply for the grant must be recited in the oath to lead the grant.

Grant Ad Colligenda Bona Defuncti

When a grant of representation is needed to administer the estate of a deceased person, or a particular part of the estate, as a matter of urgency, but a full grant cannot be extracted in time to deal with the urgency, an application may be made for an order for a grant *ad colligenda bona defuncti*. The purpose of the grant is to protect or preserve the estate until full representation can be taken.

The following are some of the circumstances in which a grant of this type may be appropriate; the list is not exhaustive:

- where contracts for sale of real property have been exchanged and the vendor dies before completion;
- to sell real property where the property is in danger of vandalism or may otherwise deteriorate, or a purchaser has been found at an advantageous price;
- to sell any stocks and shares, or any other particular assets, where to delay sale would cause loss of value to the estate;
- to a creditor, to recover a debt where those entitled to a full grant delay in applying;
- in respect of the deceased's business, to sell or allow someone to continue to run the business.

Application for the order is made on affidavit, usually by the proposed grantee(s), but, with the leave of a district judge or registrar, the affidavit may be deposed to by the solicitor instructed in the application if he has knowledge of the facts.

The affidavit

The affidavit must set out details of:

- the deceased and whether he died testate or intestate;
- if the deceased died testate, whether any testamentary document is in dispute;
- if the deceased died intestate, whether there is any dispute about title to the grant;

- why a grant is required as a matter of urgency, and why a full grant cannot be taken in sufficient time;
- the estate to be dealt with by the grant, its value and whether the estate is subject to inheritance tax; and
- any other relevant matter to assist the court in considering the application.

The affidavit concludes with a request for the order, showing the proposed limitation to be included in the grant. Although the grant, when issued, is silent as to the fact of a Will or intestacy, a copy of any testamentary document should be exhibited to the affidavit.

The proposed grantee(s) may be the person(s) entitled to a full grant, or any person considered fit and proper to act in the administration, including the solicitor instructed.

The limitation

The usual limitation in a grant *ad colligenda bona defuncti* is "for the purpose of collecting, getting in and receiving the estate and doing such acts as may be necessary for the preservation of the same until further representation be granted but not further or otherwise". The court's discretion to issue representation for specific purposes is absolute and unfettered. The limitation may therefore be tailored to suit the requirements of the particular case.

Approval of draft affidavit

Because of the discretionary nature of the order sought, it is usually wise to seek the view of the district judge or registrar, by way of a pre-lodgment enquiry, as to whether the application will be entertained. Thereafter it is also preferable for a draft affidavit to be submitted for approval (fee: £10.00). Experiences indicates that this saves time and expense. No fee is payable on the application for the order.

The grant

The procedure for applying for the grant after the order has been made is dealt with at page 165. If the estate is of such a value that an Inland Revenue Account must be delivered, an account dealing with that part of the estate passing under the *ad colligenda bona defuncti* grant must be delivered. If tax is payable, then the tax due on this part of the estate must also be paid. Enquiry should be made of IR Capital Taxes.

Special Circumstances

Section 116, Supreme Court Act 1981 provides that:

"(1) If by reason of any special circumstances it appears to the High Court to be necessary or expedient to appoint as administrator some person other than the person who, but for this section, would in accordance with probate rules have been entitled to the grant, the court may in its discretion appoint as administrator such person as it thinks expedient.

(2) Any grant of administration under this section may be limited in any way the court thinks fit."

The court's discretion to pass over prior claims to a grant is absolute and unfettered. The court may direct administration be granted to any person who can, on the evidence, satisfy the court that he is a fit and proper person to administer the estate. The grant, when issued pursuant to the order, is a full grant to the whole estate (unlike a grant *ad colligenda bona defuncti* referred to above) although it may, if necessary, be limited under paragraph (2).

Reasons for an application

The circumstances where an application may be made are:

- to pass over the right of an executor who:
  - has failed to apply for probate within a reasonable time after the death of his testator;
  - is missing, and enquiries have failed to discover his whereabouts;
  - is considered unsuitable to act in the administration of the estate;
- there is an unresolvable conflict between the executors (here, the application would be to appoint independent administrators);
- to pass over the right of an administrator who:
  - has been convicted of the murder or manslaughter of the deceased or of any other offence within the provisions of the Forfeiture Act 1982;
  - is missing, and enquires have failed to discover his whereabouts;
  - is in dispute with one or more persons equally entitled to the grant as to who should take the grant (again the application would be to appoint independent administrators);
  - is an undischarged bankrupt (the application would be to enable the receiver in bankruptcy to take the grant for the benefit of the bankrupt estate);
- the applicant wishes to bring proceedings under the Inheritance (Provision for Family and Dependants) Act 1975 and does not wish also to be the personal representative (but see now the notes to Rules of the Supreme Court 1965, Order 99, rule 4(1) in Schedule 1 to the Civil Procedure Rules 1998 in *Civil Procedure*).

The above list is not exhaustive. Section 116 may also be invoked where an executor or administrator is himself aged, or so ill that he might not survive to complete the administration. In such circumstances, the appointment of an attorney would be inappropriate since the grant would effectively cease to be operative on the donor's death.

The court has power to pass over an executor who has intermeddled in the estate (see page 113) but refuses to take probate (see *In the Estate of Biggs* [1966] P 118, [1966] 2 WLR 536, [1965] 1 All ER 358). This application is preferable to citing a dilatory executor to take probate.

The affidavit

The affidavit may be made by the proposed grantee or by the solicitor instructed if the solicitor has knowledge of the relevant facts and the leave of the district judge or registrar. If there is to be more than one grantee, at least one of them should depose to the facts (subject, as has been said, to the solicitor's being the deponent).

The affidavit should recite:

- details of the deceased and any Will;
- the persons entitled in priority to the grant under rule 20 or 22 (see pages 149 and 161);
- why the person entitled cannot or will not apply for the grant and why his title to the grant should be passed over;
- details of the enquiries which have been made to find those entitled whose whereabouts remain unknown; and
- the gross and net values of the estate.

The affidavit should conclude with a request for the order.

Any limitation to be imposed in the grant (which is known) should be included with the request for the order.

The order

If the district judge or registrar is not satisfied, he may refuse the application or give directions for further evidence. He may also direct the matter be brought before the court on summons.

But if satisfied on the evidence, the district judge or registrar directs letters of administration to issue (on application) to the persons proposed as grantees.

A copy of the order is served by the court on the solicitor for the applicant. The oath to lead the grant recites details of the order as title to take the grant.

Admission of a Copy Will or Nuncupative Will

Where the original of a testamentary document cannot be found after the testator's death, an application may be made for an order to prove a copy, draft or reconstruction. Rule 54 provides:

"*Grants in respect of nuncupative wills and copies of wills*

(1) Subject to paragraph (2) below, an application for an order admitting to

proof a nuncupative will, or a will contained in a copy or reconstruction thereof where the original is not available, shall be made to a district judge or registrar.

(2) In any case where a will is not available owing to its being retained in the custody of a foreign court or official, a duly authenticated copy of the will may be admitted to proof without the order referred to in paragraph (1) above.

(3) An application under paragraph (1) above shall be supported by an affidavit setting out the grounds of the application, and by such evidence on affidavit as the applicant can adduce as to –

(a) the will's existence after the death of the testator or, where there is no such evidence, the facts on which the applicant relies to rebut the presumption that the will has been revoked by destruction;

(b) in respect of a nuncupative will, the contents of that will; and

(c) in respect of a reconstruction of a will, the accuracy of that reconstruction.

(4) The district judge or registrar may require additional evidence in the circumstances of a particular case as to the execution of the will or as to the accuracy of the copy will, and may direct that notice be given to persons who would be prejudiced by the application."

Executed draft or copy

Sometimes the only testamentary document found is an executed draft or copy. If there is evidence to show that no engrossment or other original of the document was executed, the draft or copy may be admitted to proof without application for an order under rule 54.

It is suggested that, in these circumstances, the matter is referred as a pre-lodgment enquiry for the district judge or registrar to give directions on the procedure to be adopted. If satisfied, the district judge or registrar directs the executed draft or copy be admitted, the oath referring to the Will "as contained in an executed draft". The district judge or registrar may require notice be given to persons prejudiced by proof of the draft or copy, that is, to those persons who would receive a benefit, or greater benefit, under an earlier valid Will (which still exists) or on intestacy.

Original Will held by another court

If the original Will has been proved by a court in another country, an official copy of the Will may be admitted to proof without order under rule 54, the oath referring to the Will "as being contained in an official copy".

Lost Will

When the original Will was in the testator's possession before his death but cannot afterwards be found, there is a rebuttable presumption that the Will was revoked by the testator in his lifetime by destruction. Evidence to rebut the presumption must be included in the affidavit.

Where there is evidence to show the original Will existed after the testator's death, obviously there can be no question of revocation by the testator. The evidence must clearly establish the existence of the original Will at the date of death.

The affidavit

The affidavit must be deposed to by someone with knowledge of the facts. Where evidence to rebut the presumption of revocation is necessary, that evidence should come from family, friends or legal adviser. If the Will was lost after the death, the solicitor instructed may make the affidavit if he has knowledge of the facts of the loss of the Will.

The affidavit should contain details of:
- the deceased's address and date of death;
- the making of the Will (and any codicils);
- the place of custody of the Will;
- the loss of the Will (and if lost before the date of death and in the custody of the testator, evidence to rebut the presumption of revocation);
- attempts to find the original Will;
- the provenance of the copy;
- any persons prejudiced by proof of the copy Will; and
- who intends to prove the copy Will.

The affidavit should exhibit the copy Will to be proved and any correspondence relating to the loss of the Will and the enquiries which have been made to trace it. The affidavit concludes with a request for the order.

Copy contained in draft, unexecuted copy or reconstruction

If the copy sought to be proved is not a copy of the original made after execution, then the affidavit must also contain evidence to show the copy document or reconstruction is indeed a copy of the Will, or an accurate reconstruction of the Will, in both form and content, as when executed. This evidence needs to be especially strong when it is sought to prove a reconstruction of a Will.

Additionally, unless there is evidence from the person seeking the order which shows that the Will was duly executed, then evidence on affidavit from one of the attesting witnesses is also required. If the identity of the witnesses cannot be established then there must be evidence from another source to satisfy the court that the Will, in the form now sought to be proved, is a true and complete copy of the Will as executed.

Incomplete Will

There are occasions when the original Will, when found after the testator's death, is incomplete; i.e., parts or page(s) are missing. Subject to evidence to show the missing parts were not revoked by the testator by destruction, a complete copy may be accepted to proof.

Original Will in existence but unobtainable

Where it is known that the original Will exists, exhaustive attempts should be made to obtain it for proof.

If the original Will is held by an individual abroad, if there is evidence to show that that person refuses to deliver up the Will, coupled with the evidence, as above, of the authenticity of the copy, a copy may be admitted to proof.

If the Will is retained in the United Kingdom then a subpoena under rule 50 should be issued for the Will to be lodged in the court (see page 124). If the subpoena fails, then, subject to the district judge's or registrar's discretion, an application to prove a copy may be made.

Reconstruction

Where there is no original Will or copy in any form (i.e., carbon copy or photocopy), but there is evidence of the content of the Will when executed, an application may be made to prove a reconstruction. Evidence to support the content and form of the Will is critical to the success of such an application. Similarly, evidence to establish the Will was executed in that form is required.

Known Will: no copy or evidence of content available

Where it is known that the deceased made a Will but there is no evidence to show that it has been destroyed (other than by the deceased), and no copy is available, nor can its content be substantiated, then application must be made as on intestacy.

The application may be made on affidavit to a district judge or registrar for an order for letters of administration to be granted to the person entitled on intestacy. The oath and the grant are silent as to the deceased dying testate or intestate and the grant is limited "until the original Will or an authentic copy be proved".

Nuncupative Will

A "privileged Will", that is, a Will made, the execution of which does not conform with section 9 of the Wills Act 1837, by a soldier, seaman or airman on actual military service (see page 89), may be accepted to proof. If that Will is not written, but by oral statement, then evidence of the substance of the statement or declaration of testamentary wishes must be obtained from the person(s) to whom the declaration was made.

The declaration must be committed to paper, with evidence to support the content, and that the declaration was intended to be testamentary. This declaration must be exhibited to the affidavit.

The affidavit must establish the facts to claim the privilege and establish the content of the oral statement. It is suggested a pre-lodgment enquiry be made of the district judge or registrar as to whether the privilege is to be allowed, and, if so, the form of the Will to be submitted.

The order

If satisfied on the evidence, the district judge or registrar orders the copy Will to be admitted. The oath should refer to the Will "as being contained in the copy exhibited to the affidavit of . . . . . . sworn on the . . . . and marked ' . . . .'". The usual limitation is "until the original Will or a more authentic copy be proved", but this limitation may vary depending on the circumstances.

A copy of the order is served, and the copy Will exhibited to the affidavit is returned for marking with the oath. The oath must include the limitation.

Original Will found

If the original Will is found after the order has been made but before the application for a grant has been lodged, the original Will may be submitted to proof. The application for the grant should be accompanied by a covering letter explaining that the original Will has been found.

If the original Will is found after the grant has been issued, it may be lodged in the proving registry. No other action need be taken provided the copy Will proved was indeed a true and complete copy of the original. The order is usually "until the original Will or a more authentic copy be proved". Provided the copy is a copy of the original there is no need to prove the original; the grant, which reflects the order, remains operative to complete the administration of the estate.

Rectification

Section 20 of the Administration of Justice Act 1982 is as follows:

"*Rectification*

(1) If a court is satisfied that a will is so expressed that it fails to carry out the testator's intentions, in consequence

    (a) of a clerical error; or

    (b) of a failure to understand his instructions,

    it may order that the will shall be rectified so as to carry out his intentions.

(2) An application for an order under this section shall not, except with the permission of the court, be made after the end of the period of six months from the date on which representation with respect to the estate of the deceased is first taken out.

(3) The provisions of this section shall not render the personal representatives of a deceased person liable for having distributed any part of the estate of the deceased, after the end of the period of six months from the date on which representation with respect to the estate of the deceased is first taken out, on the ground that they ought to have taken into account the possibility that the court might permit the making of an application for an order under this section after the end of that period but this subsection shall not prejudice any power to recover, by reason of the making of an order under this section, any part of the estate so distributed.

(4) In considering for the purposes of this section when representation with respect to the estate of a deceased person was first taken out, a grant limited to settled land or to trust property shall be left out of account unless a grant limited to the remainder of the estate has previously been made or is made at the same time."

Application for rectification is governed by rule 55, which provides:

"Application for rectification of a will

(1) An application for an order that a will be rectified by virtue of section 20(1) of the Administration of Justice Act 1982 may be made to a district judge or registrar, unless a probate action has been commenced.

(2) The application shall be supported by an affidavit setting out the grounds of the application, together with such evidence as can be adduced as to the testator's intentions and as to whichever of the following matters are in issue:-

(a) in what respects the testator's intentions were not understood; or

(b) the nature of any alleged clerical error.

(3) Unless otherwise directed, notice of the application shall be given to every person having an interest under the will whose interest might be prejudiced, or such other person who might be prejudiced, by the rectification applied for and any comments in writing by any such person shall be exhibited to the affidavit in support of the application.

(4) If the district judge or registrar is satisfied that, subject to any direction to the contrary, notice has been given to every person mentioned in paragraph (3) above, and that the application is unopposed, he may order that the will be rectified accordingly."

The affidavit

The affidavit referred to in paragraph (2) above should be made by the draftsman of the Will or by someone else with knowledge of the facts. The affidavit must set out the error, how it occurred and what the testator's intentions were, i.e., the criterion to enable rectification in accordance with section 20(1)(a) and/or (b) of the Act. The affidavit should exhibit a copy of the Will as executed, and a copy of the Will in its proposed rectified form.

Paragraph (3) requires notice to any person who may be prejudiced by the proposed rectification. Notice is by letter to any person who would receive a benefit, or a greater benefit, if the proposed rectification is not effected. The Family Division's jurisdiction is limited to unopposed applications. This does not mean there has to be consent, but that no opposition has been notified. If the application is or becomes opposed, application is made by claim, under Part 57 of the Civil Procedure Rules 1998, in the Chancery Division.

Time for application

Where the error requiring rectification is known about before an application for a grant has been made, the application for rectification should be made before it is sought to prove the Will. Section 2 of the Act, however, allows an application to rectify to be made after the grant has been issued, provided it is made within six months of the issue of a full grant. An application outside that time may be made only with the leave of a district judge or registrar.

The order

On an application before a grant of representation has been issued, the court, if satisfied on the evidence, orders the Will to be proved in its rectified form: the engrossment in that form is endorsed with the district judge's or registrar's *fiat*, thereafter to form the probate and record copies. A copy of the order is served but no reference to it need be made in the oath. The original Will, not the engrossment, is marked on swearing the oath.

If the order is made after a grant has been issued, a memorandum of the order is endorsed on the original grant and a copy of the rectified Will annexed to it. The record copy grant is annotated in the same way.

No fee is payable on the application.

Interpretation

Section 21 of the Administration of Justice Act 1982 provides as follows:
"Interpretation of wills – general rules as to evidence
(1) This section applies to a will –
    (a) in so far as any part of it is meaningless;
    (b) in so far as the language used in any part of it is ambiguous on the face of it;
    (c) in so far as evidence, other than evidence of the testator's intention,

shows that the language used in any part of it is ambiguous in the light of surrounding circumstances.

(2) In so far as this section applies to a will extrinsic evidence, including evidence of the testator's intention, may be admitted to assist in its interpretation."

Jurisdiction in respect of the construction of Wills lies not with the Family Division, but with the Chancery Division under Part 57 of the Civil Procedure Rules 1998. Construction, i.e., establishing the meaning of a gift or the testator's intention regarding any gift, therefore comes within the ambit of Part 57.

Any application for interpretation to a probate registry is limited to determining title to take a grant of representation – invariably because there is a problem in the clause appointing executors.

Application is by affidavit by the Will draftsman or someone with knowledge of the testator's intention when making the Will and how the wording of the Will failed to carry out those intentions. A copy of the Will should be exhibited.

If satisfied on the evidence, the district judge or registrar directs the Will be interpreted so as to carry out the testator's intentions. No order is drawn up.

No fee is payable on the application.

Omission of Words from Probate and Record Copy Will

Where the original Will contains words which are or may be considered offensive, libellous or blasphemous, an application may be made for their omission (see page 89). If no application is made the district judge or registrar may refuse to grant probate until application is made.

The application is made on affidavit, usually before the grant has been issued, exhibiting a copy of the Will as executed and an engrossment omitting the offending words. The application is made to the district judge or registrar of the registry to which the application for the grant will be made or where it is pending.

The original Will must be marked by the deponent and a commissioner on swearing the oath, but the engrossment is copied to form the probate and record copies, and any other copy applied for subsequently.

Chapter 11

Trust Corporations

A trust corporation is defined by section 128 of the Supreme Court Act 1981, and section 115 of the Act authorises such a corporation to take grants of representation in all forms.

A trust corporation may act alone or with an individual. A grant to a trust corporation issues in the corporation's corporate name.

Resolution Authorising Person(s) to Act

Before a trust corporation may apply for a grant, the governing body of that corporation, however constituted, must pass a resolution authorising named officers, or the holders of named positions in the corporation, to swear oaths, affidavits etc. and effect renunciations or other documents required in connection with a grant of representation.

Where the trust corporation acts in numerous estates, a certified copy of the resolution may be lodged with the senior district judge of the Principal Registry, each oath to lead a grant thereafter reciting that the resolution is so lodged. Alternatively, a certified copy resolution must be lodged with each application. This also applies to persons holding an official position which acts as a trust corporation, e.g. the Public Guardianship Office.

Trust Corporation Appointed Executor

A trust corporation may take probate, with or without any other named executor, renounce probate or have power reserved to it in the same way as may an individual who has been appointed executor.

Where a local or branch office of a trust corporation is appointed executor, the appointment is deemed to be an appointment of the trust corporation, unless there is a clear contrary intention expressed in the Will.

A trust corporation which does not wish to act as executor may renounce probate through its authorised officers. If it is not known who, if anyone, is to take a grant, the renunciation and original Will may be lodged in a probate registry at any time after the testator's death (see also page 119). Alternatively, the renunciation may be lodged with the application for the grant.

Trust Corporation Appointed Attorney

Any executor entitled to probate, or other person entitled in priority under rule 20 to letters of administration (with Will annexed), or person entitled in priority under rule 22 where there is an intestacy, may appoint a trust corporation as his attorney to take the grant for his use and benefit.

Consent to a Trust Corporation Acting

Deceased testate

An executor may renounce probate and, where the residuary beneficiaries do not wish to act in the administration (in the order of priority prescribed by rule 20, see page 149), a trust corporation may take letters of administration (with Will annexed). If there is no executor or no surviving executor then, again with the consent of the residuary beneficiaries, a trust corporation may act. The residuary beneficiaries do not need to renounce (unless one or more of them is a minor – see below); only an executor, or an executor who is also a residuary beneficiary, must renounce, and, in the latter case, also consent.

Deceased intestate

Similarly, the person(s) entitled under an intestacy to take letters of administration may consent to an application by a trust corporation. All persons of equal first entitlement, e.g., issue or siblings, must consent, but do not have to renounce their title except where one or more of them is a minor. Those with no immediate beneficial interest, e.g., those entitled on an accretion, are not relevant.

Minority interests

Where all the persons entitled to the estate, whether under a Will or on intestacy, are minors, a trust corporation may take the grant with the consent of those entitled under rule 32(1) (see page 132), that is, those, including a local authority, who have parental responsibility for the minors under the Children Act 1989. If there are no persons with parental responsibility a trust corporation may apply to be appointed under rule 32(2) (see page 133). The grant is not limited for the use and benefit of the minors, but issues to the trust corporation in its own right.

Where one or more of several persons entitled is a minor the person with parental responsibility cannot consent to an application by a trust corporation. All those of full age must renounce *and* consent before the trust corporation may apply and take the grant. In these circumstances, the grant is limited until the minors, or one of them, obtains a grant. The grant does not cease to the effective when the minors, or any one of them, attains eighteen years of age.

Dispensing with renunciation and consent

Rule 36(3) is the authority for the above requirements relating to renunciation and consent. Where there are special circumstances, a district judge or registrar may, on application, dispense with any renunciation or consent. Application for the dispensation may be made by letter describing the circumstances. The district judge or registrar may require the application to be made on affidavit.

Trust Corporation a Beneficiary

Where a trust corporation is a beneficiary under a Will it may apply for a grant, its title to the grant being determined in the normal order of priority under rule 20, e.g., where a trust corporation is a legatee it may apply on the renunciation of the residuary beneficiary.

Non-Trust Corporations

A corporation which is not a trust corporation as defined by rule 2(1) may take a grant through its nominee or attorney (see rule 36(4)). Thus a non-trust corporation cannot take probate in its own right when appointed executor, but may take letters of administration (with Will annexed).

The nominee or attorney must be specifically authorised to act. The resolution appointing the nominee to act, or the power of attorney, must be executed by the governing body of the corporation, however constituted. The original or a copy, certified to be a true and complete copy of the resolution or power, must be lodged with each application for a grant.

The grant issues in the name of the nominee or attorney, for the use and benefit of the corporation, and is limited until further representation be granted.

Where a non-trust corporation is appointed executor with individuals, it may take a grant only if the individuals have predeceased or renounced, their title (to probate) being higher in priority under rule 20.

A non-trust corporation may renounce its title to a grant through its nominee authorised by the corporation to do so.

Chapter 12

Applications for Grants

Application for a Grant of Probate

The right to a grant
Where the deceased died testate, title to take the grant of representation is governed by rule 20, which provides as follows:
"Where the deceased died on or after 1 January 1926 the person or persons entitled to a grant in respect of a will shall be determined in accordance with the following order of priority, namely –
(a) the executor;
(b) any residuary legatee or devisee holding in trust for any other person;
(c) any other residuary legatee or devisee (including one for life) or where the residue is not wholly disposed of by the will, any person entitled to share in the undisposed of residue (including the Treasury Solicitor when claiming *bona vacantia* on behalf of the Crown), provided that –
   (i) unless a district judge or registrar otherwise directs, a residuary legatee or devisee whose legacy or devise is vested in interest shall be preferred to one entitled on the happening of a contingency, and
   (ii) where the residue is not in terms wholly disposed of, the district judge or registrar may, if he is satisfied that the testator has nevertheless disposed of the whole or substantially the whole of the known estate, allow a grant to be made to any legatee or devisee entitled to, or to share in, the estate so disposed of, without regard to the persons entitled to share in any residue not disposed of by the will;
(d) the personal representative of any other residuary legatee or devisee (but not one for life, or holding in trust for any other person), or of any other person entitled to share in any residue not disposed of by the will;
(e) any other legatee or devisee (including one for life or holding in trust for any other person) or any creditor of the deceased, provided

that, unless a district judge or registrar otherwise directs, a legatee or devisee whose legacy or devise is vested in interest shall be preferred to one entitled on the happening of a contingency;

(f) the personal representative of any other legatee or devisee (but not one for life or one holding in trust for any other person) or of any creditor of the deceased."

Title to the grant falls firstly to the executor, who may take a grant of probate. If the executor appoints an attorney to act for him, the attorney is entitled to letters of administration (with Will annexed). All those falling within paragraphs (b) to (f) are entitled to letters of administration (with Will annexed).

Executors

The executor's title derives from his testator's Will. On the death of the testator all property vests in his executor, even before he has taken probate of the Will.

Probate cannot be granted to more than four executors (section 114(2), Supreme Court Act 1981).

Chain of executors: Section 7 of the Administration of Estates Act 1925 provides that the executor of a sole or last surviving executor of a testator is the executor of that testator. Thus the executor, having proved the Will of his testator, is entitled to administer any estate of which his testator was the sole or last surviving executor. No further grant is required.

The chain of executorship is broken when the sole or last surviving executor:

- dies intestate;
- fails to appoint an executor in his Will; or
- his appointed executor fails to prove his Will.

Limitation or condition on appointment: Depending on the wording of the clause appointing the executor, the executor's appointment may be:

- limited to a particular part of the estate, e.g., "literary estate", "all estate outside Canada";
- contingent upon an event, e.g., "provided he has attained eighteen years of age"; "but if [*name of executor*] predeceases me or renounces probate ..."; or
- subject to a condition, e.g., "provided he remains a partner in the firm of ...".

Executor according to the tenor of the Will: The appointment clause may not expressly appoint a named person executor but, provided the Will sufficiently describes the duties of the person named, that person may be the executor "according to the tenor of the Will". For example, "I wish X to deal with the collection and distribution of my estate"; or "I want X to deal with all my requirements in this Will". The oath to lead probate of the Will should describe the person as executor according to the tenor, and this will be reflected in the grant.

Void appointment: Uncertainty in the appointment of executors renders a purported appointment void. The appointment of any "one of" or "two of" a class of persons is void for uncertainty, e.g., "any one of the partners in the firm of ...." (see *In Re Baylis' Goods* (1862) 26 JP 599). Similarly, an appointment in the alternative, e.g., "X or Y" without any words qualifying the contingency upon which the alternative appointment is effective, is also void for uncertainty.

If there is evidence to show that the appointment fails to carry out the testator's intentions, an application to rectify the Will may be made (under section 20, Administration of Estates Act 1982; see page 142), or for the appointment to be interpreted (under section 21 of the Act; see page 144).

Executor a minor: A minor executor's right to probate cannot be renounced (see rule 34(1)). A grant for the use and benefit of an executor who is a minor may be taken by the residuary beneficiary, where the minor is not also the residuary beneficiary. If the minor *is* the residuary beneficiary, administration (with Will annexed) may be granted to the person with parental responsibility for him (see rule 32, page 132). If the minor is a co-executor with a person of full age, the grant may be taken by the executor of age, with power reserved to the minor on attaining his majority.

Executor mentally incapable: Where one of several executors is mentally incapable of managing his affairs, those capable may take probate, with power reserved to the incapable executor on regaining his capacity. The giving of notice to him under rule 27(3) may be dispensed with on application to a district judge or registrar (see page 122).

Where the sole or last surviving executor is mentally incapable, letters of administration (with Will annexed) may be taken for his use and benefit by those entitled under rule 35(2); see page 133.

Executor a bankrupt: The fact that an executor is an undischarged bankrupt or is insolvent does not prevent him from acting as an executor. If it is considered inappropriate for an executor to act in such circumstances he may renounce. If the executor refuses to renounce his title, he may be passed over by application under section 116 of the Supreme Court Act 1981 (see page 136).

Executor a firm: The appointment of a trading firm, solicitors, accountants or otherwise is deemed to be an appointment of all the partners in that firm. Unless the Will expressly refers to the firm or successor firm at the date of the death, the appointment is of the partners of the firm at the date of execution of the Will.

Executor a trust corporation: Where a trust corporation is appointed, the corporation may take probate, the oath to lead the grant being deposed to by an authorised officer of the corporation (see rule 36(1) and see page 146).

If a non-trust corporation is appointed, then the appointment as executor fails, but the corporation may take letters of administration (with Will annexed) through its authorised nominee or attorney.

Executor an official: Where the appointment is of a person by his official title but not naming him, the executor is the holder of that office at the date of the testator's death, except where the Will expressly states otherwise, e.g., the appointment of "the vicar of St Mary's Church, Little Muddicombe" is an appointment of the incumbent of that office at the date of death.

Power reserved; Any executor entitled to take probate who does not renounce, but does not wish to take a grant immediately, may have power reserved to him, entitling him to apply for a grant later. The proving executor must give notice of the application for the grant to the executor to whom power is reserved (rule 27; see page 122 on dispensing with notice). A later application by the executor to whom power is reserved would be for double probate (see page 169).

Time for applying

An application for a grant of probate may be made at any time after the testator's death, but the grant cannot issue within seven days of the death (see rule 6(2)). Where there is a compelling reason for the grant to issue within the seven-day period, an application may be made to a district judge or registrar for expedition. "Compelling reasons" may include where the grant is necessary to commence or defend other legal proceedings; or where a part of the deceased's estate requires immediate administration.

Oath to lead the grant

The executor(s) deposing to the facts in the oath should be referred to by their true full names, followed by their address(es) and occupations. Rules of the Supreme Court Order 41 rule 1(4), as in force immediately before 26 April 1999, remains operative in respect of oaths and affidavits in non-contentious probate proceedings. Where the deponent is applying in a professional capacity, e.g., as a partner in a firm of solicitors, his business address may be used. The deponent's occupation should be stated, but if it is omitted, it is not fatal to the application.

The deceased's full true name, last address (including the postcode), date of death, date of birth and age must be given. The Practice Direction of 12 January 1999, [1999] 1 All ER 832, requires the name and dates to be given as they appear in the death certificate. Any difference in the names should be explained. Where assets of the deceased are registered in a different name, a statement should be included, in accordance with rule 9, so that the alternate names may be included in the grant.

Rule 8(2) requires the oath to state where the deceased was domiciled when he died. The court's jurisdiction is based on domicile so it is crucial this is sworn to. A district judge or registrar may, in exceptional circumstances, direct that domicile need not be stated.

Rule 8(3) requires that the oath contain a statement whether there was or was not settled land vested in the deceased which remained settled after his death.

The oath should conclude with the promise by the deponents to carry out the duties under section 25 of the Administration of Estates Act 1925; a statement of the values of the gross and net estate, and, in "excepted estate" cases, that there is no requirement to deliver an Inland Revenue Account.

Rule 10 provides that the Will must be marked by the signature of the deponent(s) and commissioner(s). There is no need for an exhibit clause to be added. Where there is good reason, a district judge or registrar may give leave to mark a copy, e.g., when the Will has to be sent outside the United Kingdom for a deponent to swear the oath and there is a danger of its being lost.

If the value of the estate is less than £5,000, no fee is payable, but if it exceeds £5,000, a flat fee of £50 is payable. Office copy grants issued at the time of the grant is issued are £1 each.

For the procedure where an Inland Revenue Account is required, see Chapter 4. For forms of oath, see page 308 *et seq.*

Application for Letters of Administration (with Will Annexed)
When the appointment of executors is void, or the executors have predeceased or renounced, i.e., all those entitled under rule 20(a) (see page 149) are "cleared off", an application may be made for letters of administration (with Will annexed).

Attorney of executor
An executor may appoint an attorney who may take the grant for the use and benefit of the executor, but otherwise the order of priority is as set out in paragraphs (b) to (f) of rule 20 (above). If an attorney applies on behalf of one of several executors, notice must be given to the others. The other executors do not have to consent to the application. Power is *not* reserved to the other executors, power reserved meaning power to take a like grant (i.e., of probate).

Residuary legatee or devisee in trust (rule 20(b))
Those next entitled, after the executor, are the residuary legatee(s) and/or devisee(s) in trust. The Will must contain a clear gift of the residue of the estate to named persons to hold the estate on trust. The trust(s) on which the residue is held must also be declared in the Will. If the Will contains power to the named trustee to nominate another person to act instead of him, the

substituted trustee may apply, lodging the nomination with the oath to lead the grant.

If the wording of the gift to the trustee is such that it imposes a "secret trust", the actual wording must be considered. Any question arising falls to the Chancery Division to construe, and is not a matter for the probate registry.

Residuary legatee or devisee (rule 20(c))

On clearing the executors and residuary legatees or devisees in trust, the person(s) entitled to the residue are next entitled. This class of person includes a residuary legatee or devisee for life or, where there is no gift (or no effective gift) of all the residue, to the person(s) entitled to share in the estate undisposed of by the Will. Those entitled to (share) the undisposed of estate are the person(s) being the next of kin entitled in the order of priority prescribed by rule 22 (see page 161). Thus a residuary legatee, a residuary devisee (including those for life) and a person entitled to share in undisposed of estate have equal entitlement to letters of administration (with Will annexed) without giving notice to others of equal entitlement.

Preference for vested interest: Rule 20(c)(i), however, prescribes a preference for a vested interest over a contingent interest. Thus, on a gift of part of the residuary estate to A and B, but if B predeceases, to C, A takes preference over C if B has predeceased.

Preference for persons of age: Subject to a district judge's or registrar's directing otherwise under rule 27(5), a residuary legatee or devisee of full age is preferred to the guardian of, or other person with parental responsibility for, a minor who is equally entitled to share the residue with the person of full age.

Determining whether gift is a gift of residue: Not infrequently, especially where the Will was not professionally drafted, the wording of a Will raises doubt whether there is a gift of the residuary estate. If the gift is implied sufficiently or is clear from all the surrounding words used, then the registry accepts an application for a grant by the purported residuary beneficiary. The directions of a district judge or registrar may be obtained, but the Family Division is not the court for construction of Wills. If there is a dispute, or if the wording is so unclear that no determination can be made without a trial of the matter, the Will may need to be referred to the Chancery Division by claim under Part 57 of the Civil Procedure Rules. Where there is a consensus, then the distribution may be resolved by all interested parties entering into a deed of variation or a deed of family arrangement as appropriate.

Where an intended gift of residue is to a surviving spouse with an ensuing gift on death to children, there is a presumption of an absolute gift to the surviving spouse. This applies only where the gift is to a surviving spouse and issue and there are no other words in the Will to indicate a contrary intention.

Gift in favour of child or other issue: Section 33 of the Wills Act 1837, as now in force, provides that a gift to a child or remoter descendant of the testator in his Will does not lapse if the intended beneficiary predeceases the testator leaving issue. The gift passes to the surviving issue of the intended beneficiary living at the date of death. It follows that a child *en ventre sa mere* is excluded.

The section also provides for a gift to a class of persons consisting of children or remoter descendants of the testator, where a member of the class predeceases the deceased leaving issue. The gift does not lapse, but passes to the issue of that member living at the date of death.

Section 33 operates only provided there is no contrary intention in the Will.

Grant on behalf of a minor

Where, under a Will or intestacy, a minor is entitled to the grant as a beneficiary, rule 32 applies. It provides as follows:

"(1) Where a person to whom a grant would otherwise be made is a minor, administration for his use and benefit, limited until he attains the age of eighteen years, shall, unless otherwise directed, and subject to paragraph (2) of this rule, be granted to –

(a) a parent of the minor who has, or is deemed to have, parental responsibility for him in accordance with –

(i) section 2(1), 2(2) or 4 of the Children Act 1989,

(ii) paragraph 4 or 6 of Schedule 14 to that Act, or

(iii) an adoption order within the meaning of section 12(1) of the Adoption Act 1976, or

(aa) a person who has, or is deemed to have, parental responsibility for the minor by virtue of section 12(2) of the Children Act 1989 where the court has made a residence order under section 8 of that Act in respect of the minor in favour of that person; or

(b) a guardian of the minor who is appointed, or deemed to have been appointed, in accordance with section 5 of the Children Act 1989 or in accordance with paragraph 12, 13 or 14 of Schedule 14 to that Act, provided that where the minor is sole executor and has no interest in the residuary estate of the deceased, administration for the use and benefit of the minor, limited as aforesaid, shall, unless a district judge or registrar otherwise directs, be granted to the person entitled to the residuary estate, or

(c) a local authority which has, or is deemed to have, parental responsibility for the minor by virtue of section 33(3) of the

Children Act 1989 where the court has made a care order under section 31(1)(a) of that Act in respect of the minor and that local authority is designated in that order.

(2) A district judge or registrar may by order appoint a person to obtain administration for the use and benefit of the minor, limited as aforesaid, in default of, or jointly with, or to the exclusion of, any person mentioned in paragraph (1) of this rule; and the person intended shall file an affidavit in support of his application to be appointed.

(3) Where there is only one person competent and willing to take a grant under the foregoing provisions of this rule, such person may, unless a district judge or registrar otherwise directs, nominate any fit and proper person to act jointly with him in taking the grant."

Number of grantees: Because a minority interest exists, the grant should issue to two or more grantees, or to a trust corporation, unless a district judge or registrar, if there are special circumstances, directs otherwise. Examples of "special circumstances" are where the minority will be of short duration, or where the estate is best administered by a sole grantee because there could be a conflict of interest.

Preference of persons of full age: Where, under a Will or intestacy, there is another person equally entitled to benefit and to the grant, the person of full age is preferred as grantee – the person of full age being able to take the grant without limitation – to the persons who would take the grant for the use and benefit of the minor. In special circumstances, a district judge or registrar may allow the persons with parental responsibility for the minor to apply.

Application by person having parental responsibility: Rule 32(1)(a) to (c) prescribe those who, having parental responsibility for the minor child, may take the grant for the minor's use and benefit. The procedure where a minor is appointed executor is dealt with at page 151.

Those who may apply are:
- a parent (paragraph (a));
- a person who has obtained a residence order (paragraph (aa));
- a guardian of the minor appointed by the Will of the now deceased parent (paragraph (b)); and
- a local authority which has a care order in its favour in respect of the minor (paragraph (c)).

Where the person has acquired parental responsibility under a parental responsibility order or other court order, a copy of the order must be lodged with the application for the grant. The oath must recite the authority, e.g., "the lawful adopted father of the said minor by virtue of an adoption order made under the Adoption Act 1976 by the ... court and dated ...". (see Practice Direction 26 September 1991 [1991] 4 All ER 562.)

If there is only one person with parental responsibility able to apply, that person may nominate a co-administrator under paragraph (3) of the rule. The nomination must be in writing. For a form of oath and nomination, see pages 334 and 305.

Application to be appointed to take a grant: If there is no person with parental responsibility, or the person(s) with parental responsibility cannot or will not act, then an application may be made to a district judge or registrar under paragraph (2) of rule 32 for a person to be appointed to take the grant for the minor's use and benefit. Although the rule refers to "a person" it is the usual practice of the district judges and registrars to appoint two or more persons to act, to avoid the need for the person appointed to nominate a co-administrator. See page 133 for the procedure on such an application.

Beneficiary mentally incapable
Where the residuary beneficiary, or indeed any person entitled to a grant, is mentally incapable of managing his affairs, rule 35 applies. Rule 35 provides:
"Grants in case of mental incapacity
(1) Unless a district judge or registrar otherwise directs, no grant shall be made under this rule unless all persons entitled in the same degree as the incapable person referred to in paragraph (2) below have been cleared off.
(2) Where a district judge or registrar is satisfied that a person entitled to a grant is by reason of mental incapacity incapable of managing his affairs, administration for his use and benefit, limited until further representation be granted or in such other way as the district judge or registrar may direct, may be granted in the following order of priority –
   (a) to the person authorised by the Court of Protection to apply for a grant;
   (b) where there is no person so authorised, to the lawful attorney of the incapable person acting under a registered enduring power of attorney;
   (c) where there is no such attorney entitled to act, or if the attorney shall renounce administration for the use and benefit of the incapable person, to the person entitled to the residuary estate of the deceased.
(3) Where a grant is required to be made to not less than two administrators, and there is only one person competent and willing to take a grant under the foregoing provisions of this rule, administration may, unless a district judge or registrar otherwise directs, be granted to such person jointly with any other person nominated by him.
(4) Notwithstanding the foregoing provisions of this rule, administration for the use and benefit of the incapable person may be granted to such other person as the district judge or registrar may by order direct.

(5) Unless the applicant is the person authorised in paragraph 2(a) above, notice of an intended application under this rule shall be given to the Court of Protection."

As provided by paragraph (c) above, where there is a capable person equally entitled to the grant, that person is preferred and no grant is made under the provisions of this rule unless a district judge or registrar so directs.

Person authorised: To constitute a person entitled under paragraph (2)(a) there must be an order of the Court of Protection specifically authorising the person named in the order to take the grant for the patient's use and benefit. The fact that someone has been appointed receiver for the patient does not itself provide authority to apply. If an application is to be made for a First General Order, and it is known that authority is required, an application for authority may be included in the application for that order. A copy of the authorising order must be lodged with the application for the grant and the applicant appropriately described as the person authorised in the oath.

Attorney under a registered enduring power of attorney: In the absence of a person authorised by order of the Court of Protection, an attorney acting under a registered enduring power of attorney is next entitled. Notice of the proposed application must be given to the Court of Protection in accordance with rule 35(5) and the court's acknowledgement of the notice must be lodged with the application for a grant.

The original power of attorney, or a copy certified (by the solicitors acting) to be a true and complete copy of the power, must be lodged with the application for the grant.

The oath must recite that no one has been authorised by the Court of Protection and that the applicant is acting under the registered enduring power of attorney.

Residuary beneficiary where there is a Will: If there is no one authorised and no one appointed under a registered enduring power of attorney then, where the incapable person is a sole executor or residuary legatee and devisee in trust, the residuary beneficiary may apply for the grant. In practice, however, it is usually the case that the residuary beneficiary is also the person who is mentally incapable.

Medical evidence: No evidence to substantiate the incapacity is required by the probate registry if application is made by the person authorised by the Court of Protection or the attorney under a registered enduring power of attorney, since sufficient evidence will have been lodged with the Court of Protection.

Medical evidence, by letter from the patient's general practitioner or a responsible medical officer, is required by the district judge or registrar where the application is made by a residuary legatee or devisee, or where the application is made under rule 35(4) for a person to be appointed to take the grant. The procedure for an application under rule 35(4) is set out at page 134.

Personal representative of residuary beneficiary (rule 20 (d))
After clearing off those entitled under the previous paragraphs, an application may be made by the personal representative of a residuary legatee and/or devisee. The residuary beneficiary must have survived the deceased to take his benefit under the Will. Similarly, the personal representative of a person entitled to share in estate undisposed of by the Will may take the grant. This paragraph does not apply to residuary legatees and devisees in trust or for life.

Legatee or devisee or creditor (rule 20 (e))
On clearing all those entitled under paragraphs (a) to (d), a specific legatee or devisee or creditor may apply.

Specific legatee or devisee: Where there is no gift of residue, or the residue is only partly disposed of, leaving estate to pass under a partial intestacy, but either (i) there are no known kin entitled to share in the undisposed of estate, or (ii) there are such kin but they have renounced letters of administration (with Will annexed), title falls to any person receiving a specific legacy or devise.

If there are no known kin entitled to share in the residual estate undisposed of by the Will then notice must be given to the Treasury Solicitor, the Crown being entitled to claim *bona vacantia.* The Treasury Solicitor, acting for the Crown, is entitled to take a grant in priority to a legatee or devisee.

A creditor: When all those entitled to benefit under the Will as to the estate undisposed of by the Will have been cleared off by their predecease, renunciation or citation, a grant may issue to a creditor. If there is estate which would pass to the Crown as *bona vacantia,* the Treasury Solicitor must renounce or be cited before a creditor may apply. It is suggested that the Treasury Solicitor be notified by letter that there is *bona vacantia,* and that a creditor proposes to apply for a grant. The probate registries usually accept an indication in writing by the Treasury Solicitor that he does not wish to apply, without requiring a formal renunciation.

Where it is not possible to trace kin, or the debt is likely to render the estate otherwise insolvent, an application may be made for a discretionary order for a grant to the creditor under section 116 of the Supreme Court Act 1981, passing over the title, or possible title, of others (see page 136).

If the creditor is a trading firm with partners, all the partners must join in the application. Where one or more of the partners applies, the remaining partners must consent to the application. A statement saying they consent may be included in the oath to lead the grant.

Life or minority interest

If a life or minority interest arises, the grant should issue to two or more persons or creditors. Alternatively, application may be made for a discretionary order under section 114 of the Supreme Court Act 1981 to allow the grant to issue to a sole grantee (see page 123).

Personal representative of legatee, devisee or creditor (rule 20 (f))

When all those entitled in priority as shown above have been cleared off, the personal representative of a legatee, devisee or creditor may apply. A legatee or devisee does not include one for life or holding in trust for another person. The personal representative must be so constituted by taking a grant to the estate of the legatee, devisee or creditor; details of that grant must be recited in the oath to establish title. A copy of the grant should be lodged with the application.

Trust and non-trust corporations

The procedure for taking letters of administration (with Will annexed) by a corporation is dealt with in Chapter 11.

Assignee

Rule 24 provides that:

"Right of assignee to a grant

(1) Where all the persons entitled to the estate of the deceased (whether under a will or on intestacy) have assigned their whole interest in the estate to one or more persons, the assignee or assignees shall replace, in the order of priority for a grant of administration, the assignor or, if there are two or more assignors, the assignor with the highest priority.

(2) Where there are two or more assignees, administration may be granted with the consent of the others to any one or more (not exceeding four) of them.

(3) In any case where administration is applied for by an assignee the original instrument of assignment shall be produced and a copy of the same lodged in the registry."

Any person beneficially entitled to the estate, or to share in the estate, may assign by deed his whole benefit to another or others; those to whom the benefit is assigned then take the place, in the order of priority prescribed by rule 20, which the assignor held. Title to take the grant depends upon those with a higher priority under the rule, e.g. the executor, being cleared off by renunciation. Subject to their clearing off the assignee may take the grant.

The whole interest must be transferred by the assignment. The deed may be a deed of assignment, variation or family settlement. Provided the effect of the deed is to assign a whole interest, the deed is acceptable to the probate registries. The original deed, or a copy certified to be a true and complete copy, must be lodged with the application for a grant. The deed must be stamped under the Stamp Act 1891 unless it bears a certificate in proper form that it falls within the scope of the Stamp Duty (Exempt Instruments) Regulations 1987 (SI 1987 No 516).

Where there is more than one assignee any one (or more) of them may apply with the consent of those not applying. The consent in writing must be lodged with the application for the grant, and details recited in the oath.

Application for the grant
An application for letters of administration (with Will annexed) may be made at any time after the testator's death but the grant may not issue within fourteen days of the death (see rule 6(2)).

An application may be made to a district judge or registrar for leave to abridge the time and expedite the issue of the grant. There must be good reason for the district judge or registrar to exercise his discretion under the rule, such as the commencement of litigation in another court, or to complete the urgent sale of property where the deceased had signed a contract for sale before his death.

Oath to lead the grant
The proposed administrators must depose to the relevant facts, giving proper clearings and title to the grant. The details to be included in the oath are described in the procedure for an application for probate, as are the requirements of rules 8, 9 and 10 (see pages 152 and 153). For the procedure where an Inland Revenue Account is required to be delivered, see Chapter 4. For forms of oath, see page 315 *et seq.*

Application for Letters of Administration
Letters of administration are granted when the deceased died wholly intestate. If there was a Will but it was not properly executed, or has been pronounced against in a claim in the Chancery Division, then, in the absence of any earlier Will, an intestacy ensues. Title to the grant follows the order of beneficial entitlement to (share) the estate and is prescribed by rule 22 as follows:

"(1) Where the deceased died on or after 1 January 1926, wholly intestate, the person or persons having a beneficial interest in the estate shall be entitled to a grant of administration in the following classes in order of priority, namely –

(a) the surviving husband or wife;

(b) the children of the deceased and the issue of any deceased child who died before the deceased;

(c) the father and mother of the deceased;

(d) brothers and sisters of the whole blood and the issue of any deceased brother or sister of the whole blood who died before the deceased;

(e) brothers and sisters of the half blood and the issue of any deceased brother or sister of the half blood who died before the deceased;

(f) grandparents;

(g) uncles and aunts of the whole blood and the issue of any deceased uncle or aunt of the whole blood who died before the deceased;

(h) uncles and aunts of the half blood and the issue of any deceased uncle or aunt of the half blood who died before the deceased.

(2) In default of any person having a beneficial interest in the estate, the Treasury Solicitor shall be entitled to a grant if he claims *bona vacantia* on behalf of the Crown.

(3) If all persons entitled to a grant under the foregoing provisions of this rule have been cleared off, a grant may be made to a creditor of the deceased or to any person who, notwithstanding that he has no immediately beneficial interest in the estate, may have a beneficial interest in the event of an accretion thereto.

(4) Subject to paragraph (5) of Rule 27, the personal representative of a person in any of the classes mentioned in paragraph (1) of this rule or the personal representative of a creditor of the deceased shall have the same right to a grant as the person whom he represents provided that the persons mentioned in sub-paragraph (b) to (h) of paragraph (1) above shall be preferred to the personal representative of a spouse who has died without taking a beneficial interest in the whole estate of the deceased as ascertained at the time of the application for the grant."

Rule 27, paragraph 5, referred to above, sets out the preference for a "live" interest over a "dead" interest. A living person entitled to benefit in the order of priority under this rule is preferred as grantee to the personal representative of a person of equal entitlement who, if living, would be entitled to the grant. For example, where the deceased died a widow without issue or parent or any other person entitled to share in the estate by virtue of any enactment (e.g., an adopted child), leaving two brothers of the whole blood one of whom has since died, the living brother is preferred to the personal representatives of the now deceased brother.

The distribution of an intestate's estate and title to the grant are dealt with in Chapter 6; see page 95 *et seq.*

The oath to lead the grant

For specimen forms of oath, see page 324 *et seq.* The correct wording to establish title and clearing must be set out in the oath. The following descriptions are used:

To clear	*Status of deceased*
Spouse..	widow
	widower
	bachelor (never married)
	spinster (never married)
	single man (divorced)
	single woman (divorced)
Children or remoter issue.................	without issue
Parents...	(or) parent
Brothers/sisters, nephews/	
nieces or their issue......................	(or) brother or sister of the whole blood [and/or half blood] or issue thereof
Grandparents....................................	(or) grandparent
Uncles/aunts, cousins or their issue	(or) uncle or aunt of the whole blood [and/or half blood] or issue thereof.

Where the grant is applied for by those entitled after children or remoter issue in the table above, illegitimate and adopted children must be cleared off by the addition of the words, "or any other person entitled in priority to share in the estate by virtue of any enactment".

For example, if the deceased died intestate a divorced man, leaving as his nearest relative a child of a cousin, the title and clearing to appear in the oath should be:

"died intestate a single man whose marriage with [*name of former spouse*] was dissolved by final decree of the [*name of court*] in England and Wales and that the deceased did not thereafter remarry without issue or parent or brother or sister of the whole or half blood or their issue or grandparent or uncle or aunt of the whole blood or any other person entitled in priority to share in the estate by virtue of any enactment. I am the cousin german of the whole blood once removed being the son of [*name of cousin*] who predeceased the deceased and the only person entitled to the estate of the deceased."

Rules 8 and 9, described on pages 152–153 in the context of applications for probate, apply to any oath or application and are therefore relevant on an application in an intestacy.

Application by an Attorney

Rule 31 provides:

"(1) Subject to paragraphs (2) and (3) below, the lawfully constituted attorney of a person entitled to a grant may apply for administration for the use and benefit of the donor, and such grant shall be limited until further representation be granted, or in such other way as the district judge or registrar may direct.

(2) Where the donor referred to in paragraph (1) above is an executor, notice of the application shall be given to any other executor unless such notice is dispensed with by the district judge or registrar.

(3) Where the donor referred to in paragraph (1) above is mentally incapable and the attorney is acting under an enduring power of attorney, the application shall be made in accordance with rule 35."

By virtue of paragraph (1) any person entitled to take a grant in the order of priority contained in rules 20 and 22 may appoint an attorney to apply on his behalf. The attorney may apply without leave. For application by the attorney of an executor, see page 153.

Form of power of attorney

The power of attorney may be general in form under section 10 of the Powers of Attorney Act 1971, as contained in Schedule 1 to the Act. Alternatively, the power may be specific in that it authorises the donee to take the grant and administer the estate. An enduring power of attorney which has not been registered may be used as an ordinary power of attorney. Once registered paragraph (3) of the rule above applies. If the power appoints more than one attorney jointly they must both apply, but if the appointment is joint and several, the other may apply.

Execution of power

The power of attorney must be signed by the donor before a disinterested witness who also signs the power. The date of execution must be inserted.

If the power was executed abroad then, provided it is in English and witnessed by a notary or consular officer, it is acceptable. If the power is not so witnessed, there must be evidence that the donor understood English. If the power is in a foreign language, there must be lodged an authenticated translation certified by a competent translator.

Retention of power

If the power of attorney is limited to extracting the grant it will be retained in the registry. A general power, or power for other purposes, may be returned if a copy certified to be a true and complete copy is also lodged.

Limitation in grant

The grant is usually limited until further representation is granted, i.e., it will cease to operate on the issue of another grant but need not be revoked. So, if the donor or donee dies, or the power is revoked, the grant ceases to be effective *only* from the date on which a further grant issues.

A district judge or registrar may impose any other limitation if necessary.

Limited Grants

Grant following discretionary order
Applications for discretionary orders are dealt with in Chapter 10. Following such an order, the application for the grant is made in the usual way, the oath to lead the grant reciting details of the order and any limitation in the grant imposed by the order. Generally these grants are full grants to the whole estate.

These grant applications, although not necessarily unusual, require special consideration and are dealt with below.

Letters of administration ad colligenda bona defuncti
An application for this form of grant may be made in respect of a part of the estate requiring immediate administration before a full grant is taken or, perhaps, because a full grant cannot be now taken.

In the first place, a pre-lodgment enquiry (see page 83) should be made of the district judge or registrar, to ascertain whether the application will be entertained; if so, an application for the order should then be made (see page 135).

The oath: When a discretionary order has been made, the oath to lead the grant should recite details of the order and the limitation imposed by it. The oath should not mention any Will or recite an intestacy. It must, however, contain the statements required by rule 8 – on domicile, whether a life or minority interest arises, and as to settled land.

Inland Revenue Account: Where the whole estate qualifies as an excepted estate (see page 29), no Inland Revenue Account is required. The oath to lead the limited grant should recite the appropriate gross and net figures the estate does not exceed, and that no Account is required to be delivered.

If the estate is of a value that an Account must be delivered, the Account should be delivered to IR Capital Taxes; if appropriate, form D18 (see page 59), certifying that no tax is payable, is lodged in the probate registry. The Account need deal only with that part of the estate passing under the limited grant. It is suggested that, at the time of applying for the order, IR Capital Taxes be contacted for their requirements. In some circumstances, and subject to IR Capital Taxes' agreement, the delivery of an Account at this stage may be dispensed with. But before issuing the grant, the probate registry would need to see the written agreement of IR Capital Taxes that no Account need be delivered at this stage.

Where the whole estate attracts payment of inheritance tax, the tax on that part of the estate passing under the grant must be paid before the grant may issue. Again, arrangements may be made direct with IR Capital Taxes regarding the deferment of payment at this stage. The registry must see confirmation of any agreement reached with IR Capital Taxes.

Section 109 of the Supreme Court Act 1981 prohibits the issue of any grant until the district judge or registrar is satisfied that all tax currently payable has been paid (or other arrangements are in place).

Because the grant is required urgently (and its issue is usually expedited), arrangements with IR Capital Taxes must be entered into with equivalent urgency.

The grant is always limited, *inter alia,* until further representation be granted. On the issue of the full grant, the *ad colligenda bona defuncti* grant ceases to be effective.

Grant under section 113, Supreme Court Act 1981

A grant limited to trust property where the deceased life tenant's estate is insolvent may be issued solely for the purpose of dealing with the trust property. The procedure for applying for an order to sever the estate under section 113 of the Act is dealt with at page 128. Once the order has been made, an application for the grant is made in the usual way; details of the order and limitation should be recited in the oath.

Grant pending determination of a probate claim

Where a claim has been lodged in the Chancery Division under Part 57 of the Civil Procedure Rules 1998, an application may be made, to a Master or district judge, under section 117 of the Supreme Court Act 1981, for an order for a grant of letters of administration to deal with a part of the estate requiring urgent administration. This application has, in effect, much the same result as an application for a grant *ad colligenda bona* in a non-contentious matter. Application for the order is made on application or notice in accordance with Part 57.

An application for the grant pursuant to the order must be made to the Principal Registry of the Family Division, as no grant may issue out of a district registry where there is unresolved contention (see rule 7(1)).

The oath to lead the grant must be accompanied by a copy of the order appointing the administrator and recite details of that order. If an Inland Revenue Account needs to be delivered, then form IHT200 must be lodged with IR Capital Taxes, and form D18 lodged with the application for the grant.

Grant to prosecute or defend claim

An application for a grant limited to a specific purpose may be made where:

- it is necessary to constitute a personal representative to prosecute a claim on behalf of the estate, or defend a claim against the estate, or
- to constitute a defendant for a claim under the Inheritance (Provision for Family and Dependants) Act 1975.

Such an application is required only where there is no personal representative, or the person entitled to become the personal representative refuses to apply.

An application by a person with no title to a grant is made under the court's discretionary power under section 116 of the Supreme Court Act 1981; see page 136. Once the order is made, an application for the grant proceeds in the usual way, the oath to lead the grant reciting the details of the order.

Where the grant is required so that a person may launch proceedings under the 1975 Act, there is nothing to prevent the person wishing to make the claim also being the personal representative if so entitled under the usual order of priority. For example, where the deceased dies intestate a single man leaving minor children, his former spouse, if she has parental responsibility for the minors, may take the grant for their use and benefit and then commence her application by a claim in the county court. Once the proceedings have been issued, an application to the district judge, for directions as to who will represent the minors' interests, should be made.

Where the grant is required to prosecute or defend a claim there is often little or no estate to pass under the grant. Even if the value of the estate is nil, the excepted estate provisions (see page 29) may be used to avoid the need to deliver an Inland Revenue Account. Any damages or other moneys recovered as a result of the action will not pass under a grant limited to prosecuting a claim unless the limitation imposed so provides. A full grant should be taken by the person entitled in the normal order of priority.

Grant limited to settled land

Under rule 29, no grant *including* settled land can issue. A grant of administration, limited to dealing with settled land, issues pursuant to the rule, which provides:

"(1) In this rule 'settled land' means land vested in the deceased which was settled prior to his death and not by his will, and which remained settled land notwithstanding his death.

(2) The person or persons entitled to a grant of administration limited to settled land shall be determined in accordance with the following order of priority:

    (i)   the special executors in regard to settled land constituted by section 22 of the Administration of Estates Act 1925;

    (ii) the trustees of the settlement at the time of the application for the grant; and

(iii) the personal representatives of the deceased.

(3) Where there is settled land and a grant is made in respect of the free estate only, the grant shall expressly exclude the settled land."

Where the land is vested in more than one life tenant, a settled land grant issues only on the death of the last surviving tenant.

Definition: Settled land is defined by section 1 of the Settled Land Act 1925. To require a grant in respect of settled land the *land* must have been settled by vesting assent on a person or persons, *and* remain settled land after the death of that person or of the last surviving such person. Settlements of assets other than land do not fall within the ambit of the Act and are dealt with not under rule 29, but under rules 20 and 22 (see pages 149 and 161) as appropriate.

The first matter to be determined before making an application for a grant is whether there was indeed settled land which remains settled land, i.e., that the deceased was not a life tenant such that the settlement ceases on death. Capital sums arising from the sale of settled land during the tenant's life qualify only if reinvested in land and resettled. This, and indeed settled land grants in general, will become less common since the Trusts of Land and Appointment of Trustees Act 1996 came into force on 1 July 1997. Any settlement created after the commencement of the 1996 Act cannot be a settlement for the purposes of the Settled Land Act 1925.

Special executors: The first entitled to a grant are the special executors for settled land created by section 22 of the Administration of Estates Act 1925. Obviously, "special executors" can be appointed only under the Will of the tenant for life, but even though executors may take only letters of administration limited to the settled land, the life tenant's Will is not proved on application for a grant limited to settled land. The special executors are those appointed by the tenant for life as an express appointment in his Will, but in default of an express appointment of others, the trustees of the settlement at the date of death of the tenant for life are deemed to have been appointed special executors.

Trustees of the settlement: Thus, only the trustees at the date of death may qualify as special executors. If there is no express appointment of executors and there were no trustees at the date of death (or the trustees have themselves subsequently died), the current trustees of the settlement may take the grant, such trustees being constituted under section 30 of the Settled Land Act 1925.

Life tenant's personal representatives: Where there are no special executors or trustees of the settlement, the grant limited to settled land may be taken by the life tenant's personal representatives, i.e., those who have taken a grant of representation to the life tenant's free estate.

The oath: The oath to lead the grant must set out the applicants' title to the grant, i.e., the capacity in which they apply, clearing those with prior entitlement. The oath should also recite details of any other grant taken in respect of the life tenant's free estate. The values to be inserted are those contained in the Inland Revenue Account. An Account must be delivered to IR Capital Taxes.

The oath must be accompanied by a true and complete copy of the Will or other document creating the settlement and the assent vesting the land in the life tenant.

If the estate value exceeds £5,000, the usual grant fee (£50) is payable.

Second and Subsequent Grants

The chain of executorship

An executor who proves his testator's Will also becomes the executor of any estate of which his testator was the last surviving or sole proving executor. This is by way of a chain of representation under section 7 of the Administration of Estates Act 1925. Although it may appear that a second grant may be necessary where a chain of executorship exists, no further grant is required. The chain is broken in the circumstances set out on page 150.

Where there would be a chain if the executor proved his testator's Will, but he does not do so, the chain is in abeyance. A grant of letters of administration (with Will annexed) may be made to any person next entitled under rule 20 (see page 149), limited until the executor proves the Will.

The chain of representation passes only through proving executors; it is a chain of *executorship*; no chain is created through letters of administration.

Grant of double probate

When probate has been granted to one or more of several named executors with power reserved to others, the others, or any of them, may apply for a grant of double probate at any time, *provided* the number of executors acting under the original grant and those under the double probate grant does not exceed four (section 114(1), Supreme Court Act 1981).

An application for double probate may be made to any registry, not necessarily that which issued the original grant.

The oath gives details of the former grant; to whom power was reserved; and to whom (if any) power remains reserved. The estate values may be those used originally if the estate is an excepted estate; or, if it is not, the values of the unadministered estate. If an Account was originally delivered, then an Account in Form A5C must be delivered *to the probate registry* on application for the grant.

If the oath is sworn in the registry from which the original grant issued, the original Will may be marked; otherwise an official copy should be requested and marked.

The fee for the grant is £15.

Letters of administration (with Will annexed) de bonis non
Where a grant of probate or letters of administration (with Will annexed) has issued, but the grantee dies or becomes mentally incapable of managing his affairs, a new grant is required to deal with any estate remaining unadministered.

Death of grantee: Where probate has been granted and the proving executor dies but there survives an executor to whom power had been reserved, that executor may take double probate (see above), unless a chain of executorship is created by an executor proving the Will of the now deceased proving executor (also see above).

The non-proving executor to whom power had been reserved may be cited to accept or refuse probate of the Will. If he fails properly to deal with the citation, his rights to probate are extinguished and an application for letters of administration (with Will annexed) *de bonis non* may be made. For the procedure on citations see page 112 *et seq.*

If the original grant was of letters of administration (with Will annexed) and the administrator dies, then the new grant in respect of the unadministered estate is also letters of administration (with Will annexed), taken by a person of equal or next entitlement under rule 20 (see page 149).

Incapacity of grantee: Where the grant is of probate to two or more executors, and one becomes incapable after the grant has been issued, the original grant is revoked and a new grant of probate taken by the capable executor(s), with power reserved to the incapable executor on regaining his capacity (see page 271 for the procedure for revocation).

Similarly, where letters of administration (with or without Will annexed) have been granted to two or more grantees and one becomes incapable, the original grant is revoked and a new grant issued to the capable administrator(s).

Where the grant issued to a *sole* executor or administrator and the grantee becomes incapable of managing his affairs, the grant is not revoked or impounded. Instead, a new grant may be taken by a person of equal or next entitlement for the use and benefit of the now incapable grantee. Title to the grant, when all executors have been cleared, follows the order of priority for an original grant prescribed by rule 20. The preference in paragraph (d) of the rule – for a "live" interest over a "dead" interest – also applies.

Oath to lead the grant: The oath should recite details of the original grant and clear executors and those entitled in priority in the usual way. The oath must also, where appropriate, show how the chain of executorship is broken or is in abeyance.

The estate values for the original grant, if that was an excepted estate, may be used again, although the grant is in respect of unadministered estate only. If an Inland Revenue Account was originally delivered, then an Account in Form A5C must be delivered *to the registry* with the oath and other documents.

The original Will may be marked on swearing the oath in the registry in which it is lodged (the issuing registry); otherwise the probate copy (the copy inside the original grant) may be marked, but the grant is then retained by the registry. It is usually simpler to request an official copy of the Will from the registry which issued the original grant for marking (the fee for the office copy is £5). The oath should refer to whichever form of Will is being produced and marked.

The fee for the grant is £15; official copies, £1 each.

Cessate grant

A *cessate* grant may issue to deal with estate remaining unadministered, where an original grant was issued subject to a limitation, but the limitation no longer applies, e.g., where:

- the grant issued for the use and benefit of a minor child until he attains eighteen years of age and he has attained eighteen;
- the grant issued for the use and benefit of a mentally incapable person and the person has regained capacity; or
- the grant was limited for a period of time and the time has expired.

A *cessate* grant is a grant to the whole estate, although it recites the values of the unadministered estate; a grant *de bonis non* is the appropriate grant in respect of unadministered estate only.

Original grant for the use of minor(s): Letters of administration (with or without Will) issued for the use and benefit of minor(s) are limited until the minor, or one of them, attains the age of eighteen years. The grant ceases to be operative when the minor, or the eldest, attains his majority, at which time a *cessate* grant should be taken. The minor now of age or, if a minority interest exists, the minor of age and the person with parental responsibility for the child who remains a minor, are entitled to apply.

The *cessate* grant is "limited until further representation be granted" if there remains a minority interest. The grant taken by a person now absolutely entitled remains operative even after the youngest minor attains eighteen.

Original grant for use of mentally incapable person: Letters of administration (with or without Will) issued for the use and benefit of a mentally incapable person are usually limited until further representation be granted, but may, where the grant issues to a person authorised by the Court of Protection, be limited during the patient's incapacity.

Where the grant was limited until further representation be granted, on the death of the grantee, a further grant may be made under rule 35 (see page 133) for the patient's use. If the patient dies, a grant *de bonis non* may be taken by a person entitled thereto under rule 20 or 22 (see pages 149 and 161). If the patient recovers his capacity he may apply for a grant to himself but he need not do so: the original grant remains effective and continues until a further grant is taken. On an application by the former patient, he must prove his capacity.

Where the grant was limited during the patient's incapacity, and the patient recovers, he may take a grant to himself, but must provide evidence of his recovery on application for the grant. If a patient dies before the estate is fully administered, a grant *de bonis non* may be taken by the person(s) next entitled under rule 20 or 22. If the administrator dies before completing the administration, a *cessate* grant may be taken by the person authorised to do so by further order of the Court of Protection, or by a person appointed by a district judge or registrar on application made under rule 35(4); see page 134.

Procedure: The procedure for applying for a *cessate* grant is the same as for a grant *de bonis non*. Details of the former grant must be recited in the oath and, where the deceased died testate, an office copy of the Will, marked by the commissioner and deponent, must be exhibited. The deponent swears to administer the estate, but, as in a grant *de bonis non*, the value of the unadministered estate is given. Where an Inland Revenue Account was delivered on application for the original grant, an Account in Form A5C is delivered *to the registry* with the oath. As the grant is a second grant to the same estate a fee of £15 is payable.

Representative or "leading" grants

Sometimes it is necessary to obtain a representative grant, often referred to as a "leading" grant, to establish title to take a grant where the executor or administrator has died leaving estate unadministered. For example, where probate has been taken by a sole executor who was also the sole beneficiary under the Will, and he dies intestate before completing the administration, a grant must be taken to his estate to constitute a personal representative to take the grant *de bonis non* to complete the administration. Similarly, on an intestacy, where a grant is taken by the only person entitled to the deceased's estate, and the administrator dies without completing the administration, a representative grant must be taken.

If the executor/administrator dies without any estate of his own requiring a grant, an application for a discretionary order under section 116 of the Supreme Court Act 1981 (see page 136) may be made, instead of an application for a representative grant.

Where a representative grant is required, application for both grants may be made together. If the representative grant has already been issued, the oath to lead the *de bonis non* grant recites the type and date of the representative grant, e.g., "I am the personal representative of [*name of first administrator*] letters of administration having issued out of the ... Registry on ...". If the applications are made together the oath should recite, "I am the proposed personal representative of ... letters of administration to his estate being applied for contemporaneously with this application."

The registry issues the representative grant first.

Testamentary documents found after a grant has been issued

Where a copy, draft or reconstructed Will has been proved with leave under rule 54 (see page 138) and the original Will is later found, then, provided the copy Will proved was a true and complete copy of the original, no action need be taken. The grant would have been limited until the original Will or a more authentic copy is proved, so it remains effective until the original is proved. The original Will may be lodged in the registry where the copy was proved.

Where, however, the original Will differs from the copy proved, the grant must be revoked and the original proved.

Where a codicil is in dispute, probate of the Will alone may be granted, except where the disputed codicil alters the appointment of executors. When the dispute is resolved, the codicil, if accepted as valid, may be proved alone.

Where a codicil is discovered after probate of the Will had been granted then, again, the codicil may be proved alone.

The oath to lead the grant must recite details of the original grant.

The Issue of the Grant

All grants are deemed to issue (i.e., to pass under the seal of the court) at the earliest time the registry is open for business; this is 9.30 a.m. in the district registries and 10.00 a.m. in the Principal Registry.

The grant, of whatever kind, should issue within seven working days of the receipt of the application in the registry. This is, of course, subject to the provisos that all the necessary documents are submitted and are properly completed; there is no defect in the Will and/or codicil; all fees have been paid; and there is no official impediment (e.g., a caveat) to the issue of the grant.

The grant is sent to the address or Document Exchange box number which appears on the oath to lead the grant, unless prior arrangements have been made for collection from the registry.

Although the registries endeavour to avoid errors, unfortunately they do occasionally occur. The form and content of the grant should therefore be checked. If there is an error, the grant should be returned to the registry for correction (see page 270).

Chapter 13

Scottish, Northern Irish and Colonial Grants

Scottish Confirmations and Northern Irish Grants

By virtue of section 1(1) of the Administration of Estates Act 1971, where a person dies domiciled in Scotland and a confirmation or certificate of confirmation issues from the Scottish courts, the confirmation or certificate is sufficient to administer estate throughout the UK. The confirmation or certificate must carry a notation that the deceased's domicile is in Scotland. The confirmation or certificate is not "resealed" to give it effect in England and Wales.

Similarly, under section 1(4) of the Act, a grant of representation issued in Northern Ireland, bearing a notation of the deceased's domicile there, is sufficient to administer estate throughout the UK without being "resealed".

Sections 2 and 3 of the Act provide, *inter alia,* for the recognition as sufficient, to administer estate throughout the UK, of a grant issued in England and Wales without its being resealed by the court in Scotland or Northern Ireland.

Where a confirmation or grant issues, but the deceased is not domiciled in that part of the UK whose court issued the confirmation or grant, the confirmation or grant is limited to the administration of estate in that part of the UK. So, a grant of representation issued in England and Wales to the estate of a person domiciled in Scotland would be "limited to estate in England and Wales and until representation is granted in Scotland". This is to avoid duplication of representation.

It is therefore preferable to take a confirmation or grant from the court of the place of domicile so that all estate in the UK may be administered in its entirety.

Colonial Grants

The Colonial Probates Acts of 1892 and 1927 provide for the resealing of grants issued by the courts of specified countries, with the result that the grant becomes effective to administer estate in England and Wales. The reciprocating countries, provinces and territories are specified by Order in Council and currently are:

Alberta
Antigua
Australian Capital
    Territory
Bahamas
Barbados
Belize
Bermuda
Botswana
British Antarctic
    Territory
British Columbia
British Sovereign Base
    Areas in Cyprus
Brunei
Cayman Islands
Christmas Island
Cocos (Keeling)
    Islands
Cyprus*
Dominica
Falkland Islands
Falkland Island
    Dependencies
Fiji
Gambia
Ghana
Gibraltar

Grenada
Guyana
Hong Kong
Jamaica
Kenya
Kiribati
Lesotho
Malawi
Malaysia
Manitoba
Montserrat
New Brunswick
New Guinea Territory
New South Wales
New Zealand
Newfoundland
Nigeria
Norfolk Island
Northern Territory of
    Australia
North-West Territories
    of Canada
Nova Scotia
Ontario
Papua New Guinea
Prince Edward Island
Queensland

St Christopher (Kitts)
    Nevis and Anguilla
St Helena
St Lucia
St Vincent
Saskatchewan
Seychelles (Republic)
Sierra Leone
Singapore
Solomon Islands
South Africa
South Australia
Sri Lanka
Swaziland
Tasmania
Tortola
Trinidad and Tobago
    (Republic)
Turks and Caicos
    Islands
Tuvalu
Uganda
Victoria
Western Australia
Zambia
Zimbabwe

* Only grants issued by the recognised government of Cyprus; grants issued by the courts of the Turkish Republic of North Cyprus cannot be resealed.

The procedure for resealing is governed by rule 39, as follows:

"(1) An application under the Colonial Probates Acts 1892 and 1927 for the resealing of probate or administration granted by the court of a country to which those Acts apply may be made by the person to whom the grant was made or by any person authorised in writing to apply on his behalf.

(2) On any such application an Inland Revenue affidavit or account shall be lodged.

(3) Except by leave of a district judge or registrar, no grant shall be resealed unless it was made to such a person as is mentioned in sub-paragraph (a) or (b) of paragraph (1) of Rule 30 or to a person to whom a grant could be made under sub-paragraph (a) of paragraph (3) of that rule.

(4) No limited or temporary grant shall be resealed except by leave of a

district judge or registrar.

(5)   Every grant lodged for resealing shall include a copy of any will to which the grant relates or shall be accompanied by a copy thereof certified as correct by or under the authority of the court by which the grant was made, and where the copy of the grant required to be deposited under subsection (1) of section 2 of the Colonial Probates Act 1892 does not include a copy of the will, a copy thereof shall be deposited in the registry before the grant is resealed.

(6)   The district judge or registrar shall send notice of the resealing to the court which made the grant.

(7)   Where notice is received in the Principal Registry of the resealing of a grant issued in England and Wales, notice of any amendment or revocation of the grant shall be sent to the court by which it was resealed."

Who may apply

By virtue of paragraph (3) of the rule a grant may be resealed only if the grantee was a person qualifying under:

- rule 30(1)(a) – a person entrusted with the administration by the court of the country the place of domicile;
- rule 30(1)(b) – a person beneficially entitled to (share in) the estate by the law of the place of domicile; or
- rule 30(3)(a) – the executor named in, or according to the tenor of, the Will.

A person not so qualifying may apply for resealing only with the leave of a district judge or registrar. Application for leave is made to the district judge or registrar by letter.

Thus, to qualify as above the grant must have been issued by the courts of the country of the place of domicile, and the grantee must be the person entrusted and/or beneficially entitled. The only exceptions are where the grantee is the executor, or there is separate evidence to establish beneficial entitlement. For example, the deceased died domiciled in Zimbabwe and the grant issued from the court in South Africa; the grantee is not entrusted by the court of the place of domicile so rule 30(1)(a) does not apply; if there is evidence of beneficial entitlement under the law of the place of domicile, rule 30(1)(b) may apply; or the grantee is the executor and rule 30(3)(a) applies. In the example, only a person beneficially entitled or the executor may apply to reseal.

Form of grant which may be resealed

The following may be resealed:

- the original grant;
- a duplicate sealed by the court of issue with its seal;

- a copy certified by the proper officer of the court of issue; or
- an exemplification of the original grant.

It is the practice to reseal only grants which are in English, or in a foreign language and English, e.g., grants from South Africa. Only with the leave of a district judge or registrar may a temporary or limited grant be resealed.

Documents not on the face of them appearing to be grants may be accepted for resealing. Elections to Administer sealed by the courts of Australia and New Zealand may be accepted, as may Appointments of Estate Trustees issued by the courts in Canada. Where doubt arises, the document should be submitted to the district judge or registrar for directions as to admissibility.

Will to be lodged

Whatever the form of grant, if the deceased was testate but a copy of the Will or other testamentary document is not included in the grant, a copy Will must be lodged with the grant on the application to reseal. If the testamentary document is not included in the copy grant, i.e., where they are separate documents, there must be sufficient evidence to establish that the documents are inter-related. This is usually clear from the documents themselves and the court certificates endorsed on them.

Authority to apply

Where the application to reseal is being made by someone other than the grantee, the person applying must have the grantee's written authorisation to apply. The authorisation may be in the form of a power of attorney or letter. The crucial point is that the authorisation must be in writing.

Where the grant issued to two or more grantees they must all join in the application to reseal or authorise one of them to apply. Thus, where the grantee has died after the issue of the grant, it cannot be resealed. Where one of two or more grantees has died the grant may be resealed on application by the survivor(s).

Where the grant was extracted by lawyers acting for the grantee, the district judge or registrar may accept a letter from the lawyers as sufficient authority to apply on the grantee's behalf.

Inland Revenue Accounts

As the deceased died domiciled outside the United Kingdom, an Inland Revenue Account must be delivered to IR Capital Taxes. The "excepted estate" provisions apply only if the deceased died on or after 6 April 2002; was never domiciled in the UK for tax purposes; and the estate in England and Wales does not exceed £100,000. Where these conditions are met, the letter accompanying the application to reseal must confirm that that is the case.

Form IHT200, together with form D18, must be delivered to IR Capital Taxes. D18 will be returned stamped (and, if necessary receipted) to show the Account has been controlled and any tax due paid. The D18 must be lodged with the grant on application to reseal.

Making the application
Application may be made to any registry or sub-registry by lodging the following documents:
- the original grant, court-certified copy, duplicate or exemplification;
- a court-certified copy of all testamentary documents;
- copies of each of the above documents for retention by the court;
- the power of attorney or other written authority of the grantee;
- if the estate does not qualify as an excepted estate, form D18 (stamped and, where appropriate, receipted).

Where the value of the net estate exceeds £5,000, a fee of £50 is payable for resealing. No fee is payable where the net estate is less than £5,000. Office copies are £1 each. These are the same fees as for a full "English" grant.

Chapter 14

Applications on Summons

Under the Non-Contentious Probate Rules 1987, certain matters which *are* contentious may be brought before a district judge or registrar on summons, supported by an affidavit of facts. The Civil Procedure Rules 1998 do not apply to proceedings (save in respect of costs) brought under the 1987 Rules. The Rules of the Supreme Court 1965 (SI 1965 No 1776), as in force as at 26 April 1999, continue to apply.

Disputes

Between persons of equal entitlement

Rule 27(4) allows a grant of administration (with or without Will annexed) to be granted without notice to any other person entitled in the same degree. One of several residuary beneficiaries under a Will, or one of several classes of person entitled under an intestacy, may simply apply for the grant. The giving of notice is restricted to executors capable of proving, i.e. taking probate.

Rule 27(6) allows for a dispute between persons entitled to a grant in the same degree to be brought before a district judge or registrar for determination. Either party to the dispute may issue a summons, supported by an affidavit of facts. Each party to the dispute must have equal entitlement under rule 20 or 22 (see pages 149 and 161).

The affidavit must set out:
- details of the claimant's title to the grant;
- the reason the applicant should be preferred; and
- details of any others also entitled, and their views or preferences. For example, three siblings, A, B and C, are entitled to administer their mother's estate; A applies for a grant; B opposes it and C supports A. A says in affidavit that C wants A to administer the estate; the dispute is settled in favour of A since two out of the three support him. On the other hand, if C supports B, A would probably not refer to that in his affidavit.

The court has unfettered discretion to override several supportive interests if it considers the administration would be better achieved by another interested party.

The application may be made whether or not either of the disputing parties has applied for the grant. To avoid a grant issuing as of right to another person entitled, it may be necessary to enter a caveat (see page 107).

Between administrators

Applications to resolve disputes between administrators are the most common types of application under the rule. They are made where one party considers the other unfit to act because of:

- an incompatible interest;
- ill-health;
- financial instability;
- distance of place of residence;
- the ease of or cost to the estate of administration.

Where no real ground for preference is established, the court usually favours the earliest application, or the application supported by the majority of those entitled.

Between executors

It was held in *Smethurst v Tomlin and Bankes* (1861) 2 SW & Tr 143 that the court should not intervene in a dispute between executors as to which should take probate, the testator's choice of those named to be his executors being sacrosanct. The courts do, however, entertain disputes between executors if they are based on the issues listed above in respect of administrators.

Appointment of independent administrators

When dealing with disputes between persons of equal entitlement, the court may exercise its discretion under section 116 of the Supreme Court Act 1981 to appoint "independent" administrators – persons with no title to a grant but who are prepared to take on the administration.

Before issuing a summons under the rule, consideration should be given to a consent application under section 116 (perhaps appointing a solicitor to represent each of the disputing parties). The application is made on affidavit (see page 136) which should recite the details of the dispute, the proposed applicants and the latter's consent to act.

Passing over

See also pages 137–138 for the procedure for applying for an order to pass over a person entitled to a grant. Where the district judge or registrar directs that notice be given to a person(s) whose right is to be passed over, and that person opposes the application, the matter should be brought before the court on summons. The affidavit to lead the *ex parte* order may be used as the affidavit to support the summons.

The court is now more likely to require notice to be given, because of the right of the respondent, under the Human Rights Act 1998, to be heard on any matter affecting him.

Application to Remove a Caveat

For the procedure on caveats, see page 107 *et seq.*

Rule 44(6) provides for a caveator, who has no interest contrary to that of the applicant for the grant, but who nevertheless opposes the issue of the grant to the applicant, to issue a summons seeking an order preventing the grant from issuing to the applicant. A contrary interest means, *inter alia,* a question over the Will or a dispute as to a relationship.

The summons must be supported by an affidavit of facts. The summons is usually issued out of the registry at which the application for a grant is pending. If no application for a grant is pending, the summons may issue out of any registry but may, under rule 62A, be transferred for hearing to a more convenient registry.

The summons should issue within eight days of the service on the caveator of the warning to the caveat, but may issue at any time provided the applicant has not filed his affidavit in the Leeds Probate Registry (see page 110) and no appearance to the warning has been entered.

It is for the caveator to show cause (i.e., good reason) why the applicant should not have the grant; for example, that the proposed applicant is of bad character, or there is real concern that he would not administer the estate properly.

After an appearance has been entered the caveat remains in force until the determination of the probate claim in the Chancery Division.

Where no probate claim has been issued, either the applicant or the caveator may seek the removal of the caveat and discontinuance of the proceedings by issuing a summons returnable before a district judge of the Principal Registry. Where the application is by consent it may be dealt with by a registrar.

Application for an Order for a Person to Attend for Examination

Section 122 of the Supreme Court Act 1981 provides for application to be made by summons, supported by an affidavit of facts, for an order that a person with knowledge of a Will attend to be examined regarding that Will. The application is not restricted to witnesses giving evidence of execution, but may be directed to a person with knowledge of the whereabouts of a Will or other testamentary document. The summons and affidavit must be served personally.

Application for the order to attend is made to a district judge or registrar and may issue out of any registry. The initial hearing may be before a district judge or registrar, but the order may, if the district judge or registrar is satisfied that it should be heard by a judge, direct attendance before a High Court judge of the Family Division.

The court may make an order for the production of the testamentary document. Where it is known a person holds a testamentary document but refuses or neglects to release it for proof, a subpoena may be issued for its lodgment in court (see page 124).

Summons for Delivery of an Inventory and Account

Rule 8 requires every application for a grant to be made on oath. Every oath must contain the statement of the duties of, and undertakings by, a personal representative prescribed by section 25, Administration of Estates Act 1925:

"when required to do so by the High Court exhibit on oath in the court a full inventory of the estate and when so required render an account of the administration of the estate to the court."

Any person having a beneficial interest in the estate, or a creditor of the estate, may issue a summons, supported by an affidavit of facts, out of the registry which issued the grant of representation, calling on the personal representative to deliver an inventory of the estate and an account of his administration (see rule 61).

There is no requirement for any particular period of time to elapse between the issue of the grant and the application by summons. The summons may issue before the "executor's year" (see page 197) has expired.

On hearing, the court may make an order for the delivery of an inventory and account. On receiving the documents, the applicant is in a position to consider further action in another court, if there appears to have been fraud or maladministration.

Summons after Citation Proceedings

Where the person cited to accept or refuse a grant, to take probate, or to propound a testamentary document, enters an appearance but thereafter fails to prosecute his application for the grant with due diligence, a summons may be issued by the citor for an order to strike out the appearance and for a grant to issue to the citor. The summons should be entered at the registry where the citation proceedings are pending, returnable before the district judge or registrar of that registry. The summons must be supported by an affidavit of facts setting out the chronology of events to show the lack of proceeding with reasonable diligence.

The court may order a grant to issue (where the citation related to taking a grant) to the citor; or direct that the Will sought to be propounded is valid and for a grant to issue accordingly.

Procedure

Venue

The district judge or registrar may direct any matter be brought before the court on summons (rule 61(1)). Unless the matter is one which must be heard by a district judge of the Principal Registry, the summons should issue out of the registry in which the application for a grant is pending, or to which it is intended to apply. Any summons for hearing before a High Court Judge must issue out of the Principal Registry. The summons must set out clearly and concisely the order sought and whether costs are to be asked for.

Service

All summonses must be supported by an affidavit, usually deposed to by the applicant. The summons must be lodged in duplicate in the registry. One copy is returned, sealed and endorsed with the date of hearing. The copy summons and copy affidavit must be served on the person(s) named as respondents not less than two clear days before the hearing date. Summonses should be served in accordance with Rules of the Supreme Court Order 65 rule 5 – personally, by post or FAX (if service is so accepted). The district judge or registrar must be satisfied at the hearing that service was properly effected.

Transfer

Rule 62 allows a registrar to transfer any application to another registry. Rule 62A allows any registrar to hear and dispose of any matter which would normally fall to be heard by another registrar. Rule 62A applies on application by either party or by the court of its own motion.

Orders

All orders are drawn up by the court and copies served by post. Any order requiring a penal notice must be endorsed appropriately by the person in whose favour the order was made and must be served personally.

Appeal

Any order, direction or requirement of a district judge or registrar is subject to appeal to a High Court Judge of the Family Division.

Rule 65 deals with appeals and provides that any appeal is made by summons issued within seven days of the making of the order. The summons is issued by the Clerk of the Rules to the Family Division in the Royal Courts of Justice.

Costs

Parts 43 to 48 of the Civil Procedure Rules 1998 (SI 1998 No 3132) apply to a bill of costs, and proceedings relating thereto, delivered after 24 February 2002. A registrar may deal with costs and has full power to determine by whom, and to what extent, costs are to be paid. Costs orders for detailed assessment made by a registrar may be assessed by him. Rule 60 of the 1987 Rules, introduced by the Non-Contentious Probate (Amendment) Rules 2003 (SI 2003 No 185), means that the same procedure relating to costs and the assessment of costs applies in non-contentious probate matters as in any other proceedings in the Family Division.

Chapter 15

Collecting in the Assets

Time for Collecting in Assets

Once the grant of representation has been obtained, the personal representatives may proceed to collect in all of the deceased's outstanding assets that could not be accessed without production of a grant. In *In Re Tankard* [1942] Ch 69, [1941] 3 All ER 458 it was held that once the personal representatives have obtained the grant they should collect in the deceased's assets as quickly as reasonably practicable given the nature of the assets, and pay the deceased's debts with due diligence, having regard to the circumstances of the case. This is particularly important in respect of assets that are vulnerable to fluctuations in value, such as shares in public limited companies. If the personal representatives delay in collecting in such assets, they must have a good reason for doing so, or they may be liable to the beneficiaries for any resulting loss to the estate.

Consultation with the Beneficiaries

As a matter of good practice, the personal representatives should consult the beneficiaries of the estate as to which assets are to be liquidated and which transferred *in specie*, although they are not bound to comply with the beneficiaries' wishes. It is generally advisable to start this consultation process early on in the administration of the estate so that by the time the grant has been issued, the personal representatives already know how they are to dispose of each asset.

The capital gains tax effects of a sale of assets by the personal representatives and beneficiaries are discussed at page 241 *et seq*. Before deciding to sell an asset and collect in the cash, the personal representatives should consider whether the capital gains tax consequences could be more favourable if the assets are appropriated to the beneficiaries themselves and sold by them in their personal capacities.

Authority of the Personal Representatives

Where there is more than one personal representative, technically any one of them has the authority to bind all the personal representatives in relation to personalty, but not real property. Good communication between the personal representatives is vital to ensure that they do not commit themselves to dealing with the same asset in different ways, and any solicitor acting on behalf of the personal representatives should encourage them to act only upon unanimous decisions. In any event, most institutions require the signature of all the personal representatives before they will deal with any asset.

The formalities for collecting in each asset vary depending on the type of asset. Some useful examples are given below.

Bank Accounts

A bank account can generally be closed using a written authority signed by all the personal representatives. If, though, the account is one into which dividends on the deceased's shares are paid, the account should not be closed, but cleared out and left open, so that dividends can continue to be collected until the deceased's shares are sold. Even after that, dividends can continue to be paid on shares until two or three months after their sale so it may be wise to keep the account open until the personal representatives are sure it is dormant.

When closing a bank account, the personal representatives should ask for a certificate of the interest paid on the account for the period from the date of death onwards, together with the income tax deducted from that interest. This will be useful to them when completing the income tax returns for the period of administration.

Building Society Accounts

Building society accounts are usually closed using the society's standard forms, or a written authority signed by all the personal representatives. Any restrictions on the account regarding the notice period that must be given before a withdrawal can be made cease to apply once the account holder has died. The points made above in relation to keeping the account open to collect dividends, and about the provision of a tax certificate, apply.

The personal representatives should consider whether the closure of a building society account will jeopardise any benefits available upon any proposed demutualisation of the building society.

Premium Bonds

Premium bonds cannot be transferred directly to a beneficiary but must instead be encashed. They may, however, remain in the prize draw for a period of one year from the date of death and the personal representatives must decide whether this would delay the administration of the estate. In any event, a direction for the bonds to remain in the draw can be revoked at any time and the bonds encashed.

National Savings Certificates
National savings certificates can be transferred *in specie*, or encashed using the prescribed forms.

TESSAs, ISAs and PEPs
TESSAs, ISAs and PEPs lose their special tax status on the death of the holder and are treated in the same manner as any other savings or share holding account. They can be liquidated using a written authority from the personal representatives. The rules of the provider may permit any shares to be transferred *in specie*.

A statement, showing the income accruing on the account from the date of death onwards, should be requested. If the account comprises shares, dividends should be shown on this statement. The statement may show entries marked "income tax rebate". This is the rebate of income tax already paid on income payments made during the deceased's lifetime. These rebates are in fact assets to which the deceased was entitled during his lifetime and should be included as part of his capital estate for inheritance tax purposes.

Life Assurance Policies and Pension Scheme Death Benefits
Any benefit due under a life assurance policy or pension scheme is paid to the personal representatives, or trustees if the death benefit was written into trust. If the deceased was the sole trustee of any trust, the death benefit cannot be obtained until a grant has been issued, as it is the personal representatives who are entitled to claim it. The paying company usually provides forms for claiming death benefit.

Interest should be payable on any policy proceeds not paid out immediately upon death; a tax deduction certificate, showing the interest credited and income tax paid, should be requested.

Interests in Trusts and Other Estates
Interests in trusts and other estates are paid directly from the trust or estate on production of the grant of representation to the trustees/personal

representatives of the estate. A set of trust or estate accounts, showing how the payment is made up as to income and capital, should be requested; this is relevant to the income tax position of the personal representatives. If the deceased was using any trust property, it should have been returned to the trustees upon his death.

Land

If the personal representatives are unsure what is to be done about land that was in the deceased's sole name, they can register it in their own names as legal owners. To do this, the following must be sent the Land Registry:
- a completed form AP1 (Application to change the register);
- the grant of representation;
- the land or charge certificate; and
- the appropriate fee.

Often, however, it is more convenient to leave the title in the name of the deceased until it is sold or assented to a beneficiary. Rule 170 of the Land Registration Rules 1925 provides that the personal representatives need not transfer legal title into their names before a sale takes place.

If the land is to be assented to a beneficiary, a land registry form AS1 (Assent of whole of registered title(s)) is used.

If the land was in the deceased's name jointly with a third party, legal title is transferred into the name of that party automatically upon the deceased's death. If the land was held as joint tenants, no further action need be taken – the co-owner can apply to be registered as sole owner of the land immediately; or a death certificate can be placed with the title deeds for production on later sale.

If the beneficial interest was held as tenants-in-common, there must be at least two owners of the legal title before the legal interest can be dealt with. Thus, if the deceased was co-owner with one other person, a new trustee must be appointed. The two legal owners may then execute, in relation to the legal title to the land, a form TR1 (Transfer of whole of registered title(s)) if the deceased's interest is to be sold; or AS1 if it is to be assented to a beneficiary. The personal representatives should deal with the beneficial interest by executing a separate form of assent.

If the land (whether held in the deceased's sole name or in joint names) was unregistered, an assent leads to an automatic first registration (section 4, Land Registration Act 2002), in the same way as does a transfer on sale. In addition, the personal representatives must demonstrate the validity of their action in assenting the land by providing a copy of the Will to the Land Registry; or, in the case of an intestacy, swearing a statutory declaration explaining how the estate devolves under the intestacy rules.

Leasehold Property

Obligations in respect of any leasehold property bind the personal representatives, although the lease itself may be an asset within the estate. If the personal representatives enter into possession of leasehold property (for example, by allowing a business to continue to be run from the property), they may become personally liable for the breach of any covenants in the lease during the administration of the estate. If they do not enter into possession, they are liable only in their capacity as personal representatives and thus any penalty for a breach would be borne by the estate. Personal representatives must carefully consider their actions in relation to the property, and whether those actions could be construed as "entering into possession".

The most favourable manner of dealing with leasehold property may be to surrender the lease, as all obligations of the personal representatives and estate would cease at that point. Alternatively, the personal representatives might consider assigning the lease, but, should the assignee default under its terms, the landlord may seek damages from the personal representatives in their personal capacity if there are insufficient funds in the estate to meet the claim. On the other hand, section 26, Trustee Act 1925 gives some protection to personal representatives, providing that they are not personally liable in relation to any claim under a lease that has been assigned if they first set aside a fund sufficient to meet any future claim.

Business Interests of a Sole Trader

The business interests of a sole trader may be more difficult to deal with because the deceased was himself the business. If the business is to be sold, the personal representatives must decide whether the business assets are to be sold off piecemeal, in which case they simply need to be maintained until sold; or whether the business is to be sold as a going concern. In the latter case, an agent should be appointed to manage the business until it is ready to be sold. If the sale proceeds are to pass to a single beneficiary, it may be wise for that beneficiary to act as manager, or participate in the choice of manager, to avoid any suggestion of negligence on the part of the personal representatives. If the business is to be assented to a beneficiary, this should take place as soon as possible to reduce any risk that the business may diminish in value.

If the personal representatives carry on the deceased's business otherwise than with a view to its sale, they are liable for all the trade debts incurred, unless the Will gives them specific authority to carry on the business (*Dowse v Gorton* [1891] AC 190); or to postpone a sale (*Re Crowther* [1895] 2 Ch 56). Further, they may not use, for the purposes of the business, any of the deceased's assets which he did not himself use for those purposes unless the Will permits it (*McNeillie v Acton* [1853] 4 DGM & G 744). If the deceased's creditors have not authorised the continuation of the business, debts owed to them take precedence over the personal representatives' right of indemnity against the deceased's estate for liabilities incurred in the business (*In Re Oxley* [1914] 1 Ch 604 (CA)).

The personal representatives are in an invidious position – if they do nothing, the value of the business will diminish and they may find themselves under attack by the estate beneficiaries, but if they allow the business to continue trading they may become liable to existing and future creditors. Bearing all the above points in mind, the personal representatives would be wise to obtain the consent of the beneficiaries of the estate and the creditors of the deceased's business before they arrange for it to continue after the deceased's death.

If the business is to continue trading, the personal representatives must:

- inform Customs and Excise, the Inland Revenue and any insurers;
- make the position clear on all trading documents seen by creditors and customers;
- notify banks and employees, and anyone with whom the deceased held a contract; and
- review health and safety issues affecting staff and customers.

On the sale of the business, the personal representatives must consider the warranties and indemnities they are both willing and able to give to prospective purchasers, and ensure that all relevant contracts are transferred to the purchaser.

Partnership Assets

Partnership assets are distributed according to the partnership deed. The deed may set out the criteria for valuing a partner's share in the business on his death. It may also stipulate that the partnership must purchase the deceased partner's share from his estate according to that valuation.

Partnership deeds relating to professional firms, such as accountancy or the law, commonly state that the personal representatives of a deceased partner are not permitted to make any enquiries as to how the share was valued, but that, in effect, they must take the amount passed over to them with no knowledge of whether or not it has been calculated on a fair basis. The only reassurance in this situation is that each partner must have agreed to this basis for valuing the shares, and therefore the personal representatives are simply abiding by the agreement the deceased partner made.

In *Re White (deceased)* [2001] Ch 393, [2000] 3 WLR 855, [2000] 3 All ER 618 (Ch D), it was held that the amount required to buy out a deceased partner's share need be based only on the historic value of the land belonging to the partnership, as this had always been the basis on which the partnership accounts were prepared.

Assets at Lloyds

Lloyds assets can be collected in and distributed, subject to the retention at Lloyds of a fund sufficient to meet the excess on any estate protection plan (see page 23), and subject to obtaining a *Re Yorke* order (see page 257) if necessary.

There may be questions of how profits should be distributed and losses paid. Many Wills specifically deal with the bequest of Lloyds assets; even if this is not the case, providing the relevant definition in the Will is sufficiently wide to cover assets held at Lloyds as well as all profits and losses, there may be no issue. But if the capital of the Lloyds assets passes in one manner and the income in another (for example, if the assets pass into a life interest trust), there may be a problem. Most Wills contain anti-apportionment clauses so that the profits derived from participation in Lloyds are treated as income arising in the year in which they are paid, and thus pass to the life tenant of the trust. But anti-apportionment clauses generally extend only to income, not to liabilities, so that losses arising in relation to a deceased's Lloyds participation during his lifetime are treated as capital liabilities and thus paid from the capital of the trust fund. The impact of those losses will be felt by the remaindermen rather than the life tenant (although this does mean that his income reduces as the amount in the trust fund reduces). This can cause conflict between remaindermen and the life tenant, unless profits are paid net after deduction of losses, which may rectify the situation.

Stocks and Shares

Most estates contain stocks and shares. It is worth considering these in some detail, since they are often the assets that the beneficiaries of the estate are least likely to wish to sell.

The principle behind dealing with stocks and shares is the same whether they are a portfolio of quoted shares or a holding of shares in a private family company. The principle is that all the beneficiaries must be treated equally. Clearly, there is little risk of any difficulty where there is a single, residuary beneficiary of the shares – the beneficiary asks the personal representatives either to appropriate the shares to him *in specie*, or to sell the shares and remit the proceeds. Likewise, where the shares are specifically bequeathed to one or more persons, problems should not arise because those persons have the right to have the shares appropriated to them directly.

Where, however, the shares are bequeathed to more than one person, or where they fall into residue, the personal representatives may be faced with the difficult choice between selling or appropriating the shares, and, if the latter, how the appropriation should be made. In the commentary below, a distinction is drawn between quoted shares and unquoted shares in a private company, because their likely treatment is different.

Quoted shares

As mentioned elsewhere, the personal representatives should liaise with the beneficiaries of the estate to ascertain their wishes. The personal representatives cannot be compelled to appropriate shares to beneficiaries in satisfaction of a residuary interest, but it is good practice at least to seek their opinions and to meet their wishes where possible.

All in favour of sale: If all the beneficiaries wish the shares to be sold the decision is simple and it would be unusual for the personal representatives to disagree. The only real consideration is whether the shares should be sold by the personal representatives, or whether the beneficial interest in them ought to be appropriated to the beneficiaries so that the sale is made by them. The choice depends on the capital gains tax position of the personal representatives and beneficiaries, and the personal representatives should consider this carefully.

All in favour of appropriation: On the other hand, the beneficiaries may wish the shares to be appropriated to them *in specie.* If the shares are the subject of a specific bequest the personal representatives cannot deny this wish unless the shares need to be sold to pay the debts of the estate, but they do have discretion if the shares fall into residue. Each shareholding should be split between the beneficiaries, in the proportions to which they are entitled to them or to the residuary estate. There may be holdings that cannot be split exactly equally, but the personal representatives must undertake the division as fairly as possible. If the shares fall into residue, they should be appropriated at their market value on the date on which the appropriation takes place, not the probate value. This allows the personal representatives to ascertain how much each beneficiary has received, and then any beneficiary who has received slightly less can receive a balancing payment from the residue of the estate.

If the shares are the subject of a specific bequest but cannot be divided equally between the beneficiaries entitled (for example, 100 shares between three people), the personal representatives must decide what to do, in consultation with them. They may agree to an unequal division, or one beneficiary may decide to "buy" the extra shares he receives from the other beneficiaries (the transaction would be subject to stamp duty). A third alternative is for the extra shares that cannot be divided equally to be sold and the sale proceeds split between the beneficiaries, although this is unlikely to be cost-efficient if the number and value of shares is small.

Mixed wishes: If any residuary beneficiary does not wish to receive the shares *in specie*, the personal representatives can either sell the shares that would have been appropriated to him on the open market and remit the sale proceeds to him; or, if all the beneficiaries are agreeable, his shares can be appropriated to the other beneficiaries and he will receive a greater cash sum from the residue. If shares are being sold on behalf of one beneficiary and being appropriated to others, the appropriation date should generally be taken as the date upon which the shares are sold, to preserve equality between all the beneficiaries.

Very small holdings: The share portfolio may comprise a number of small holdings that are not worth subdividing between the beneficiaries. It may be logical for each beneficiary to take all the shares in one or more of the individual holdings, so that the holdings are not fragmented. But the effect may be that a particular beneficiary perceives that he is receiving an asset of less value than another beneficiary, so it is strongly recommended that personal representatives attempt an appropriation of this kind only if all the beneficiaries are in complete agreement over which holding(s) each of them is to receive.

Complicated appropriation calculations can be time-consuming and this should be explained to the beneficiaries. It may be more cost- and time-effective for the entire portfolio to be sold and the cash proceeds distributed. The registrars of some companies offer a cheap dealing facility for particularly small holdings and it may be worthwhile checking whether this is available before stockbrokers' dealing fees are incurred.

Cost-ineffective holdings: Some holdings may not be cost-effective to deal with at all. A good example is holdings in African small mining companies that occasionally come to light. The fees for, and paperwork involved in, dealing with holdings such as these can be out of proportion to their value. If these holdings are not producing any dividend (and frequently they are not), it is not financially viable to deal with them. They should be left in the name of the deceased, providing all the beneficiaries agree that this is the most sensible course of action. Alternatively, it may be possible to gift these shareholdings to a charity if the charity is willing to take them on.

Settlement date: If shares are to be sold, the personal representatives may need to think about what the settlement date of the sale should be. Most sales are undertaken on a "T plus 3" or "T plus 5" basis. This means that the settlement date for the delivery of the signed stock transfer form and the remittance of the monies by the purchaser is three or five working days after the transaction is undertaken. But where the number of personal representatives is such that it may take some time for a stock transfer form to be circulated for signature, and the personal representatives particularly wish to agree the sale as soon as possible (for example because of fears that the share price will fall), stockbrokers can agree a sale on a "T plus 15" basis. This effectively gives the personal representatives three weeks before the signed stock transfer forms must be produced, although it does of course delay receipt of the sale proceeds.

Loan stock: If the deceased owned loan stock that requires encashment rather than sale, there may be only two dates in the year upon which encashment may take place. The personal representatives should ascertain these dates as early as possible in the administration, to ensure that encashment is not delayed by missing a date.

Unquoted shares

Unquoted shares are often shares in "family companies" and more often than not are specifically dealt with in the Will, if one exists. They should be dealt with carefully to avoid pitfalls. Consider the situation where a father owns all the shares in a family business that he runs with his son. Upon the father's death, his entire estate is to be divided equally between his son and daughter. The daughter would like one half of the family company shares, but the son wants them all to be appropriated to him and the daughter to take a balancing payment from the estate.

In the first place, the articles of association of the company should be checked for any restrictions on the transfer of the deceased's shares. The directors of the company may have power to refuse to register a new shareholder in the company's statutory books. This can lead to deadlock between the beneficiaries of the deceased's estate and the directors of the company, if they are different people. In this situation, unless the deadlock can be broken, the personal representatives have no option but to apply to court for guidance.

The articles may provide that on the deceased's death the remaining shareholders have rights of pre-emption over his shares. If so, the beneficiaries cannot require the shares to be transferred into their names until those rights have been properly dealt with.

The points raised above regarding the sale or appropriation of shares apply to private as to public company shares.

Chapter 16

The Powers and Duties of the Personal Representatives

The personal representatives derive their powers from two sources – statute, and, if the deceased died testate, the Will. For many years, most of the personal representatives' powers were set out in the Trustee Act 1925, which was highly restrictive. Since the commencement of the Trustee Act 2000, on 1 February 2001, personal representatives have greater powers under statute and are much less reliant on the provisions of the deceased's Will for the powers they need to administer the estate effectively.

The Trustee Act 2000 applies to all deaths, whether they occurred before or after the commencement of the Act, apart from the sections on the remuneration of personal representatives, which apply only in respect of deaths after 1 February 2001. The application of each of these sections is subject to any contrary intention in the Will, if any, although a Will would have to specifically state that a section is not to apply, rather than simply being more narrowly drafted than the section. Examples of common alterations of the statutory provisions are given in this chapter.

The more important powers conferred by the Trustee Act 2000 are discussed below.

Powers to Deal with Property
Section 39, Administration of Estates Act 1925 stated that personal representatives have the power to sell, mortgage or charge any property comprised in the estate. This was altered in relation to real property by the Trusts of Land and Appointment of Trustees Act 1996, so that personal representatives have all the powers of an absolute owner when deciding how to deal with land.

Section 33 of the Administration of Estates Act 1925 provided that where a person died intestate, a trust for sale over his property was created. Section 5 of the Trusts of Land and Appointment of Trustees Act 1996, in force from 1 January 1997, provides that if an estate contains real property, a trust of land with a power to postpone sale, rather than a trust for sale, arises in respect of that land.

In addition, section 212, Inheritance Tax Act 1984 states that, to fund the inheritance tax due in relation to an estate, the personal representatives may sell, mortgage or charge the property upon which the tax is payable.

Section 3 of the Trustee Act 2000 allows trustees a general power of investment as though they were the absolute beneficial owner of monies held by them. It is arguable whether this should apply to personal representatives, as their duty is to distribute the estate, rather than invest monies held in it, unless they are actually holding those monies as trustee.

Power to Insure

Section 19 Trustee Act 1925 allowed personal representatives to insure against fire and for only three-quarters of the value of an asset. Section 34 of the Trustee Act 2000 replaced this to allow personal representatives to insure against any risk, and for the full value of the property. The only restriction on the personal representatives now is that if an asset is held as bare trustee for a beneficiary, and that beneficiary directs the personal representatives not to insure the asset, they are obliged not to do so.

Power to Postpone Distribution

Section 44, Administration of Estates Act 1925 established the "executor's year". It allows the personal representatives one year from the date of the deceased's death within which they should realise the estate and pay out any legacies. If they postpone distribution beyond that year, interest becomes payable on the legacies.

A testator cannot alter this in his Will by requiring the personal representatives to make payments earlier, although he could, for example, provide that interest is to be paid on a legacy from the date of death.

Power to Appropriate

Under section 41 of the Administration of Estates Act 1925, the personal representatives may appropriate any asset towards the satisfaction of a legacy or interest in residue, whether the legacy or interest is absolute or settled in trust. They may make such an appropriation only with the consent of the beneficiary entitled. Where the beneficiary is under the age of eighteen or is mentally incapacitated and therefore unable to give consent, consent may be given by a parent or guardian, or by the beneficiary's receiver, respectively.

If the asset is to pass into a life interest trust, consent need be given by the life tenant only, not the remaindermen. A difficulty may arise if the beneficiary is a discretionary trust, as the class of beneficiaries is wide and not all the potential beneficiaries of the trust may be alive at that time to give consent. Often the Will dispenses with the need for such consent.

Finally, if the personal representative is also the beneficiary to whom the asset is being appropriated, there may be a concern about self-dealing. The Will may specifically allow the appropriation to take place in these circumstances.

Power to Distribute to a Minor

Under section 21, Law of Property Act 1925, an unmarried minor cannot give a good receipt for either income or capital; a married minor can give a valid receipt for income only. In such a situation the personal representatives would have to hold a legacy or share of residue due to a minor until the minor is eighteen. To avoid this, section 42, Administration of Estates Act 1925 allows the personal representatives to appoint trustees to hold a legacy or share of residue to which a minor beneficiary is absolutely entitled, and to obtain a proper discharge from the trustees. The Will may extend the power in section 42 to allow the personal representatives to accept the receipt of the minor's parent or guardian for any capital or income paid over to him, to which the minor is absolutely entitled.

If the entitlement of the minor is contingent, section 42 does not avail the personal representatives, as it does not apply to contingent interests. The personal representatives must continue to hold the legacy or share in residue for the minor until he satisfies the contingency.

Power to Maintain

Where a beneficiary has a vested interest in an estate, the personal representatives or trustees holding the interest in trust for him may use the income generated by it for the maintenance, education or benefit of the beneficiary, at their discretion, while he is under the age of eighteen (section 31(1)(i), Trustee Act 1925). The section requires the trustees to take into account various factors when deciding whether or not to make the distribution, and provides that the payment of income must "... in all the circumstances, be reasonable ...". The Will often modifies this, so that the trustees need not take the listed items into account, but may pay out income at their unfettered discretion.

Once the beneficiary reaches the age of eighteen, he is entitled to the income generated by that interest (section 31, Trustee Act 1925).

Section 42 also applies where the beneficiary has only a contingent interest in the legacy if the legacy itself carries a right to intermediate income. This is the case if:

- the legacy is not pecuniary;
- the legacy is a pecuniary legacy but the deceased was the parent of, or someone standing *in loco parentis* to, the beneficiary;
- the Will specifies that the right to intermediate income applies or demonstrates a general intention to maintain the beneficiary.

If income is not paid out it must be accumulated and the accumulations paid out once the beneficiary becomes entitled to the capital or to a life interest in it, whether that entitlement is at age eighteen or later. The accumulated income may, however, be paid in a later year than the year in which it was generated as though it was income arising in the year of payment (section 31(2)).

Power to Advance Capital

Section 32, Trustee Act 1925 allows trustees to pay over capital to which a beneficiary is entitled, whether the interest is vested or contingent, to that beneficiary. The payment must be for the advancement or benefit of the beneficiary to whom it is paid, and it may not exceed one half of the monies to which he would be entitled in total. Any monies paid to him must be brought into account at the time at which he would become absolutely entitled to any remaining monies within the trust.

This section is often modified in a Will to state that the personal representatives may pay over the whole interest to which a beneficiary would become entitled, not just half.

Power to Charge

Until the Trustee Act 2000, personal representatives did not have a statutory power to charge for their professional services. This is altered by sections 28 and 29 of that Act for deaths since the commencement of the Act. Section 28 provides that where a Will allows a personal representative to be paid, that charging clause does not take effect as a gift for the purposes of section 15 of the Wills Act 1837 (which states that gifts to beneficiaries who witness the Will are invalid) or section 34(3) of the Administration of Estates Act 1925 (which refers to Part II of Schedule 1, stating the order in which debts are to be paid from an insolvent estate). This means that the fees of a professional personal representative are treated as an administration expense of the estate for insolvency purposes, and that a professional executor may now act as witness to a Will without invalidating his charging clause.

Section 29, Trustee Act 2000 allows a trust corporation or personal representative other than a sole personal representative to charge for his services even if this is not permitted in the Will. The other personal representatives must agree to such remuneration for it to be permissible.

Both these sections take effect subject to any contrary intention expressed in the Will, and do not apply to sole personal representatives. In any event, rule 15 of the Solicitors Practice Rules 1990 obliges the solicitor acting on behalf of an estate to write to the client (in this case the personal representatives) setting out the terms of his engagement and his charging structure. This rule should always be followed, to prevent any argument later as to the appropriate level of the solicitor's fees. If the solicitor is also the personal representative, it would be wise to address this letter to the beneficiaries of the estate, again to reduce the risk of conflict.

Power to Recoup Expenses

Section 31 of the Trustee Act 2000 specifies that any personal representative is entitled to be reimbursed for any expenses properly incurred by him when acting on behalf of the estate.

Power to Delegate

Section 11, Trustee Act 2000 allows personal representatives to appoint agents to exercise any "delegable function". The section goes on to clarify what is not a "delegable function", broadly:
- any decision regarding the distribution of the estate;
- any decision as to whether fees should be paid from income or capital;
- any power to appoint trustees (for example as trustee of a legacy holding for a minor);
- the delegation of any "delegable function" or the appointment of a nominee or custodian. This simply means that once a function has been delegated by the personal representatives, they cannot allow the delegatee to delegate his powers.

Section 22 of the Act states that the appointment must be kept under review and section 23 sets out the circumstances in which the personal representatives are not liable for the actions of the agent.

Power to Appoint an Attorney

The Trustee Delegation Act 1999 (section 5) amended section 25, Trustee Act 1925 to allow a personal representative to appoint an attorney to act in his stead. Such an appointment must be renewed every twelve months. A sample form of appointment is given in the section. The attorney is permitted to be a sole co-personal representative. If an attorney is appointed, the co-personal representatives must be notified of the appointment within seven days of its being made, although failure to give this notice does not render the actions of the attorney invalid. In any event, the Will may contain a power for an executor to appoint an attorney.

Powers Conferred by a Will

Other powers not provided for by statute, but often found specifically within a Will are discussed below.

Power to permit self-dealing

The personal representative may appropriate or sell assets to himself provided this is done at a proper value. If power to do so is not given in the Will the transaction may be voidable at the instance of the beneficiary, or the personal representative may have to account for any profit made resulting from the transaction.

Power to carry on the deceased's business

The personal representatives should carry on the deceased's business only with a view to its sale, generally within the "executor's year". If the business is continued for longer than that, the personal representatives may become personally liable for the debts of the business. On the other hand, the Will may permit the personal representatives to carry on any business in which the deceased participated for such period of time as they deem necessary or expedient.

Power to lend and borrow

The Will may specifically authorise the personal representatives to lend money, generally to a beneficiary of the estate, or to borrow money on any terms they think fit. This power can be especially useful in confirming the personal representatives' ability to take out a loan to pay any inheritance tax due.

Power to permit enjoyment of land and chattels

The personal representatives may be specifically authorised to allow any beneficiary to occupy land or use chattels comprised in the estate for as long as they think fit and on any terms. This may be relevant where a person who is not a beneficiary under the Will was living in a property with the deceased. The personal representatives will be able to allow that person to live in the property and use all the chattels that are kept there without payment of rent, at least until the person finds a new home (providing the person is also a beneficiary under the Will).

The Duties of Personal Representatives

The duty of the personal representatives is to the beneficiaries and it is an overriding duty to administer the estate properly and with all due expediency. Its exact nature varies according to the stage the administration of the estate has reached. For example, at the beginning of the administration the personal representatives must ensure they locate the deceased's last Will and any codicil(s). Once the grant has been received, they have the duty to collect in the assets and pay the debts as quickly as possible. The duties of the personal representatives at all the various stages are discussed in detail throughout this book.

Section 1(1) of the Trustee Act 2000 imposes an overriding duty on all personal representatives:

"Whenever the duty under this subsection applies to a trustee, he must exercise such care and skill as is reasonable in the circumstances, having regard in particular –

(a) to any special knowledge or experience that he has or holds himself out as having, and

(b) if he acts as trustee in the course of a business or profession, to any special knowledge or experience that it is reasonable to expect of a person acting in the course of that kind of business or profession."

Chapter 17

Paying the Debts of the Estate

Personal representatives should pay the debts of the estate as soon as possible after obtaining the grant. *In Re Tankard* [1942] Ch 69 requires them to pay the debts with "due diligence", having regard to the assets in their hands properly applicable for that purpose. As a practical measure, debts should always be paid quickly to stop interest accruing on them.

All debts of the estate must be paid in full before any distribution of legacies or residue can be made. There are two main considerations regarding the payment of debts, firstly the order in which they are paid, which is particularly relevant for insolvent estates, and, secondly, the property that may be used to pay them.

Identifying the Debts

Identifying the creditors of the deceased, and the enquiries that should be made of them, have been discussed in Chapter 2. The personal representatives must take steps to ensure that all debts claimed against the estate were genuinely incurred by the deceased. For example, a false claim may be submitted in response to a newspaper advertisement for creditors, a bogus invoice being sent to the personal representatives with a claim that the deceased incurred the debt during his lifetime. The amount claimed is often not significant, so as to excite little interest by the personal representatives. If the personal representatives receive a claim of this nature, they should check with the family of the deceased and write to the creditor asking for further details. If the personal representatives pay a debt such as this without making proper enquiries, and it later becomes apparent that the claim was fraudulent, they may become personally liable to the beneficiaries for the loss to the estate.

It is suggested that if the personal representatives are not entirely satisfied that a debt is genuine, but decide to pay it, they should take an indemnity from the residuary beneficiaries that they will not make a claim against the personal representatives if the debt later turns out to be false.

Another difficulty arises where the personal representatives suspect a debt exists, but have received no claim from the creditor. If the debt has not become statute-barred, they cannot distribute the funds required to pay the debt in case it is claimed later, but they ought not to pay a liability that has not been claimed since again this would cause a loss to the estate. The most practical course is to retain sufficient funds to meet the debt until the time limit passes for it to become statute barred, or distribute the funds to the estate beneficiaries but take an indemnity from them against the debt being claimed at a later date.

Order of Priority for Payment

There is a specific statutory order in which debts of the estate must be paid. This ranks creditors by class and requires that all the debts in the highest class must be paid in full before debts in the next highest class are paid, and so on.

The order is not strictly relevant if the estate is solvent, as the assets are sufficient to meet all the deceased's debts. The Administration of Insolvent Estates of Deceased Persons Order 1986 (SI 1986 No 1999) sets out the order of priority, which cannot be varied. It is:

1. secured creditors;
2. funeral, testamentary and administration expenses;
3. debts preferred by statute;
4. preferential debts (listed in Schedule 6 to the Insolvency Act 1986);
5. ordinary debts;
6. interest on debts;
7. deferred debts.

The amount of funeral expenses properly allowable as a debt for these purposes may be different from the amount which is deductible for inheritance tax purposes. Section 172, Inheritance Tax Act 1984 states that "reasonable" expenses are allowable for inheritance tax purposes. Both provisions generally include mourning expenses, newspaper advertisements and tombstones.

If the personal representatives have placed their advertisements under section 27 of the Trustee Act 1925 (see page 256) and undertaken any other action required to ascertain the debts of the estate, and are sure that the estate is solvent, the statutory order of priority need not be followed, as the estate is sufficient to pay all the debts in full. But if the personal representatives are at all unsure whether the estate will cover all the liabilities, they should pay the deceased's debts in accordance with the order of priority above. If they do not, and find that they have paid an "inferior" debt leaving insufficient funds to pay a "superior" debt, they become personally liable to pay the "superior" debt.

The personal representatives should also be careful to establish whether they have sufficient funds to pay all the debts in each class. If they pay one debt in a class in full, and then discover that they do not have enough to pay all the debts in that class in full, they may be personally liable for the rest of the debts in that class. On the other hand, section 10(2) Administration of Estates Act 1971 may provide a defence if the personal representatives had no reason to believe that the estate was insolvent, and payment was made in good faith. The section does not, however, provide a defence to a claim by creditors in a superior class who have not been paid in full.

Order of Priority of Property

The order in which property is to be used to pay the debts of a deceased whose estate is solvent is set out in Part II of Schedule 1 to the Administration of Estates Act 1925. The order of property is:

1. property undisposed of by the Will, subject to the retention of a fund to meet the pecuniary legacies;
2. property included in a residuary gift, subject to the retention of a fund to meet pecuniary legacies to the extent that they have not already been provided for above;
3. property specifically appropriated, devised or bequeathed by the deceased for the payment of debts;
4. property charged with, or devised or bequeathed subject to, the payment of debts;
5. the fund retained to meet pecuniary legacies;
6. property specifically devised or bequeathed, rateably according to value;
7. property appointed by Will under a general power.

Personal representatives taking out a loan to pay inheritance tax (see page 80) usually give an undertaking that the loan is to be treated as a first charge on the deceased's assets. This does not fit completely with the statutory order given above. But given that inheritance tax is payable on the value of the deceased's net estate, it is difficult to envisage a situation in which inheritance tax would be payable and yet the estate would not be sufficient to meet the debts chargeable on it. In practice, therefore, there would appear to be no irregularity in the personal representatives' giving such an undertaking.

Contrary intention in the Will

The statutory order in which the deceased's property should be used to pay the debts of the estate is subject to any contrary intention in the deceased's Will, so the personal representatives should always read the Will carefully before deciding how the liabilities are to be paid.

Section 35 goes on to state that if a debt was charged on a specific asset, that asset must be used to discharge the debt, unless the Will expresses a contrary intention. The best example is a house owned by the deceased, upon which a mortgage is secured. If the deceased left the house to his wife in his Will "subject to mortgage" (or without making any reference to the mortgage at all), the wife could either take the house from the personal representatives, sell it to pay off the mortgage and retain the excess proceeds; or she could take the house and continue to pay the mortgage herself. If the house is left to the wife "free of mortgage", the mortgage would first be discharged from the residue of the deceased's estate and the house transferred to the wife, debt-free. If the deceased's Will directs a specific fund from which the debt is to be paid, and that fund is insufficient, the burden of the undischarged debt falls back onto the charged asset.

The usual direction in a Will that the deceased's assets should be collected in and used to pay off his debts before the residue is paid out is not enough to constitute a "contrary intention" for the purposes of section 35. The Will must directly contemplate that the debt secured on a specific asset should not be discharged by that asset.

Taking the example a step further, a problem may arise where the deceased left his house to his wife, and left the residue of his estate to his son. If he took out a life assurance policy to pay off the mortgage on his death, but failed to assign the policy to the mortgagee or his wife, the life assurance policy would fall into the residue of the estate and thus to the son, and would not be available to pay off the mortgage. In that situation the personal representatives may suggest that the son and mother execute a deed of variation (see page 261) to pass the proceeds of the life assurance to the mother.

Assets falling outside the statutory categories

Certain assets in the deceased's estate may not fall into any of the statutory categories set out above. For example, the deceased may, in his Will, have left someone an option to purchase an asset. If the asset is sold under the option, the proceeds of sale fall into one of the classes above. But if the Will provided for the sale to be at an undervalue, the asset may instead, if the personal representatives so choose, be sold for its full value free of the option and the proceeds of sale used to discharge the debt. Indeed, they would be bound to do so if, without the proceeds of sale at full market value, the estate would be insufficient to meet its debts. Any other action would be a breach of the personal representatives' duty to the creditors of the estate. Assets gifted by way of *donatio mortis causa* (see page 13) or nominated assets may also be used. In each case, the assets should be used as a last resort only, if all the assets listed are insufficient to discharge the deceased's debts.

Marshalling

A creditor is not concerned to establish whether he has been paid from the correct fund; his main concern is to obtain satisfaction of his invoice. If the deceased's funds are used in the wrong order, any adverse effect on the interests of the beneficiaries must be rectified. This is a process known as "marshalling" and is achieved by compensating each beneficiary for what he would have received at the time he would have received it from the fund that should have been used to pay the debt.

Insolvent Estate

Where the deceased was insolvent at the time of his death and an individual voluntary arrangement had been approved by the court, the estate is administered in accordance with that arrangement. But if the arrangement had not been approved by the court, even if it had been agreed by the deceased's creditors, it cannot be enforced after death.

If a bankruptcy petition had been presented before death, but no order had been made, the bankruptcy proceedings may continue as though the deceased were alive.

If a petition had not been presented but the deceased's estate is insolvent the personal representatives have three options:

- they can administer the estate themselves according to the rules (the Administration of Insolvent Estates of Deceased Persons Order 1986, SI 1986 No 1999 and section 421, Insolvency Act 1986);
- they can obtain an insolvency administration order from the court and administer the estate under the court's direction (under Part 50 of and Schedule 1 to the Civil Procedure Rules 1998); or
- they (or a creditor of the deceased) can present a bankruptcy petition to the court and obtain an insolvency administration order. The estate would then vest in the Official Receiver until a trustee in bankruptcy takes over and administers the estate.

The applicant for the grant

In practical terms, the administration of an insolvent estate can be difficult, notably in ensuring that the right debts are paid in the right amount at the right time. A personal representative who has no personal interest in the administration of the estate would do well to consider renouncing the right to probate or letters of administration and leaving the estate to be administered by someone who does have such an interest, such as a creditor of the deceased. If a creditor does not wish to take out a grant, he can present a bankruptcy petition so that a trustee in bankruptcy can be appointed to administer the estate, as mentioned above.

If the personal representatives have already taken out the grant of representation and it then becomes apparent that the estate is insolvent, they can apply to be removed or replaced, under section 50, Administration of Justice Act 1985. The court cannot, however, remove all the personal representatives without appointing others in their place.

Onerous property

If the deceased was insolvent, some of the assets in the estate may cause problems for the personal representatives. For example, a lease under which the deceased was the tenant may in fact be a burden on the estate, rather than of benefit to it. The personal representatives should try to surrender or assign the lease, although any assignment may render the estate liable for any acts of default of the assignee (see page 190). If the estate is subject to an insolvency administration order the trustee in bankruptcy may disclaim any onerous property such as a lease, which is often the most practical course.

Joint property

An insolvency administration order serves to sever any joint tenancies held by the deceased with another person, so that his share in the joint property is available to meet his liabilities. In *Re Palmer (Deceased) (a debtor)* [1994] Ch 316, [1994] 3 WLR 420, [1994] 3 All ER 835 (CA), however, it was held that such an order, granted after death, is treated as made immediately after the deceased's death, by which time the property held by the deceased as joint tenant has already passed by survivorship and is therefore not available to meet the deceased's liabilities.

Property gifted or sold for less than market value

Section 339, Insolvency Act 1986 provides that, if the deceased made any gifts or transactions at an undervalue in the two years prior to the presentation of a successful bankruptcy petition, those gifts or transactions may be set aside during his lifetime. If the gift or transaction was made within five years of the presentation of the petition and the deceased became insolvent as a result of it, that gift or transaction may also be set aside. Section 423 of the same Act goes even further, providing that if the deceased undertook any transaction, the purpose of which was to put his assets beyond the reach of his creditors, the transaction may be set aside no matter when it was undertaken.

Section 341 (as amended by the Administration of Insolvent Estates of Deceased Persons Order 1986) confirms that each of the above sections applies to a deceased's estate, but that the relevant time period does not end with the presentation of a bankruptcy petition, but on the date of death. Any application to set aside a transaction cannot be made by the personal representatives of a deceased, but must be made by a trustee in bankruptcy.

Chapter 18

Paying the Legacies

There are three main matters to be established before making payments of legacies and of residue under the deceased's estate:
- identifying the beneficiary entitled;
- establishing what each beneficiary is entitled to receive; and
- the time at which each legacy should be paid.

Identifying the Beneficiaries Entitled

Identifying the beneficiaries is straightforward when they are named in a Will. It may be more difficult where they are referred to in the Will or under the intestacy rules as members of a certain class; here, all the members of the class must be located. Unless it is specifically excluded by the Will, the Family Law Reform Act 1987 provides that illegitimate and legitimated children are all treated as children of their biological parents, and adopted children are treated as the natural children of their adoptive parents. Step-children are not treated as children of their step-parents unless they have been adopted. Personal representatives should therefore be careful, in particular, to establish whether the deceased had any illegitimate children, although if they have made the proper advertisements for creditors under section 27 of the Trustee Act 1925 (see page 256), this will provide protection against a later claim by any illegitimate children of whom they were unaware.

Problems have arisen in recent years in connection with claims in estates by children born by artificial insemination, where the identity of a parent has not been established. An order specifying parentage may have been made after the birth of the child. If such an order has not been made or cannot be located, the personal representatives may need to apply to the court for further information and directions.

If the gift is to a class of persons, the point at which entry to the class closes must be established. This may be specified in a Will, but if not, the gift is subject to the "class closing rules" which derive from common law. If the gift is made to a class and at least one person is already absolutely entitled to his share of the gift (for example, a gift to "my grandchildren as shall attain the age of 25" and one grandchild is aged 25 at the date of death), the class closes at the date of death. If there are potential beneficiaries alive at the date of death but no one in the class has become absolutely entitled at that time, the class closes when the first beneficiary to do so attains an absolute entitlement, such as when the first grandchild reaches the age of 25. If there are no potential beneficiaries living at the date of death, for example if the deceased had no living grandchildren, the class remains open indefinitely. This is also the case if the class takes only the income generated by a pool of capital; here the income is distributed between those falling into the class each year.

If a life interest was created and the gift of capital is to a class, the class closing rules do not come into operation until the life interest ceases.

Any reference to a living person includes an unborn child *en ventre sa mère*.

If a beneficiary is described by reference to his status or relationship to the deceased, subject to any contrary intention in the Will, the person who occupied that status or relationship at the time the Will was executed is the person entitled. So a gift to "my housekeeper" would be a gift to the deceased's housekeeper at the date of the Will, but a gift to "my housekeeper at the date of my death" takes effect to the person occupying that position when the testator died. The intestacy rules also describe a person by reference to relationship to the deceased, again meaning the person having that relationship at the date of death.

If a beneficiary cannot immediately be located at the date of the deceased's death, any expenses incurred in finding him are payable out of his legacy. But if the difficulties arise from ambiguity in the Will (in which case they are likely to relate to establishing the identity of the beneficiary rather than to finding a beneficiary who is thought to exist), the costs of resolving the ambiguity must be met from the deceased's estate.

Establishing What Each Beneficiary is Entitled to Receive

Specific legacies
A specific legacy is a gift of a particular asset, not cash. A specific gift of personal property is referred to as a bequest, and a specific gift of real property, a devise. If a specific gift is of a physical asset, a beneficiary who is absolutely entitled must bear the cost of insuring the asset from the date of death, and the costs of maintenance and storage, and of transporting it to him. Personal representatives should carefully check the scope of the legacy. For example, if a house is devised, does the gift include any land adjacent to the house but which was not purchased at the same time? Or is a gift of

shares a gift of all the deceased's shares in a company, or of the ordinary shares only?

Pecuniary legacies
A pecuniary legacy is a legacy of an amount of money. A legacy does not become pecuniary simply because it consists of money, but rather because it is a stated sum. So for example, a gift of "the contents of my HSBC account" would be specific because it is of a specific asset, not pecuniary even though the account comprises cash. Expenses incurred by the personal representatives in the payment of these legacies are payable out of residue.

Residuary gifts
A residuary gift is a gift of the remainder of the deceased's assets after the other legacies and debts have been paid; see page 223 *et seq.*

These distinctions are not particularly significant in many estates, but they become important if the residue is insufficient to pay the deceased's debts, as they govern the order of property used to meet the remaining liabilities (see page 205).

General legacies
Specific and pecuniary legacies can be subdivided into two categories – general and demonstrative. A general legacy is paid out of the deceased's general estate. It can be pecuniary in nature, in that it is simply of cash, or it can be of an asset that is not within the deceased's estate at the time of his death, and therefore must be purchased by the personal representatives for a beneficiary. For example, a gift of "a Rolex watch" is not dependent upon the deceased's having owned a Rolex watch at his death. If he did not, the personal representatives must buy a Rolex watch for the beneficiary named.

Demonstrative legacies
A demonstrative legacy is one directed to be paid out of a specific fund. If that fund is insufficient to meet the legacy, it is paid out of the deceased's other assets. To the extent that it can be paid out of the intended fund, it is classed as a specific legacy. Any amount that cannot be met out of the fund and is paid from the deceased's general estate falls into the category of pecuniary legacy.

Cumulative and substitutional legacies
If a beneficiary has been left two legacies in the deceased's Will and codicils, it must be established whether or not the legacy is cumulative. If legacies of a different asset or amount are made in the same document, or if legacies of the same amount are made in two different documents, the

legacies are presumed to be cumulative and both are permitted, unless the later gift is interpreted as in substitution for the earlier gift. If the same amount is gifted more than once to the same person in a single document, only one legacy of that amount may take effect.

If a Will makes a gift to a beneficiary, and a codicil makes a further gift to the same person, the documents must be read to discover whether there is any evidence that the testator intended the second gift to replace the first gift, or whether the gifts should be treated as cumulative.

The Will or intestacy may impose requirements on a legacy before it becomes vested, i.e., before the beneficiary is absolutely entitled to the asset as against the personal representatives. Examples of the different categories of such requirement are given below.

Contingent gifts

The beneficiary becomes entitled to a contingent gift only on satisfying a specified requirement. The most common requirement is that the beneficiary should attain a particular age.

Conditional gifts

The beneficiary becomes entitled to the conditional gift only if a certain event, such as marriage, takes place.

It is sometimes difficult to distinguish between a contingent legacy and a conditional legacy. Generally, contingencies are events which will be fulfilled over the passage of time, providing the beneficiary lives long enough to do so, whereas contingencies require action on the part of the beneficiary or a third party.

Gifts in trust

While contingent and conditional gifts are simple forms of trust, in that the legacy is held in trust for the beneficiary until the contingency or condition is satisfied, legacies may also be held upon more complex forms of trust; see page 223.

Gifts to executors

A legacy to an executor in a Will is presumed to be conditional upon that person's acting as executor, unless the Will identifies the executor as a relative or friend of the testator. This does not, however, apply in relation to gifts of residue to an executor (*Griffiths v Pruen* (1840) 11 Sim 202).

Gifts to debtors

If a general legacy or share in residue is given to a debtor of the deceased, the debt must be set off against the legacy, unless the Will releases the debt.

Annuities

An annuity is general if the Will does not specify the fund from which it is to be paid, or demonstrative if it does. If only a certain amount is to be paid under the annuity, and the fund retained to meet it produces excess income in any year, that excess income can be paid to the residuary beneficiaries of the estate or retained to meet any income shortfall in the future. If the personal representatives are directed in the Will to purchase an annuity, rather than simply pay the income of a particular fund to the annuitant, the gift is treated as a pecuniary legacy of the amount required to buy the annuity at the date of the deceased's death. In that situation the annuitant can elect to take the capital sum required to buy the annuity if he wishes to do so, rather than having the annuity bought for him.

The way a clause gifting an annuity is worded can greatly affect the exact amount to which the annuitant is entitled. If the beneficiary is bequeathed "£100 per annum", this is the gross amount due to him, but the personal representatives must deduct basic rate income tax before paying the annuity, and provide the annuitant with a tax deduction certificate. If the gift is of "such sum as after the deduction of income tax amounts to £100 per annum", the personal representatives must pay over an annuity, net of basic rate income tax, of £100 per annum. Finally, if the Will gifts "£100 per annum free of all income tax", again the beneficiary can demand £100 after the payment of basic rate income tax; if he is a higher rate taxpayer, he can recover the higher rate tax from the personal representatives.

Precatory trusts

A Will may deal with the testator's chattels in three different ways:
- it can gift them specifically to someone;
- it can make no reference to them and allow them to fall into residue; or
- it can pass them to a precatory trust.

The intestacy rules provide for the first two of these options only, depending on whether or not the deceased left a widow(er). A precatory trust is a trust whereby one or more people (often the personal representatives) are given the deceased's chattels beneficially. As they receive them as legatees, not as trustees, they can choose to keep the chattels or do with them as they wish. But in a precatory trust, the Will goes on to request that the beneficiaries dispose of the deceased's chattels in accordance with any letter of wishes written by him during his lifetime. These wishes are not binding, but they do impose a moral obligation on the "trustees".

Precatory trusts are often useful because they allow the deceased much more flexibility when dealing with his chattels. The letter of wishes can be as long or short as he desires, and can be changed at any time without changing the Will. There are usually fewer problems of misdescription in a letter of wishes because legal terminology need not be used. The transfer of a chattel by the "trustee" to the intended recipient is read back into the deceased's Will for inheritance tax purposes providing it is made within two years after death (section 144, Inheritance Tax Act 1984). But it is a disposal by the "trustee" for capital gains tax purposes, although a marked increase in the value of a chattel over so short a period of time is unlikely.

Secret trusts

A Will may provide for the creation of a secret trust. This can be one of two types – fully secret or half secret.

A fully secret trust arises where a gift is expressed to be made to one beneficiary absolutely, but that beneficiary was made aware, before the Will was executed, that he is to hold the asset on trust for a third party. In this situation the personal representatives must treat the gift like any other; they are not necessarily aware of the existence of the trust. Therefore, if the secret trustee witnesses the Will or predeceases the deceased, the gift and the trust fail.

Under a half secret trust, the gift is made in the Will but is expressed to be made to a person "upon trust". The terms of the trust are not specified in the Will. As the trustee is not stated to be a beneficiary, the gift does not fail if the trustee predeceases the deceased or witnesses the Will.

Time for Payment of Legacies

Section 44, Administration of Estates Act 1925 creates the "executor's year". It provides that no interest is due on unpaid pecuniary legacies until one year after the date of the deceased's death. After that year, gross interest must be paid on the value of the legacies at the rate of 6 per cent (Rules of the Supreme Court (Amendment No 2) 1983, SI 1983 No 1181). This is subject to any contrary intention expressed in the deceased's Will. A pecuniary legacy charged on an interest in land carries interest from the date of death.

A legacy given in satisfaction of a debt owed by the deceased carries interest from the date of death if the debt itself bore interest.

The first instalment of an annuity is due on the first anniversary of the death.

A specific legatee with a vested interest is entitled to all the income generated by the asset until it is passed to him.

If a specific gift is contingent or conditional, the wording of the Will and statute govern whether the beneficiary is entitled to the income of the asset from the date of death onwards. Under section 31(3), Trustee Act 1925 a legacy from parent to child (or to someone to whom he stands *in loco parentis*) carries a right to the intermediate income from the asset if the gift is to vest when the beneficiary reaches the age of eighteen or marries under that age, and if the Will makes no other provision for the maintenance of that child (*Re Pollock* [1943] Ch 338 (Ch D)). In any event, a contingent legacy to an infant not falling within the criteria above carries a right to intermediate income if the Will showed an intention for the child to be maintained out of the legacy and the Will provided no other fund for his maintenance (*Re Churchill* [1909] 2 Ch 431).

Personal representatives must be careful about the inter-relationship between these provisions and those under the Apportionment Act 1870, where that statute is not excluded by the Will. The Act states that for the purposes of deciding the beneficiary to whom it must be paid, any income paid in relation to an asset after the date of the deceased's death must be allocated between capital and income beneficiaries depending on the date upon which the income arose. For example, the deceased died on 30 June and a dividend on his shareholding in ABC plc was paid on 31 July for the period 1 June to 31 July. If the Apportionment Act 1870 had not been excluded by the Will, the beneficiary to whom the shares had been gifted would be entitled to 31/61sts of the income, being the proportion of the income arising from the date of death to 31 July. The other 30/61sts of the income would be allocated to the capital of the estate. If the Will had excluded the Act, the entire dividend would be payable to the recipient of the shares. The income tax rules do not, however, follow the Apportionment Act, and so for income tax purposes the personal representatives would be taxed as having received the entire dividend. This should have no impact as the personal representatives are liable to income tax only at the basic rate, which should have already been satisfied by the 10 per cent tax credit given with most dividends.

The rules under the Apportionment Act 1870 are not excluded on an intestacy, although it would be open to the beneficiaries of the estate to agree that they are not to apply.

Failure of Legacies

There are several ways in which a legacy may fail, in whole or in part.

Ademption

Section 24 of the Wills Act 1837 provides that, on a gift of property under a Will, the property is ascertained at the deceased's death unless a contrary intention is shown. In *Re Sikes* [1927] 1 Ch 364 (Ch D), it was confirmed that the use of the word "my" when describing an asset showed such a contrary intention, because the testator must have been thinking of the property he owned at the time he made the Will. Therefore a specific legacy of an asset referred to in the Will as belonging to the deceased will adeem if that exact asset does not form part of the deceased's estate upon his death. For example, a gift of "my Rolls Royce" will take effect as a gift of the Rolls Royce the deceased owned at the date he signed his Will. If he does not own that Rolls Royce on the day he dies, the gift adeems, even if he owns a different Rolls Royce at that time. On the other hand, if the gift had been of "such Rolls Royce as I shall own at the date of my death", the gift would not fail. The final possibility is that the Will could have made a gift of "a Rolls Royce". In that situation it would be of no consequence whether the deceased owned a Rolls Royce at the date he signed the Will or the date he died. If there was not one in his estate at his death, the personal representatives would have to purchase a Rolls Royce for the beneficiary from the deceased's estate.

In this context, it is important to distinguish a change in the *substance* of the gift from a change in its *form*. If an asset changes in form, such as on the re-organisation of a company, so that the 50 x £1 shares held by the deceased become 100 x 50p shares, the asset can be seen to be substantially the same, so that the gift does not fail. But if the asset changes in substance, as where the deceased elected to redeem the shares on the re-organisation and take cash in exchange, the gift would not take effect.

If a contract had been made for the sale of an asset gifted in the Will, and that contract had not been completed prior to death, the gift does not take effect as though it were of the proceeds of sale unless the Will specifically allows this.

If the testator granted an option over property already specifically bequeathed in his Will, the proceeds of sale under the option fall into the residue of the deceased's estate. But if the option was granted before the execution of the Will, or if a codicil was executed, republishing the Will after the option was signed, the gift takes effect subject to the option and the proceeds of sale pass to the beneficiary receiving the asset under the Will.

Abatement
If the deceased's residuary estate is insufficient to discharge its liabilities, the legacies under the Will must abate. The order in which gifts abate is the same as the order of priority to pay debts; see page 205. If there is more than one gift in the class that abates, the abatement is calculated proportionately.

Lapse
If an intended beneficiary predeceases the testator, the gift to him lapses and does not take effect, although it may take effect as a gift to a substitutional beneficiary. A Will may extend this doctrine so that the beneficiary has to outlive the deceased for a specified period of time, such as a calendar month, before the gift becomes effective. The intestacy rules make a similar provision in that a husband or wife must survive the deceased by 28 days to

attain a vested interest in the estate (section 46(2A), Administration of Estates Act 1925).

Section 33(1), Wills Act 1837 may apply to rescue a gift to the children or remoter issue of the deceased who predecease him. It states that if a gift is made to a child or remoter issue of the testator in his Will, and that beneficiary predeceases the testator, the gift takes effect as a gift to the beneficiary's children or issue *per stirpes*. This section has effect subject to any contrary intention in the deceased's Will. Often such an intention is expressed because the Will does not provide for the situation in which the beneficiary survives the testator but does not live to a specified age or fulfil any other contingency imposed.

The intestacy rules also provide for the issue of any class of relative who would be entitled to a share in the deceased's estate, but who predeceases the deceased, to take the parent's share in the estate (section 47, Administration of Estates Act 1925).

Forfeiture
It is a rule of common law, embodied in the Forfeiture Act 1982, that one cannot profit from one's own wrongdoing. Therefore, if the deceased was murdered by a beneficiary under his Will or intestacy, the gift to that beneficiary lapses (*In the Estate of Crippen* [1911] P 108, [1911-13] All ER Rep 207). See also page 105.

A beneficiary disentitled under the Forfeiture Act can make an application for provision from the deceased's estate under the Inheritance (Provision for Family and Dependants) Act 1975, providing he has not become disentitled because he murdered the deceased. Such an application should be made within three months of the applicant's conviction for the offence in question.

Witnessing the Will
Any person, and the spouse of that person, taking a beneficial interest under a Will is barred from taking the interest if he also acted as witness to the Will (section 15, Wills Act 1837). This does not apply if the trustee of a trust created in the Will acts as a witness, as the witness has no beneficial interest in the bequest.

If the trust was secret in nature (whether fully or half secret, see page 214) the beneficiary of the trust may witness the Will because on the face of it he is not a beneficiary (*Re Young, Young v Young* [1951] Ch 185, [1950] 2 All ER 1040). Likewise, the trustee of a half-secret trust may act as a witness because the Will states that he is merely a trustee and not a beneficiary. However, if a trustee of a fully secret trust witnesses the Will, the gift is invalid, as on the face of the Will that person is the intended beneficiary.

A Will is republished on the execution of a codicil to it, so that if a beneficiary under the original Will witnessed the signature of the Will, the gift to him is reinstated after the execution of the codicil, providing he does not also act as witness to that.

Divorce

Section 18A, Wills Act 1837 (as amended by section 3, Law Reform (Succession) Act 1995) states that when a marriage ended in divorce or annulment, the following do not take effect, unless there is a contrary intention in the Will:

- any appointment of the former spouse as executor,
- any power of appointment conferred on the former spouse; and
- any gift to the former spouse in the Will.

The former spouse is treated as though he died on the date the divorce or annulment was made final. This section does not apply to a judicially separated spouse, who is still treated as a "full" spouse for the purposes of the legislation.

The intestacy rules in the Administration of Estates Act 1925 do not mention a former husband or wife, who is therefore not entitled to anything on the deceased's intestacy.

Satisfaction of legacy by portion

Where a legacy or share of residue has been left to a child of the deceased (or someone to whom the deceased stood *in loco parentis*), but the deceased had made provision for the child during his lifetime (such provision being known as a "portion"), the beneficiary's entitlement under the estate may be deemed to be satisfied to the extent of the portion. This may be the case even if the donee does not know about the *inter vivos* gift or the provision made for him under the Will or intestacy, and even if the gift is not made directly to the donee but is instead made for his benefit (*Re Cameron* [1999] Ch 383, [1999] 3 WLR 394, [1999] 2 All ER 924 (Ch D)).

A gift of "pure bounty" does not amount to a portion; a portion is a sum the donee receives to establish him in life or similar.

If a gift may constitute a portion, the question of whether it adeems a gift made under the deceased's Will or intestacy depends on the donor's intention.

Uncertainty

If a beneficiary, or the gift a beneficiary is to receive, cannot be identified with certainty, the gift may be declared invalid for uncertainty. If the personal representatives are at all unsure about the nature of a legacy or the identity of an intended beneficiary they must consider their situation carefully as they may be personally liable for any incorrect payment made. If the uncertainty is not substantial, the personal representatives may choose to deal with the matter by paying out what they consider to be the correct legacy to the correct beneficiary and taking an indemnity from that beneficiary against any later claim against the estate.

If the problem cannot be resolved in this manner, the personal representatives may apply to the court for directions under the Rules of the Supreme Court 1965, Order 93 rule 21, by making an *ex parte* application under section 48, Administration of Justice Act 1985. The application should be made to the High Court, and the resulting order authorises the personal representatives to act on the written opinion of Counsel, of at least ten years' call, on the construction of the Will. If any person objects to the proposed construction of the Will, the case proceeds as though an application had been made to the High Court regarding the construction of the Will (see page 145).

If a gift is exclusively charitable but the personal representatives cannot properly ascertain the identity of the charitable beneficiary intended, the gift may be "rescued" by the doctrine of *cy-près*. A detailed discussion of the doctrine is outside the scope of this book, but if *cy-près* applies, the personal representatives make an application to the court for the approval of a scheme for the administration of the legacy. Under section 16, Charities Act 1993 the Charity Commission has power to establish such a scheme, but it cannot decide that a gift is charitable to the detriment of others. It must wait until the court orders that a gift is charitable and asks the Commission to establish a scheme for the application of the monies bequeathed.

Alternatively, the personal representatives can approach the Treasury Solicitor for a "Sign Manual Direction" as to who is to receive the legacy. This procedure is available only if the deceased made a gift (not upon trust) in his Will for charitable purposes, but no specific charitable object has been named, or where a charity has been named but it does actually exist (e.g., "The Donkey Fund"). The Treasury Solicitor investigates and makes a recommendation to the Attorney General as to the charity that would be a suitable recipient of the legacy. If the Attorney General agrees, the direction is given to the personal representatives, who must pay the legacy in accordance with it. Such a direction does not, however, protect the personal representatives from a claim by a beneficiary that a legacy should not be paid out, and so should be sought only where all the beneficiaries are in agreement.

Election

The doctrine of election is important when the deceased, in his Will, bequeathed to a beneficiary an asset that did not belong to him, and then left another asset, that did belong to him, to the owner of the first asset, as compensation. The beneficiary whose asset has been given away in the Will takes the asset bequeathed to him only if he agrees to give his own asset to the other beneficiary named in the Will. For example, Thomas dies and leaves "Bluefield" to Roger. His Will also states that he leaves "Greenfield" to Peter. Thomas owns Bluefield, but does not own Greenfield, and never has done. Roger owns Greenfield. The doctrine of election would apply here so that Roger is permitted to take the gift of Bluefield only if he agrees to give Greenfield to Peter.

The bankruptcy of the beneficiary

If a beneficiary under a Will or intestacy has been declared bankrupt at the date of death, or between death and receipt of the legacy, this does not affect the validity of the gift. The gift may, though, be claimed by his trustee in bankruptcy, by serving written notice on the personal representatives under section 307, Bankruptcy Act 1986. If such a written notice has not been served on the personal representatives and they do not know the beneficiary is a bankrupt, they cannot be held liable for the payment of any legacy directly to the beneficiary.

Mental incapacity

The lack of capacity of a beneficiary does not affect his entitlement under a Will or intestacy, although he is unable to provide a proper receipt for the legacy or share of residue when it is paid over to him. It should instead be paid over to his receiver or attorney.

The Assets From Which the Legacies are Paid

Once it has been established that the gift may actually take effect, the practicalities of transferring the legacy must be examined.

If a legacy is of a specific asset that the deceased held at the date of his death, the asset itself must be transferred to the beneficiary. But where the legacy is pecuniary in nature, the personal representatives must consider the fund from which the legacy is to be paid. Most Wills contain a direction that the deceased's estate must be sold and the cash proceeds used to pay any debts and taxes, as well as any legacies, before the residue is transferred to the residuary beneficiary. A partial intestacy in relation to the residue is of no consequence because the legacies have been directed to be paid before the amount of the residue is established.

If the Will contains no direction as to the sale of the deceased's assets and payment of his debts and legacies, and there is a partial intestacy in the estate, the personal representatives will not know whether to pay the debts and legacies from the disposed of, or from the undisposed of, residue. Section 33 of the Administration of Estates Act 1925 (as amended by the Trusts of Land and Appointment of Trustees Act 1996) states that the property undisposed of by the deceased's Will is held on trust by the personal representatives with a power for them to sell it. The proceeds of that sale are to be used to discharge the deceased's debts and legacies, and only to the extent that they are insufficient to do so is the disposed of residue used.

Section 33 does not, however, apply if a contrary intention has been expressed, such as an express direction in the Will for the personal representatives to sell the deceased's assets, but no direction regarding the payment of legacies. In this situation, the personal representatives have no guidance on paying the legacies (how the debts are to be paid is explained at page 204 *et seq*). The rules are unclear as to whether the legacies should still be paid from the undisposed of residue, or whether the rules in force before 1926 should be applied. These stated that legacies could be paid from residuary personalty only, not from real property, unless a contrary intention was expressed in the Will, and that legacies would abate to the extent that personal property was insufficient to meet them. A contrary intention could, however, be inferred from the deceased's leaving the entire residue to one beneficiary (*Greville v Browne* [1859] 7 HLC 689) or by directing in his Will that the pecuniary legacies were to be paid from a mixture of real property and personalty (*Roberts v Walker* [1830] 1 R & M 752).

There is an argument that, rather than applying the pre-1925 rules, the personal representatives should apply the rules in section 34(3) of the Administration of Estates Act 1925, on the payment of debts, to paying the legacies. These rules are outlined at page 205.

If the personal representatives find themselves in this position of uncertainty, and cannot resolve it by agreement with the beneficiaries, they would be well advised to seek direction from the court.

Inheritance Tax on Gifts

The personal representatives should ascertain whether each gift is "free of" or "subject to" any inheritance tax payable on it. If the Will does not specify, the gift is deemed to be free of inheritance tax. Whether or not a gift bears its own tax is important, as it determines whether the inheritance tax payable on the legacy is deducted from the legacy itself or from the residue. This also affects the total amount of inheritance tax payable. The rules regarding the calculation and grossing up of legacies are complex and a detailed consideration of them is outside the scope of this book; a brief summary of the more usual situations is given below.

Legacies within nil rate band; residue exempt
Here no grossing-up calculations are required as there is no inheritance tax to pay.

Legacies exceed nil rate band, subject to tax; residue exempt
Here the inheritance tax payable on the legacies is deducted from them before they are paid to the beneficiaries. For example, Bob leaves an estate worth £855,000 in total, with £355,000 to his daughter Claire subject to tax and the residue to his wife Sarah. The nil rate band of £255,000 is deducted from the legacy to Claire, leaving a taxable legacy of £100,000, upon which Claire must pay inheritance tax at 40 per cent, which equals £40,000. Claire receives £315,000 after tax. Sarah receives £500,000.

Legacies exceed nil rate band, free of tax; residue exempt
In these circumstances the legacy must be grossed up and the inheritance tax payable is deducted from the residue before it is paid out. Using the example above, the gift to Claire must be grossed up, so that after paying the inheritance tax on it, Claire is left with £355,000. The taxable part of the legacy is grossed up (multiplied by 100/60) and added back to the value of the legacy before this is deducted from the residue of his estate. So £100,000 x 100/60 + £255,000 = £421,666. Inheritance of £66,666 is payable. Claire receives £355,000 and Sarah receives £433,334.

Legacies within or exceeding the nil rate band, subject to tax; residue taxable
Here no grossing up of the legacies is required because the entire estate is taxable.

Legacies within or exceeding the nil rate band, free of tax; residue taxable
Again, no grossing up of the legacies is required because the entire estate is taxable.

The Will may provide for combinations of the situations mentioned above, where the legacies are a mixture of those bearing their own tax and those free of tax, or where the residue is partially taxable and partially exempt.

Receipts
The personal representatives should always be careful to obtain a receipt from any beneficiary following the payment of a legacy to him, to avoid any question of whether or not the legacy has been paid in full.

Chapter 19

The Distribution of the Residue

Before distributing the residue of the deceased's estate the personal representatives should take careful steps to ascertain the nature of each residuary beneficiary's interest. Like legacies (see page 212), interests in residue can be vested, contingent or conditional. They can fail in the same ways as have been described above (page 215 *et seq*). If a gift of any part of residue under a Will fails in its entirety, that part of residue passes according to the rules of intestacy.

Creation of a Will Trust or Trust on Intestacy

Legacies and shares in residue can be held in trust. A detailed discussion of the different types of trust is beyond the scope of this book, but a short summary of the main types of trust is given below.

Interest in possession (or life interest) trusts

This arrangement gives a certain person, or class of persons, the right to take the trust income for a certain period of time, such as the person's lifetime, or until a certain event happens, such as marriage. On the expiration of that period of time or the happening of the event, the life interest terminates and the assets in the trust pass to the remaindermen outright, or into a further trust for them.

This type of trust is generally used where the deceased wished a certain person to benefit from his estate for the rest of that person's life, but wanted to ensure that the capital would pass elsewhere in the long term. A common example of the circumstances in which a life trust is established is where a husband and wife have both been previously married and wish to protect the capital in their estates for the children of their first marriages. They may choose to leave the residue of their estates on a life interest trust for the survivor of them, with the capital passing to the children from the first marriage upon the death of the survivor.

The intestacy rules also create a life interest trust for the surviving spouse when the deceased died intestate with a free estate of over £125,000, and was survived by a spouse and issue.

Discretionary trusts

A discretionary trust can have a wide class of beneficiaries, none of whom has a right to take anything from the trust. The decision as to who is allocated income or capital from the trust is left to the trustees, who are often guided by a letter of wishes written by the deceased during his lifetime. Such a letter is not binding, but provides assistance to the trustees in understanding why the trust was created.

This type of trust is often found in the context of inheritance tax planning for a husband and wife. Their Wills may provide for the creation of a discretionary trust on the death of the first of them to die, to hold assets to the value of the nil rate band. In this manner, the survivor can be a beneficiary of the discretionary trust and thus take a benefit from the assets in the trust during his lifetime, without the trust assets falling into that person's estate for inheritance tax purposes upon that person's death.

Further, section 144, Inheritance Tax Act 1984 provides that where property is settled by the deceased's Will on a discretionary trust, distributions from that trust within two years of the deceased's death are "read back" for inheritance tax purposes into the Will as though they were distributions made under it. In this manner, the deceased can leave his entire estate into such a trust and allow the trustees of the trust flexibility to distribute his estate as they see fit, depending on the circumstances at his death, without losing the possibility of invoking the surviving spouse or charity exemptions. This type of trust can be more useful than relying on a deed of variation or disclaimer to alter the distribution of the estate after the testator's death, because any minor or incapacitated beneficiaries would not be able to give their consent to such documents.

Accumulation and maintenance trusts

To some extent, accumulation and maintenance trusts are a hybrid of discretionary and interest in possession trusts. Accumulation and maintenance trusts have many of the characteristics of a discretionary trust, but more favourable tax consequences, although the rules on their use and operation are restrictive and complex. They are often used by a grandparent wishing to benefit his grandchildren. They provide for a class of beneficiaries of the trust, the constitution of which is restricted by section 71, Inheritance Tax Act 1984. While each beneficiary is under a specified age, generally 25, the trustees can choose how to allocate income and capital between the class of beneficiaries. Once a beneficiary has attained the specified age, he either becomes absolutely entitled to his share of the trust assets, or the assets are held on a life interest trust for him.

Protective trusts

A protective trust may be created pursuant to section 33 of the Trustee Act 1925. This provides that a specified person may have a life interest in the trust until an event occurs that would deprive the beneficiary of the right to the income from the trust, for example, he becomes bankrupt or attempts to sell his life interest. In that situation, the life interest trust automatically terminates and the trust becomes discretionary in nature. The class of discretionary beneficiaries is listed in the section, and comprises the beneficiary, his spouse, children and remoter issue.

This type of trust is generally used where the deceased doubted the intended beneficiary's financial wisdom, and wished to protect the beneficiary's interest in the trust fund no matter what the beneficiary's own financial position might be in the future.

What to Distribute

The deceased's estate usually comprises all types of asset, including cash, shares and land. Some of these assets must be liquidated to pay the debts, the tax due on the estate, and any legacies. The remaining assets are the residue. It is rare that the residue consists solely of a sum of money. The personal representatives must decide whether to sell the deceased's assets and make a cash transfer of the residue, or appropriate assets *in specie*. The decision is governed in part by their powers. Section 41, Administration of Estates Act 1925 gives the personal representatives power to appropriate assets to a beneficiary only with that beneficiary's consent (see page 197). Most modern Wills, however, extend this power to allow personal representatives to appropriate assets to a beneficiary at their discretion.

No beneficiary has a right to any asset in the residue of the deceased's estate – they have only a *chose in action* to ensure that the estate is properly administered. It is, though, good practice to consult the residuary beneficiaries and find out what their preferences are; indeed, section 11, Trusts of Land and Appointment of Trustees Act 1996 imposes a duty on personal representatives, where the estate comprises land, to consult beneficiaries of an estate as to their wishes regarding the administration of the estate, and to give effect to those wishes so far as possible. This can be unduly onerous, and is often excluded by a Will.

The fact that the personal representatives can or do consult the residuary beneficiaries does not oblige them to comply with the beneficiaries' wishes. In *Lloyds Bank v Duker* [1987] 1 WLR 1324, [1987] 3 All ER 193 the deceased held 999 shares in a private limited company. One of the residuary beneficiaries had been bequeathed 46/80 of the estate, the remainder being split between a number or other beneficiaries. It was held that the beneficiary taking the largest proportion of the estate could not compel the personal representatives to transfer 574 of those shares to him, where the personal representatives were of the opinion that to appropriate that number of shares to him would be to confer a much greater benefit than the transfer of the sale proceeds of 574 shares would do.

Value for Appropriation

If an asset is to be appropriated *in specie*, the value for administration purposes is the value of the asset at the date on which the appropriation takes place, not the probate value. This is less important where assets are being appropriated to all the residuary beneficiaries as the position should be roughly equal between them. Where, however, the personal representatives are selling assets on behalf of one beneficiary but appropriating similar assets to a different beneficiary, the value is crucial. In this situation, to ensure equality, the date of appropriation should generally be taken to be the same as the date of sale.

For example, the deceased's residuary estate comprises £10,000 and 500 shares in ABC plc. At the date of death, the shares are worth £20 each, giving a total value of £10,000. The residue is split equally between Bob and Jim. Bob would like his proportion of the shares in ABC plc *in specie,* but Jim would like the cash proceeds of sale and instructs the personal representatives to sell 250 shares on his behalf. They are sold for £10 per share. If the appropriation value were taken to be the same as the probate value, Bob would receive 250 shares worth £5,000 (at probate prices), and Jim would receive the sale proceeds – £2,500. Jim would then be "compensated" by giving him £2,500 in cash, and the remaining £7,500 would be split between them – £3,750 each. The value of assets in Bob's possession would actually be shares worth £2,500 and cash of £3,750, giving him £6,250 in total. However, Jim would have £8,750 in cash. Had the shares been appropriated to Bob at the same value as Jim's shares were sold, Jim would not have received any "compensation" and thus their positions would have been equal.

The Will should be studied carefully – it may allow personal representatives to appropriate assets at probate value, at the value at the date of appropriation, or at any other value they deem suitable, although this does not detract from the personal representatives' obligation to treat the residuary beneficiaries equally, which cannot be achieved if unfair appropriation values are used.

Treating the Beneficiaries Equally

The above point demonstrates the importance of treating the residuary beneficiaries equally. There may be a problem where one beneficiary wishes to receive one entire asset held by the deceased and another beneficiary wishes to receive an entirely different asset. For example, the deceased held two plots of land, Bluefield and Redfield. Both were valued at £10,000 for the purposes of probate. The residue of the deceased's estate is to be divided equally between Mary and Susan. Technically, each piece of land ought to be assented to them jointly. However, if Mary wishes to receive Bluefield and Susan wishes to receive Redfield the personal representatives can choose to appropriate one piece of land to each of them.

If Bluefield had instead been worth £12,000, Mary would be receiving more than her fair share of the estate. If there is no cash in the estate with which to compensate Susan, Mary can still receive Bluefield but she must purchase part of it from the estate for £2,000. That £2,000 is then divided equally between herself and Susan as residuary beneficiaries. This operates as a partial disposal by the personal representatives for capital gains tax and stamp duty purposes.

Time for Distribution

When dealing with the residue of an estate, the personal representatives should not wait until they have ascertained the exact *quantum* that each beneficiary will receive, before making a distribution. Administering an estate can be a lengthy affair and it is good practice to make interim distributions to the residuary beneficiaries as soon as possible. On the other hand, the personal representatives should not allow themselves to be pressured into transferring too much or too early. It is preferable to distribute on a small scale as and when possible, than to make a large distribution and then have to ask the residuary beneficiaries to return some money because an unexpected debt has been discovered. The personal representatives should be concerned to distribute to each residuary beneficiary the same amount at the same time, unless all the beneficiaries agree otherwise. A fair balance must be kept between all beneficiaries at all times.

Before any interim distribution is made it is good practice to prepare a first set of estate accounts. This gives the personal representatives a good picture of the financial situation of the estate and highlights any outstanding issues.

If the residuary beneficiary is not yet entitled to his interest in residue absolutely as against the personal representatives, no distribution should be made unless the personal representatives are certain they have the power to do so; the asset may instead need to be held by trustees (see below).

To Whom the Residue is Distributed

If the residuary beneficiary is absolutely entitled, the distribution can be made to him directly. If the residue passes into trust, the personal representatives must pass the assets to the trustees named in the Will or arising under the intestacy. If no trustees were specifically appointed (and if in the case of a minor, the parent or guardian is not permitted to give a valid receipt), section 42 of the Administration of Estates Act 1925 allows a trust corporation or two individuals to be appointed as trustees of residue and for the personal representatives to receive a full discharge from their responsibilities relating to the assets held in trust.

Making the Distribution

Making the distribution requires the personal representatives to decide how title to each asset is to pass. There are two types of interest to be transferred, beneficial and legal. A beneficial interest in any asset can be transferred by the execution of a simple assent of beneficial interest by the personal representatives. For assets other than land, an assent is a resolution signed by the personal representatives evidencing their intention to transfer the beneficial ownership in the stated asset to the relevant beneficiary. To convey a beneficial interest in land, the personal representatives must execute a deed.

Following an assent, the personal representatives hold the legal title as bare trustees for the beneficiary entitled. If an asset is to be sold, but it has been decided, for capital gains tax purposes, that the sale is to be made by the beneficiary rather than by the personal representatives, the personal representatives need only assent the asset to the beneficiary and then sell as bare trustees for him; they do not need to transfer the legal title to the asset to him as well.

If the personal representatives are to act as trustees of an interest in residue, they must evidence this change in the nature of their ownership by completing some form of document, so that the date upon which the asset concerned became held in trust can easily be identified. In the case of land, the document required is an assent (see below); in the case of other assets, the personal representatives may make a simple resolution listing the assets passing to them as trustees.

The method of transferring legal title in an asset depends on the nature of the asset, and takes effect as a transfer of the beneficial interest if that has not already been dealt with, unless a contrary intention appears in the document effecting the transfer. For capital gains tax purposes, a transfer is read back as though it occurred at the date of death (section 62(1), Taxation of Chargeable Gains Act 1992).

Transferring Legal Title

Land

Land is transferred using a land registry form AS1 (Assent of whole of registered title(s)). Section 36(4) of the Administration of Estates Act 1925 provides that the transfer of title to land must be in writing, signed by the personal representatives, and must name the person in whose favour it is given. A notice of the assent should be endorsed on the grant of representation; the assentee is entitled to insist on this (section 36(5), Administration of Estates Act 1925). If no notice of assent is endorsed on the grant, a *bona fide* purchaser for value of the land takes the land free of any assentee's interest. A purchaser buying land from an assentee is likewise permitted to rely on the assent as proper evidence of the assentee's entitlement to the land.

Shares

Shares are transferred using a stock transfer form (or "Crest" transfer form if the legal title to them is in the name of a nominee).

Bank and building society accounts

Cash held in bank and building society accounts is transferred by the completion of the appropriate form supplied by the bank or building society, or by the personal representatives submitting their own written authorisation.

National Savings investments

Prescribed forms for transferring national savings products should be obtained from National Savings and are simple to use.

Chattels

Chattels can generally be transferred by simple delivery, although some chattels, such as cars, have registration documents that should be completed. If chattels are particularly valuable it is suggested that an assent is completed as formal evidence of the transfer.

It is good practice for all the personal representatives to sign any transfer, and this is generally required by the transferring institutions in any event.

Taxation of Residue

If the residue of the deceased's estate passes entirely to exempt, or entirely to non-exempt, beneficiaries, calculating the inheritance tax payable should be simple. If, on the other hand, the residue is divided between exempt and non-exempt beneficiaries (see page 74 *et seq*), such as the spouse and children of the deceased, careful attention must be paid to the inheritance tax calculation. Section 41, Inheritance Tax Act 1984 provides that none of the tax payable on a non-exempt share of residue may be borne by the exempt residue.

A Will normally specifies whether the distribution of residue between exempt and non-exempt beneficiaries is to take place before or after the payment of inheritance tax. Where the residue is divided between the beneficiaries and then the tax payable is calculated, the position is relatively simple. But in *Re Benham's Will Trusts* [1995] STC 210 (Ch D) the deceased's Will specified that the exempt and non-exempt beneficiaries should receive the same after the inheritance tax due had been paid. This leads to a circular problem – the amount to be divided cannot be ascertained until the tax has been calculated, but the tax payable cannot be calculated until it is known how much the beneficiaries will receive. The solution is to "gross up" the non-exempt beneficiary's share in residue. This can be a highly complicated calculation, outside the scope of this book. The Inland Revenue website offers practical guidance, and a formula for the grossing up calculation. Very basically, if grossing up takes place, the exempt beneficiary receives less, and the non-exempt beneficiary receives more, than if the residue were divided and then the tax paid.

Often a Will does not state whether the share of each beneficiary is to be calculated by reference to the estate before or after inheritance tax, and the personal representatives do not know what the deceased intended. This was considered in *Re Ratcliffe* [1999] STC 262. The result of the cases is that if the Will is of a standard form, directing the payment of debts, taxes etc., and then the distribution of residue, the residue of the estate is calculated and divided between the beneficiaries in the appropriate shares; and then the inheritance tax payable is ascertained. This means that no grossing up calculations are necessary.

If the Will specifically refers to the *Re Benham* situation or directs that the shares should be calculated only after the inheritance tax has been paid, the residue passing to the non-exempt beneficiary must be grossed up.

If the Will is unclear, the most practical solution is for the personal representatives to ask the beneficiaries to agree the interpretation of the Will. If this is not possible, the *Re Benham* calculation should be prepared. The exempt beneficiary should receive his share of residue on this basis, and the non-exempt beneficiary should be given what he would receive if grossing up were not undertaken (i.e., each beneficiary receives that which would be payable to him under the least favourable scenario). Inheritance tax should be paid as though *Re Benham* does not apply (which gives the lesser of the two amounts of inheritance tax payable), and the rest of the money in the estate should be retained until the court has decided how the Will should be interpreted, and thus how much inheritance tax is payable and how much each residuary beneficiary should receive.

Practical Points

Receipts
As in the case of legacies, a residuary beneficiary should always be asked to provide a receipt for all distributions made to him.

Accounts
As mentioned above, the personal representatives should prepare a set of interim accounts before the first interim distribution is made. Ideally, copies should be given to the residuary beneficiaries so they can see how the administration of the estate is progressing. They will also be able to raise any queries regarding assets during the course of the administration rather than at the end, which should help avoid delay. Once the administration of the estate has been finalised and the final distribution is made to the residuary beneficiaries, they should each be asked to sign a set of estate accounts (see page 245) and return them to the personal representatives as evidence that they fully understand and approve of how the estate has been administered.

Capital gains tax
If assets in the estate are to be sold, the simplest course is usually for the personal representatives to sell them and divide the proceeds. This may not, however, have the most advantageous capital gains tax consequences. Capital gains tax in the context of the administration of the estate is discussed in Chapter 21. The personal representatives need to consider whether better use could be made of the beneficiaries' annual capital gains tax exemptions if assets were to be appropriated to beneficiaries and sold by them, rather than being sold by the personal representatives. This is particularly important if the residuary beneficiary is a charity. Charities do not pay capital gains tax on gains realised on assets sold by them, but personal representatives do. Likewise, a beneficiary may intend to move into property which comprises part of the estate, in which case it may be possible for the "principal private residence" exemption to apply on any gain made on any future sale of the property by the beneficiary in residence.

Chapter 20

Finalising Liability to Inheritance Tax

The inheritance tax calculated as due when form IHT200 is originally submitted (see page 60) is unlikely to be the same as the amount finally payable. There can be many reasons for this – the value of an asset as originally submitted may transpire to be higher or lower than first thought; assets may be discovered that were not known about at the outset of the administration; or assets may be sold for less than their original valuation.

Discovery of Further Assets
As mentioned elsewhere, if, during the course of the estate administration, an asset is discovered to have belonged to the deceased of which the personal representatives were previously unaware, they should take steps to notify IR Capital Taxes as soon as possible, to avoid any penalty being imposed. A valuation of the asset as at the date of death should be produced quickly, and it is recommended that any extra inheritance tax payable is forwarded to IR Capital Taxes at the same time as they are notified of the asset, to avoid any criticism of the personal representatives. Notification can be by way of letter; a new account or corrective account need not be filed.

Updating the Values of Assets
Occasionally it becomes apparent that the value of an asset as originally submitted on form IHT200 was incorrect, or a provisional valuation may need to be updated. If so, the personal representatives should again notify IR Capital Taxes by way of letter as soon as possible and pay any additional inheritance tax.

Where new assets are discovered, or their values are updated, with the result that extra inheritance tax is payable, interest is also due if the time for paying the tax has passed.

Filing a Corrective Account
As an alternative to notifying IR Capital Taxes of changes in the value of

assets or the discovery of further assets by letter, the personal representatives may complete a corrective account, form C4, and forward it to IR Capital Taxes. This may be useful if the changes are discovered towards the end of the administration and the personal representatives believe that once IR Capital Taxes has been notified of the changes, the inheritance tax position will be finalised.

On the other hand, it may be inappropriate to file several corrective accounts. Therefore, if alterations are discovered some time before the administration of the estate has been finalised, it is simpler to keep IR Capital Taxes appraised of those changes by letter. This minimises the interest on the additional inheritance tax due, by paying the tax as quickly as possible, and reduces the likelihood that IR Capital Taxes will seek to impose a penalty for failing to declare the alteration as early as possible.

In addition, for a solicitor appointed to act on behalf of the personal representatives it is administratively more convenient to send a letter to IR Capital Taxes than to prepare a corrective account, circulate it to the personal representatives for signature and then forward it to IR Capital Taxes.

Loss on Sale of Shares

Section 179, Inheritance Tax Act 1984 allows for relief from inheritance tax where "qualifying investments" are sold within twelve months of the date of death for a price lower than the probate value. If the relief is allowed, the price for which the investments were sold becomes the value upon which inheritance tax payable is calculated. This means that the personal representatives may reclaim any excess inheritance tax paid. In addition, the sale price becomes the base cost of the shares for capital gains tax purposes.

"Qualifying investments" are defined in section 178(1) as quoted shares or securities, holdings in an authorised unit trust, and shares in a common investment fund.

The relevant date of sale is the date on which the sale is agreed, not the date on which the purchase monies are paid over. If the sale is pursuant to an option, the sale date is the date the option was granted (section 189, Inheritance Tax Act 1984).

However, the relief is available only if all the qualifying investments sold within the twelve month period have produced an overall loss – the personal representatives cannot pick and choose the investments in respect of which they wish to claim the relief.

The expenses of sale and other items, such as stamp duty, cannot be taken into account – the prices compared must be the gross probate value as against the gross selling price. Interest on loan stock is taken into account as part of the sale price or probate value, but the value of a dividend if the share was "ex-dividend" at the date of death or sale is not.

If a holding is cancelled within twelve months of the date of death, the personal representatives are treated as though they made a sale of the holding for the nominal consideration of £1 per share (section 186A, Inheritance Tax Act 1984).

If the holding, when sold, is not the same as it was at the date of death, for example because of a re-organisation, sales are dealt with as provided in sections 181 to 184 of the Act. Obviously, if all the new holdings have been sold, the position is broadly the same as if the shares held at the date of death were sold. It becomes more complicated if not all the new shareholdings are disposed of.

The relief is limited if the personal representatives purchase shares in the same company any time before the expiry of two months after the last sale has taken place (section 180, Inheritance Tax Act 1984).

To claim the relief, the "appropriate person" must complete form IHT35 (Claim for relief – loss on sale of shares). The "appropriate person" is the person paying the inheritance tax – usually the personal representatives. The form must be signed by that person, not someone acting on his behalf.

The personal representatives must be careful about when to complete the form. It should not be filed within twelve months of the date of death unless all the deceased's investments have been sold and the personal representatives are certain they are in a position to make the claim. If the form is submitted within the twelve month period and not all the qualifying investments have been sold, the relief granted is provisional until that twelve month date has passed.

If the personal representatives have suffered a loss within the twelve months from the date of death and they want to claim relief, they should defer the crystallisation of any other sales that will produce a gain until after the twelve months have expired.

Even if a relievable loss has arisen, the personal representatives should consider whether they would prefer to set it against gains on the sale of other assets, such as the deceased's house, to mitigate the capital gains tax due. It is suggested that the personal representatives consider all the possible tax permutations and calculate the tax payable and repayable in the different scenarios before taking a final decision.

Loss Relief on the Sale of a Property

Relief from liability to inheritance tax in respect of a loss incurred on selling property operates in a manner similar to that in relation to the sale of qualifying investments, discussed above. It is granted by section 191, Inheritance Tax Act 1984 and applies to the sale of an "interest in land" owned by the deceased. An "interest in land" does not extend to interests in land arising by way of mortgage or other security (section 190).

For the purposes of the relief, a sale is made once contracts are exchanged, unless the sale is made pursuant to an option that was granted within six months of the exchange. In that case, the date of sale is the date the option was granted (section 198).

To qualify for the relief, the sale must be made within three years of the date of death and cannot be to someone with an existing interest in the land sold, the spouse, children or remoter issue of such a person, or the trustees of any trust under which any of the persons listed above has an interest in possession (section 191(3)). If the land was sold pursuant to a compulsory purchase order, the time period is extended indefinitely, providing the notice to treat in relation to the order was served within three years from the date of death (section 197).

For deaths after 15 March 1990, a sale made in the fourth year after death can also be taken into account if it realised a loss compared with the probate value, but not if it realised a gain (section 197A, Inheritance Tax Act 1984).

The values taken into account are the probate value compared with the gross sale price. The expenses of sale are not deductible.

If the person making the claim also buys any interest in the land sold at any time between the date of death and four months from the date of the last sale, that is taken into account for the purposes of the relief, which is then restricted (section 192, Inheritance Tax Act 1984).

If the difference between the sale price and the probate value is smaller than the lesser of £1,000 or 5 per cent of the probate value, the relief cannot be claimed.

If the property sold is a lease with less than 50 years to run, section 194, Inheritance Tax Act 1984 operates to adjust the sale price by reference to the amount of time left to run on the lease.

Again the person who makes the claim and signs the claim form (IHT38, Claim for relief – loss on sale of land), must be the "appropriate person" responsible for the payment of inheritance tax on the land. Relief is available on all sales made within the relevant time period, so the personal representatives should not make the claim within the four year period unless all the deceased's land has been sold already, particularly as the claim cannot be withdrawn once it has been made.

Overpayment or Underpayment

Once any revised values have been submitted and agreed by IR Capital Taxes, the personal representatives may reclaim any overpaid inheritance tax. If the forms IHT35 or 38, or form C4 (Corrective account/inventory), have been submitted, these are automatically treated as applications for repayment of tax, but if IR Capital Taxes has simply been notified of alterations in value by letter, the personal representatives must formally ask for any overpaid inheritance tax to be returned to them. Alternatively, they can wait until they make the application for clearance (see below), which should act as a trigger for IR Capital Taxes to return any outstanding inheritance tax.

In any event, any repayment due that is less than £25 must be specifically applied for within six years of becoming due, or it will not be paid.

When IR Capital Taxes makes a repayment, it is paid with interest, at the same rate as that payable on an underpayment of inheritance tax. For income tax purposes, however, the repayment is not income in the hands of the personal representatives and so is not liable to income tax.

If the personal representatives have not paid enough inheritance tax, but they have received a clearance certificate, or the amount underpaid is small (a decision made by IR Capital Taxes case by case), or more than six years have passed since the later of the date for payment or the date upon which payment was made, IR Capital Taxes cannot claim any further payment of inheritance tax (section 240, Inheritance Tax Act 1984). But if underpayment is a result of fraud, wilful default or neglect by the person liable to pay the tax, the period of six years does not begin to run until that fraud, wilful default or neglect came to the attention of IR Capital Taxes.

Double Tax Treaties

A detailed consideration of double tax treaties is outside the scope of this book. But if the estate qualifies for relief under a double tax treaty, or the unilateral relief given by the Inheritance Tax Act 1984 in relation to foreign property (see page 73), it may be possible to reclaim UK inheritance tax which has been paid. Such a claim is usually made by letter to IR Capital Taxes.

Clearance Certificate

Once the personal representatives are satisfied that they have paid all the inheritance tax due in relation to the estate, they can make an application for clearance under section 239, Inheritance Tax Act 1984. The application is made on form IHT30 (Application for a clearance certificate), which must be signed by each of the personal representatives and sent in duplicate to IR Capital Taxes. If IR Capital Taxes agrees that all the inheritance tax due has been paid, both copies of the certificate are stamped and one is returned to the personal representatives.

If tax on instalment option property is outstanding, an application for clearance can be made only in relation to non-instalment option property,

Once the certificate is given, the personal representatives cannot be held liable for any further inheritance tax in relation to the property comprised in the application for clearance, and nor can anyone else, unless:

- there was fraud or failure to disclose material facts;
- any further property comes to light; or
- any extra inheritance tax becomes payable as a result of a deed of variation or other variation of the estate under section 142, Inheritance Tax Act 1984 (see page 262).

It is always advisable to obtain a clearance certificate on behalf of the personal representatives; they can then proceed to make the final distributions from the estate in the knowledge that there will be no further inheritance tax demands made of them.

Life tenancies

Problems can arise if the deceased was the life tenant of an interest in possession trust. The assets in the trust form part of the deceased's estate for inheritance tax purposes, and the nil rate band is apportioned between the free estate and the trust. This means that as the value of the estate alters, so the proportion of the nil rate band allocated to the estate changes. An application by the personal representatives for clearance of the free estate cannot be examined until an application by the trustees has been made, as the two tax situations are linked. The consequence is that one party may be delayed in the distribution of the trust or estate, if the other party is slower in making its application. There is very little that can be done about this and the beneficiaries may simply have to be patient.

If clearance has been given to both the trust and the estate, and then a further asset is discovered – say in relation to the trust – the overall inheritance tax payable by the trust is increased, but so is the nil rate band allocated to the trust, and so the inheritance tax due by the estate is greater. IR Capital Taxes deals with matters such as these case by case. It may be persuaded to write off the additional inheritance tax payable by the estate if it is small, or the personal representatives may be willing to pay the tax due if they still hold estate funds. Alternatively, the trustees may be persuaded to pay the entire additional inheritance tax since they are at fault. The trust beneficiaries might be dissatisfied and might seek to raise a claim against the trustees if this is the case. Thus, any party applying for a clearance certificate must be as certain as possible that all the outstanding assets have been declared at their correct values before the application is made.

Chapter 21

Taxation During the Administration

There are two elements of income tax and capital gains tax to be paid during the estate administration. The first is the tax due for the period up to the date of death, the second is the tax arising during the period of the administration.

Income and Capital Gains Tax to the Date of Death
As part of the administration process the personal representatives must ascertain whether it is necessary to complete a tax return for the deceased to the date of his death, or to reclaim any overpaid income tax. The deceased's accountant (if he had one) should be able to help. If the deceased did not normally complete a tax return, it is unlikely that the personal representatives need to complete one for the period from 5 April last to the date of death, but they should nevertheless check the income and gains arising during that time. If income or capital gains tax does need to be claimed or repaid, this is a capital liability or asset and must be shown as such on form IHT200 (see Chapter 3).

If a tax return for the period is submitted, and any liability to tax has been established and the amount due paid, the personal representatives should ask the Inland Revenue for written confirmation that their files in relation to the deceased during his lifetime have been closed. This provides the personal representatives with some assurance that there should be no additional liability, unless any income or gains not previously declared to the Inland Revenue come to light.

Income Tax During the Administration
Personal representatives need to keep track of the estate income and gains passing through their hands. If they receive income or realise gains that are taxable, they are required to submit a return for the estate.

Personal representatives pay income tax at the basic rate, no matter how much income they receive. On the other hand they receive no allowances – all income is taxable.

Interest on a loan to pay inheritance tax

If the personal representatives took out a loan to pay the inheritance tax due, any interest payable on that loan during the twelve months from the date on which it was taken out can be deducted from the gross income of the estate for income tax purposes (section 364, Income and Corporation Taxes Act 1988). In the first instance, the interest is deducted from the income arising in the estate in the same tax year. If this is insufficient, it can be set against previous years' income, and if it exceeds that, it can be set against later years' income. This provision applies only to loans taken out to pay inheritance tax; it does not apply to an overdraft used to pay inheritance tax or to interest at a rate greater than a normal commercial rate (section 353, Income and Corporation Taxes Act 1988). Further, it applies only to personal representatives, and to the deceased's personal property alone – not to trustees or trust property. It applies to a loan taken out to pay the inheritance tax due on the initial delivery of the account, but not to any loans taken out to pay any inheritance tax due later, such as on instalment option property (section 364(1)). Further, it does not apply to interest arising on inheritance tax itself, such as where the inheritance tax is paid late (section 233, Inheritance Tax Act).

Apportioned income

If the Apportionment Act 1870 applies to the estate, the income arising within it must be apportioned between capital and income, depending on the period to which it relates. This is discussed in more detail at page 215. The Apportionment Act 1870 does not, however, apply for income tax purposes. This means that the personal representatives may have to pay income tax on that which is actually classed as capital for estate administration purposes.

Bonds

Detailed rules apply to the transfer of bonds, as the income on these assets is treated as accruing from day to day. Interest on a bond is paid to the person in whose name the bond is registered a certain number of days before the interest payment date. This means that if a bond is sold close to the interest payment date, the seller may still receive the entire interest payment, even though he does not own the bond for the final part of that period. Accordingly he should rebate to the purchaser an amount equal to the income arising during the period for which the purchaser owned the bond. Alternatively, if the bond is sold in sufficient time for the purchaser to be registered as the new owner before the next interest payment date, the purchaser would receive some interest that relates to the period during which the seller owned the bond. He may have to pay the seller an amount equal to this accrued income.

The provisions on the sale of bonds are in sections 710 to 738, Income and Corporation Taxes Act 1988. Very briefly, they require that if a bond is sold and the seller has to rebate interest to the purchaser, the seller is entitled to deduct that rebate from the net interest on the bond declared as received by him, and the purchaser must declare this as his own income. Similarly, if the purchaser has to pay accrued income to the seller, the purchaser can deduct this accrued income from the interest on the bond shown on his tax return, but the seller must show it as interest received on his tax return. These provisions apply to personal representatives as to individuals.

Income tax effects for beneficiaries

Situations in which a beneficiary is entitled to income from an estate or from a particular asset are discussed at page 214 *et seq.* Income arising to the estate that is paid to a legatee should always be paid net of basic rate tax, even if the beneficiary is not resident in the UK. In that situation, the beneficiary may reclaim any income tax credited as paid by him. The only circumstance in which payment is made gross is when it is statutory interest on a pecuniary legacy that is being paid more than a year after the deceased's death. Interest is then paid at the gross rate of 6 per cent unless the beneficiary is non-UK resident, when it should be paid net of basic rate tax.

Whenever income is paid to a beneficiary, the personal representatives should also supply the beneficiary with a completed form R185E (Estate income). This is a statement, signed by the personal representatives or someone on their behalf, showing how much income tax has been paid in the estate on the income passed to the beneficiary, and the nature of the income. The beneficiary will need the form when completing his own tax return for the year in which he receives the income from the estate.

Income paid to beneficiaries is usually treated as received by them in the tax year in which it is actually paid. This may not correspond with the tax year when it is received by the estate. The only circumstance in which this principle does not apply is in relation to life interest trusts created within the estate. Where the income is paid to the life tenant, the income is treated as received by him in the same year as it is received by the personal representatives. This is because the life tenant is absolutely entitled under the terms of the trust to receive all the income, even though the assets generating the income may not have been formally appropriated to the trust at that point.

Where a distribution is made to a beneficiary entitled to both income and capital, for example where the beneficiary is absolutely entitled to residue, it is necessary to distinguish between the amount distributed as income and the amount distributed as capital. If income has accrued to the residue and a distribution is made to the residuary beneficiary, that beneficiary is treated as though he received income to the extent of the accrued income within the estate. Any excess of the amount distributed over the amount of the income accrued is treated as a capital distribution. For this reason the personal representatives should, where there is accrued income in the estate, ask the residuary beneficiaries if they have any preference as to the tax year in which a distribution is made.

Tax relief for accrued income

If there was accrued income in the estate at the date of death, for example a dividend on a share that was quoted as "ex-dividend" at the date of death, that accrued income is subject to inheritance tax in the estate. When the income is paid to a beneficiary, if the beneficiary is a higher rate taxpayer, he then pays 40 per cent income tax on the dividend as well. This leads to a double charge to 40 per cent tax. Section 699, Income and Corporation Taxes Act 1988 contains provisions to avoid this double charge arising. To declare this potential double charge to tax, the personal representatives should complete a form 92A (Statement of residuary income). The relief may be claimed only if one of the residuary beneficiaries is a higher rate income tax payer. The relief is given to the personal representatives by a deduction from the residuary income of the estate.

Capital Gains Tax

The personal representatives must pay capital gains tax on any gains accruing on the sale of an asset which forms part of the estate. Their base cost of such an asset is its value at the date of the deceased's death, as agreed with IR Capital Taxes.

Reduction in gain

Inland Revenue Statement of Practice 8/94 sets out an allowance under which the personal representatives may, for capital gains tax purposes, reduce the gain made on the sale of an asset to allow for their administration costs of establishing title to the asset concerned. The amount of reduction allowable depends on the entire value of the estate, as follows:

Gross value of estate	*Reduction allowable*
Less than £40,000	1.75 per cent of the probate value of the asset sold;
£40,001 – £70,000	£700 divided between all the assets sold in proportion to their probate value;
£70,001 – £300,000	1 per cent of the probate value of the asset sold;
£300,001 – £400,000	£3,000 divided between all the assets sold in proportion to their probate value;
£400,001 – £750,000	0.75 per cent of the probate value of the asset sold;
Over £750,000	to be negotiated with the Inland Revenue inspector.

In addition, the costs of ascertaining the market value of the asset at the date of death are deductible from the gain made before the taxable gain is calculated (section 38, Taxation of Chargeable Gains Act 1992). This does not extend to the cost of any negotiation with the Inland Revenue or IR Capital Taxes about the value of the asset.

Rates and allowances

Personal representatives pay capital gains tax at the rate of 34 per cent. They have an annual allowance, the same as any individual, for the remainder of the tax year in which the deceased died, and the following two tax years. After that they have no annual allowance. If possible, therefore, disposals by the estate should be made in the tax year of death and the following two tax years, to ensure that the allowances are fully utilised.

Allowances and exemptions

The sale of an asset by the personal representatives is always a disposal by them, but a transfer to a beneficiary is not. In the latter situation, the base cost at which the beneficiary takes the asset is the market value at the date of the deceased's death. If an asset is appropriated to the beneficiary by reference to a different value, for example as a proportion of residue, the appropriation value has no effect for capital gains tax purposes.

If a gain is to be realised on a sale, the personal representatives should consider whether the gain would be better realised by the beneficiary directly rather than by them. This may be advantageous if the beneficiary is a lower rate taxpayer, or a charity that does not have to pay capital gains tax; if the beneficiary is non-resident; or if the expected gain would fall within the beneficiary's annual allowance.

If the sale of an asset is expected to realise a loss, the personal representatives cannot transfer the loss to the beneficiary; they may set it off only against gains made during the course of the administration of the estate. They may therefore be better off appropriating the asset to a beneficiary and allowing the beneficiary to realise the loss in his personal capacity so that he can set it off against his personal gains.

Personal representatives are entitled to taper relief on an asset in the same manner as an individual, the amount of the gain subject to capital gains tax reducing the longer the asset has been held. The period of ownership commences with the date of death. If the asset is transferred to an individual, the transferee is also entitled to taper relief, and again the qualifying period commences with the date of death. The personal representatives should, though, consider whether the asset would qualify as a business asset either in their hands or the beneficiary's – it may be more or less advantageous for them, rather than the beneficiary, to dispose of the asset, as business assets accrue relief more quickly than non-business assets.

Agreeing a valuation

If the personal representatives need to fill in a capital gains tax return, they should complete form SA905 (Trust and estate capital gains), in addition to completing the estate income tax return. They should tick the relevant box in response to the question whether an estimate or valuation has been used, as the probate value will have been used as the base cost of the asset. The Inland Revenue should accept this as the base cost if it has been accepted by IR Capital Taxes as an accurate value of the asset at the date of death. But a query may arise in relation to an asset that was relieved from tax, either because it qualified for relief (as a business asset, for example) or because the beneficiary (the spouse of the deceased, say) receiving the asset was exempt from inheritance tax. In such a situation IR Capital Taxes may not have enquired in any detail into the market value of the asset at the date of death, and the personal representatives may be concerned that the Inland Revenue will query whether the valuation of the asset at the date of death is correct. To forestall such queries and resolve the issue as soon as possible, the personal representatives may complete a form CG34 (Application for post-transaction valuation check) with details of the asset and the base cost they wish to submit. Although this form may not be completed and submitted until after the disposal of the asset, it does facilitate agreeing the market value of the asset at the date of death as soon as possible, helping to avoid delays in the administration.

The deceased's home

The deceased's home is often of particular concern. It may appreciate in value between the time of the deceased's death and the time of sale. Any gain made on a sale by the personal representatives is subject to capital gains tax and is not exempt from tax simply because it was the deceased's main residence. Further, if the sale price is substantially higher than the probate value, IR Capital Taxes is likely to seek to increase the market value at the date of death. Additional inheritance tax then becomes payable on the increase in probate value, and capital gains tax is calculated by reference to the revised probate value.

If the deceased lived in the property with another person as their joint residence, and the deceased's share in the property passes to that person under the Will, then the beneficiary should qualify for the principal private residence exemption on the property in relation to the deceased's share from the date of death. Any disposal should therefore be made by the beneficiary to ensure that all exemptions are fully utilised. If the co-owner was married to the deceased, the co-owner is in any event treated as though he had owned the property throughout the entire period of the marriage.

If the long term plan is to sell the home, but one of the beneficiaries of the estate is willing and does not have a home of his own, it may be possible for the beneficiary to move into the deceased's home and treat it as his main residence, providing there is nothing in the Will to prevent this. As long as the beneficiary lives there for a reasonable period of time, and treats the property as his principal residence, either he or the personal representatives may then sell the home and claim relief from capital gains tax on the basis of the principal private residence exemption.

Joint ownership deduction
As noted on page 24, if the deceased owned a property in conjunction with a third party, it may be possible for the personal representatives to claim a deduction in the value of the property in the estate for inheritance tax purposes. If such a deduction has been claimed, it is the reduced value that operates as the base cost of the home for the purposes of capital gains tax. The personal representatives should bear in mind the long term capital gains tax consequences when deciding how much to claim by way of such a deduction.

The deceased's chattels
Section 262, Taxation of Chargeable Gains Act 1992 provides that if a chattel is sold for less than £6,000, no capital gains tax is payable on any gain made in relation to that sale. This applies equally to individuals and personal representatives.

Chapter 22

Completing the Administration

Estate Accounts

Section 25 of the Administration of Estates Act 1925 imposes an obligation on personal representatives, when required to do so, to exhibit a full inventory of the estate and render an account of the administration to the court. This obligation is recited in the wording used in the oath sworn by the personal representatives on the application for a grant (see page 153). The effect is that accounts in relation to the deceased's estate must be prepared.

The accounts should be supplied to the residuary beneficiaries as a matter of good practice, so that they can examine how their entitlement has been calculated. The case of *In Re Tillott, Lee v Wilson* [1892] 1 Ch 86 (Ch D) confirms that all beneficiaries and creditors are entitled to inspect the accounts free of charge upon request. It is not necessary to supply a copy of the accounts to any creditor or non-residuary beneficiary unless they specifically ask for it.

If the personal representatives are uncooperative in supplying a copy of the accounts to those entitled, a beneficiary can issue an originating summons under the Non-Contentious Probate Rules 1987, rule 61(2), for an order that the accounts be prepared by the personal representatives and submitted to court for examination.

Personal representatives often seem daunted by the prospect of creating a set of accounts. The key is to keep full records of all transactions throughout the estate administration. It is advisable to start drafting the accounts as soon as possible, and not to wait until towards the end of the administration. Firstly, it is much easier to add to the accounts as time goes on, and, secondly, the residuary beneficiaries are often keen to see interim accounts, to give them a rough idea of what their final entitlement will be. An example of a set of accounts relating to a straightforward estate is given at pages 249–250.

Accounts can be an extremely valuable tool in the swift and accurate administration of an estate if they are prepared and used correctly. The four main sections in an accurate set of accounts are listed below.

The capital account

The capital account should show the original market value of each asset at the date of death, together with any increase or decrease in this value when sold or appropriated. For the sake of simplicity, shares (or properties, if there are several) should be shown on a separate schedule and the total carried forward to the capital account.

The deceased's liabilities at the date of death should be shown, together with any liabilities charged against capital arising during the estate administration, including inheritance tax and capital gains tax. The net total of the capital assets must be sub-totalled and carried forward to the distribution account.

The income account

The income account should show all the income due to the estate during the administration. It may also be helpful to confirm the income tax paid on each element of the income, as this can be useful when completing forms R185E (see page 248). It is helpful to separate the income between the various tax years in which it arose, to assist when filling in the estate tax return. Again, different types of income, such as dividend income or rents, should be shown on supporting schedules and carried forward to the income account. Whether or not the Apportionment Act 1870 has been excluded (see page 215) affects the division of notional income between the capital and income accounts of the estate.

Expenses charged against income and income tax payable should be deducted from income, to give the net amount of income carried forward to the distribution account. Examples of the charges that may be raised against income are:

- interest on inheritance tax,
- interest on loans taken out to pay inheritance tax and legacies;
- the cost of running repairs to real property;
- rents and utility bills arising after the deceased's death.

The distribution account

The distribution account shows how all the assets in the estate have been distributed. The first entry should be the total of the capital and income accounts – the overall value of the estate.

From this total are deducted the legacies, so that the amount falling into residue can be established. Finally, the residue is shown as apportioned between the residuary beneficiaries, with the value of interim payments, together with their nature (cash, land appropriated etc.), and the date of each distribution.

The balance sheet

It is not vital to include a balance sheet but it can be useful for checking the accuracy of the accounts as the administration progresses. One half of the balance sheet comprises the sub-total of the capital and income accounts combined, to show the net value of the estate. The other half shows the value of the estate that has already been distributed, together with the value of the assets remaining in the personal representatives' hands awaiting distribution or liquidation. The two halves should equal each other.

Items to be included in the accounts
It is a matter of preference for the personal representatives whether the accounts include all the estate assets, or only those that actually pass through their hands. Incorporating in the accounts joint assets passing by survivorship can give a fuller picture of the estate, but since the personal representatives have no access to such an asset nor any real control over it, it may be simpler to leave it out.

Again, it is a matter for the personal representatives to decide whether they wish simply to provide a basic set of accounts or whether they prefer a fuller document, perhaps including the deceased's full name, address, dates of birth and death, together with a summary of the provisions of the Will.

The Final Distribution

The final distribution should not be made until the administration of the estate has been completely finished. This is the time at which the personal representatives divest themselves of the last of the monies in the estate and therefore they must be certain they have no further obligations to meet. There are various checks that the personal representatives should make before they make the final distribution.

Inheritance tax clearance certificate
If inheritance tax was payable in relation to the estate, IR Capital Taxes should be asked to supply a clearance certificate to confirm that all outstanding inheritance tax has been paid. If inheritance tax is still due in relation to instalment option property, a certificate can still be applied for in relation to the non-instalment option assets.

If an Inland Revenue account was submitted, but no inheritance tax was due on the estate, the personal representatives should send a form D19 to IR Capital Taxes for stamping and return. This confirms that no inheritance tax was payable.

Indemnity from beneficiaries
If, as mentioned above, there remains instalment option property on which inheritance tax is being paid by instalments, and the assets are being transferred to the beneficiaries, the personal representatives need to ensure

that the beneficiaries will meet the future inheritance tax due. They should do this by obtaining the signatures of the relevant beneficiaries to an agreement that binds them to pay all future inheritance tax due on the instalment option property and confirms that they indemnify the personal representatives against any claims in respect of that inheritance tax.

Closure of Inland Revenue records

The Inland Revenue should be asked for written confirmation that they have closed their records in relation to the deceased's income and capital gains tax affairs, and also those of the estate. This is again to protect the personal representatives against future tax claims in relation to the deceased or his estate.

Discharge of debts

The personal representatives should double check that they have discharged all outstanding debts of the deceased or the estate. They should ensure that the final distribution is not made within the two months that must elapse to obtain protection under section 27, Trustee Act 1925 (see page 256) and that any claims made pursuant to the advertisement have been investigated and paid where due.

Inheritance claims

Under the Inheritance (Provision for Family and Dependants) Act 1975, anyone wishing to make a claim for financial provision from the deceased's estate must bring the claim within six months of the date the grant is issued. If the personal representatives anticipate such a claim, they would be wise not to make any distributions from the estate within that six month timescale. In any event, it may be unwise for the estate to be fully distributed within such a period.

Expenses and fees

The personal representatives must ensure they have recouped all out-of-pocket expenses and professional fees before the final distribution is made. The fees of a solicitor or other professional person acting on their behalf should also be reserved from the final amount to be distributed.

Documents to accompany the final distribution

As mentioned above, any beneficiary receiving income from an estate should be supplied with a form R185E, confirming the gross income paid to him, together with the income tax deducted therefrom during the final tax year of the administration.

Each residuary beneficiary should be supplied with a set of final estate accounts. The residuary beneficiaries should each be asked to sign a form confirming that they accept the accounts as correct and have received the entirety of their entitlements from the estate. Some beneficiaries are conscientious and sign and return these forms upon receipt; others may be less diligent. This should not trouble the personal representatives too greatly; if a beneficiary cashes the final cheque sent to him and does not contact the personal representatives with any query in relation to it, he is estopped from raising any issues regarding that distribution. On the other hand, the personal representatives may be concerned about not hearing from a beneficiary, particularly if the beneficiary has been troublesome or uncooperative during the administration. In such a situation the personal representatives may prefer to send the form to the beneficiary for signature, along with the final accounts, explaining that as soon as they receive back the signed documents, they will send a cheque in settlement of the outstanding sum due. This can slightly prolong the administration of the estate, and does lead to a little more work for the personal representatives, but may be wise in the long run.

Sample Estate Accounts

Donald Smith dies leaving various assets, including his house at 2 Moss Street, valued at £100,000. This is sold for £108,700. He left his shares in HSBC to his nephew Derek Smith, and the residue of his estate equally between his daughter Susie and his son Neville.

CAPITAL ACCOUNT

Assets	£	£
2 Moss Street	100,000	
Plus gain on sale	8,700	
Abbey National account	150,000	
National Savings certificates	20,000	
HSBC plc shares	5,000	
		283,700

Liabilities		
Pre-death:		
Credit card	444	
Electricity bill	56	
Post-death		
Council tax	100	
Funeral	2,000	
Inheritance tax	9,800	
Capital gains tax	340	
	12,740	
Carried forward to Distribution Account		<u>270,960</u>

INCOME ACCOUNT

	£	£
Interest on Abbey National account	500	
Dividend on HSBC shares	30	
		530
Less interest on loan to pay inheritance tax	400	
Carried forward to distribution account		130

DISTRIBUTION ACCOUNT

	£	£
Carried forward from Capital Account		270,960
Carried forward from Income Account		130
Total		271,090

Distributed as to:
Derek Smith

HSBC plc shares	5,000	
plus dividend	30	
		5,030

Residue:
Susie Smith (one half)

Interim payment (21 January 2003)	75,000	
		75,000

Neville Smith (one half)

Interim payment (21 January 2003)	75,000	
		75,000
Amount remaining to be distributed		116,060

BALANCE SHEET

Amount remaining to be distributed	116,060
Made up as to:	
Solicitors Client Account	116,060

Chapter 23

Claims By and Against the Estate

Various types of claim may be made by and against a deceased's estate. Some of the more common claims are considered in this chapter.

If a claim is brought by or against the estate, the personal representatives have the power, under section 15(c), Trustee Act 1925, to "pay or allow any debt or claim on any evidence that he or they think sufficient". In addition, under section 15(f), the personal representatives may "compromise, compound, abandon, submit to arbitration, or otherwise settle any debt, account, claim, or thing whatever relating to the testator's or intestate's estate". A compromise made by one personal representative binds all of them. The section goes on to provide that no personal representative is responsible for any loss occasioned in relation to any act or thing done by him (which includes compromising a claim), providing that he has complied with the duty of care set out in section 1(1) to the Trustee Act 2000 (see page 202). That duty of care calls for a conscious decision by the personal representatives; it is not sufficient for the personal representatives to say they decided not to pursue a matter if in fact they simply failed to consider it properly.

Having said this, personal representatives should, to avoid any complaint against them, liaise with the residuary beneficiaries wherever possible regarding the most appropriate form of defence to a claim, or whether to continue to prosecute an action. Litigation can be extremely expensive and personal representatives are well advised to weigh up the potential cost against the likely benefits. They can also be required to act as a "cool head of reason", where one or more beneficiaries expresses a wish to pursue a claim to obtain "justice", particularly if this may be at the expense of the residuary estate.

If the personal representatives reach a compromise of any claim by or against the estate, they would be wise to obtain an indemnity from the beneficiaries of full age and capacity that no personal representative will be pursued in respect of that compromise at any later time. In any event, personal representatives should take professional legal advice when bringing or defending an action, to ensure that their actions are reasonable.

Claims in Relation to the Validity of the Will

A third party may bring a claim against the estate on the basis that the Will (or a codicil) was invalid. This could be for several reasons.

Will improperly executed

A Will may be invalid if it was not duly executed; see page 84.

Undue influence

A third party may claim that the deceased was unduly influenced in making his Will. This does not apply where the beneficiary became friends with the deceased in the hope that the deceased would remember him in his Will, but rather where the deceased was forced into making the Will by the actions or persuasion of the beneficiary.

Lack of testamentary capacity

The test for capacity to make a Will was set down in *Banks v Goodfellow* (1870) LR 5 QB 549. The testator must:
- understand the nature and effects of the Will he is making;
- understand the extent of the property that he has to dispose of;
- appreciate the moral claims that may be made on his estate (i.e., the people he ought to provide for).

A Will may be valid if the testator had capacity at the time of giving instructions for the Will to be made, but had lost that capacity by the time he executed the Will (*Parker v Felgate* (1883) 8 PD 171).

Providing that, on the face of it, the Will appears to have been properly executed, by a testator of full capacity acting of his own free will, it is for the third party to prove the claim, not for the personal representatives or beneficiaries to prove that the Will was valid.

Inheritance Act Claims

In England and Wales, everybody has complete freedom of testamentary disposition. This means that the law does not stipulate any class of persons who must benefit from the estate of a deceased. The Inheritance (Provision for Family and Dependants) Act 1975 was introduced to allow a person who believes he ought to have been named as a beneficiary of a deceased's estate, either under the Will or the intestacy rules, to make a claim for financial provision from that estate. The class of potential claimants under the Act is limited by section 1 to:
- the spouse of the deceased;
- a former spouse who has not remarried;
- a person who was cohabiting with the deceased as his spouse in the two years before his death;

- a child of the deceased;
- a person who was treated as a child of the deceased's marriage;
- any person who was being maintained by the deceased before his death.

A successful claimant receives only such sum as would make reasonable financial provision for his needs, except that the deceased's spouse may receive such sum as is reasonable in all the circumstances, whether or not that is the sum required for his maintenance (section 1(2)).

A claim under the Act must be brought within six months of the grant of representation being issued, although the court has discretion to extend this time limit. Claims cannot be brought before the grant is given, although a potential claimant would be well advised to notify the personal representatives of his intention to bring an action. Negotiations can then be started to compromise the claim quickly, if at all possible.

To ascertain when a grant of representation is issued, the potential claimant should lodge a standing search at the Principal Probate Registry (see page 275). This has effect for one year and the person lodging the search is notified when the grant is issued. A caveat (see page 107) should not be lodged, as this will only delay the administration of the estate.

Orders made under this Act vary widely, and include orders for the payment of a lump sum or regular income, or that assets should be transferred into a trust for the claimant.

The effect of any order under this Act is that the transfer of assets to the claimant takes effect as though, for inheritance tax purposes, the deceased's estate had devolved in accordance with the order (section 146, Inheritance Tax Act 1984). In addition, if the outcome of the claim is determined by the court (rather than by a compromise agreed between the parties), the effect of the order is that, for income tax and capital gains tax purposes, the disposition takes effect as though made by the deceased's Will (section 19(1), Inheritance (Provision for Family and Dependants) Act 1975).

Limitation Periods

An action against an estate cannot accrue indefinitely. Limitation periods are set out in the Limitation Act 1980. A creditor wishing to bring a claim must do so within six years of the date on which the loss occurred. The loss arises only when sufficient of the estate has been distributed that the creditor can no longer be paid. But if the Will charges a particular asset with the repayment of a debt, that debt does not become statute-barred until twelve years after the date of death.

If a beneficiary wishes to make a claim against an estate, he has twelve years from the date of accrual of his right (the date of death) in which to bring it, although interest can be claimed for only six years from the date of accrual of the right.

If a beneficiary wishes to bring an action for fraud against a personal representative, or make a claim that a personal representative has received estate property and converted it for his own use (not as a beneficiary), there is no limit. If, though, the beneficiary knew of the potential claim for some time and did nothing about it, the personal representatives may be able to raise a defence of acquiescence to their actions.

Personal representatives have twelve years to claim the assets of an estate that are in the hands of a third party; the period starts when the existence of the assets comes to their attention.

Chapter 24

The Liabilities of the Personal Representatives

Personal Liability

A personal representative is personally liable for any tort he commits as a personal representative during the administration of the estate. He is likewise personally liable for a contract he enters into as a personal representative to the extent that it cannot be met by the estate, or is found to have been entered into improperly.

If the personal representative causes loss to a third party by an act or omission during the administration of the estate, and that act or omission was reasonable, the personal representative is entitled to an indemnity from the estate for any action brought against him in relation to that loss.

If a personal representative acts in breach of duty as a personal representative and causes loss to the estate, he is personally liable for that loss. But the position is different where a loss arises without any breach of duty by the personal representative, or where the loss arises from his negligence but not his wrongdoing.

Some of the mechanisms delimiting the liabilities and obligations of personal representatives are examined below.

Express Clause in the Will

Many modern Wills expressly limit the personal liability of personal representatives to actions that are fraudulent or which comprise wrongdoing. Such a provision often stipulates that a personal representative is not liable for loss to the estate resulting from mere negligence.

Acquiescence or Agreement of Creditor or Beneficiary

If the personal representatives act in breach of their duty to the estate and thereby caused loss to the estate, or, as a result, a creditor cannot be paid in full, the personal representatives may still be protected from liability. This is so if the beneficiary of the estate or the unpaid creditor can be shown to have been fully aware of the breach of duty and to have acquiesced in it. The rule applies to breaches resulting from both acts or omissions of the personal representatives.

If the beneficiary or creditor went even further and agreed to the personal representatives' breach, section 62 of the Trustee Act 1925 operates to impound the interest of that creditor or beneficiary to provide protection to the personal representatives.

Agents, Nominees and Custodians

Under section 23 of the Trustee Act 2000, a personal representative is not liable for the action or default of any agent, nominee or custodian appointed by him, providing he complied with the duty of care imposed on him when appointing that agent, nominee or custodian and when reviewing its activities. The scope of the duty of care is laid out in section 1 of the Act.

Limitation of Liability

Under section 30 of the Trustee Act 1925, each personal representative was responsible for the correct application only of the estate assets that passed through his hands, and not of those assets that passed through the hands of a co-personal representative. This section was repealed by the Trustee Act 2000, although it is possible that the courts would still apply the rule, for example, by invoking section 61, Trustee Act 1925 to produce the same result.

Advertising

It is entirely possible that if the personal representatives of an estate distribute the estate and are then unable to meet debts of the estate of which they later become aware, they are personally liable to pay those debts without recourse against the beneficiaries. Section 27 of the Trustee Act 1925 provides that if the personal representatives place a notice of their intention to distribute the estate in the *London Gazette*, and in a newspaper local to the place where any land in the estate is situated, together with any other notices that a court might order, the personal representatives may distribute the estate free from any claims of which they have not been notified. The notice should specify:

- the name of the deceased;
- the personal representatives' intention to distribute the estate;
- the time period (at least two months) within which any claim must be made; and
- the address to which notice of the claim must be made.

It is advisable also to specify the deceased's address and date of death.

The personal representatives should also make such other searches as a prudent purchaser would make, for example bankruptcy searches, local land charges searches and searches of the Land Registry and Land Charges Register.

If these searches are made, the personal representatives are then not liable for any claims by creditors or beneficiaries of which they have received no notification. Those creditors or beneficiaries may still, however, follow the assets into the hands of the beneficiaries receiving them on distribution, and claim against them. Knowledge that a debt exists (even if it has not been claimed), or that a beneficiary exists but not how to trace him, means that the personal representatives have no protection under this section.

Relief from Personal Liability

If a personal representative is found to be personally liable for an action in breach of trust, but the court feels that he acted honestly and reasonably, and ought fairly to be excused for the breach, the court can relieve the personal representative from the personal liability, either wholly or in part. The fact that the personal representative acted in accordance with legal advice is not necessarily sufficient to qualify for relief under this section (*Marsden v Regan* [1954] 1 WLR 423, [1954] 1 All ER 475 (CA)).

Lloyds Estates

The personal representatives of a Lloyds Name must be aware that the estate may have a future liability to Lloyds, but they have no means to quantify the liability. Most Lloyds Names purchase estate protection plans that will meet all Lloyds liabilities, subject to an excess. But there is still a remote possibility that the company providing the estate protection plan may become insolvent and unable to meet the liability. In that case, the responsibility to discharge the debt would fall back on the personal representatives. To administer the estate properly, the personal representatives ought not to make any distributions until the final Lloyds liability has been quantified and paid. But in practice, this would delay the administration by a number of years.

The case of *Re Yorke deceased* [1997] 4 All ER 907 (Ch D) provides a solution. It allows the personal representatives to make an application to the court to seek directions as to the distribution of the estate. Pursuant to the application, the court may sanction the distribution of the deceased's estate without taking an indemnity from the beneficiaries or making a retention pending future Lloyds liabilities. If the personal representatives comply with the directions given, they are protected from personal liability should any future Lloyds debts arise which they cannot meet. This would not, however, absolve the beneficiaries from liability to pay the Lloyds debt.

A Practice Note of 25 May 2001, [2001] 3 All ER 765, governs the process for applying for *Re Yorke* directions.

General Administration Order

Rules of the Supreme Court, Order 85 allows the personal representatives to apply to the court for a general administration order. Such an order governs the manner in which the estate must be administered; and the personal representatives cannot carry out any action without the prior approval of the court. This provides them with full protection in relation to any action they undertake. But because of its onerous nature, such an order is not given readily and the personal representatives should normally try to find an alternative manner of administering the estate. If they are in sufficient doubt about a specific issue, they should instead apply to the court for directions on that issue.

The Inland Revenue

As mentioned elsewhere, it is the responsibility of the persons liable to pay the inheritance tax in relation to an estate to make full disclosure. In the first instance, these duties fall to the personal representatives. If full disclosure is not made, or the inheritance tax due is not paid in full, interest and penalties accrue. There may be substantial problems in relation to transfers made by the deceased during his lifetime, which are not always easily discoverable, the personal representatives having to rely largely on information from third parties.

The Inland Revenue's press release of 13 March 1991 confirmed that the Inland Revenue does not generally press personal representatives for payment from their personal reserves if the personal representatives:
- made the fullest enquiries reasonably practicable in the circumstances to discover lifetime transfers;
- did everything in their power to make a full disclosure of those transfers to IR Capital Taxes;
- obtained a certificate of discharge and divided the estate between the beneficiaries before the transfer came to light.

Dealing with the Interests of Beneficiaries

Many problems can arise when dealing with beneficiaries' interests, for example: in tracing beneficiaries who are known to exist; dealing with incapacitated beneficiaries; and establishing the exact interests of different beneficiaries.

Payment into court

Under section 63 of the Trustee Act 1925, personal representatives may pay assets held by them into court, and the receipt of the court officer provides them with a proper and full discharge in relation to those assets. This can be useful, for example, if a beneficiary is a minor and the personal representatives do not want to continue to hold assets for him until he reaches the age of eighteen, or if assets are due to a beneficiary who is mentally incapable but no receiver or attorney has been appointed.

If an issue arises as to the person actually entitled to the estate, or if a beneficiary cannot be traced, one of the other options discussed below may be more practical.

Benjamin order

If a beneficiary of the estate cannot be traced, the personal representatives can apply to court for a *Benjamin Order*. This arises from the case of *Re Benjamin* [1902] 1 Ch 723, but the order is now applied for under Order 85, rule 2, Rules of the Supreme Court 1985. The personal representatives must show the court the steps they have taken, including instructing title research agents or private investigators, to establish whether the beneficiary is still alive, and any evidence they have regarding his whereabouts or last known actions.

Providing the court agrees that the personal representatives have done all they can to trace the beneficiary, it can make an order allowing them to distribute the estate on the basis that the beneficiary predeceased the deceased, leaving no issue.

Seeking a *Benjamin* order can be a costly exercise, and in most instances is not the most practical solution.

Indemnity

An indemnity can be used to resolve a number of issues – where the personal representatives are not completely sure of the correct interpretation of the Will, or where a beneficiary cannot be traced, for example. In situations such as these the personal representatives can agree to distribute the estate on a particular basis, taking an indemnity from each recipient, to the effect that if any third party challenges the basis upon which the distribution was made, that recipient will fund the costs of answering that challenge and any amount payable to the third party as a result.

This may be an appropriate course where the amounts in question are relatively low, or where the basis for the distribution is unlikely to be challenged. An indemnity is only useful, however, if the party giving it is solvent and able to meet the required costs if and when the indemnity is called in. If the beneficiary no longer has the monies to fund the indemnity, the personal representatives could find themselves personally liable. Further, a minor beneficiary cannot give an indemnity.

Indemnity insurance

Indemnity insurance is most commonly used to deal with a missing beneficiary. If the personal representatives do not wish to apply for a *Benjamin* order, but the sums involved are too great to be satisfied with taking an indemnity, the personal representatives may take out insurance to cover the possibility of the missing beneficiary claiming his share of the estate in the future. The premium is payable out of the estate. The known beneficiaries usually prefer this course to setting aside funds with which to meet any claim by the disappointed beneficiary. The courts have often referred to insurance as a sensible, practical solution (*Evans v Westcombe* [1999] 2 All ER 777 (Ch D)), although the personal representatives must be careful to ensure that the policy covers the amount that the disappointed beneficiary would have received, together with any interest payable on it.

Chapter 25

Variations, Disclaimers and Other Opportunities

A deed of variation or a disclaimer may be executed to alter the distribution of the deceased's estate. This may be because the intended beneficiaries wish to modify the provisions of the Will or intestacy, or because they wish to make them more tax-efficient.

Deed of Variation

Purpose

A deed of variation is an instrument by which the intended recipient of an asset ("beneficiary 1") can direct that the asset passes to a different person ("beneficiary 2"). Beneficiary 1 stipulates in the deed that the asset will pass to beneficiary 2 in his stead. Beneficiary 1 could of course simply give the asset to beneficiary 2 after he has received it from the estate. The advantage of a deed of variation, is that, if it is signed within two years of the deceased's death, and contains an election (i.e., a statement) that the personal representatives wish it to do so, the estate is treated for inheritance tax and capital gains tax purposes as though the deceased had executed a Will containing the gift made in the deed. This means that the gift by beneficiary 1 to beneficiary 2 is not a potentially exempt transfer or lifetime chargeable transfer by him for inheritance tax purposes (see page 43), nor is it a disposal by him for capital gains tax. The statutory provisions allowing this are sections 142(1), Inheritance Tax Act 1984 and 62(6), Taxation of Chargeable Gains Act 1992.

Signatories

The deed must be signed by every beneficiary who thereby gives up something. For example, if an asset was directed in the Will to be held on trust for A for life, remainder to B, and it is decided that the asset should instead pass to C outright, both A and B would have to sign the deed of variation.

A deed of variation cannot be executed by a minor beneficiary, nor can it be signed by his parent, but must be approved by the court on behalf of the minor.

Further, if the execution of the deed leads to a greater amount of inheritance tax becoming payable, it must also be signed by the personal representatives. They may not refuse to execute the deed unless they hold insufficient assets to pay the additional tax. Other persons who may be adversely affected by the deed, such as trustees of an interest in possession trust under which the deceased had a life interest, do not need to join in the election, even though the result may be that the trust has to pay more inheritance tax.

Conditions

More than one deed of variation can be executed in relation to an estate, but each asset can be subject to only one variation. Thus, if the deceased's Will passed his house to A, and A used a deed of variation to pass the house to B, B could not execute a deed of variation to pass the house on to C. For this reason it is important to give full consideration to the effects of a proposed deed of variation, and to whether the beneficiary under the deed actually wishes to receive the asset.

A deed of variation can be used even if beneficiary 1 has accepted and received the asset left to him under the Will or intestacy. It can also be executed in relation to part only of the asset gifted. In these respects it differs from a deed of disclaimer (see page 265).

A deed of variation can be used only in relation to assets in the deceased's free estate at his death. This means that it cannot be used in relation to gifts with reservation of benefit, or to alter the terms of any trust under which he was a beneficiary (section 142(5), Inheritance Tax Act 1984), unless the trust assets were subject to a general power of appointment exercisable by the deceased under his Will, as the assets could then be disposed of by the deceased's Will.

It can, however, be used to bring into the estate assets that the deceased could dispose of by Will, by severing the joint tenancy of any asset held by the deceased with a third party. The third party must sign the deed of variation to signify his consent.

Taxation

As already mentioned, the Inheritance Tax Act 1984 and the Taxation of Chargeable Gains Act 1992 operate to "re-write" the dispositions effected by the deed back into the deceased's Will, if the appropriate election is made in the deed. This is particularly important as, once an election has been made, it cannot be revoked. The election is a statement made within the deed (and therefore deemed to be made by the parties executing the deed) that the provisions of section 142(1) Inheritance Tax Act 1984 or section 62(6),

Taxation of Chargeable Gains Act 1992 should apply, and therefore that the gift should be treated as though it were made by the deceased in his Will.

Deeds of variation call for careful planning to ensure they achieve the desired result. For example, if the deceased left his shares in ABC plc (valued at £100,000 at the date of his death) to his wife in his Will, they would qualify for the surviving spouse exemption from inheritance tax. If the wife wishes to pass the shares on to their child, she would have to decide whether to make the inheritance tax election in the deed. If the deceased had used his entire inheritance tax nil rate band before his death and the election were made, the gift would be treated as passing to his child under his Will and inheritance tax would be payable accordingly. In that situation, it would probably be advisable not to make the election. The gift would then be treated as a potentially exempt transfer by the wife and, providing she survives for seven years from the date of that gift, its value should fall out of her estate for inheritance tax purposes upon her death.

On the other hand if the deceased's inheritance tax nil rate band were available on his death, the election should be made so that the gift of the shares is treated as having been made by the deceased's Will. No inheritance tax would be payable as the gift would fall within the nil rate band, and the wife would not have to survive seven years for it to become non-chargeable.

Whether or not the inheritance tax election is made has no bearing on whether a capital gains tax election should be made, and *vice versa*. These are independent decisions. In the example above, if the shares were valued at £105,000 when they were to be passed to the child, and the wife has her full capital gains tax allowance available for the year, it would probably be inappropriate to make the capital gains tax election. The gift would be treated as a disposal by the wife for capital gains tax purposes, but if the gain fell within her allowance, no capital gains tax would be payable. But if the gain on the shares were £20,000, it would probably be advisable to make the election. The child's base cost of the shares for capital gains tax purposes would then be the probate value of £100,000.

If the deed is used to create a trust, the beneficiary disposing of the asset under the deed is not the settlor of the trust for inheritance tax purposes (the settlor is the deceased), but he is the settlor for income tax and capital gains tax purposes. This means that if he is also a beneficiary of that trust, all its income and capital gains are taxed in his hands.

Consideration

Sections 142(3), Inheritance Tax Act 1984 and 62(8), Taxation of Chargeable Gains Act 1992 specifically state that if the beneficiary making the gift under the deed receives any form of consideration, whether in money of money's worth, for the execution of the deed, the deed has no effect for the purposes of inheritance tax or capital gains tax.

Income arising before the variation

A deed of variation is effective only for inheritance tax and capital gains tax purposes, not for income tax purposes. This means that any income paid to the original beneficiary before the variation was signed does not need to be declared by him for income tax purposes. Once the deed of variation has been signed, the future income must be distributed in accordance with it.

Notice of election

For many years notices of elections under the Inheritance Tax Act 1984 or the Taxation of Chargeable Gains Act 1992 had to be given to IR Capital Taxes and the Inland Revenue respectively. More recently, the tax authorities require written notice only if additional inheritance tax or capital gains tax becomes payable.

The "real world"

A recent development concerning deeds of variation relates to so-called "real world" situations. Suppose A dies and leaves his entire estate on a life interest trust to B, remainder to C. Within two years, B dies and the assets in the trust pass to C. If inheritance tax were payable on the assets in A's estate, and then also on the trust assets in B's estate, C may ask B's personal representatives to execute a deed of variation in relation to A's estate, whereby the estate is left outright to C, thereby avoiding the double charge to inheritance tax. This is similar to the situation that arose in *Soutter v IRC* [2002] STC (SCD) 385. The Inland Revenue argued that the variation had no "real world" effect, as, by the time the deed was executed, C was beneficially entitled to the trust assets. In that case, the Special Commissioners agreed with the Inland Revenue – that there were no assets upon which the deed of variation could "bite", because the deed sought to bring into effect that which would have happened anyway. There is some argument whether a disclaimer by B's personal representatives might have been effective as an alternative, providing he had not received any income from the life interest trust. This is a developing area of the law and personal representatives should consider current case law carefully if they are contemplating a deed of variation in a situation such as this.

Stamp duty

A deed of variation is exempt from stamp duty under category M of the Schedule to the Stamp Duty (Exempt Instruments) Regulations 1987 (SI 1987 No 516), but the deed must contain a certificate to that effect.

Tax planning

Some examples of when a deed of variation may be used for tax planning purposes are:

- to create a discretionary trust of the deceased's inheritance tax nil rate band or to make an outright gift of it;
- to give assets qualifying for relief from inheritance tax to non-exempt beneficiaries, such as the deceased's children;
- to give additional assets to the deceased's spouse so that they qualify for the exemption from inheritance tax.

Order Pursuant to an Inheritance Act Claim

Section 146, Inheritance Tax Act 1984 states that where an order is made under section 2 of the Inheritance (Provision for Family and Dependants) Act 1975, for the purposes of inheritance tax the deceased's estate is treated as though it had devolved in accordance with the provisions of the order.

Disclaimer

A disclaimer is made where a person entitled to assets from the deceased's estate, either under a Will or an intestacy, does not wish to accept them. It differs from a deed of variation in both the requirements relating to it, and the effects.

Requirements

A disclaimer need not be made in writing; it can be inferred from the conduct of the disclaimant. For practical purposes, however, it is recommended that a disclaimer is always evidenced by deed. A disclaimer is not effective once the asset has been accepted by the intended beneficiary – he cannot choose to reject it later. The asset in question must be accepted or rejected in its entirety. This is why some Wills break down each gift into a number of gifts of £1 each, so that a gift of an asset can be partially disclaimed, by accepting or rejecting individual gifts of £1.

Effects

A disclaimant has no control over the destination of the gift he disclaims. The estate is administered as though the disclaimant had predeceased the deceased, so that any substitutional gift takes effect.

A disclaimer by a beneficiary with a prospective entitlement under a testator's estate which is executed during the testator's lifetime has no effect (*Smith v Smith* [2001] 1 WLR 1937, [2001] 3 All ER 552 (Ch D)).

Taxation implications

The taxation implications of a disclaimer are also different from those of a variation. If the disclaimer is made within two years of the deceased's death, sections 142, Inheritance Tax Act 1984 and 62, Taxation of Chargeable

Gains Act 1992 take effect automatically. There is no need for any written election to be made.

The personal representatives do not need to join in any disclaimer, even if extra inheritance tax becomes payable – they can do nothing about this.

If the assets subject to the disclaimer pass into a trust when the disclaimer becomes effective, the disclaimant is not the settlor of that trust for income tax or capital gains tax purposes. This may be advantageous if the disclaimant or his minor children are to be beneficiaries of that trust, as the income and capital gains of it are not assessable on him.

Income arising before the disclaimer
Any income that arose on the asset before the disclaimer becomes effective should not be paid to the disclaimant. If it is, and the disclaimant accepts the asset, he receives a benefit from the asset and is unable to disclaim it. All the income arising on the asset must therefore pass to the new beneficiary.

Joint property, trust assets and gifts with reservation of benefit
A person holding property as joint tenant with the deceased can disclaim the assets passing to him under the joint tenancy. If there are other joint owners, the disclaimer operates to transfer the disclaiming beneficiary's share to the other joint owners – his share does not revert to the deceased's estate.

Like a deed of variation, a disclaimer cannot be used in relation to assets subject to a gift with reservation of benefit. It can be used in relation to trust property under section 93, Inheritance Tax Act 1984, but only by the life tenant of an interest in possession trust, to accelerate the interest of the remainderman. It cannot be used by the remaindermen, as, at the point they become entitled, the property is no longer held in a life interest trust, but belongs to them absolutely or contingently.

Stamp duty
A disclaimer is not subject to stamp duty.

Two-year Discretionary Trusts
To preserve flexibility in his estate, a testator may, in his Will, create a discretionary trust, into which certain assets, or his entire estate, may pass. If a distribution is made from this trust within two years of the deceased's death and before an interest in possession subsists in the asset distributed, that disposition is treated as though it had been made by the deceased in his Will for inheritance tax purposes (section 144, Inheritance Tax Act 1984). This means that assets can be appointed out of the trust to exempt beneficiaries, such as the deceased's spouse, and any inheritance tax paid on those assets is refunded, because they qualify for the surviving spouse

exemption from inheritance tax.

The disadvantage is that the inheritance tax must have been paid in the first instance, until the appointment was made. In addition, the personal representatives must wait at least three months from the date of death before they make such a distribution or the desired inheritance tax consequences will not be achieved (*Frankland v IRC* [1996] STC 735 (Ch D)).

The final disadvantage is that there is no reciprocal provision in the Taxation of Chargeable Gains Act 1992. This means that any appointment from the trust is a disposal for capital gains tax purposes by the personal representatives, although it should automatically qualify for holdover relief from this tax under section 260, Taxation of Chargeable Gains Act 1992.

Precatory Trusts

It is common for a testator to leave his chattels to certain specified persons, with a direction that those persons distribute the chattels in accordance with a letter of wishes written by him during his lifetime. Under section 143, Inheritance Tax Act 1984, inheritance tax is payable on those chattels as though they were gifted absolutely to the specified persons. But if those persons dispose of the chattels within two years of the death, the estate is taxed as though the Will made the same distribution.

Other Opportunities

Once the administration of an estate has been finalised, the beneficiaries may need further professional advice. For example, they may be advised to make their own Wills, perhaps with some inheritance tax planning advice. Alternatively, they may wish to consider executing enduring powers of attorney to ensure that their affairs can be properly dealt with, should they lose capacity. These are all matters which a solicitor acting for the personal representatives may be able to deal with.

Finally, beneficiaries taking substantial sums of money under an estate may need investment advice; the solicitor for the personal representatives may be able to recommend an advisor.

Chapter 26

Notation, Amendment and Revocation of Grants

Notation

In certain circumstances an original grant must be notated with an event or order which affects the use of the grant in the administration of the estate.

Domicile

Rule 8(2) of the Non-Contentious Probate Rules 1987 provides that the oath to lead a grant shall, unless otherwise directed by a district judge or registrar, contain a statement of the deceased's domicile at death. The domicile is recited in the grant. A grant issued in England and Wales, referring to domicile in England and Wales, is effective to administer estate throughout the UK.

If an oath was, with leave, silent as to the place of the deceased's domicile, the grant is likewise silent, but the grant may later be notated with the domicile. Entitlement to benefit from an estate may vary depending on the deceased's domicile, e.g., if the deceased died domiciled in France, French law requires that statutory legacies must be paid to members of kin, even if there is a Will. In such a case, the executor, or, if more than one, any one of them, or *all* the administrators, must first make an affidavit deposing to the place of the deceased's domicile at death. The affidavit must be lodged in the registry with the original grant. If satisfied, the district judge or registrar directs notation of the domicile to be made on the grant, together with a note of his direction and the date of it.

Election to redeem life interest

The surviving spouse of an intestate, whose estate exceeded the value of the spouse's statutory legacy (see page 100), may elect to redeem the life interest to which he is entitled, being property then in possession. Redemption is effected by paying the appropriate amount determined by reference to the Intestate Succession (Interest and Capitalisation) Order 1977 (SI 1977 No 1491), as amended.

Notice of the election to redeem is served on the personal representatives or, where the surviving spouse is the sole personal representative, on the Senior District Judge. Notice in Form 6 of Appendix 1 to the 1987 Rules (see page 306) is lodged in the Principal Registry, or, in duplicate, in the district registry from which the grant issued. The original grant must be lodged. The notice must be lodged within one year of the issue of the grant unless, in special circumstances, the court extends the time for lodging.

If satisfied, the registry notates the original grant and the record copy (the copy retained in the registry) of the filing of the election and returns the grant to the grantee.

Further personal representative
When an order has been made following an application under rule 26 for the appointment of an additional personal representative (see page 124), the original grant must be notated with the additional personal representative's name and address. The original grant and the record copy are notated in red ink, and details of the order added as a marginal note. The registry notifies the Probate Records Centre (see page 275) and thereafter returns the original grant to the extracting solicitors.

Substituted personal representative
Application may be made under section 50 of the Administration of Justice Act 1985 for the removal and substitution of an executor or administrator. The application is made under Part 57, Civil Procedure Rules 1998, to the Chancery Division.

When an order has been made for the removal and/or substitution of a personal representative, the original grant (which will have been lodged in the Chancery Registry with the application under section 50) is forwarded to the issuing probate registry for notation. The original grant and record copy are notated in red ink with the effect of and details of the Chancery order. Thereafter the original grant is returned, as appropriate, to the extracting solicitors or those representing the substituted personal representative. The registry notifies the Probate Records Centre.

Bankruptcy administration order
Where the deceased died bankrupt, the bankruptcy court may order the powers of the personal representative be transferred, usually to the receiver in bankruptcy, by order under the Insolvency Act 1986. The effect of such order, called an administration order, is notated on the original grant and record copy by the registry from which it issued. The registry notifies the Probate Records Centre.

Rectification of Will
The procedure to apply to rectify a Will is dealt with at page 142 *et seq.* Where an order is made to rectify after the grant has issued, the original grant must be notated with the effect of the order. If the order is made by a

district judge or registrar the original grant should have been lodged with the application. Where the application was opposed, but an order to rectify was made by the Chancery Division, the original grant is sent to the issuing registry. The original grant is notated with a marginal note of the order, and a memorandum of its effect on the Will, or a copy of the Will as rectified, is annexed. The registry notifies the Probate Records Centre.

Second or subsequent grant
There is no notation on the original grant of the issue of a grant of double probate, a grant *de bonis non*, or a *cessate* grant.

Amendment
Rule 41 deals with the procedure for applications to amend grants. Where the grant contains an error, that is, a clerical error arising from a mistake in the application or by the registry in preparing the grant, it may be amended. Where the defect in the application affects title to the grant then the grant must be revoked (see page 271).

Error by registry
The personal representatives should, immediately on receiving the grant from the registry, check it to ensure it is in proper form and contains the correct names and addresses of the deceased and the personal representatives. If an error has been made by the registry, the grant and all office copies should be returned within 28 days of issue. Provided it is returned within this time a new grant is issued, but if after that time, the original grant is manually amended in red ink and notated with the district judge or registrar's order to amend. Where the probate copy Will in the grant is incomplete, the original grant should be returned for the full testamentary document to be annexed.

Error by applicant
Where the oath to lead the grant was defective in that it failed to give full correct names or addresses, an application for amendment may be made by the applicant or the extracting solicitors. The application should be made on affidavit, deposed to by the person with best knowledge of the error. The district judge or registrar has discretion to accept a less formal method of application, by letter, depending on the circumstances.

Provided the application is made within 28 days of the date of the original grant, a new grant is issued in proper form. Where application is made after 28 days have elapsed the original grant is manually notated with the amendment and order to amend.

Error in limitation
Where there is an error in a limitation on a grant, whether the error was made in the probate registry or arose from a defect in the application, the limitation is amended. This may be done without affidavit evidence in support if the grant fails to follow the limitation imposed in a discretionary order.

Codicil found after Will proved
Where a codicil to a Will is found after probate of the Will has been granted, the original grant is not amended, nor is the original grant notated. Instead, an application for a grant in respect of the codicil alone is made. Only where the codicil changes the appointment of executors, or affects the title of the person who took the grant, is the original grant recalled and revoked.

Changes in estate value
Where, after the issue of a grant, it is discovered that the estate values quoted in the oath or Inland Revenue Account were wrong, the grant may be amended to show the correct figures.

As a general rule, it is not the practice of the probate registries to amend the values of the gross and/or net estate appearing in the grant. Where correction is necessary, an application should be made to IR Capital Taxes with an explanation or corrective account (see page 232). The original grant should be lodged with IR Capital Taxes for that office to control the estate value figures.

Revocation
Rule 41 provides for the revocation of a grant on application to a district judge or registrar. Other than in exceptional circumstances a grant is revoked only with the consent of the grantee.

No fee is payable to the probate registry on application to revoke.

Grant issued on false premise
A grant of probate is revoked where:
- the Will proved was not the last valid Will of the deceased;
- a codicil, or further codicil, is found which affects the appointment of executors;
- evidence is produced which clearly shows the Will was not duly executed;
- there is evidence to show that the testator revoked the original Will, a copy having been accepted to proof.

A grant of letters of administration is revoked where:
- a valid Will is found after letters of administration had been taken on

an intestacy;
- the grantee is found not to be the nearest of kin to the deceased and therefore not beneficially entitled to the estate.

In addition, there are cases common to testacy and intestacy where a grant issued on a false basis must be revoked:
- where leave to swear to the death of the deceased was given by order under rule 53 but the "deceased" is subsequently found to be alive;
- where the applicant for the grant himself dies before the grant is issued.

A grant is deemed to be issued when "passed under seal of the court" at the earliest time the registry is open to the public on the day of issue, i.e., 10.00 a.m. in the Principal Registry and 9.30 a.m. in a district registry. Thus, if there is evidence to show the grantee died at 2.00 p.m. on the date the grant was issued, it was properly issued and a grant *de bonis non* may be taken. But if the grantee died at 8.00 a.m. on the day of issue, the grant must be revoked and a new original grant taken by a person of equal or next entitlement.

Grantee incapable of managing his affairs

Where a sole grantee, in whatever capacity he was entitled to the grant, becomes incapable of managing his affairs through mental incapacity, the grant is not revoked. Instead, a new grant may be applied for in the order of priority provided by rule 35(2) or by discretionary order under rule 35(4) (see page 133). The grant is a grant *de bonis non* for the use and benefit of the former grantee. The only exception to this general rule is where the grant issued to one of several appointed executors, the others having power reserved. These others may take a grant of double probate (see page 169).

Several grantees

Where one of two or more proving executors becomes mentally incapable of managing his affairs the grant must be revoked and a new grant of probate issued to the capable executors. Power is reserved to the incapable executor on regaining his mental capacity.

Similarly, where letters of administration with or without Will annexed have been taken out and one of the grantees becomes incapable, the grant must be revoked. A new grant may be taken by those persons with the same entitlement under rule 20 or 22. The application for revocation and for the new grant may be combined in one affidavit if the grant issued to one or more executors, one of whom is now incapable of managing his affairs.

Where there is a conflict in the administration of the estate between the grantees, or between the grantee(s) and the beneficiaries, the grantee may apply for revocation of the grant. Similarly, where the grantee becomes ill or incapacitated (other than mental incapacity) in some way he may apply to be relieved of his duties by having the grant to him revoked. Any person who takes on the mantle of personal representative is relieved of those duties only in exceptional circumstances, even if all interested parties agree to the revocation of the grant. An order for revocation in these circumstances is in the discretion of the district judge or registrar and orders are not lightly made.

Grant issued too soon

Rule 6(2) provides that no grant of probate or letters of administration (with Will annexed) may issue within seven days of the deceased's death, and no grant of letters of administration may issue within fourteen days of the deceased's death. A district judge or registrar has power to abridge these times in extenuating circumstances.

If a grant has issued without leave before the expiry of the necessary times it is not usually revoked. The court does, however, of its own motion, revoke a grant if any person can show that he was prevented from objecting to the grant being issued and/or from entering a caveat because of the registry's error in issuing the grant before time without leave.

Grantee's disappearance or failure to administer

Where representation has been granted but the grantee disappears leaving part of the estate unadministered, or fails to administer it fully, an application to revoke the grant may be made.

This situation usually falls into the "exceptional circumstance" criterion for revocation without the grantee's consent. The application may, by way of exception to the usual rule, be made without lodging the original grant. It is suggested that an enquiry be made of the district judge or registrar before applying to revoke. If the district judge or registrar agrees to entertain the application, an affidavit of facts to lead the order should be drafted and lodged.

The alternative, in this situation, is to apply to the Chancery Division under section 50 of the Administration of Justice Act 1985 (see below).

Removal or substitution of grantee

Where the problem lies not with grant, but with the grantee, an application may be made to the Chancery Division under section 50 of the Administration of Justice Act 1985 for the removal and/or substitution of the grantee.

If the grantee (or one of them) fails to participate in the administration of the estate or maladministers the estate, that grantee may be removed, and, if appropriate, another substituted. Clearly, if the offending grantee is a sole grantee, then there must be substitution.

Application under section 50 is a probate claim, the procedure for which is governed by Part 57, Civil Procedure Rules 1998. The procedure for issue follows Part 7. The application may be made to the Central Office in London or to any of the designated district registries with Chancery jurisdiction.

Revocation opposed

Where it is said that the grant should not have issued because there is a dispute about the validity of the Will or the grantee's title to the grant, and the application to revoke is opposed, the application must be made to the Chancery Division. See Parts 7 and 57, Civil Procedure Rules.

Application for new grant

Whether the order to revoke is made by the Family Division or the Chancery Division, any consequent application for a new grant may be made to any probate registry. The oath to lead the new grant must recite details of, and the order revoking, the former grant.

The new grant is a full grant to the whole estate, although the estate values referred to in the oath relate only to the estate remaining unadministered.

Chapter 27

Searches and Copies

Records of Grants of Representation

A record of every grant of representation issued between 1858 and 1995 is maintained in indexes (called "calendars") available for search and inspection in the probate registries. Generally, district probate registries hold calendars for the last fifty years only; searches for earlier documents may be made in the Principal Registry. Some of these records (those since 1972) are on microfiche, but otherwise are in book form. Records of grants issued since 1995 are held in the *Probateman* computer system.

Registries hold the files on grants which have issued for two years. Older files are archived in the Probate Records Centre and may be retrieved for inspection at a registry. These files comprise original Wills and any other documents required before the grant could issue.

Standing Search for a Grant

Rule 43 of the Non-Contentious Probate Rules 1987 provides that any person who wishes to be notified of the issue of a grant may enter a standing search for the grant in any registry or sub-registry. The application is made by lodging Form 2 of the forms prescribed by the Rules 1987 (see page 349). The full information required by the form must be given or the search will not be entered.

Thus, if proceedings under section 1 of the Inheritance (Provision for Family and Dependants) Act 1975, or any other litigation against the estate, is contemplated, a standing search should be entered. Similarly, a creditor of the deceased may wish to know when representation is granted so that he may make his claim to the personal representatives.

A copy of any grant issued in the twelve months before the entry of the search, or which issues within the six months after the entry of the search, is sent to the person who entered the search.

A standing search remains effective for six months after entry, but may be extended on application in writing made within the last month of the six month period, and so on *ad infinitum.*

A fee of £5 is payable for the entry of a standing search and for each extension.

Copies of Wills and Grants

From the time a Will is proved it becomes a "public" document and copies of it, and of any grant of representation, may be obtained by any person on request and on payment of the requisite fee.

Rules 58 and 59, which deal with copies of documents held by probate registries, also provide for Wills to be open to inspection or refused inspection, at the discretion of a district judge or registrar.

Copies of grants and Wills may be requested from the registry which issued the grant or from the Principal Registry. Where it is known from which registry the grant issued, the application should be made to that registry. Where that information is not known, the application should be made to the York Probate sub-Registry (for the address, see Appendix B).

Types of copy supplied

Plain copies, i.e., copies neither sealed not certified, of Wills:
- which have been refused admission to probate;
- which are inoperative and not proved;
- which have been proved in part;
- which were proved in the form of an engrossment endorsed with the court's *fiat,*

in which the grant of probate or letter of administration (with Will annexed) has been revoked (and the Will has not been proved again) may be obtained from the registry in which they are held. Similarly, a plain copy of a revoked grant or of a copy of a power of attorney (where the original is not held by the registry) may be obtained from the registry in which it is held.

Sealed, but not certified copies of:
- oaths;
- affidavits;
- orders (except for orders giving leave to swear death);
- powers of attorney (where the original is held); and
- renunciations

may be obtained from the registry holding the records of the issue of the grant. Office copies of grants and oaths may be obtained at the time of application for the grant.

Once a grant of representation has issued, sealed and certified copies of the grant and proved testamentary documents may be obtained. Each document is sealed with the seal of the High Court, Family Division and certified by a district judge or registrar as a true copy of the grant and proved Will and/or codicil. Sealed and certified copies may be obtained on the issue of the grant.

Copies for use abroad

Apostilles: Usually, a sealed and certified copy of a grant or Will endorsed with the "apostille" is sufficient evidence for use in countries which are signatories to the Hague Convention on Recognition of Documents dated 5 October 1961.

The endorsement of the apostille is made on application to the Legalisation Department of the Foreign and Commonwealth Office (see Appendix B for the address). A sealed and certified copy of the relevant documents to be enclosed should be sent with the fee of, currently, £15. The fee includes the cost of secure postage return after endorsement.

Exemplification: An exemplification is sometimes required as evidence in the courts of other countries. An exemplification is a statement of the details of the grant of representation. It contains a resumé of the grant and an exact copy of all testamentary documents proved. A certificate verifying authenticity of the documents is signed by a district judge or registrar.

An application for an exemplification must be made to the registry from which the grant issued on payment of the requisite fee.

Special copies: A "special copy" or "special certificate" is again sometimes required by courts of foreign countries. A special copy is an exemplification signed by a district judge or registrar and countersigned by the President of the Family Division.

Duplicate grants

Where the original grant had been lost or inadvertently destroyed and an original grant is required for administrative purposes, a duplicate may be issued.

An application may be made only by the original grantee. It is made by letter setting out how (if known) the original has been lost or destroyed and the reasons why a duplicate grant (and not a plain or certified copy) is required.

A duplicate grant is an exact replica of the original and bears the original date of issue, but it is noted in the margin that it is a duplicate of the original, and with the date of issue of the duplicate.

Fees

The following fees are payable for copies and are prescribed by Fee 8 of the Non-Contentious Probate Fees Order 1999 (SI 1999 No 688) as amended:
On a request for a copy of any document whether or not provided as a certified copy:

- for the first copy, £5.00;
- for every copy of the same document if supplied at the same time, £1.00.
  In practice, the registries charge £1 for *each* copy applied for at the time the grant is issued;
- where copies of any document are made available on a computer disk or in other electronic form, for each copy, £3.00;
- where a search of the index is required, in addition to the fees above as appropriate, for each period of four years searched after the first four years, £3.00.

The fee for a duplicate grant, prescribed by Fee 2 of the Order, is £15.00.

Deposit of Wills for Safe Keeping

It is strongly recommended that a Will is executed in the offices of the solicitors who drafted it and retained by those solicitors. But if the testator cannot be persuaded to leave his Will, it may be lodged for safe custody in the Principal Registry. The Wills (Deposit for Safe Custody) Regulations 1978 (SI 1978 No 1724) apply.

A Will may be lodged for deposit personally by the testator or his authorised agent at any district registry or the Principal Registry, but may be lodged at the Principal Registry by post only. The Will must be sealed up in the envelope provided by the registry. A certificate of deposit is provided. Wills lodged in a district probate registry are forwarded to the Principal Registry.

The registry immediately records the deposit on the *Probateman* computer system.

A fee of £15 is payable for the deposit of a Will.

Withdrawal

After deposit, a testator may withdraw his Will on written request, supported by the certificate of deposit, to the Principal Registry. A district judge must be satisfied before the original Will is released (a copy is retained). Except on the written request of the testator the original is not released during his lifetime.

Death of the testator

After the testator's death the original Will may be released by a district judge on production of the certificate of deposit and proof of death. No fee is payable for the withdrawal of a will.

Appendix A

Checklist of Information and Documents

The following may be used a checklist when taking instructions and when gathering the information and documents needed before applying for a grant.

1. Deceased's personal details
- Name;
- Address;
- Dates of birth and death (obtain death certificate);
- National insurance no., tax self-assessment no. and Inland Revenue office;
- Brief summary of family situation.

2. Will and Codicils
- Dates of Will and codicils;
- Current location (if not handed over);
- Check whether funeral wishes mentioned;
- Names and addresses of executors.

3. Assets
Details and approximate values of all property owned by the deceased (ascertain whether property owned in deceased's sole name or jointly with another person):
- Deceased's home;
- Location of title deeds;
- Other properties owned by the deceased;
- Location of title deeds;
- Bank/building society accounts (obtain up to date statements);
- National Savings certificates (obtain certificates);
- Premium bonds (obtain holder's card);
- Other National Savings investments;
- Stocks and shares (obtain certificates or confirm identity of nominee name);
- Life assurance policies (obtain original policy documents);
- Cash, e.g., cash found at home;

- Furniture and personal possessions;
- Other assets and location of title documents.

4. Liabilities

All money owed by the deceased together with any relevant documents, for example:

- Mortgages (obtain last statement);
- Outstanding bills, e.g., gas, electricity, council tax;
- Funeral director's invoice;
- Other debts.

5. Trusts

- Details of any trusts made by the deceased;
- Details of any trusts in which the deceased had an interest.

6. Gifts and Receipts

- Details of gifts made by the deceased in the seven years before death;
- Details of money and property inherited by the deceased in the last five years.

7. Miscellaneous

- Copy of last tax return and name of accountant;
- Pension book (obtain);
- Social security benefits received;
- Insurance policies relating to house, contents and car.

Appendix B

Useful Addresses

Association of British Insurers
51 Gresham Street
London EC2V 7HQ
Telephone: (020) 7600 3333

Attendance Allowance
Disability Benefits Unit
Warbreck House
Warbreck Hill
Blackpool FY5 3AW
Telephone: (08457) 123456

Benefits Agency (Recovery from Estates)
A Wing
Government Buildings
Otley Road
Lawnswood
Leeds LS16 5PU

British Government Stock held on the Bank of England Register
Registrars Department
Southgate House
Southgate Street
Gloucester GL1 1UW

Foreign and Commonwealth Office
Legalisation Department
Old Admiralty Building
The Mall
London SW1A 2LG
DX 123243 St James' Park
Telephone: (020) 7008 1111

General Register of Births and Deaths
General Register Office
PO Box 2
Southport PR8 2JT
Telephone: (0151) 471 4800
FAX: (01704) 550013

Applications in person:
Family Record Centre
1 Myddleton Street
Islington
London EC1R 1UW

IR Capital Taxes
Helpline: 0845 30 20 900

IR Capital Taxes Nottingham
Ferrers House, PO Box 38
Castle Meadow Road
Nottingham NG2 1BB
DX 701201 Nottingham 4
DX 701202 Nottingham 4 (pre-grant)
Telephone: (0115) 974 2424

IR Capital Taxes Belfast
Level 3, Dorchester House
52-58 Great Victoria Street
Belfast BT2 7QL
DX 2001 NR Belfast 2
Telephone: (028) 9050 5342

IR Capital Taxes Edinburgh
Meldrum House
15 Drumsheugh Gardens
Edinburgh EH3 7UG
DX Edinburgh 542001 Edinburgh 14
Telephone: (0131) 777 4214

IR Capital Taxes Shares Valuation
Fitz Roy House, PO Box 46
Castle Meadow Road
Nottingham NG2 1BD
DX 701203 Nottingham 4
Telephone: (0115) 974 2203
Helpline: (0115) 974 2222

Leeds District Probate Registry
Third Floor, Coronet House
Queen Street
Leeds LS1 2BA
DX 26451 Leeds North Square
Telephone: (0113) 243 1505

*London Stock Exchange Historic
  Price Service*
4th Floor Tower
London Stock Exchange
Old Broad Street
London EC2N 1HP
Telephone: (020) 7797 1206

National Savings
*Bank accounts; capital and deposit
  bonds; children's bonus bonds; first
  option bonds*
National Savings Bank
Carglen
Glasgow G58 1SB

*National Savings certificates; SAYE
  and year plans*
Savings Certificates and SAYE Office
Milburngate House
Durham DH99 1NS

*Premium bonds; National Savings
  income bonds; pensioners'
  guaranteed income bonds*
Bonds and Stock Office
Marton
Blackpool FY3 9YP

Pensions and Overseas Directorate
Department of Social Security
Tyne View Park
Whiterley Road
Newcastle-upon-Tyne N98 1BA
Telephone: (0191) 203 0203

Principal Probate Registry
First Avenue House
42–49 High Holborn
London WC1V 6NP
Telephone: (020) 7947 7000

Public Guardianship Office
Protection Division
Archway Tower
2 Junction Road
London N19 5SZ
DX 141150 Archway 2
Telephone: (020) 7664 7300

Treasury Solicitor
Queen Anne's Chambers
28 Broadway
London SW1H 9SJ
Telephone: (020) 7210 3000

York Probate sub-Registry
First floor, Castle Chambers
Clifford Street
York YO1 9RG
Telephone: (01904) 666777

Appendix C

Specimen Forms

1. Affidavit of Condition of Will or of Alterations to Will

In the High Court of Justice
Family Division
[Principal] [...................... District Probate] Registry
In the Estate of ...., Deceased

I, [1] make oath and say that:
1.   I am [2] named in the last Will and Testament of [3] deceased the said Will being dated the ..... day of .... 20 .. and now produced to me marked ..... and having perused the said Will and in particular observed [4].
2.   The said Will is now, in all respects, in the same condition as when found by me as aforesaid.[5]

Sworn by the above-named deponent ....
at .... on [date] ....
Before me, ... A Commissioner for Oaths/Solicitor.

2. Affidavit of Search for Will

In the High Court of Justice, *etc., as in Form 1.*

I, [1] make oath and say that:
1.   I am [2] named in the last Will and Testament of [3] deceased, the said Will [being undated] [being incompletely dated] [dated the ..... day of .... 20 ..] being now produced to me and marked .....
2.   I have made all possible searches and enquiries for any other Will including a search of the home of the deceased and of all places where it is likely that he kept his important papers or valuable personal belongings.
3.   I have been unable to discover any testamentary document other than the said Will.
4.   I have made enquiries of [6].

---

[1] Insert the full name, address and occupation or description of the deponent.
[2] Insert title to grant, e.g., "the sole executor"; "one of the residuary legatees and devisees".
[3] Insert the deceased's full name and last permanent address.
[4] Describe the circumstances of the finding of the Will and its then condition together with (if known) an explanation for its condition. If the Will has been damaged since being found, set out details of how the damage occurred. If the Will contains unauthenticated alterations this affidavit may need supplementing by evidence from a witness to the Will with knowledge of the alteration at execution.
[5] If another document was attached but subsequently removed, add a further paragraph dealing with the attachment, the nature of it and its removal.
[6] Insert details of the enquiries made, e.g., of solicitors, bankers, accountants, relatives or friends who might have been entrusted with the original Will.

5.   I believe the deceased died without having left any Will or testamentary document other than the said Will referred to above.

Sworn, *etc. as in Form 1.*

3.   Affidavit of Handwriting

In the High Court of Justice, *etc., as in Form 1.*

I, [1] make oath and say that:
1.   I am [7] of .... deceased. I [worked with the deceased for many years [8]] and frequently received correspondence from him and saw him sign his name to documents so that I am well acquainted with his handwriting and signature.
2.   I have examined the paper writing now produced to me and marked ..... which purports to contain the last Will and Testament of the deceased dated the ..... day of .... 20.. and being subscribed thus [9] .
3.   I believe [the whole of the said Will together with] the signature of [10] to be in the true and proper handwriting of the deceased.

Sworn, *etc. as in Form 1.*

4.   Affidavit of Due Execution

In the High Court of Justice, *etc., as in Form 1.*

I, [1] make oath and say that:
1.   I am one of the subscribing witnesses to the last Will and Testament of [11] deceased.
2.   [The said Will] [A copy of the said Will] is now produced to me and marked ...... and dated the ...... day of .... 20... The deceased executed the said Will on [12] by signing his name [at the foot or end thereof as

---

[7] Insert the relationship of the deponent to the deceased, e.g., "the brother", "a friend", "a work colleague".

[8] Or as may be.

[9] Insert details of the signature, e.g., "I M A Forgery".

[10] Insert the deceased's name.

[11] Insert the deceased's full name and last permanent address. Where the deponent is not a subscribing witness this paragraph should state "I was present at the execution of ...." or whatever the situation is enabling the deponent to give evidence of execution. An explanation of why a subscribing witness is not making the affidavit (e.g. his death) must be included.

[12] Insert the date the Will was executed. If it is wrongly dated or undated, insert the true date of execution or an estimated date.

the same now appears] thereon [in the presence of me [13] and .... the other subscribing witness thereto] both of us being present at the same time and we then both attested the said Will [in the presence of the deceased] [in the presence of .... [who have predeceased the deceased] [whose whereabouts are unknown]].

[3. Before the execution of the said Will by the deceased the same was read over to him by [14] and at the time he seemed perfectly to understand the same and its contents.]

[4. The deceased died a [15] and that I am [16] being one of the persons entitled to the deceased's estate if he had died intestate and that [17] are all *sui juris* and have consented to the admission of the said Will to proof without further proof of execution as appears from the consents now produced to and marked by me ......]

[5. The deceased executed the said Will on the date stated thereon by signing his name at the foot or end thereof as the same now appears in the presence of me and .... both of us being present at the same time and that after the deceased had signed we attested and subscribed the said Will in the presence of the deceased but that [18] and I signed our names above that of the deceased because there was insufficient space for us to sign below the deceased's signature.]

[6. The deceased executed his last Will on the date stated thereon by acknowledging his signature as the same now appears thereon to be his signature in the presence of me and [18] both of us being present at the same time by indicating his signature on the said Will and asking us to witness his signature and we then attested and subscribed the said Will in the presence of the deceased.]

Sworn, *etc. as in Form 1.*

5. Affidavit of Executor's Identity

In the High Court of Justice, *etc., as in Form 1.*

I, [1] make oath and say that:

---

[13] Insert the names of the witnesses; if the deponent was a witness, insert the deponent's name first.

[14] Insert the name of the witness or other person who read over the Will.

[15] Insert status, e.g., widower without issue, parent, brother, sister of the whole blood or any other person entitled in priority to share in the estate by virtue of any enactment.

[16] Insert relationship to the deceased.

[17] Insert the names of the other persons entitled to share; if none, delete "one of the persons" and insert "the only person".

[18] Insert the name(s) of the other subscribing witness(es).

1. [3] deceased, died on the ...... day of .... 20.. having made and duly executed his last Will and Testament dated the ...... day of ....
20.., wherein he appointed [19] as [his sole executor] [one of his executors].
2. I was at the date of execution of the said Will living at [20] [and was the only person of that name living at that address at the time [21]].
3. The deceased told me he had appointed me as his executor.
4. [I am sometimes known] [the deceased always referred to me] as [22].

Sworn, *etc. as in Form 1.*

6. Affidavit of Alias

In the High Court of Justice, *etc., as in Form 1.*

I, [1] make oath and say that:
[1. [23] otherwise [24] of [25] died on the ...... day of .... 20.. [having made and duly executed his last Will and Testament dated the ...... day of .... 20 .. and thereof appointed me [26]].]
[2. I am the lawful son [21] of [23] otherwise [24] of [25] deceased who died on the ...... day of .... 20 .. intestate].
[3. The true name of the deceased was [23] .]
[4. The deceased made and executed his said Will in the name of [24]].
[5. The deceased held [27] in the name of [24]].
In the circumstances it is desired that the grant should issue in the name of [23] otherwise [24] .

Sworn, *etc. as in Form 1.*

7. Affidavit in Support of Application for Leave to Swear Death

In the High Court of Justice, *etc., as in Form 1.*

I, [1] make oath and say that:

---

[19] Insert the name of the executor as it appears in the Will.
[20] Insert the address.
[21] Or as may be.
[22] Insert the name appearing in the Will.
[23] Insert the deceased's true name.
[24] Insert the alias name(s).
[25] Insert the deceased's last permanent address.
[26] Insert the deponent's name and capacity, e.g., "one of the executors", or the deponent's relationship to the deceased.
[27] Identify the asset(s) held in the alias name.

1. [28]
2. The presumed deceased was last seen alive on the ...... day of
.... 20 .. [29] .
3. The presumed deceased died [testate] [intestate].[30]
4. The presumed deceased had [31] .
5. The presumed deceased had accounts with [32] and that these accounts
have not been used since the presumed deceased disappeared. [33]
6. I believe the presumed deceased died on or since [34] .

Sworn, *etc. as in Form 1.*

8. Affidavit in Support of Application to Pass Over Right to Grant

In the High Court of Justice, *etc., as in Form 1.*

I, [1] make oath and say that:
1. [3] deceased, died on the ...... day of .... 20.. [having made and
duly executed his last Will and Testament dated the ...... day of ....
20.. [wherein he appointed [35] his sole executor]] [intestate] a bachelor

---

[28] Insert the full name, address, occupation or description, and age or date of birth, of
the presumed deceased.

[29] Where death is alleged to have occurred in a common disaster, e.g. in an air
accident, details of the presumed deceased's being aboard and the view taken by the
airline's insurers should be included; reports of rescue services (if any) should be
exhibited or put on separate affidavit, as should any supporting evidence by other
persons. Insert details of the time and place at which the presumed deceased was last
seen and by whom; if known, include the deceased's reason for being in that place.
Describe inquiries made by the police or any other official body, and of
advertisements inserted in newspapers with a view to tracing the presumed deceased
and the results. Insert details of any letters and/or telephone calls received from the
presumed deceased since his disappearance. Exhibit any relevant correspondence,
reports, newspapers or other documents.

[30] If the presumed deceased died testate the Will should be lodged with this affidavit.
If he died intestate, or the residue of the estate is not fully disposed of by the Will,
insert the names of persons entitled to share in the estate, or in the undisposed of
residue, and their relationship to the presumed deceased.

[31] Insert details of all insurance policies on the presumed deceased's life and recite the
views of the insurers, exhibiting relevant correspondence.

[32] Insert the names of the bank(s) and/or building society(ies) with which the
presumed deceased held accounts.

[33] Insert the amounts in the accounts, and details of all assets which comprise the
estate.

[34] Insert the date of the presumed death.

[35] Insert the name of the executor.

without issue or parent leaving .... his brother of the whole blood.[36]

2. The said [37] cannot now be traced. Despite extensive enquiries, his whereabouts cannot now be determined. [38]

3. I am the [39] .

4. The gross value of the estate amounts to £ ......

5. No life or minority interest arises in the estate.

I apply for an order under section 116 of the Supreme Court Act 1981 directing that letters of administration be granted to me.

Sworn, *etc. as in Form 1.*

9. Affidavit in Support of Application to Prove a Copy Will

In the High Court of Justice, *etc., as in Form 1.*

I, [1] make oath and say that:

1. [3] deceased, died on the ...... day of .... 20.., domiciled in England and Wales having made and duly executed his last Will and Testament dated the ...... day of .... 20.. [with ...... codicil[s] thereto].

2. Following execution the Will was [retained by his solicitors and there is an entry in their wills register of this fact] [deposited with ...... Bank] [handed to the deceased].

3. Following the death of the deceased the original of the said Will [and/or codicil] cannot be found.

4. [40]

I produce herewith marked ...... a [carbon copy] [copy draft] [photocopy] [reconstruction] [41] .

I request the court to make an order under and pursuant to Rule 54 of the Non-Contentious Probate Rules 1987 admitting the said copy Will to proof; the grant to be limited until the original Will or a more authentic copy be

---

[36] Or as may be.

[37] Insert the name of the executor or person entitled on intestacy, or as may be.

[38] Or as may be, giving the reason for passing over the right of the person entitled to the grant.

[39] Insert the relationship of the applicant to the deceased, if any, and all other relevant information to enable the court to determine whether the applicant is a proper person to be granted administration.

[40] Insert details of the loss of the original document. Where the Will had been in the testator's possession immediately before death, include evidence to rebut the presumption that the testator revoked it by destruction.

[41] Where no copy of the Will is available and the application is to prove a reconstruction, set out the evidence to establish that the proposed reconstruction is an accurate reflection of the original Will as executed.

proved [42].

Sworn, *etc. as in Form 1.*

10. Affidavit in Support of Application for Grant of Administration Limited Until Will Proved

In the High Court of Justice, *etc., as in Form 1.*

I, [1] make oath and say:

1. That [3] died on the ...... day of .... 20.. domiciled in England and Wales.

2. That the deceased is [known] [believed] to have made and executed a Will on [or about] the ...... day of .... 20.. [43] but following his death neither the original nor any copy can be found. There is no, or insufficient, evidence of the content or tenor of the Will to create a reconstruction. [44]

I request the court to order that letters of administration be granted to [me] [....................] the said grant to be limited until the original Will or an authentic copy be proved.

Sworn, *etc. as in Form 1.*

11. Affidavit in Support of Application to Rectify a Will

In the High Court of Justice, *etc., as in Form 1.*

I, [1] make oath and say that:

1. [3] deceased, died on the ...... day of .... 20.. having made and duly executed his last Will and Testament dated the ...... day of .... 20.. [with a codicil thereto dated the ...... day of .... 20..] a copy of which is exhibited hereto marked ..... [and therein named me sole executor] [and that I am one of the partners in the firm of ...., Solicitors] [which firm drew up the said Will [and codicil] and that I am the draftsman of the said Will [and codicil]].

[2. [In the said Will the appointment of executors [has been omitted] [is defective [45]]] [Clause ...... has been omitted from the said Will] [Clause ...... of the said Will was not intended by the testator to be revoked by the said codicil.]]

---

[42] This is the usual limitation, but the court may impose a further or different limitation if the circumstances so warrant.

[43] Insert the reason for the belief that there was a Will and the date, or approximate date, of its execution.

[44] Insert details of the enquiries made to find the Will and/or a copy.

[45] Insert details of the defect.

[2. Since the sealing of the grant of probate on the ...... day of ....
20.. it has been discovered that the original last Will and Testament of the
deceased dated the ...... day of .... 20.. is defective in that [46] .]
3.   It is clear from the [draft] [Will] [codicil] [exhibited hereto and marked
......] [instructions taken from the deceased] that the words ....
should be [inserted] [excluded] [amended to read ....].
4.   The error arose because [47] .
5.   [No one is prejudiced by the rectification sought.] [The consent[s]] [The
reply/ies to notice] of ...., being the persons prejudiced by the
rectification, are exhibited hereto and marked ...... [48]].

I request an order be made to rectify the said [Will] [Codicil] accordingly
pursuant to section 20 of the Administration of Justice Act 1982.

Sworn, *etc. as in Form 1.*

12. Affidavit in Support of Application for Interpretation of a Will

In the High Court of Justice, *etc., as in Form 1.*

I, [1] make oath and say that:
1.   [3] deceased, died on the ...... day of .... 20.. having made and
duly executed his last Will and Testament dated the ...... day of ....
20.. [with a codicil thereto dated the ...... day of .... 20..] [and
therein named me sole executor] [and that I am one of the partners in the
firm of ...., Solicitors] [which firm drew up the said Will [and
codicil] and that I am the draftsman of the said Will [and codicil]].
2.   [In the said Will the appointment of executors is defective because [49] .]
[That the gift of .... is meaningless or ambiguous because [50]].

I request the court to interpret the Will under section 21 of the
Administration of Justice Act 1982 accordingly to give effect to the
testator's intention.

Sworn, *etc. as in Form 1.*

---

[46] Insert details of the defect; this paragraph is to be completed where rectification is
sought after the Will has been proved.
[47] Insert how the error occurred, e.g., clerical error or failure to understand
instructions.
[48] Rule 55 requires notice to be given to persons prejudiced by the rectification, unless
the court directs otherwise.
[49] Describe the defect in the appointment clause; the testator's intention must be clear
and unequivocal and the clause must fail to give effect to that intention.
[50] Describe how the gift fails to carry out the testator's intention. The probate
registrar's jurisdiction to construe a gift is limited to establishing title to the grant
through that gift.

13. Affidavit in Support of Application for the Appointment of a Person to Take Administration for the Use and Benefit of a Person Mentally Incapable

In the High Court of Justice, *etc., as in Form 1.*

I, [1] make oath and say that:

1. [3] deceased, died on the ...... day of .... 20.. domiciled in England and Wales [having made and duly executed his last Will and Testament dated the ...... day of .... 20.. [and therein appointed .... his sole executor and residuary legatee and devisee]] [intestate leaving ...., the only person entitled to his estate [51]] who is now by reason of mental incapacity incapable of managing his affairs.

2. No one has been authorised by the Court of Protection to apply for letters of administration [(with Will annexed)] of the estate of the deceased and there is no one acting under a registered enduring power of attorney.

3. I am the [52].

4. I have given notice of the proposed application to the Public Guardianship Office (Court of Protection) pursuant to rule 35(5) [53].

I exhibit hereto [54].

I apply to the court for an order directing that letters of administration [(with Will annexed)] be granted to me under and pursuant to Rule 35(4) of the Non-Contentious Probate Rules 1987 for the use and benefit of the said .... and until further representation be granted.

Sworn, *etc. as in Form 1.*

14. Affidavit in Support of Application for the Appointment of Persons to Take Administration for the Use and Benefit of a Minor

In the High Court of Justice, *etc., as in Form 1.*

I, [1] make oath and say that:

1. [3] deceased, died on the ...... day of .... 20.. domiciled in

---

[51] Insert the title and clearing of the order of priority under rule 22 down to the incapable person.

[52] Insert the relationship of the deponent to the deceased and/or whether the applicant is, or intends to become, the receiver for the patient.

[53] Notice of the application (by letter) must be given to the Public Guardianship Office; its acknowledgement of the notice must be exhibited to the affidavit or lodged with the application for a grant.

[54] Exhibit medical evidence to establish the incapacity. A letter or report from the patient's GP is usually sufficient, or, if the patient is in an institution, a certificate by a responsible medical officer of the institution.

England and Wales [55] who is now a minor aged ...... years.

[2. The marriage of the deceased with .... was dissolved by final decree of the .... court in England and Wales and the deceased did not thereafter remarry [56].]

[3. [57], the person with parental responsibility for the said minor [has renounced administration for the use and benefit of the said minor] [refuses or neglects to apply for letters of administration for the use and benefit of the said minor.] [58]]

4.   There is no person [save ....] having parental responsibility for the said minor under section 2(1), 2(2) or 4 of or paragraph 4 or 6 of Schedule 14 to the Children Act 1989 or by virtue of an adoption order made under the Adoption Act 1976 and there is no person appointed or deemed to be appointed guardian of the said minor under section 5 or paragraph 12, 13 or 14 of Schedule 14 to the Children Act 1989.

5.   The said minor has not been made a ward of court and there are no proceedings pending to make the said minor a ward of court nor have there been or are there pending any proceedings in any court to which the Children Act 1989 Applies.[59]

6.   We are [60] .

7.   The said minor resides at [61] .

8.   The gross value of the estate is £ ..... and the net value, £ ......

We apply for an order under Rule 32(2) of the Non-Contentious Probate Rules 1987 directing that letters of administration be granted to us for the use and benefit of the said minor and until he shall attain the age of eighteen years.

Sworn, *etc. as in Form 1.*

---

[55] Insert "having made his last Will and Testament in which he appointed .... the executor] [and/or residuary beneficiary]"; "intestate [status, e.g., "a single man"] leaving .... his daughter and only person entitled to his estate"; or as may be.

[56] If the decree or order was made by a court outside England and Wales, insert evidence to show that it is capable of recognition under section 46, Family Law Act 1986.

[57] Insert the name of the former spouse or other person with parental responsibility.

[58] Or as may be.

[59] If there have been proceedings, insert details of them and of any order(s) made.

[60] Set out the relationship, if any, to the minor child and/or the deceased.

[61] Insert the minor's current address and who presently cares for him.

15. Affidavit to Establish Validity of Will: Foreign Domicile

In the High Court of Justice, *etc., as in Form 1.*

I, [1] make oath and say that:

1. I am [the sole executor] [one of the executors] [62] named in the [last Will and Testament] [Codicil] bearing date the ...... day of .... 20.. of [3] who died on the ...... day of .... 20, the said [Will] [Codicil] being now produced to and marked by me ....

2. [The said [Will] [Codicil] was executed at [63]].

[At the time of execution of the said [Will] [Codicil] the deceased was domiciled in or had his habitual residence in [63]].

[At [the time of execution of the said [Will] [Codicil]] [the date of his death] the deceased was a national of [63]].

3. Of the systems of internal law in force in [63] relating to the formal validity of wills at the time of execution of the said [Will] [Codicil] or at the time of the deceased's death the deceased was most closely associated with the .... internal system of law by reason of [64] .

4. The said [Will] [Codicil] is therefore valid under section 1 of the Wills Act 1963 and admissible to proof in England and Wales.

Sworn, *etc. as in Form 1.*

16. Affidavit to Establish Validity of Will or Beneficial Entitlement: Foreign Law

In the High Court of Justice, *etc., as in Form 1.*

I, [1] [an advocate [62]] make oath and say that:

1. I am fully conversant with the laws and constitutions of [63] and [practised] as an [advocate [62]] in that [country] [state] [province] for ...... years.[65]

2. I am informed and verily believe that [3] deceased died on the ...... day of .... 20.., domiciled in [63] [having made his last Will and Testament dated the ...... day of .... 19..] [intestate].

[3. I have referred to the [official] [notarial] [certified] copy of the last Will and Testament of the deceased, which is now produced to and marked by me

---

[62] Or as may be.

[63] Insert the country, or where the state or territories of that country have separate systems of law, the state or territory.

[64] Insert the basis for the connection, e.g., residence, religion, place of birth, ownership of property. To validate a Will in "English form" where the deceased was a British national, it must be shown that he was most closely connected with the system of law in England and Wales.

[65] Insert any other qualifications to establish the deponent's knowledge of the law concerned.

..... and I say that the said Will was made in conformity with and is valid by the said laws and constitutions.[66]

[4. In accordance with the said laws and constitutions the original of the said Will is deposited [at] [with] .... and cannot be removed from such custody. The said copy produced to and marked ...... by me is acceptable as evidence of the contents of the original Will in the Court of [63].]

5. In the circumstances I say that [67] [is] [are] beneficially entitled to [share in] the said estate by the said laws and constitutions of [63].

Sworn, *etc. as in Form 1.*

17. Affidavit in Support of Application for a Subpoena for the Production of a Testamentary Document

In the High Court of Justice, *etc., as in Form 1.*

I, [1] make oath and say that:

1. [3] deceased, died on the ...... day of .... 20.. domiciled in England and Wales having made and duly executed his last Will and Testament dated the ...... day of .... 20.., and therein appointed .... his [executor] and appointed me [one of] the residuary legatees and devisees.

2. The said Will is now in the possession, custody or power of [68] and that [he] [they] have neglected or declined to prove the said Will or renounce probate thereof. [69]

3. The said [68] reside at .... [respectively].

I request that the said Will be brought in to the [Principal] [.................... District Probate] Registry in order that I may prove the same or otherwise act as I may be advised.

Sworn, *etc. as in Form 1.*

18. Affidavit of Service of Warning

In the High Court of Justice, *etc., as in Form 1.*

I, [1] make oath and say that:

On the ...... day of .... 20.. I duly served [70] with a true copy of the

---

[66] Where the Wills Act 1963 is relied on, recite the law which validated the Will in the place where the deceased died domiciled.

[67] Insert the name(s) of the person(s) beneficially entitled to share the estate.

[68] Insert the name(s) of the person(s) having custody of the Will.

[69] Or as may be.

[70] Insert the full name of the caveator or his solicitors.

warning now produced to and marked by me ..... [by delivering to and leaving the same with [71] [a clerk in the firm of ....] [before the hour of 4 in the afternoon] [before the hour of 12 noon on a Saturday] [by sending the same by [prepaid] [registered] [recorded delivery] post to the address for service given in the caveat] [by leaving the same at the ....
Document Exchange for box number .... at .... Exchange]
[by leaving the same at the .... Document Exchange for transmission to the .... Document Exchange, box number ....] included in the address for service given in the caveat.

Sworn, *etc. as in Form 1.*

19. Affidavit of Service of Citation

In the High Court of Justice, *etc., as in Form 1.*

I, [1] make oath and say that:
1. I served [72] with a true copy of the citation issued out of the [73] by delivering to and leaving the same with him. A sealed copy of the citation is exhibited hereto marked ......
2. I established the identity of the person served by [74] .

Sworn, *etc. as in Form 1.*

20. Affidavit in Support of Application for an Order Amending a Grant of Representation

In the High Court of Justice, *etc., as in Form 1.*

I, [1] make oath and say that:
1. On the ...... day of .... 20.. a grant of [probate] [letters of administration [(with Will annexed)]] of the estate of [3] deceased [was] [were] granted at the [Principal] [.................... District Probate] Registry to me this deponent [the sole executor named in the Will of the deceased] [the residuary legatee and devisee named in the Will of the deceased] [the lawful widow and the only person entitled to share in the estate of the deceased] [75]
2. In the said grant of [probate] [letters of administration [(with Will

---

[71] Insert name of person served.

[72] Insert the full name, address and occupation or description of the citee.

[73] Insert the name of the registry which issued the citation.

[74] Recite how identity was established, e.g., the citee identified himself by producing his driving licence.

[75] Insert the grantee's title to the grant.

annexed)]] [76] whereas [77] .

3.   The error arose [78] .

I apply for an order that the said grant of [probate] [letters of administration [(with Will annexed)]] be amended by [79] .

Sworn, *etc. as in Form 1.*

21. Affidavit in Support of Application for an Order Revoking a Grant of Representation

In the High Court of Justice, *etc., as in Form 1.*

I, [1] make oath and say that:

1.   On the ...... day of .... 20.. a grant of [probate] [letters of administration [(with Will annexed)]] of the estate of [3] deceased [was] [were] granted at the [Principal] [.................... District Probate] Registry to me this deponent [the sole executor named in the Will of the deceased] [the residuary legatee and devisee named in the Will of the deceased] [the lawful widow and the only person entitled to share in the estate of the deceased] [80]

2.   The said grant of [probate] [letters of administration [(with Will annexed)]] issued on the basis that [the Will dated .... was the last Will of the deceased] [the deceased died intestate a bachelor without issue] [81] whereas [the deceased had in fact made a later Will dated ....] [was married to .... who remained his lawful wife] [the grantee died before the grant of .... issued] [81] .

I hereby apply for an order that the said grant of [probate] [letters of administration [(with Will annexed)]] issued on the ...... day of .... 20.. be revoked and declared null and void.

Sworn, *etc. as in Form 1.*

⅃

---

[76] Recite the error or omission appearing in the grant.

[77] Insert what should have appeared in the grant.

[78] Explain how the error or omission arose.

[79] Insert the correction sought.

[80] Insert the grantee's title to the grant.

[81] Or as may be.

22. Caveat

The Non-Contentious Probate Rules 1987, Schedule 1, Form 3

In the High Court of Justice, *etc., as in Form 1.*

Let no grant be sealed in the estate of [82] deceased, who died on the ...... day of .... 20.. without notice to [83]

Dated the ...... day of .... 20..
Signed .... [84]
whose address for service is ....
[Solicitor for the said ....]

23. Warning to Caveator

The Non-Contentious Probate Rules 1987, Schedule 1, Form 4

In the High Court of Justice
Family Division
The Leeds District Probate Registry
In the Estate of ...., Deceased

To .... of .... a party who has entered a caveat in the estate of .... deceased.

You have eight days (starting with the day on which this warning was served on you):

(i) to enter an appearance either in person or by your solicitor or probate practitioner at the Leeds District Probate Registry, Third Floor, Coronet House, Queen Street, Leeds LS1 2BA setting out what interest you have in the estate of the above-named .... of .... deceased contrary to that of the party at whose instance this warning is issued; or

(ii) if you have no contrary interest but wish to show cause against the sealing of a grant to such party, to issue and serve a summons for directions by a District Judge of the Principal Registry or a Registrar of a District Probate Registry.

   If you fail to do either of these the court may proceed to issue a grant of probate or administration in the said estate notwithstanding your caveat.
Dated the ...... day of .... 20..
Issued at the instance of [85].

---

[82] Insert the full name and address of the deceased. The deceased's names as they appear in the death certificate should be given (see Practice Direction 22 March 2002 [2002] 1 WLR 1303). Failure to give the full true name may mean that an application for a grant will not be matched to the caveat.

[83] Insert the name of the party by whom or on whose behalf the caveat is entered.

[84] To be signed by the caveator's solicitor or by the caveator if acting in person.

[85] Here set out the name and interest (including the date of the Will, if any, under which the interest arises) of the party warning, the name of his solicitor and the address for service. If the party warning is acting in person, this must be stated.

24. Appearance to Warning
The Non-Contentious Probate Rules 1987, Schedule 1, Form 5

In the High Court of Justice
Family Division
The Leeds District Probate Registry
In the Estate of ...., Deceased

Caveat number .... dated the ...... day of .... 20..
Full name and address of deceased: ....
Full name and address of person warning: .... [86]
Full name and address of caveator: .... [87]
Enter an appearance for the above-named caveator in this matter.

Dated the ...... day of .... 20..
Signed .... [Solicitor for the said ....][................... in person]
whose address for service is ....

25. Citation to take Probate Against an Executor who has Intermeddled

In the High Court of Justice, *etc., as in Form 1.*

ELIZABETH THE SECOND by the Grace of God, of the United Kingdom of Great Britain and Northern Ireland and of the Other Realms and Territories, Queen, Head of the Commonwealth, Defender of the Faith. To [88]
TAKE NOTICE that [89] has stated in an affidavit sworn on the ...... day of .... 20.. that [90] died on the ...... day of .... 20.. domiciled in England and Wales, having made and duly executed his last Will and Testament dated the ...... day of .... 20.. now remaining in [the Principal Registry of the Family Division of the High Court of Justice] [the .... District Probate Registry], that you the said [88] are appointed sole executor in that Will, that the said [89] is interested in the estate of the said deceased under the said Will and that you the said [88] have intermeddled in the estate of the said deceased.

NOW THIS IS TO COMMAND YOU the said [88] that within eight days after service hereof on you, inclusive of the day of such service, you do cause an appearance to be entered in the [Principal Registry of the Family Division, First Avenue House, 42–49 High Holborn, London WC1V 6NP]

---

[86] Here set out the interest of the person warning as shown in the warning.
[87] Here set out the interest of the caveator, stating the date of the Will (if any) under which such interest arises.
[88] Insert the name of the intermeddling executor (the citee).
[89] Insert the name of the beneficiary (the citor).
[90] Insert the name and address of the deceased.

[the .... District Probate Registry at ....] and show cause why you should not be ordered to take probate of the said Will.

Dated the ...... day of .... 20..
Extracted by .... of ...., Solicitor
Signed .... District Judge/Registrar

26. Citation Against Executor to whom Power was Reserved, to Accept or Refuse Probate

In the High Court of Justice, *etc., as in Form 1.*

ELIZABETH THE SECOND, *etc., as in Form 25.*
To [91]

TAKE NOTICE that [92] has stated in an affidavit sworn on the ...... day of .... 20.. that probate of the Will of [93] was on the ...... day of .... 20.. granted by our High Court of Justice at [the Principal Registry of the Family Division of the High Court of Justice] [the .... District Probate Registry] thereof to [94] one of the executors named therein, power of making a like grant being reserved to [95] the other executor named therein, that the said [94] died on the ...... day of .... 20 .. leaving part of the estate of the said deceased unadministered and that on the ...... day of .... 20 .. probate of the Will of the said [94] was granted by this court at the said Registry to [96] the sole executor thereof.

NOW THIS IS TO COMMAND YOU the said [95] that within eight days after service hereof on you, inclusive of the day of such service, you do cause an appearance to be entered in [The Principal Registry of the Family Division, First Avenue House, 42–49 High Holborn, London WC1V 6NP] [the .... District Probate Registry at ....] and accept or refuse probate of the said Will of the said .... deceased.

AND TAKE FURTHER TAKE NOTICE that, in default of your so appearing and accepting or extracting probate of the said Will, your rights as such executor will wholly cease, and the representation to the said .... deceased will devolve as if you had not been appointed executor.

Dated the ...... day of .... 20..
Extracted by .... of ...., Solicitor
Signed .... District Judge/Registrar

---

[91] Insert the full name and address of the executor cited (the citee).
[92] Insert the name and address of the citor.
[93] Insert the name and address of the deceased.
[94] Insert the name of the proving executor.
[95] Insert the name of the citee.
[96] Insert the name of the sole executor.

27. Citation to Accept or Refuse a Grant

In the High Court of Justice, *etc., as in Form 1.*

ELIZABETH THE SECOND, *etc., as in Form 25.*
To [97]

Whereas it appears by the affidavit of [92] sworn on the ...... day of ....
20 .. that [93] died on the ...... day of .... 20 ..

[having made and duly executed his last Will and Testament dated the ......
day of .... 20 .. [now remaining in [the Principal Registry of the
Family Division of the High Court of Justice] [the .... District
Probate Registry]] and [98] [thereof appointed you the sole executor] [wherein
he named you the residuary legatee and devisee.]

[intestate a [widow] [widower] [99] or any other person entitled in priority to
share in the estate by virtue of any enactment] leaving [95] the lawful [100] and
[one of] [101] the person[s] entitled to share in the estate of the said deceased.]

NOW THIS IS TO COMMAND YOU the said [95] that within eight days
after service hereof on you, inclusive of the day of such service, you do
cause an appearance to be entered in the [Principal Registry of the Family
Division, First Avenue House, 42–49 High Holborn, London WC1V 6NP]
[the .... District Probate Registry at ....] and accept or
refuse [a grant of probate of the said Will] [letters of administration (with
Will annexed)] [letters of administration] of all the estate which by law
devolves to and vests in the personal representatives of the said deceased or
show cause why a grant should not be granted to [102].

AND TAKE NOTICE that in default of your appearing and accepting
and extracting [a grant of probate of the said Will] [letters of administration
[(with Will annexed)]] our said Court will proceed to grant letters of
administration [(with Will annexed)] to the said [102] notwithstanding your
absence.

Dated the ...... day of .... 20..
Extracted by .... of ...., Solicitor
Signed .... District Judge/Registrar

---

[97] Insert the full name and address of the person cited.
[98] Insert the title to the grant.
[99] Insert any further clearings.
[100] Insert the relationship to the deceased.
[101] Or as may be.
[102] Insert the name of the citor.

28. Citation to Propound Paper Writing

In the High Court of Justice, *etc., as in Form 1.*

ELIZABETH THE SECOND, *etc., as in Form 25.*
To [97]
Whereas it appears by the affidavit of [102] sworn on the ...... day of
.... 20 .. that [93] died on the ...... day of .... 20 .. domiciled
in England and Wales a [widow] [widower] leaving the said [102] his [100] and the
only person entitled to his estate and that the said deceased left a certain
paper writing dated the ...... day of .... 20 .. purporting to be a Will
now remaining in [the Principal Registry of the Family Division of the High
Court of Justice] [the .... District Probate Registry], whereby he
appointed you the said [95] sole executor and residuary legatee and devisee.

NOW THIS IS TO COMMAND YOU the said [95] that within eight days
after service hereof on you, inclusive of the day of such service, you do
cause an appearance to be entered in the [Principal Registry of the Family
Division, First Avenue House, 42–49 High Holborn, London WC1V 6NP]
[the .... District Probate Registry at ....] and propound
the said paper writing should you think it in your interest to do so, or to
show cause why letters of administration of all the estate which by law
devolves to and vests in the personal representative of the said deceased
should not be granted to the said [102].

AND TAKE NOTICE that in default of your appearing and doing as
aforesaid our said Court will proceed to issue a grant of representation of the
said estate as if the said purported Will were invalid, notwithstanding your
absence.

Dated the ...... day of .... 20..
Extracted by .... of ...., Solicitor
Signed .... District Judge/Registrar

29. Appearance to Citation
The Non-Contentious Probate Rules 1987, Schedule 1, Form 5

In the High Court of Justice, *etc., as in Form 1.*

Caveat number .... dated the ...... day of .... 20..
Citation dated the ...... day of .... 20 ..
Full name and address of deceased: ....
Full name and address of citor: .... [103]
Full name and address of person cited: .... [104]

---

[103] Here set out the interest of the citor, as shown in the citation.

[104] Here set out the interest of the person cited, stating the date of the Will (if any)
under which such interest arises.

ENTER AN APPEARANCE for the above-named person cited in this matter.

Dated the ...... day of .... 20..
Signed .... [Solicitor for the said ....] [................ in person] whose address for service is ....

30. Consent to Will Being Proved

In the High Court of Justice, *etc., as in Form 1.*

1.   WHEREAS [105] died on the ...... day of .... 20 .. having made and duly executed his last Will and Testament dated the ...... day of .... 20 .. and in the said Will appointed .... [the sole executor] [the residuary legatee and devisee] thereof.
2.   The following [alterations [106]] appear in the said Will namely [107]
3.   [108] [are dead] [cannot be found]. [106]
4.   The said deceased died a [109] or any other person entitled in priority to share in his estate by virtue of any enactment leaving [110]
5.   I, [111] do hereby give my consent to [probate of the Will] [letters of administration (with Will annexed)] being granted to [112].

Signed by the said ....
in the presence of .... of ....
the ...... day of .... 20 ..

31. Consent to Trust Corporation Applying

In the High Court of Justice, *etc., as in Form 1.*

Whereas [105] died on the ...... day of .... 20 .. domiciled in England and Wales [intestate [113] leaving [114] the only person entitled to his estate]

---

[105] Insert the full name and address of the deceased.
[106] Or as may be.
[107] Describe the alteration or other apparent irregularity giving rise to the need for consent by those who could be prejudiced.
[108] Insert the names of the witnesses.
[109] Insert deceased's status, e.g., a widower, clearing kin down to the person(s) entitled to share if the deceased had died intestate.
[110] Insert the names of all persons, and their interests, who would be prejudiced if the Will were to be accepted to proof in its correct form.
[111] Insert the name of the person consenting.
[112] Insert the name of the applicant.
[113] Insert the deceased's status, e.g., a widow.
[114] Insert the names of the next of kin entitled to share in the estate.

[having made and duly executed his last Will and Testament dated the ......
day of .... 20 .. wherein he named .... sole executor and
residuary legatee and devisee].

Now [I] [we], the said [115] hereby consent to letters of administration [with
the said Will annexed] of the estate of the said deceased being granted to [116]

Signed by the said ....
in the presence of .... of ....
the ...... day of .... 20 ..

32. Nomination of Second Administrator, Minority Interest Arising

In the High Court of Justice, *etc., as in Form 1.*

Whereas [105] deceased died on the ...... day of .... 20 .. domiciled in
England and Wales intestate, [117] leaving [118] the only person[s] entitled to
[share in] his estate.

And whereas the said [119] [is] [are] [a] [minor[s]] aged ...... [and ......
respectively].

And whereas there is no [other person with parental responsibility for]
[guardian of] the said minor[s].

Now I, the said [120] do hereby nominate and appoint [121] to be my co-
administrator in the estate of the said intestate, he being a fit and proper
person to act in that capacity.

Signed by the said ....
in the presence of .... of ....
the ...... day of .... 20 ..

---

[115] Insert the name(s) of the beneficiary/ies consenting.

[116] Insert the name of the trust corporation.

[117] Insert the deceased's status, e.g., "a widow".

[118] Insert the names of the minor(s) entitled to share and their relationship to the
deceased, e.g., "his sons".

[119] Insert the names of the minor(s).

[120] Insert the name of the applicant.

[121] Insert the name and address of the proposed second co-administrator, his
relationship to the children and the capacity in which parental responsibility was
obtained.

33. Nomination of Person by Resolution to Act on Behalf of Non-Trust Corporation

At the meeting of the [122] of [123] on the ...... day of .... 20 .. it was resolved that [124] be nominated to act on behalf of .... in [all matters relating to the estate of persons in which [125] has an interest] [in the estate of .... deceased][126].

Signed .... [127]
the ...... day of .... 20 ..

34. Notice of Election to Redeem Life Interest
The Non-Contentious Probate Rules 1987, Schedule 1, Form 6

In the High Court of Justice, *etc., as in Form 1.*

Whereas .... of .... died on the ...... day of .... 20 .. [wholly] [partially] intestate leaving [his] [her] lawful [wife] [husband] and .... lawful issue of the said deceased.

And whereas [probate] [letters of administration] of the estate of the said .... were granted to me the said ....[and to .... of ....] at the.............. Probate Registry on the ...... day of .... 20 ..

And whereas [the said .... has ceased to be a personal representative because ....] and I am [now] the sole personal representative.

Now I, the said .... hereby give notice in accordance with section 47A of the Administration of Estates Act 1925 that I elect to redeem the life interest to which I am entitled in the estate of the late .... by retaining £ ...., its capital value, and £ ...., the costs of the transaction.

Dated the ...... day of .... 20 ..
Signed ....
To the Senior District Judge of the Family Division.

---

[122] Insert the title of the governing body, e.g., "board of directors".

[123] Insert the name of the charity, or as may be, the non-trust corporation.

[124] Insert *either* the name(s) of the person(s) appointed *or* the positions of officers entitled to act by virtue of holding those positions, e.g., secretary, chief executive, legacy officer.

[125] Insert the name of the charity, or as may be.

[126] Delete as appropriate for general authorisation or for authorisation limited to a specific estate.

[127] Signature of authorising officer, e.g., the company secretary.

35. Notice to Executor Having Power Reserved

In the Estate of ...., Deceased

TAKE NOTICE that [128] died on the ...... day of .... 20 .. having appointed [129] as executors of his Will, [130] being [one] [two] [131] of the executors intend to apply for probate with power reserved to you [132].

Signed ....
the ...... day of .... 20 ..

36. Notice of Application for a Standing Search

In the High Court of Justice, *etc., as in Form 1.*

[I] [We] apply for the entry of a standing search so that there shall be sent to [me] [us] an office copy of every grant of representation in England and Wales in the estate of [128].
Alternative or alias name: [133]
Exact date of death: [134]
which either has issued not more than twelve months before the entry of this application or issues within six months thereafter.

Signed: .... Name in block letters: ....
Address: .... Reference (if any): ....

---

[128] Insert the full name and address of the deceased.

[129] Insert the names of all the executors appointed (except where the appointment is of partners in a firm, when "the partners in the firm of ....." should be inserted.

[130] Insert the name(s) of the proving executor(s).

[131] Or as may be.

[132] Insert the name(s) of the executor(s) to whom power is reserved.

[133] If the deceased was known by an alternative forename or surname, insert the alternative name(s).

[134] Insert the date of death as it appears in the death certificate, or, if not known, a span of dates, e.g. "1st to 7th March 2003".

37. General Form of Oath for Executors

In the High Court of Justice, *etc., as in Form 1.*
[I] [We] [135] of [136] make oath and say:
1. That [I] [we] believe the paper writing now produced to and marked by [me] [us] to be the true and original last Will and Testament [137] of [138] deceased, who was born on the ...... day of .... 19 .. and died on the ...... day of .... 20 ..[139] aged ...... domiciled in [England and Wales].
2. That to the best of [my] [our] knowledge and belief there was [no] land vested in the said deceased immediately before his death which was settled previously to his death (and not by his Will [and codicil[s]) and which remained settled land notwithstanding his death.[140]
3. That [I am the [sole] [surviving] executor] [We are the [surviving] executors] [141] named in the said Will [142].
[4. That notice of the application has been given to .... the

---

[135] Insert the full and correct names of each executor applying. If any name is different from that given in the Will, an explanation must be given; e.g., following a change of name on marriage, "formerly ...... having married ...... since the date of the Will". Further evidence may be required if any difference is not properly explained.

[136] Insert the full, permanent postal address (including postcode) of each executor. An executor acting in a professional capacity may give his business address.

Following the address of each executor, insert his occupation or description, e.g., "journalist", "retired".

[137] Where the Will to be proved comprises more than one document, insert the words "as contained in the paper writings marked ....". Add, if appropriate, "together with [a] [two] [three] codicil[s]". Each executor and the commissioner must mark the documents with their signatures.

[138] Insert the full true name and address (including postcode) of the deceased (see Practice Direction 22 March 2002 [2002] 1 WLR 1303). If the deceased held property in a former name or alias, insert "formerly or otherwise known as .....". Any substantial discrepancy in the name must be explained in the oath, as must the reason for including the alternative or alias name in the grant. The last residential address of the deceased should be given.

[139] Insert the dates of birth and death as they appear in the death certificate (see Practice Direction 12 January 1999). The death certificate need not be lodged.

[140] Where there is such settled land and the grant is in respect of free estate only, the word "no" should be omitted and the words "save and except settled land" added.

[141] Or as may be.

[142] The deponent(s) must swear that they are the executor(s) named in the Will in accordance with their appointment. Where one or more executor(s) has renounced probate, add " [name] having renounced probate". The form(s) of renunciation must be lodged with the other documents.

executor[s] to whom power is to be reserved [143] [save ....]] [144] [145].

5.   That [I] [we] will collect, get in and administer according to law the real and personal estate of the said deceased; when required to do so by the Court, exhibit in the Court a full inventory of the said estate and render an account thereof to the Court; and when required to do so by the High Court, deliver up to that Court the grant of probate.

6.   That to the best of [my] [our] knowledge, information and belief the gross value of the estate passing under the grant [amounts to] [does not exceed] £ .... and the net value [amounts to] [does not exceed] £ .... [and that this is not a case in which an Inland Revenue Account is required to be delivered]. [146]

Sworn by the above-named deponent[s] ....
at .... on [date]
Before me, ... A Commissioner for Oaths/Solicitor.

38. Oath for Executors who are Partners in a Firm

In the High Court of Justice, *etc., as in Form 1.*

[I] [We] [135] of [136] make oath and say:

1.   That [I] [we] believe the paper writing now produced to and marked by [me] [us] to be the true and original last Will and Testament [137] of [138] deceased, who was born on the ...... day of .... 19 .. and died on the ...... day of .... 20 ..[139] aged ...... domiciled in [England and Wales].

2.   That to the best of [my] [our] knowledge and belief there was [no] land vested in the said deceased immediately before his death which was settled previously to his death (and not by his Will [and codicil[s]]) and which remained settled land notwithstanding his death. [140]

3.   That the said deceased appointed in the said Will [and codicil[s]] the partners at the date of his death in [the firm of ....] [the firm which at the date of his death had succeeded to and carried on the practice of the firm of ....] to be the executors [and trustees] of the said Will.

4.   That [I am] [we are] [one] [two] of the partners in the firm of

---

[143] Where power is to be reserved to executors who are partners in a firm, notice need not be given, nor need their names be recited.

[144] Where a district judge or registrar has dispensed with giving such notice, add "after the giving of notice to whom was dispensed with by direction dated ......".

[145] If the appointment is limited in any way, e.g., to literary estate, the limitation should be set out.

[146] When an Inland Revenue Account is required, insert the actual gross and net values of the estate; where an Account is not required, insert the appropriate gross value. The net estate figure should be the actual value rounded up to the nearest £1,000; see Practice Direction 22 March 2002 [2002] 1 WLR 1303.

.... [being the successor firm to ....] at the date of death of the said deceased and as such [one] [two] of the executors named in the said Will.

[5. That power is reserved to all the other partners in the said firm of .... at the said date of death and as such the other executors.]

6.   That [I] [we] will collect, get in and administer according to law the real and personal estate of the said deceased; when required to do so by the Court, exhibit in the Court a full inventory of the said estate and render an account thereof to the Court; and when required to do so by the High Court, deliver up to that Court the grant of probate.

7.   That to the best of [my] [our] knowledge, information and belief the gross value of the estate passing under the grant [amounts to] [does not exceed] £ .... and the net value [amounts to] [does not exceed] £ .... [and that this is not a case in which an Inland Revenue Account is required to be delivered.] [146]

Sworn *etc, as in Form 37.*

39. Oath for Double Probate

In the High Court of Justice, *etc., as in Form 1.*

[I] [We] [135] of [136] make oath and say:

1.   That [I] [we] believe the paper writing now produced to and marked by [me] [us] to be [an official copy of] the true and original last Will and Testament [and codicil[s]] of [138] deceased, who was born on the ...... day of .... 19 .. and died on the ...... day of .... 20 ..[139] aged ...... domiciled in [England and Wales].

2.   That to the best of [my] [our] knowledge and belief there was [no] land vested in the said deceased immediately before his death which was settled previously to his death (and not by his Will [and codicil[s]) and which remained settled land notwithstanding his death. [140]

3.   That on the ...... day of .... 20 .. probate of the said Will was granted to [147] at the [Principal Registry] [.................... District Probate Registry] [one] [two] of the executors named in the said Will [power being reserved of making the like grant to [148] the other executor[s] named in the said Will.

4.   That [I am] [we are] [one of] [two of] the other executor[s] named in the said Will.

5.   That notice of the application has been given to .... the

---

[147] Insert the names of the proving executors.

[148] Insert the names of the executor(s) to whom power was reserved.

executor[s] to whom power is to be reserved [149].

6.   That [I] [we] will collect, get in and administer according to law the real and personal estate of the said deceased; when required to do so by the Court, exhibit in the Court a full inventory of the said estate and render an account thereof to the Court; and when required to do so by the High Court, deliver up to that Court the grant of probate.

7.   That to the best of [my] [our] knowledge, information and belief the gross value of the estate now unadministered passing under the grant [amounts to] [does not exceed] £ .... and the net value [amounts to] [does not exceed] £ .... [and that this is not a case in which an Inland Revenue Account is required to be delivered.] [146]

Sworn *etc, as in Form 37.*

40. Oath for Trust Corporation Appointed Executor

In the High Court of Justice, *etc., as in Form 1.*

I [150] in the employ of [151] whose registered office is at .... make oath and say:

1.   That I believe the paper writing now produced to and marked by me to be the true and original last Will and Testament [and codicil[s]] of [138] deceased, who was born on the ...... day of .... 19 .. and died on the ...... day of .... 20 ..[139] aged ...... domiciled in [England and Wales].

2.   That to the best of my knowledge and belief there was [no] land vested in the said deceased immediately before his death which was settled previously to his death (and not by his Will [and codicil[s]) and which remained settled land notwithstanding his death.[140]

3.   That the said deceased appointed in the said Will [and codicil[s]] the said corporation [and [152]] to be the [sole] executors of the said Will.

4.   That the said company by a resolution dated the ...... day of .... 20 .. [a certified copy of which is lodged herewith appointed me for the purpose of applying for a grant] [a certified copy of which has been lodged with the Senior District Judge and is still in force authorised persons holding my position to apply for grants of representation] and that the said company is a trust corporation as defined by Rule 2(1) of the Non-Contentious Probate

---

[149] Where power is to be further reserved to another executor, this should be recited and a statement that notice has been given should be added (see paragraph 4 of form 37, above).

[150] Insert the deponent's full name and address, which may be the business address. Insert also the deponent's occupation if necessary as authority to swear the oath.

[151] Insert the name and address of the trust corporation.

[152] Insert the full names of any other executor(s) appointed.

Rules 1987 and has power to accept the grant now applied for.

5.   That the said company will collect, get in and administer according to law the real and personal estate [save and except settled land] of the said deceased; when required to do so by the Court, exhibit in the Court a full inventory of the said estate and render an account thereof to the Court; and when required to do so by the High Court, deliver up to that Court the grant of probate.

6.   That to the best of my knowledge, information and belief the gross value of the estate passing under the grant [amounts to] [does not exceed] £ ....
[and that this is not a case in which an Inland Revenue Account is required to be delivered.] [146]

Sworn *etc, as in Form 37.*

41. Oath for Executors: Lost or Reconstructed Will

In the High Court of Justice, *etc., as in Form 1.*

[I] [We] [135] of [136] make oath and say:

1.   That [I] [we] believe the paper writing now produced to and marked by [me] [us] to contain the last Will and Testament as contained in the [carbon copy] [draft] [photocopy] [reconstruction] exhibited to the affidavit of [153] sworn on the ...... day of .... 20 .. and marked "..." of [138] deceased, who was born on the ...... day of .... 19 .. and died on the ...... day of .... 20 ..[139] aged ...... domiciled in [England and Wales].

2.   That to the best of [my] [our] knowledge and belief there was [no] land vested in the said deceased immediately before his death which was settled previously to his death (and not by his Will [and codicil[s]) and which remained settled land notwithstanding his death. [140]

3.   That by order of [Mr Registrar] [District Judge] .... of this Division dated the ...... day of .... 20 .. it was ordered that the last Will and Testament of the said deceased be admitted to proof as contained in the said [carbon copy] [draft] [photocopy] [reconstruction].

4.   That [I am the [sole] [surviving] executor] [we are the [surviving] executors] [141] named in the said Will [142].

5.   That notice of the application has been given to .... the executor[s] to whom power is to be reserved [143] [save ....]] [144] [145]

6.   That [I] [we] will collect, get in and administer according to law the real and personal estate of the said deceased limited until the original Will or a more authentic copy be proved; when required to do so by the Court, exhibit in the Court a full inventory of the said estate and render an account thereof to the Court; and when required to do so by the High Court, deliver up to

---

[153] Insert the name of the deponent to the affidavit pursuant to which the order to admit the copy was made.

that Court the grant of probate.

7.   That to the best of [my] [our] knowledge, information and belief the gross value of the estate passing under the grant [amounts to] [does not exceed] £ .... and the net estate [amounts to] [does not exceed] £ .... [and that this is not a case in which an Inland Revenue Account is required to be delivered.] [146]

Sworn *etc, as in Form 37.*

42. Oath for Special Executors

In the High Court of Justice, *etc., as in Form 1.*

[I] [We] [135] of [136] make oath and say:

1.   That [I] [we] believe the paper writing now produced to and marked by [me] [us] to be the true and original last Will and Testament [137] of [138] deceased, who was born on the ...... day of .... 19 .. and died on the ...... day of .... 20 .. [139] aged ...... domiciled in [England and Wales].

[2.   That on the ...... day of .... 20 .. probate of the said Will in respect of all the estate save and except [his publishing business [154]] was granted at the .... District Probate Registry to [155] , his general executors.] [156]

3.   That [I am] [we are] [one] [two] [of] the special executor[s] named in the said Will in respect of the deceased's [publishing business].

4.   That notice of the application has been given to .... the other special executor[s] to whom power is to be reserved [143] [save ....]] [144] [145].

5.   That to the best of [my] [our] knowledge and belief there was [no] land vested in the said deceased immediately before his death which was settled previously to his death [and not by his Will] and which remained settled land notwithstanding his death.

6.   That [I] [we] will collect, get in and administer according to law the real and personal estate of the said deceased limited to the deceased's [publishing business]; when required to do so by the Court, exhibit in the Court a full inventory of the said estate and render an account thereof to the Court; and when required to do so by the High Court, deliver up to that Court the grant of probate.

7.   That to the best of [my] [our] knowledge, information and belief the gross value of the estate passing under the grant limited as aforesaid [amounts to] [does not exceed] £ .... and the net estate [amounts to] [does

---

[154] Or as may be.

[155] Insert the names of the general executors.

[156] Include this paragraph only if a grant in respect of the general estate has already been issued.

not exceed] £ .... [and that this is not a case in which an Inland Revenue Account is required to be delivered.] [146]

Sworn *etc, as in Form 37.*

43. Oath for Executors: Will Pronounced for in a Probate Claim

In the High Court of Justice, *etc., as in Form 1.*

[I] [We] [135] of [136] make oath and say:

1. That [I] [we] believe the paper writing now produced to and marked by [me] [us] to be the true and original last Will and Testament [137] of [138] deceased, who was born on the ...... day of .... 19 .. and died on the ...... day of .... 20 ..[139] aged ...... domiciled in [England and Wales].

2. That to the best of [my] [our] knowledge and belief there was [no] land vested in the said deceased immediately before his death which was settled previously to his death (and not by his Will [and codicil[s]) and which remained settled land notwithstanding his death.

3. That on the ...... day of .... 20 .. the Honourable [Mr] [Mrs] Justice ...., one of the Justices of the Chancery Division of the High Court of Justice, in a claim entitled [157] pronounced for the force and validity of the said Will [and codicil[s]] dated .... [respectively] and ordered that the said Will [and codicil[s]] be admitted to proof and probate thereof be granted to ....]

[and against the validity of the Will [and codicil[s]] dated .... [and the ...... day of .... 19/20 ..] respectively].

4. That [I am] [we are] [the sole] [surviving] executor[s] named in the said Will.

[5. That notice of this application has been given to .... the other executor[s] named in the said Will.]

6. That [I] [we] will collect, get in and administer according to law the real and personal estate of the said deceased; when required to do so by the Court, exhibit in the Court a full inventory of the said estate and render an account thereof to the Court; and when required to do so by the High Court, deliver up to that Court the grant of probate.

7. That to the best of [my] [our] knowledge, information and belief the gross value of the estate passing under the grant [amounts to] [does not exceed] £ .... and the net estate [amounts to] [does not exceed] £ .... [and that this is not a case in which an Inland Revenue Account is required to be delivered.] [146]

Sworn *etc, as in Form 37.*

---

[157] Insert the title and number of the claim.

44. Oath for Attorney of an Executor

In the High Court of Justice, *etc., as in Form 1.*

I [158] make oath and say:

1.   That I believe the paper writing now produced to and marked by me to contain the true and original last Will and Testament [and [one] [two] codicil[s]] of [138] deceased, who was born on the ...... day of .... 19 .. and died on the ...... day of .... 20 ..[139] aged ...... domiciled in [England and Wales] wherein he appointed [159] his sole executor [160].

2.   That no minority or life interest arises in the estate.[161]

3.   That to the best of my knowledge and belief there was no land vested in the said deceased immediately before his death which was settled previously to his death (and not by his Will [and codicil[s]]) and which remained settled land notwithstanding his death.

4.   That I am the lawful attorney of the said [159] [162]

5.   That I will collect, get in and administer according to law the real and personal estate of the said deceased for the use and benefit of the said [159] and until further representation be granted; when required to do so by the Court, exhibit in the Court a full inventory of the said estate and render an account thereof to the Court; and when required to do so by the High Court, deliver up to that Court the grant of letters of administration (with Will annexed).

6.   That to the best of my knowledge, information and belief the gross value of the estate passing under the grant [amounts to] [does not exceed] £ .... and the net value [amounts to] [does not exceed] £ .... [and that this is not a case in which an Inland Revenue Account is required to be delivered.] [146]

Sworn *etc, as in Form 37.*

45. Oath for Administration (with Will Annexed)

In the High Court of Justice, *etc., as in Form 1.*

[I] [We] [163] of [164] make oath and say:

1.   That [I] [we] believe the paper writing now produced to and marked by

---

[158] Insert the full names and permanent address of the applicant.

[159] Insert the name of the executor.

[160] Or as may be.

[161] Where a minority or life interest arises, the grant must issue to at least two grantees, i.e., two attorneys or a trust corporation must be appointed. The district judge or registrar may, in special circumstances, allow the grant to issue to a sole grantee under s. 114, Supreme Court Act 1981.

[162] Clear off any other executor(s).

[163] Insert the full and correct names of each applicant.

[164] Insert the full, permanent postal address (including postcode) of each applicant, followed by his occupation or description, e.g., "journalist" or "retired".

[me] [us] to be the true and original last Will and Testament [137] of [138] deceased, who was born on the ...... day of .... 19 .. and died on the ...... day of .... 20 ..[139] aged ...... domiciled in [England and Wales].

2. That no minority or life interest arises in the estate.[161]

3. That to the best of [my] [our] knowledge and belief there was no land vested in the said deceased immediately before his death which was settled previously to his death (and not by his Will [and codicil[s]]) and which remained settled land notwithstanding his death. [140]

4. [That the said deceased did not in his Will name any executor.]
[That the purported appointment of an executor in the said Will is void for uncertainty.]
[That .... the sole executor named in the said Will survived the said deceased but has since died without having proved the said Will.]
[That .... one of the executors named in the said Will died during the lifetime of the deceased and .... the other executor named in the said Will has renounced probate thereof.]
[That .... the [sole] [surviving] executor named in the said Will has renounced probate thereof.]

5. That I am the [residuary legatee and devisee in trust in the said Will] [[residuary] [legatee] [and] [devisee]] [substituted [residuary legatee and devisee] [residuary legatee] [devisee]].

6. [165]

7. That [I] [we] will collect, get in and administer according to law the real and personal estate of the said deceased; when required to do so by the Court, exhibit in the Court a full inventory of the said estate and render an account thereof to the Court; and when required to do so by the High Court, deliver up to that Court the grant of letters of administration (with Will annexed).

8. That to the best of [my] [our] knowledge, information and belief the gross value of the estate passing under the grant [amounts to] [does not exceed] £ .... and the net value [amounts to] [does not exceed] £ .... [and that this is not a case in which an Inland Revenue Account is required to be delivered.] [146]

Sworn *etc, as in Form 37.*

---

[165] Insert the deponent's capacity, clearing off those with a prior entitlement to the grant. Where the deponent is one of two or more persons entitled to apply, add the words "one of the persons entitled".

46. Oath for Administration (with Will annexed) by Legatee where (substantially) the Whole Estate is Disposed of by the Will

In the High Court of Justice, *etc., as in Form 1.*

I [158] make oath and say:

1.   That I believe the paper writing now produced to and marked by me to be the true and original last Will and Testament [137] of [138] deceased, who was born on the ...... day of .... 19 .. and died on the ...... day of .... 20 ..[139] aged ...... domiciled in [England and Wales].

2.   That no minority or life interest arises in the estate.[161]

3.   That to the best of my knowledge and belief there was no land vested in the said deceased immediately before his death which was settled previously to his death [and not by his Will] and which remained settled land notwithstanding his death. [140]

4.   [That the said deceased did not in his Will name any executor.]

[That the purported appointment of an executor in the said Will is void for uncertainty.]

[That .... the sole executor named in the said Will survived the said deceased but has since died without having proved the said Will.]

[That .... one of the executors named in the said Will died during the lifetime of the deceased and .... the other executor named in the said Will has renounced probate thereof.]

[That .... the [sole] [surviving] executor named in the said Will has renounced probate thereof.]

5.   That [166] the residuary legatee(s) and devisee(s) named in the said Will [[has] [have] renounced letters of administration with Will annexed] [died in the lifetime of the said deceased]. [167]

6.   That I am a [legatee] [devisee] named in the said Will. The said Will disposes of [substantially] the whole known estate. [£.................... of the total value of the known estate of £.................... is disposed of by the said Will.][168]

7.   That I will collect, get in and administer according to law the real and personal estate of the said deceased; when required to do so by the Court, exhibit in the Court a full inventory of the said estate and render an account thereof to the Court; and when required to do so by the High Court, deliver up to that Court the grant of letters of administration (with Will annexed).

8.   That to the best of my knowledge, information and belief the gross value of the estate passing under the grant [amounts to] [does not exceed] £ ....

---

[166] Insert name(s).

[167] Insert the manner by which the residuary legatee(s) and devisee(s) has/have been cleared off.

[168] Insert the capacity in which the grant is applied for, and the manner in which all others with a prior entitlement to a grant are cleared off.

and the net value [amounts to] [does not exceed] £ .... [and that this is not a case in which an Inland Revenue Account is required to be delivered.] [146]

Sworn *etc, as in Form 37.*

47. Oath for Administration (with Will annexed) by Person Entitled to the Estate not Disposed of by the Will

In the High Court of Justice, *etc., as in Form 1.*

I [158] make oath and say:

1. That I believe the paper writing now produced to and marked by me to be the true and original last Will and Testament [137] of [138] deceased, who was born on the ...... day of .... 19 .. and died on the ...... day of .... 20 ..[139] aged ...... domiciled in [England and Wales].
2. That no minority or life interest arises in the estate.[161]
3. That to the best of my knowledge and belief there was no land vested in the said deceased immediately before his death which was settled previously to his death (and not by his Will [and codicil[s]]) and which remained settled land notwithstanding his death. [140]
4. [That [169] died in the lifetime of the said deceased.] [That [170] renounced probate of the said Will and [171] died in the lifetime of the said deceased.] [172]
5. That the said deceased died a [173] [or any other person entitled in priority by virtue of any enactment.]
6. That I am [174] and [one of] [the only] person[s] entitled to share in the estate now undisposed of by the said Will.
7. That I will collect, get in and administer according to law the real and personal estate of the said deceased; when required to do so by the Court, exhibit in the Court a full inventory of the said estate and render an account thereof to the Court; and when required to do so by the High Court, deliver up to that Court the grant of letters of administration (with Will annexed).
8. That to the best of my knowledge, information and belief the gross value of the estate passing under the grant [amounts to] [does not exceed] £ .... and the net value [amounts to] [does not exceed] £ .... [and that this is not a case in which an Inland Revenue Account is required to be delivered.] [146]

Sworn *etc, as in Form 37*

---

[169] Insert the name of the executor and residuary legatee and devisee.

[170] Insert the name of the executor.

[171] Insert the name of the residuary legatee and devisee.

[172] Or as may be, to establish the applicant's title to a grant.

[173] Insert the status of the deceased at death and clearings down to the applicant's relationship.

[174] Insert the relationship to the deceased.

48. Oath for Personal Representative of Residuary Legatee and Devisee

In the High Court of Justice, *etc., as in Form 1.*

I [158] make oath and say:

1. That I believe the paper writing now produced to and marked by me to be the true and original last Will and Testament [137] of [138] deceased, who was born on the ...... day of .... 19 .. and died on the ...... day of .... 20 ..[139] aged ...... domiciled in [England and Wales].

2. That no minority or life interest arises in the estate.[161]

3. That to the best of my knowledge and belief there was no land vested in the said deceased immediately before his death which was settled previously to his death (and not by his Will [and codicil[s]) and which remained settled land notwithstanding his death. [140]

4. [That the said deceased did not in his Will name any executor.]
[That the purported appointment of an executor in the said Will is void for uncertainty.]
[That [175] the sole executor named in the said Will survived the said deceased but has since died without having proved the said Will.]
[That [175] one of the executors named in the said Will died during the lifetime of the deceased and [175] the other executor named in the said Will has renounced probate thereof.]
[That [175] the [sole] [surviving] executor named in the said Will has renounced probate thereof.]

5. That [175] the residuary legatee[s] and devisee[s] predeceased the deceased.

6. That I am the [executor of the Will of [175]] [the administrator of the estate of [175]], the residuary legatee(s) and devisee(s), [probate of his Will] [letters of administration of his estate] having been granted to me out of the .... Registry on the ...... day of .... 20 ...

7. That I will collect, get in and administer according to law the real and personal estate of the said deceased; when required to do so by the Court, exhibit in the Court a full inventory of the said estate and render an account thereof to the Court; and when required to do so by the High Court, deliver up to that Court the grant of letters of administration (with Will annexed).

8. That to the best of [my] [our] knowledge, information and belief the gross value of the estate passing under the grant [amounts to] [does not exceed] £ .... and the net estate [amounts to] [does not exceed] £ ....
[and that this is not a case in which an Inland Revenue Account is required to be delivered.] [146]

Sworn *etc, as in Form 37.*

---

[175] Insert the name and manner of clearing.

49. Oath for Legatee or Devisee

In the High Court of Justice, *etc., as in Form 1.*

I [158] make oath and say:

1.   That I believe the paper writing now produced to and marked by me to be the true and original last Will and Testament [137] of [138] deceased, who was born on the ...... day of .... 19 .. and died on the ...... day of .... 20 ..[139] aged ...... domiciled in [England and Wales].

2.   That no minority or life interest arises in the estate.[161]

3.   That to the best of my knowledge and belief there was no land vested in the said deceased immediately before his death which was settled previously to his death (and not by his Will [and codicil[s]]) and which remained settled land notwithstanding his death. [140]

4.   [That the said deceased did not in his Will name any executor.]
[That the purported appointment of an executor in the said Will is void for uncertainty.]
[That [175] the sole executor named in the said Will survived the said deceased but has since died without having proved the said Will.]
[That [175] one of the executors named in the said Will died during the lifetime of the deceased and [175] the other executor named in the said Will has renounced probate thereof.]
[That [175] the [sole] [surviving] executor named in the said Will has renounced probate thereof.]

5.   That [175] the residuary legatee[s] and devisee[s] named in the said Will [has] [have] renounced letters of administration [with Will annexed] [That [175] the residuary legatee(s) and devisee(s) named in the said Will died in the lifetime of the said deceased.] [176]

6.   That I am a [[legatee] [devisee] named in the said Will] [creditor of the said deceased.] [177]

7.   That I will collect, get in and administer according to law the real and personal estate of the said deceased; when required to do so by the Court, exhibit in the Court a full inventory of the said estate and render an account thereof to the Court; and when required to do so by the High Court, deliver up to that Court the grant of letters of administration (with Will annexed).

8.   That to the best of my knowledge, information and belief the gross value of the estate passing under the grant [amounts to] [does not exceed] £ .... and the net value [amounts to] [does not exceed] £ .... [and that this is not a case in which an Inland Revenue Account is required to be delivered.] [146]

Sworn *etc, as in Form 37.*

---

[176] Insert the manner in which the residuary beneficiaries are cleared off.
[177] Insert the capacity in which the grant is applied for, clearing off those with a prior entitlement.

50. Oath for Administration for the Use and Benefit of an Executor or Residuary Legatee who is Mentally Incapable

In the High Court of Justice, *etc., as in Form 1.*

[I] [We] [178] make oath and say:

1. That [I] [we] believe the paper writing now produced to and marked by [me] [us] to be the true and original last Will and Testament [137] of [138] deceased, who was born on the ...... day of .... 19 .. and died on the ...... day of .... 20 ..[139] aged ...... domiciled in England and Wales.

2. That no minority or life interest arises in the estate.[161]

3. That to the best of [my] [our] knowledge and belief there was no land vested in the said deceased immediately before his death which was settled previously to his death (and not by his Will [and codicil[s]) and which remained settled land notwithstanding his death. [140]

4. That in his said Will the said deceased appointed [179] leaving [180] the residuary legatee and devisee who is now by reason of mental incapacity incapable of managing his affairs.

5. [That by order dated the ...... day of .... 20 .. of the Public Guardianship Office (Protection Division) I was authorised to apply for letters of administration (with Will annexed) either alone or with a co-administrator for the use and benefit of [180] .]

[That [I am] [we are] the lawful attorney[s] of the said [180], acting under an enduring power of attorney which has been registered with the Public Guardianship Office (Protection Division).]

[By order of [Mr] [Mrs] [District Judge] [Registrar] .... dated the ...... day of .... 20 .. made under and by virtue of Rule 35(4) of the Non-Contentious Probate Rules 1987, [I was] [we were] appointed to apply for letters of administration (with Will annexed).]

6. That [I] [we] will collect, get in and administer according to law the real and personal estate of the said deceased for the use and benefit of the said [180] [during his incapacity] [until further representation be granted]; when required to do so by the Court, exhibit in the Court a full inventory of the said estate and render an account thereof to the Court; and when required to do so by the High Court, deliver up to that Court the grant of letters of administration (with Will annexed).

8. That to the best of [my] [our] knowledge, information and belief the gross value of the estate passing under the grant [amounts to] [does not exceed] £ .... and the net value [amounts to] [does not exceed] £ .... [and that this is not a case in which an Inland Revenue Account is required to be delivered.] [146]

Sworn *etc, as in Form 37.*

---

[178] Insert the full names and addresses of the applicant(s).

[179] Insert the name(s) of the executor(s) and the manner of clearing.

[180] Insert the name of the residuary beneficiary.

51. Oath for Nominee of Residuary Legatee and Devisee which is a Non-trust Corporation

In the High Court of Justice, *etc., as in Form 1.*

I [158] make oath and say:

1.   That I believe the paper writing now produced to and marked by me to be the true and original last Will and Testament [137] of [138] deceased, who was born on the ...... day of .... 19 .. and died on the ...... day of .... 20 ..[139] aged ...... domiciled in England and Wales.

2.   That no minority or life interest arises in the estate.[161]

3.   That to the best of my knowledge and belief there was no land vested in the said deceased immediately before his death which was settled previously to his death (and not by his Will [and codicil[s]) and which remained settled land notwithstanding his death. [140]

4.   [That the said deceased did not in his Will name any executor.]

[That the purported appointment of an executor in the said Will is void for uncertainty.]

[That [175] the sole executor named in the said Will survived the said deceased but has since died without having proved the said Will.]

[That [175] one of the executors named in the said Will died during the lifetime of the deceased and [175] the other executor named in the said Will has renounced probate thereof.]

[That [175] the [sole] [surviving] executor named in the said Will has renounced probate thereof.]

[5.   That [181] the residuary legatee and devisee named in the said Will is not a trust corporation as defined by rule 2(1) of the Non-Contentious Probate Rules 1987.]

6.   That by a resolution dated the ...... day of .... 20 .. I was duly appointed by the said [181] as its nominee for the purpose of applying for letters of administration (with Will annexed) to the estate of the said deceased.[182]

7.   That I will collect, get in and administer according to law the real and personal estate of the said deceased for the use and benefit of the said [181] and until further representation be granted; when required to do so by the Court, exhibit in the Court a full inventory of the said estate and render an account thereof to the Court; and when required to do so by the High Court, deliver up to that Court the letters of administration (with Will annexed).

8.   That to the best of my knowledge, information and belief the gross value of the estate passing under the grant [amounts to] [does not exceed] £ .... and the net value [amounts to] [does not exceed] £ .... [and that this is not a case in which an Inland Revenue Account is required to be delivered]. [146]

Sworn *etc, as in Form 37.*

---

[181] Insert the name of the non-trust corporation.

[182] Amend this paragraph as appropriate if the authority is a general authority applying also to estates other than the estate in question.

52. Oath for Administration (with Will annexed): Gift Saved under Section 33, Wills Act 1837

In the High Court of Justice, *etc., as in Form 1.*

I [158] make oath and say:

1.   That I believe the paper writing now produced to and marked by me to be the true and original last Will and Testament [137] of [138] deceased, who was born on the ...... day of .... 19 .. and died on the ...... day of .... 20 ..[139] aged ...... domiciled in England and Wales.

2.   That no minority or life interest arises in the estate.[161]

3.   That to the best of my knowledge and belief there was no land vested in the said deceased immediately before his death which was settled previously to his death (and not by his Will [and codicil[s]) and which remained settled land notwithstanding his death. [140]

4.   [That the said deceased did not in his Will name any executor.]
[That the purported appointment of an executor in the said Will is void for uncertainty.]
[That [175] the sole executor named in the said Will survived the said deceased but has since died without having proved the said Will.]
[That [175] one of the executors named in the said Will died during the lifetime of the deceased and [175] the other executor named in the said Will has renounced probate thereof.]
[That [175] the [sole] [surviving] executor named in the said Will has renounced probate thereof.]

5.   That [183] the son of the said deceased and the residuary legatee and devisee named in the said Will predeceased the deceased leaving issue who survived the said deceased.

6.   That I am [one of] the issue of the said [183], being his daughter and [one of the persons] [the person] now entitled to share in the residue under the said Will by virtue of section 33 of the Wills Act 1837.

7.   That I will collect, get in and administer according to law the real and personal estate of the said deceased; when required to do so by the Court, exhibit in the Court a full inventory of the said estate and render an account thereof to the Court; and when required to do so by the High Court, deliver up to that Court the letters of administration (with Will annexed).

8.   That to the best of my knowledge, information and belief the gross value of the estate passing under the grant [amounts to] [does not exceed] £ ....
and the net value [amounts to] [does not exceed] £ .... [and that this is not a case in which an Inland Revenue Account is required to be delivered].[146]

Sworn *etc, as in Form 37.*

---

[183] Insert the name of the residuary legatee and devisee.

53. Oath for Administration: Surviving Spouse

In the High Court of Justice, *etc., as in Form 1.*

I [158] make oath and say:

1. That [137] of [138] was born on the ...... day of .... 19 .. and died on the ...... day of .... 20 ..[139] aged ...... domiciled in England and Wales intestate.

2. That no minority or life interest arises in the estate.[161]

3. That to the best of my knowledge and belief there was no land vested in the said deceased immediately before his death which was settled previously to his death and which remained settled land notwithstanding his death. [140]

4. That I am the lawful [widow] [husband] of the deceased and the only person [now] entitled to [his] [her] estate.

5. That I will collect, get in and administer according to law the real and personal estate of the said deceased; when required to do so by the Court, exhibit in the Court a full inventory of the said estate and render an account thereof to the Court; and when required to do so by the High Court, deliver up to that Court the letters of administration.

6. That to the best of [my] [our] knowledge, information and belief the gross value of the estate passing under the grant [amounts to] [does not exceed] £ .... and the net value [amounts to] [does not exceed] £ .... [and that this is not a case in which an Inland Revenue Account is required to be delivered]. [146]

Sworn *etc, as in Form 37.*

54. Oath for Administration: Child or Other Issue with Beneficial Interest, Spouse having Survived but since Died

In the High Court of Justice, *etc., as in Form 1.*

[I] [We] [178] make oath and say:

1. That [137] of [138] was born on the ...... day of .... 19 .. and died on the ...... day of .... 20 ..[139] aged ...... domiciled in England and Wales intestate, leaving [his lawful widow] [her lawful husband] [the only] [one of the] person[s] entitled to share [his] [her] estate who has since died without obtaining letters of administration of [his] [her] estate.

2. That no minority or life interest arises in the estate.[161]

3. That to the best of [my] [our] knowledge and belief there was no land vested in the said deceased immediately before [his] [her] death which was settled previously to [his] [her] death and which remained settled land notwithstanding [his] [her] death. [140]

4. That I am the grandson of the said deceased and one of the persons beneficially entitled to share the estate, being the son of .... the

only daughter of the said deceased who predeceased the said deceased [184].

5.   That [I] [we] will collect, get in and administer according to law the real and personal estate of the said deceased; when required to do so by the Court, exhibit in the Court a full inventory of the said estate and render an account thereof to the Court; and when required to do so by the High Court, deliver up to that Court the letters of administration.

6.   That to the best of [my] [our] knowledge, information and belief the gross value of the estate passing under the grant [amounts to] [does not exceed] £ .... and the net value [amounts to] [does not exceed] £ .... [and that this is not a case in which an Inland Revenue Account is required to be delivered]. [146]

Sworn *etc, as in Form 37.*

55. Oath for Administration: Spouse Entitled to Whole Estate having Survived but since Died

In the High Court of Justice, *etc., as in Form 1.*

I [158] make oath and say:

1.   That [137] of [138] was born on the ...... day of .... 19 .. and died on the ...... day of .... 20 ..[139] aged ...... domiciled in England and Wales intestate, leaving [185] [his lawful widow] [her lawful husband] the only person entitled to [his] [her] estate who has since died without obtaining letters of administration of [his] [her] estate.

2.   That no minority or life interest arises in the estate.[161]

3.   That to the best of my knowledge and belief there was no land vested in the said deceased immediately before [his] [her] death which was settled previously to [his] [her] death and which remained settled land notwithstanding [his] [her] death. [140]

4.   That I am the [proposed] [executor] [administrator] of the estate of [185], [probate of [his] [her] Will] [letters of administration of [his] [her] [estate] [having been granted to me out of the .... [Probate] Registry on the ...... day of .... 20 ..] [being applied for contemporaneously with the application for the grant.] [186]

5.   That I will collect, get in and administer according to law the real and personal estate of the said deceased; when required to do so by the Court, exhibit in the Court a full inventory of the said estate and render an account thereof to the Court; and when required to do so by the High Court, deliver up to that Court the letters of administration.

---

[184] Insert the title and clearing according to the circumstances.

[185] Insert the name of the surviving spouse.

[186] An application for the "representative" or "leading" grant may be made before or together with the application for the grant.

6. That to the best of my knowledge, information and belief the gross value of the estate passing under the grant [amounts to] [does not exceed] £ .... and the net value [amounts to] [does not exceed] £ .... [and that this is not a case in which an Inland Revenue Account is required to be delivered]. [146]

Sworn *etc, as in Form 37.*

56. Oath for Administration: Surviving Child

In the High Court of Justice, *etc., as in Form 1.*

I [158] make oath and say:
1. That [135] of [136] deceased was born on the ...... day of .... 19 .. and died on the ...... day of .... 20 ..[139] aged ...... domiciled in England and Wales intestate a widow[er].
2. That no minority or life interest arises in the estate.[161]
3. That to the best of my knowledge and belief there was no land vested in the said deceased immediately before [his] [her] death which was settled previously to [his] [her] death and which remained settled land notwithstanding [his] [her] death.[140]
4. That I am the [son] [daughter] of the said deceased and [one of the persons] [the only person] entitled to share [his] [her] estate.
5. That I will collect, get in and administer according to law the real and personal estate of the said deceased; when required to do so by the Court, exhibit in the Court a full inventory of the said estate and render an account thereof to the Court; and when required to do so by the High Court, deliver up to that Court the letters of administration.
6. That to the best of my knowledge, information and belief the gross value of the estate passing under the grant [amounts to] [does not exceed] £ .... and the net value [amounts to] [does not exceed] £ .... [and that this is not a case in which an Inland Revenue Account is required to be delivered]. [146]

Sworn *etc, as in Form 37.*

57. Oath for Administration: Parents

In the High Court of Justice, *etc., as in Form 1.*

[I] [We] of [158] make oath and say:
1. That [137] of [138] deceased was born on the ...... day of .... 19 .. and died on the ...... day of .... 20 ..[139] aged ...... domiciled in England and Wales intestate a [bachelor] [spinster] [single man] [single woman] [187]

---

[187] If the deceased died a single person, i.e., was divorced, insert details of the decree absolute.

326

without issue or any other person entitled in priority to share [his] [her] estate by virtue of any enactment.

2.   That no minority or life interest arises in the estate.[161]

3.   That to the best of [my] [our] knowledge and belief there was [no] land vested in the said deceased immediately before [his] [her] death which was settled previously to [his] [her] death and which remained settled land notwithstanding [his] [her] death. [140]

4.   That [I am] [we are] the [mother] [father] [parents] of the said deceased and the only person[s] entitled to [his] [her] estate.

5.   That [I] [we] will collect, get in and administer according to law the real and personal estate of the said deceased; when required to do so by the Court, exhibit in the Court a full inventory of the said estate and render an account thereof to the Court; and when required to do so by the High Court, deliver up to that Court the letters of administration.

6.   That to the best of [my] [our] knowledge, information and belief the gross value of the estate passing under the grant [amounts to] [does not exceed] £ .... and the net value [amounts to] [does not exceed] £ .... [and that this is not a case in which an Inland Revenue Account is required to be delivered]. [146]

Sworn *etc, as in Form 37.*

58. Oath for Administration: Brother and Sister

In the High Court of Justice, *etc., as in Form 1.*

[I] [We] of [158] make oath and say:

1.   That [137] of [138] deceased was born on the ...... day of .... 19 .. and died on the ...... day of .... 20 ..[139] aged ...... domiciled in England and Wales intestate a widow[er] without issue or parent or any other person entitled in priority to share [his] [her] estate by virtue of any enactment.

2.   That no minority or life interest arises in the estate.[161]

3.   That to the best of [my] [our] knowledge and belief there was no land vested in the said deceased immediately before [his] [her] death which was settled previously to [his] [her] death and which remained settled land notwithstanding [his] [her] death.[140]

4.   That [I am] [we are] the [brother] [sister] [brother and sister] of the said deceased and [two of the persons] [the only persons] entitled to [his] [her] estate. [188]

5.   That [I] [we] will collect, get in and administer according to law the real and personal estate of the said deceased; when required to do so by the

[188] Where there are no surviving brothers, sisters, nieces or nephews of the whole blood, a brother, sister, niece or nephew of the half blood may apply; the form should be reworded appropriately.

Court, exhibit in the Court a full inventory of the said estate and render an account thereof to the Court; and when required to do so by the High Court, deliver up to that Court the letters of administration.

6.   That to the best of [my] [our] knowledge, information and belief the gross value of the estate passing under the grant [amounts to] [does not exceed] £ .... and the net value [amounts to] [does not exceed] £ .... [and that this is not a case in which an Inland Revenue Account is required to be delivered]. [146]

Sworn *etc, as in Form 37.*

59. Oath for Administration: Nephew

In the High Court of Justice, *etc., as in Form 1.*

I [158] make oath and say:

1.   That [137] of [138] deceased was born on the ...... day of .... 19 .. and died on the ...... day of .... 20 ..[139] aged ...... domiciled in England and Wales intestate a widow without issue or parent or brother or sister of the whole blood or any other person entitled in priority to share his estate by virtue of any enactment.

2.   That no minority or life interest arises in the estate.[161]

3.   That to the best of my knowledge and belief there was no land vested in the said deceased immediately before his death which was settled previously to his death and which remained settled land notwithstanding his death.[140]

4.   That I am the nephew of the whole blood of the said deceased and [one of the persons] [the only person] entitled to [share] his estate.

5.   That I will collect, get in and administer according to law the real and personal estate of the said deceased; when required to do so by the Court, exhibit in the Court a full inventory of the said estate and render an account thereof to the Court; and when required to do so by the High Court, deliver up to that Court the letters of administration.

6.   That to the best of my knowledge, information and belief the gross value of the estate passing under the grant [amounts to] [does not exceed] £ .... and the net value [amounts to] [does not exceed] £ .... [and that this is not a case in which an Inland Revenue Account is required to be delivered]. [146]

Sworn *etc, as in Form 37.*

60. Oath for Administration: Cousin German

In the High Court of Justice, *etc., as in Form 1.*

I [158] make oath and say:

1. That [137] of [138] deceased was born on the ...... day of .... 19 .. and died on the ...... day of .... 20 ..[139] aged ...... domiciled in England and Wales intestate a spinster without issue or parent or brother or sister of the whole or half blood or their issue or grandparent or uncle or aunt of the whole blood or any other person entitled in priority to share her estate by virtue of any enactment.

2. That no minority or life interest arises in the estate.[161]

3. That to the best of my knowledge and belief there was no land vested in the said deceased immediately before her death which was settled previously to her death and which remained settled land notwithstanding her death. [140]

4. That I am the cousin german of the said deceased and [one of the persons] [the only person] entitled to [share] her estate.

5. That I will collect, get in and administer according to law the real and personal estate of the said deceased; when required to do so by the Court, exhibit in the Court a full inventory of the said estate and render an account thereof to the Court; and when required to do so by the High Court, deliver up to that Court the letters of administration.

6. That to the best of my knowledge, information and belief the gross value of the estate passing under the grant [amounts to] [does not exceed] £ .... and the net value [amounts to] [does not exceed] £ .... [and that this is not a case in which an Inland Revenue Account is required to be delivered]. [146]

Sworn *etc, as in Form 37.*

61. Oath for Administration: Assignee(s)

In the High Court of Justice, *etc., as in Form 1.*

[I] [We] [178] make oath and say:

1. That [137] of [138] deceased was born on the ...... day of .... 19 .. and died on the ...... day of .... 20 ..[139] aged ...... domiciled in England and Wales intestate leaving [189] [his] [her] lawful [widow] [husband] and the only person now entitled to [his] [her] estate.[190]

2. That no minority or life interest arises in the estate.

3. That to the best of [my] [our] knowledge and belief there was no land vested in the said deceased immediately before [his] [her] death which was settled previously to [his] [her] death and which remained settled land notwithstanding [his] [her] death. [140]

4. By a Deed of Assignment [191] dated the ...... day of .... 20 .. the said [189] assigned to [me] [us] [and to ....] all [his] her] right and title to and interest in the estate of the said deceased.

---

[189] Insert the name of the surviving spouse.

[190] Insert any other status of the deceased, the title of the deponents, and any clearings.

[191] The deed of assignment, or a certified true and complete copy, must be lodged.

5.   That [I] [we] will collect, get in and administer according to law the real and personal estate of the said deceased; when required to do so by the Court, exhibit in the Court a full inventory of the said estate and render an account thereof to the Court; and when required to do so by the High Court, deliver up to that Court the letters of administration.

6.   That to the best of [my] [our] knowledge, information and belief the gross value of the estate passing under the grant [amounts to] [does not exceed] £ .... and the net value [amounts to] [does not exceed] £ .... [and that this is not a case in which an Inland Revenue Account is required to be delivered]. [146]

Sworn *etc, as in Form 37.*

62. Oath for Administration: Person Entitled on Accretion

For use only where the net estate does not, at the date of death, exceed the spouse's statutory legacy.

In the High Court of Justice, *etc., as in Form 1.*

I [158] make oath and say:

1.   That [137] of [138] deceased was born on the ...... day of .... 19 .. and died on the ...... day of .... 20 ..[139] aged ...... domiciled in England and Wales intestate leaving [192] [his] [her] lawful [widow] [husband] and the only person now entitled to [his] [her] estate who has renounced letters of administration of the estate.

2.   That no minority or life interest arises in the estate.

3.   That to the best of my knowledge and belief there was no land vested in the said deceased immediately before [his] [her] death which was settled previously to [his] [her] death and which remained settled land notwithstanding [his] [her] death. [140]

4.   That I am the [son] [daughter] of the said deceased and a person who may have a beneficial interest in [his] [her] estate in the event of an accretion thereto.

5.   That I will collect, get in and administer according to law the real and personal estate of the said deceased; when required to do so by the Court, exhibit in the Court a full inventory of the said estate and render an account thereof to the Court; and when required to do so by the High Court, deliver up to that Court the letters of administration.

6.   That to the best of my knowledge, information and belief the gross value of the estate passing under the grant [amounts to] [does not exceed] £ .... and the net value [amounts to] [does not exceed] £ .... [and that this is not a case in which an Inland Revenue Account is required to be delivered]. [146]

Sworn *etc, as in Form 37.*

[192] Insert the name of the surviving spouse.

63. Oath for Administration: Creditor

In the High Court of Justice, *etc., as in Form 1.*

I [158] make oath and say:

1. That [137] of [138] deceased was born on the ...... day of .... 19 .. and died on the ...... day of .... 20 ..[139] aged ...... domiciled in England and Wales intestate leaving [192] [his] [her] lawful [widow] [husband] and the only person now entitled to [his] [her] estate who has renounced letters of administration of the estate.[193]

2. That no minority or life interest arises in the estate.

3. That to the best of my knowledge and belief there was no land vested in the said deceased immediately before [his] [her] death which was settled previously to [his] [her] death and which remained settled land notwithstanding [his] [her] death. [140]

4. That I am a creditor of the said deceased.

5. That I will collect, get in and administer according to law the real and personal estate of the said deceased; when required to do so by the Court, exhibit in the Court a full inventory of the said estate and render an account thereof to the Court; and when required to do so by the High Court, deliver up to that Court the letters of administration.

6. That to the best of my knowledge, information and belief the gross value of the estate passing under the grant [amounts to] [does not exceed] £ .... and the net value [amounts to] [does not exceed] £ .... [and that this is not a case in which an Inland Revenue Account is required to be delivered]. [146]

Sworn *etc, as in Form 37.*

64. Oath for Administration: Attorney

In the High Court of Justice, *etc., as in Form 1.*

I [158] make oath and say:

1. That [137] of [138] deceased was born on the ...... day of .... 19 .. and died on the ...... day of .... 20 ..[139] aged ...... domiciled in England and Wales intestate [194] and without any person entitled in priority to share in [his] [her] estate leaving [195] [one of the persons] [the person] entitled to share in [his] [her] estate.

2. That no minority or life interest arises in the estate.[161]

3. That to the best of my knowledge and belief there was no land vested in the said deceased immediately before [his] [her] death which was settled previously to [his] [her] death and which remained settled land notwithstand-

---

[193] Insert any other status of the deceased and the appropriate clearings.

[194] Insert the deceased's status, e.g., "a widow".

[195] Insert the name and relationship of the person beneficially entitled.

331

ing [his] [her] death. [140]

4.   That I am the lawful attorney of the said [196].

5.   That I will collect, get in and administer according to law the real and personal estate of the said deceased for the use and benefit of the said [196] limited until further representation be granted; when required to do so by the Court, exhibit in the Court a full inventory of the said estate and render an account thereof to the Court; and when required to do so by the High Court, deliver up to that Court the letters of administration.

6.   That to the best of my knowledge, information and belief the gross value of the estate passing under the grant [amounts to] [does not exceed] £ .... and the net value [amounts to] [does not exceed] £ .... [and that this is not a case in which an Inland Revenue Account is required to be delivered]. [146]

Sworn *etc, as in Form 37.*

65. Oath for Administration: Child and Attorney of Another Child

In the High Court of Justice, *etc., as in Form 1.*

We [178] make oath and say:

1.   That [137] of [138] deceased was born on the ...... day of .... 19 .. and died on the ...... day of .... 20 ..[139] aged ...... domiciled in England and Wales intestate a widow leaving .... and .... her son and daughter the only persons entitled to share her estate.

2.   That no minority or life interest arises in the estate.

3.   That to the best of our knowledge and belief there was no land vested in the said deceased immediately before her death which was settled previously to her death and which remained settled land notwithstanding her death.[140]

4.   That I the said [197] am the daughter of the said deceased and I, [198] am the lawful attorney of .... , the son of the deceased.

 5.   That we will collect, get in and administer according to law the real and personal estate of the said deceased limited until further representation be granted; when required to do so by the Court, exhibit in the Court a full inventory of the said estate and render an account thereof to the Court; and when required to do so by the High Court, deliver up to that Court the letters of administration.

6.   That to the best of our knowledge, information and belief the gross value of the estate passing under the grant [amounts to] [does not exceed] £ .... and the net value [amounts to] [does not exceed] £ .... [and that this is not a case in which an Inland Revenue Account is required to be delivered]. [146]

---

[196] Insert the name of the person entitled who has executed the power of attorney.

[197] Insert the name of the first deponent.

[198] Insert the name of the second deponent.

7. I, [199] consent to the grant being limited as aforesaid.

Sworn *etc, as in Form 37.*

66. Oath for Administration for the Use and Benefit of a Mentally Incapable Person

In the High Court of Justice, *etc., as in Form 1.*

I [158] make oath and say:

1. That [137] of [138] deceased was born on the ...... day of .... 19 .. and died on the ...... day of .... 20 ..[139] aged ...... domiciled in England and Wales intestate [200] or any other person entitled in priority to share in [his] [her] estate by virtue of any enactment leaving [201] [202] who is now by reason of mental incapacity incapable of administering [his] [her] affairs.

2. [That by an order of the Court of Protection dated the ...... day of .... 20 .. I was authorised to apply for letters of administration for the use and benefit of [201] and during [his] [her incapacity.]

[That no one has been authorised by the Court of Protection to apply for letters of administration. I am the lawful attorney of the said [201] acting under an enduring power of attorney which was registered in the Court of Protection on the ...... day of .... 20 ...]

[That no one has been authorised by the Court of Protection to apply for letters of administration for the use and benefit of the said [201] and there is no one acting under a registered enduring power of attorney.]

[That by order dated the the ...... day of .... 20 .. made by [District Judge] [District Probate Registrar] .... of this Division it was ordered under and pursuant to Rule 35(4) of the Non-Contentious Probate Rule 1987 that letters of administration be granted to me for the use and benefit of the said [201] and until further representation be granted.]

3. That no minority or life interest arises in the estate. [203]

4. That to the best of my knowledge and belief there was no land vested in the said deceased immediately before his death which was settled previously to his death and which remained settled land notwithstanding his death.

5. That I will collect, get in and administer according to law the real and personal estate of the said deceased for the use and benefit of the said [201] [during [his] [her] incapacity] [limited until further representation be granted]; when required to do so by the Court, exhibit in the Court a full inventory of the said estate and render an account thereof to the Court; and

---

[199] Insert the name of the daughter.

[200] Insert the status of the deceased, e.g., "widow without issue", "parent".

[201] Insert the name of the incapable person.

[202] Insert the relationship to the deceased, e.g., "brother of the whole blood".

[203] Or as may be.

when required to do so by the High Court, deliver up to that Court the letters of administration.

6.   That to the best of my knowledge, information and belief the gross value of the estate passing under the grant [amounts to] [does not exceed] £ ....
and the net value [amounts to] [does not exceed] £ .... [and that this is not a case in which an Inland Revenue Account is required to be delivered]. [146]

Sworn *etc, as in Form 37.*

67. Oath for Administration: Person with Parental Responsibility and Nominated Co-administrator for the Use and Benefit of Minor(s).

In the High Court of Justice, *etc., as in Form 1.*

We [204] and [205] make oath and say:

1.   That [137] of [138] deceased was born on the ...... day of .... 19 .. and died on the ...... day of .... 20 ..[139] aged ...... domiciled in England and Wales intestate a single [man] [woman] [206] leaving [207] [his] [her] [son[s]] [daughter[s]] and the only person[s] entitled to [his] [her] estate who [is] [are] now [a] minor[s] aged .... [and .... respectively].

2.   [That the marriage of the said deceased with [208] was dissolved by final decree of the .... Court dated the ...... day of .... 20 .. and the said deceased did not remarry.]

3.   That the said [209] is the [210] of the said minor[s] and that there is no other person [having parental responsibility for] [appointed guardian of] the said minor[s].

4.   That the said [209] has nominated by a nomination dated the ...... day of .... 20 .. the said [211] to be [his] [her] co-administrator, [he] [she] being a fit and proper person to act in that capacity.

5.   That a minority [and a] [but no] life interest arises under the intestacy.

6.   That to the best of our knowledge and belief there was no land vested in the said deceased immediately before [his] [her] death which was settled previously to [his] [her] death and which remained settled land

---

[204] Insert the full and correct names of the person with parental responsibility applying, and his/her full, permanent postal address (including postcode).

[205] Insert the full names and address of the nominated co-administrator.

[206] Or as may be.

[207] Insert the names of the deceased's surviving child(ren).

[208] Insert the name of the surviving parent.

[209] Insert the name of the applicant with parental responsibility.

[210] Insert the relationship to the minor(s) and title under rule 32(1) (a) to (c), e.g., "the parent of the minor having parental responsibility pursuant to section 2(1) or 2(2) of the Children Act 1989".

[211] Insert the name of the co-administrator.

notwithstanding [his] [her] death.

7.   That we will collect, get in and administer according to law the real and personal estate of the said deceased for the use and benefit of the said minor[s] until [he] [she] [one of them] shall attain the age of eighteen years; when required to do so by the Court, exhibit in the Court a full inventory of the said estate and render an account thereof to the Court; and when required to do so by the High Court, deliver up to that Court the letters of administration.

8.   That to the best of our knowledge, information and belief the gross value of the estate passing under the grant [amounts to] [does not exceed] £ .... and the net value [amounts to] [does not exceed] £ .... [and that this is not a case in which an Inland Revenue Account is required to be delivered]. [146]

Sworn *etc, as in Form 37.*

68. Oath for Administration: Persons Appointed to take Letters of Administration for the Use and benefit of Minors

In the High Court of Justice, *etc., as in Form 1.*

We [178] make oath and say:

1.   That [137] of [138] deceased was born on the ...... day of .... 19 .. and died on the ...... day of .... 20 ..[139] aged ...... domiciled in England and Wales intestate a widow[er] [single man] [single woman] leaving [212] [his] [her] child[ren] and the only persons entitled in priority to [share in] [his] [her] estate who [is a minor aged ....] [are minors aged .... and .... respectively].

2.   [That there is no person or body with or deemed to have parental responsibility and that there is no person or body appointed or deemed to be appointed guardian of the said minor[s].]

3.   That [178] were appointed by order of [District Judge] [Registrar] .... dated the ...... day of .... 20 .. for the purpose of taking letters of administration of the estate of the said deceased for [his] [her] [their] use and benefit until [he] [she] [one of them] shall attain the age of eighteen years.

4.   That a minority [and a] [but no] life interest arises under the intestacy.

5.   That to the best of our knowledge and belief there was no land vested in the said deceased immediately before [his] [her] death which was settled previously to [his] [her] death and which remained settled land notwithstanding [his] [her] death.

6.   That we will collect, get in and administer according to law the real and personal estate of the said deceased for the use and benefit of the said minor[s] until [he] [she] [one of them] shall attain the age of eighteen years;

[212] Insert the full names of the surviving minor child(ren).

when required to do so by the Court, exhibit in the Court a full inventory of the said estate and render an account thereof to the Court; and when required to do so by the High Court, deliver up to that Court the letters of administration.

7.   That to the best of our knowledge, information and belief the gross value of the estate passing under the grant [amounts to] [does not exceed] £ ....
and the net value [amounts to] [does not exceed] £ .... [and that this is not a case in which an Inland Revenue Account is required to be delivered]. [146]

Sworn *etc, as in Form 37.*

69. Oath for Administration Ad Colligenda Bona Defuncti

In the High Court of Justice, *etc., as in Form 1.*

I [213] make oath and say:

1.   That [137] of [138] deceased was born on the ...... day of .... 19 .. and died on the ...... day of .... 20 ..[139] aged ...... domiciled in England and Wales. [214]

2.   That [no] [a] minority [and a] [but no] life interest arises in the estate.

3.   That by order of [District Judge] [Registrar] .... dated the ...... day of .... 20 .. it was ordered that letters of administration of the estate of the said deceased be granted to me limited to [215]

4.   That to the best of my knowledge and belief there was no land vested in the said deceased immediately before his death which was settled previously to his death and which remained settled land notwithstanding his death.

5.   That I will collect, get in and administer according to law the real and personal estate of the said deceased limited to collecting, getting in and receiving the estate and doing such acts as may be necessary for the preservation of the estate and until further representation be granted but no further or otherwise [216] ; when required to do so by the Court, exhibit in the Court a full inventory of the said estate and render an account thereof to the Court; and when required to do so by the High Court, deliver up to that Court the grant of letters of administration.

6.   That to the best of my knowledge, information and belief the gross value of the estate passing under the grant [amounts to] [does not exceed] £ ....
and the net value [amounts to] [does not exceed] £ .... [and that this is not a case in which an Inland Revenue Account is required to be delivered]. [146]

Sworn *etc, as in Form 37.*

---

[213] The applicant is the person named in and authorised by the order.

[214] This form of grant is always of letters of administration. The oath and the grant are silent as to the deceased's having been testate or intestate.

[215] Recite the limitation imposed in the order.

[216] Or as may be, according to the order.

70. Oath for Administration Pursuant to Order under Section 116, Supreme Court Act 1981

In the High Court of Justice, *etc., as in Form 1.*

[I] [We] [178] make oath and say:

1. That [[I] [we] believe the paper writing now produced to and marked by [me] [us] to be the true and original last Will and Testament] [137] of [138] deceased, who was born on the ...... day of .... 19 .., and died on the ...... day of .... 20 ..[139] aged ...... domiciled in [England and Wales] [intestate].

2. That no minority or life interest arises in the estate.[161]

3. That to the best of [my] [our] knowledge and belief there was no land vested in the said deceased immediately before his death which was settled previously to his death [and not by his Will] and which remained settled land notwithstanding his death. [140]

4. That by order of [District Judge] [Registrar] .... dated the ...... day of .... 20 .. it was ordered that letters of administration of the estate of the said deceased be granted to [me] [us] pursuant to Section 116 of the Supreme Court Act 1981.

5. That [I] [we] will collect, get in and administer according to law the real and personal estate of the said deceased [217]; when required to do so by the Court, exhibit in the Court a full inventory of the said estate and render an account thereof to the Court; and when required to do so by the High Court, deliver up to that Court the grant of letters of administration.

6. That to the best of [my] [our] knowledge, information and belief the gross value of the estate passing under the grant [amounts to] [does not exceed] £ .... and the net value [amounts to] [does not exceed] £ .... [and that this is not a case in which an Inland Revenue Account is required to be delivered]. [146]

Sworn *etc, as in Form 37.*

71. Oath for Administration De Bonis Non

In the High Court of Justice, *etc., as in Form 1.*

[I] [We] [178] make oath and say:

1. That [[I] [we] believe the paper writing now produced to and marked by [me] [us] to be [the true and original] [an office copy of the] last Will and Testament] [137] of [138] deceased, who was born on the ...... day of .... 19 .., and died on the ...... day of .... 20 ..[139] aged ...... domiciled in England and Wales [wherein he did not name any executor] [wherein he

---

[217] Recite any limitation imposed by the order.

named .... the sole executor who died on the ...... day of
.... 20 ...] [intestate.]

That on the ...... day of .... 20 .. letters of administration [(with Will annexed)] were granted to [218] [the residuary legatee and devisee in trust [219]] named therein and that the said [218] died on the ...... day of .... 20 .. leaving part of the estate of the said deceased unadministered [220]

2.   That no minority or life interest arises in the estate.[161]

3.   That to the best of [my] [our] knowledge and belief there was no land vested in the said deceased immediately before his death which was settled previously to his death [and not by his Will] and which remained settled land notwithstanding his death. [140]

4.   That [I am] [we are] the residuary legatee[s] [221] named in the said Will. [222]

5.   That [I] [we] will collect, get in and administer according to law the real and personal unadministered estate of the said deceased; when required to do so by the Court, exhibit in the Court a full inventory of the said estate and render an account thereof to the Court; and when required to do so by the High Court, deliver up to that Court the grant of letters of administration.

6.   That to the best of [my] [our] knowledge, information and belief the gross value of the estate passing under the grant [amounts to] [does not exceed] £ .... and the net value [amounts to] [does not exceed] £ .... [and that this is not a case in which an Inland Revenue Account is required to be delivered]. [146]

Sworn *etc, as in Form 37.*

72. Oath for Cessate Grant of Administration

In the High Court of Justice, *etc., as in Form 1.*

I [158] make oath and say:

1.   That I believe the paper writing now produced to and marked by me to be the true and original last Will and Testament [137] of [138] deceased, who was born on the ...... day of .... 19 .., and died on the ...... day of .... 20 ..[139] aged ...... domiciled in England and Wales [wherein he

---

[218] Insert the name of the grantee.

[219] Or as may be.

[220] Insert details of the previous grant; the grantee(s); the title to the previous grant; and the reason the original grant has ceased to be effective. Where the application is made to a registry other than the registry which issued the original grant, the original grant or an office copy must be lodged with this oath.

[221] Or as may be.

[222] Insert the applicant's title to the grant and any other clearings of persons with prior entitlement other than those already mentioned.

did not name any executor] [wherein he named [223] the sole executor] [who predeceased the said deceased] [who survived the deceased but died without proving the said Will] [who has renounced probate of the said Will] and wherein he named me [224] [the residuary legatee and devisee [225] [226]] [intestate].

2. That on the ...... day of .... 20 .. letters of administration (with Will annexed) [227] of the estate of the said deceased were granted out of the [Principal] [District Probate] Registry to [228] for my use and benefit [229].

3. [That I have regained my mental capacity.] [That on the ...... day of .... 20 .. I attained the age of eighteen years] [227] by reason of which the said grant has ceased and expired.

4. That no minority or life interest [now] arises in the estate.

5. That to the best of my knowledge and belief there was no land vested in the said deceased immediately before his death which was settled previously to his death [and not by his Will] and which remained settled land notwithstanding his death.

6. That I am [the lawful widow] [the residuary legatee and devisee] [227] [named in the said Will].

7. That I will collect, get in and administer according to law the real and personal estate [save and except settled land] of the said deceased [230]; when required to do so by the Court, exhibit in the Court a full inventory of the said estate and render an account thereof to the Court; and when required to do so by the High Court, deliver up to that Court the grant of letters of administration [(with Will annexed)].

8. That to the best of my knowledge, information and belief the gross value of the estate passing under the grant [amounts to] [does not exceed] £ .... and the net value [amounts to] [does not exceed] £ .... [and that this is not a case in which an Inland Revenue Account is required to be delivered]. [146]

Sworn *etc, as in Form 37.*

---

[223] Insert the full name of the executor.

[224] Insert the name of the beneficiary.

[225] Or as may be.

[226] Insert the relationship of the applicant to the deceased and the capacity in which the grant is applied for; persons with a prior entitlement must be cleared off.

[227] Or as may be.

[228] Insert the name of the previous grantee and his relationship to the applicant.

[229] Insert the appropriate eventuality, e.g., "until I regained my mental capacity"; "until I attained the age of eighteen years".

[230] Recite any limitation imposed by the order.

73. Oath for Administration: Trust Corporation

In the High Court of Justice, *etc., as in Form 1.*

I [231] make oath and say:

1. That [I believe the paper writing now produced to and marked by me to be the true and original last Will and Testament of] [137] of [138] deceased [who] was born on the ...... day of .... 19 .. and died on the ...... day of .... 20 ..[139] aged ...... domiciled in England and Wales [intestate] leaving [232] who have consented to a grant of letters of administration [with Will annexed] to [233]

2. That the said [233] is a trust Corporation as defined by rule 2(1) of the Non-Contentious Probate Rules 1987 and has power to accept the grant now applied for and that the said [233] by a resolution dated the ...... day of .... 20 .. [a certified copy of which is annexed hereto] [which has been lodged with the Senior District Judge of the Family Division in which I am identified by the position I hold and which resolution is still in force] appointed me for the purpose of applying for letters of administration [(with Will annexed)] of the said deceased's estate.

3. That no minority or life interest [now] arises in the estate.[161]

4. That to the best of my knowledge and belief there was no land vested in the said deceased immediately before his death which was settled previously to his death [and not by his Will [and codicil[s]] and which remained settled land notwithstanding his death. [140]

5. That the said [233] will collect, get in and administer according to law the real and personal estate of the said deceased; when required to do so by the Court, exhibit in the Court a full inventory of the said estate and render an account thereof to the Court; and when required to do so by the High Court, deliver up to that Court the letters of administration [(with Will annexed)].

6. That to the best of my knowledge, information and belief the gross value of the estate passing under the grant [amounts to] [does not exceed] £ .... and the net value [amounts to] [does not exceed] £ .... [and that this is not a case in which an Inland Revenue Account is required to be delivered]. [146]

Sworn *etc, as in Form 37.*

---

[231] Insert the full name and address of the deponent; the business address or registered office of the trust corporation; and the deponent's position in the trust corporation, by virtue of which he is authorised to act, e.g., "manager".

[232] Set out the title of those with a prior right to a grant and the manner of clearing them off; e.g., "spinster without issue leaving ..... her mother and only person entitled to her estate".

[233] Insert the name of the trust corporation.

74. Oath for Administration: Foreign Domicile

In the High Court of Justice, *etc., as in Form 1.*

I [158] make oath and say:

1. That [I believe the paper writing now produced to and marked by me to contain [an official copy] [a notarially certified copy of [234] the true and original last Will and Testament [and codicil[s]] of] [137] of [138] deceased, who was born on the ...... day of .... 19 .. and died on the ...... day of .... 20 ..[139] aged ...... domiciled in [235] .

2. That [236] is [the person] [one of the persons] [entrusted with the administration of the estate of the said deceased by the Court having jurisdiction at the place where the deceased died domiciled] [beneficially entitled to [share] in the estate of the deceased by the law of the place where the deceased died domiciled]. [That by order of Mr [District Judge] [Registrar] .... dated the ...... day of .... 20 .. it was ordered that letters of administration [(with Will annexed)] of the estate of the said deceased be granted to me under and by virtue of Rule 30(1)[(a)] [(b)] [(c)] of the Non-Contentious Probate Rules 1987. [237] [238]

3. That no minority or life interest [now] arises in the estate.[239]

4. That to the best of my knowledge and belief there was no land vested in the said deceased immediately before his death which was settled previously to his death [and not by his Will] and which remained settled land notwithstanding his death. [140]

5. That I will collect, get in and administer according to law the real and personal estate of the said deceased [240] ; when required to do so by the Court, exhibit in the Court a full inventory of the said estate and render an account thereof to the Court; and when required to do so by the High Court, deliver up to that Court the letters of administration [(with Will annexed)].

6. That to the best of my knowledge, information and belief the gross value of the estate in England Wales passing under the grant amounts to £ ....

---

[234] Or as may be.

[235] Insert the country, or, if appropriate, the state or territory, of domicile.

[236] Insert the name of the person entrusted or beneficially entitled.

[237] Where an attorney applies for the grant, this should be stated; and the words "for the use and benefit of the said .... and until further representation be granted" added after the word "deceased".

[238] Where an order under rule 30(1)(a) or (b) has not been made, a request for such an order may be made in the oath by adding the appropriate words, e.g., "that I am the person entrusted with administration by the court of the place having jurisdiction where the deceased died domiciled as evidenced by the affidavit made by .... and I hereby apply for an order under Rule 30(1)[(a)] [(b)]".

[239] If such an interest does arise, at least two applicants will be required.

[240] Recite any limitation imposed by the order.

and the net value of the estate amounts to £ ....[241]

Sworn *etc, as in Form 37.*

75. Power of Attorney to Take Letters of Administration (with Will annexed)

In the High Court of Justice, *etc., as in Form 1.*

1.   [242] was born on the ...... day of .... 19 .. and died on the ...... day of .... 20 .. domiciled in [England and Wales] [having made and duly executed his last Will and Testament dated the ...... day of ....
20 .. and in the said Will appointed [243] [the sole executor] [one of the executors] thereof [residuary legatee and devisee] [244]].
[intestate a [widow[er]] [spinster without issue] [244] leaving [243] .
2.   I [243] of.................... do hereby nominate constitute and appoint [245] to be my lawful attorney for the purpose of obtaining letters of administration [(with Will annexed)] of the estate of the said deceased to be granted to him for my use and benefit until further representation be granted and I hereby promise to ratify and confirm whatever my said attorney shall lawfully do or cause to be done in the premises.

Signed by the said ....
the ...... day of .... 20 ..
in the presence of

---

[241] Where the deceased died domiciled outside England and Wales, an Inland Revenue Account must be delivered before a grant may issue. The gross and net values in the oath must be as in the Account and form D18. Where the deceased died on or after 6 April 2002, was never domiciled in the UK for tax purposes, and the estate in England and Wales was less than £100,000, no Account need be delivered, the excepted estate provisions applying.
[242] Insert the full name and address of the deceased.
[243] Insert the name of the donor.
[244] Or as may be.
[245] Insert the full name and address of the attorney.

76. Enduring Power of Attorney

This form is prescribed by The Enduring Powers of Attorney (Prescribed Form) Regulations 1990, Statutory Instrument 1990 No 1376.

Part A: About using this form

1. **You may choose one attorney or more than one.** If you choose one attorney then you must delete everything between the square brackets on the first page of the form. If you choose more than one, you must decide whether they are able to act:
   - Jointly (that is, they must all act together and cannot act separately) or
   - Jointly and severally (that is, they can all act together but they can also act separately if they wish).
   On the first page of the form, show what you have decided by crossing out one of the alternatives.

2. **If you give your attorney(s) general power** in relation to all your property and affairs, it means that they will be able to deal with your money or property and may be able to sell your house.

3. **If you don't want your attorney(s) to have such wide powers,** you can include any restrictions you like. For example, you can include a restriction that your attorney(s) must not act on your behalf until they have reason to believe that you are becoming mentally incapable; or a restriction as to what your attorney(s) may do. Any restrictions you choose must be written or typed where indicated on the second page of the form.

4. **If you are a trustee** (and please remember that co-ownership of a home involves trusteeship), you should seek legal advice if you want your attorney(s) to act as a trustee on your behalf.

5. **Unless you put in a restriction preventing it** your attorney(s) will be able to use any of your money or property to make any provision which you yourself might be expected to make for their own needs or the needs of other people. Your attorney(s) will also be able to use your money to make gifts, but only for reasonable amounts in relation to the value of your money and property.

6. **Your attorney(s) can recover the out-of-pocket expenses** of acting as your attorney(s). If your attorney(s) are professional people, for example solicitors or accountants, they may be able to charge for their professional services as well. You may wish to provide expressly for remuneration of your attorney(s) (although if they are trustees they may not be allowed to accept it).

7. **If your attorney(s) have reason to believe** that you have become or are becoming mentally incapable of managing your affairs, your attorney(s) will have to apply to the Court of Protection for registration of this power.

8. **Before applying to the Court of Protection for registration** of this power, your attorney(s) must give written notice that that is what they are going to do, to you and your nearest relatives as defined in the Enduring Powers of Attorney Act 1985. You or your relatives will be able to object if you or they disagree with registration.

9. **This is a simplified explanation** of what the Enduring Powers of Attorney Act 1985 and the Rules and Regulations say. If you need more guidance, you or your advisers will need to look at the Act itself and the Rules and Regulations. The Rules are the Court of Protection (Enduring Powers of Attorney) Rules 1986 (Statutory Instrument 1986 No. 127). The Regulations are the Enduring Powers of Attorney (Prescribed Form) Regulations 1990 (Statutory Instrument 1990 No. 1376).

10. **Note to Attorney(s)**
   After the power has been registered you should notify the Court of Protection if the donor dies or recovers.

11. **Note to Donor**
   Some of these explanatory notes may not apply to the form you are using if it has already been adapted to suit your particular requirements.

YOU CAN CANCEL THIS POWER AT ANY TIME BEFORE IT HAS TO BE REGISTERED

Part B: To be completed by the "donor" (the person appointing the attorney(s))

Don't sign this form unless you understand what it means

Please read the notes in the
margin which follow and
which are part of the form
itself.

Donor's name and address.

I _____

of _____

Donor's date of birth

born on _____

appoint _____

of _____

See note 1 on the front of this
form. If you are appointing
only one attorney you should
cross out everything between
the square brackets. If
appointing more than two
attorneys please give the
additional name(s) on an
attached sheet.

• [and _____

of _____

Cross out the one which does
not apply (see note 1 on the
front of this form).

• jointly
• jointly and severally]
to be my attorney(s) for the purpose of the Enduring
Powers of Attorney Act 1985

Cross out the one which does
not apply (see note 2 on the
front of this form). Add any
additional powers.

• with general authority to act on my behalf
• with authority to do the following on my behalf:

If you don't want the
attorney(s) to have general
power, you must give details
here of what authority you are
giving the attorney(s).

Cross out the one which does
not apply.

in relation to
• all my property and affairs
• the following property and affairs:

Please read the notes in the margin which follow and which are part of the form itself.

• subject to the following restrictions and conditions:

If there are restrictions or conditions, insert them here; if not, cross out these words if you wish (see note 3 on the front of this form).

If this form is being signed at your direction:-
• the person signing must not be an attorney or any witness (to Parts B or C)
• you must add a statement that this form has been signed at your direction.
• a second witness is necessary (please see below).

I intend that this power shall continue even if I become mentally incapable

I have read or have had read to me the notes in part A which are part of, and explain, this form.

Your signature (or mark).

Signed by me as a deed and delivered

Date.

on _____

Someone must witness your signature.

Signature of witness.
Your attorney(s) cannot be your witness. It is not advisable for your husband or wife to be your witness.

in the presence of   _____
Full name of witness   _____
Address of witness   _____
                          _____
                          _____

A second witness is only necessary if this form is not being signed by you personally but at your direction (for example, if a physical disability prevents you from signing).

Signature of second witness.

in the presence of   _____
Full name of witness   _____
Address of witness   _____
                          _____
                          _____

345

Part C: To be completed by the attorney(s)

Notes 1. This form may be adapted to provide for execution by a corporation
2. If there is more than one attorney additional sheets in the form as shown below must be added to this Part C.

Please read the notes in the margin which follow and which are part of the form itself.

Don't sign this form before the donor has signed Part B or if, in your opinion, the donor was already mentally incapable at the time of signing Part B.

If this form is being signed at your direction:-

• the person signing must not be an attorney or any witness (to Parts B or C)
• you must add a statement that this form has been signed at your direction.
• a second witness is necessary (please see below)

I understand that I have a duty to apply to the Court for the registration of this form under the Enduring Powers of Attorney Act 1985 when the donor is becoming or has become mentally incapable.

I also understand my limited power to use the donor's property to benefit persons other than the donor.

I am not a minor.

Your signature (or mark).

Signed by me as a deed and delivered

Date.

on _____

Someone must witness your signature.

Signature of witness.

Your attorney(s) cannot be your witness. It is not advisable for your husband or wife to be your witness.

in the presence of _____

Full name of witness _____

Address of witness _____

_____

_____

A second witness is only necessary if this form is not being signed by you personally but at your direction (for example, if a physical disability prevents you from signing).

Signature of second witness.

in the presence of _____

Full name of witness _____

Address of witness _____

_____

_____

77. General Form of Renunciation

In the High Court of Justice, *etc., as in Form 1.*

1. [246] deceased died on the ...... day of .... 20 .. [having made and duly executed his last Will and Testament dated the ...... day of .... 20 ..] [intestate] [wherein he appointed [247] [the sole executor] [and residuary legatee and devisee] [one of the executors] [who has since died without proving the said Will] [wherein he did not appoint any executor but named me [247] [as residuary legatee and devisee]. [248]
[wherein he named me residuary legatee and devisee]
[leaving me [247, 249]]
I, the said [247] declare that I have not intermeddled in the said deceased's estate and will not hereinafter intermeddle therein with the intent of defrauding creditors and do hereby renounce all my right and title to [probate and execution of the said Will] [and to letters of administration [(with Will annexed)]] of the estate of the said deceased.

Signed by the said ....
the ...... day of .... 20 ..
in the presence of [250]

78. Renunciation of Probate by Partners for Themselves and Other Partners in a Firm

In the High Court of Justice, *etc., as in Form 1.*

[251] deceased died on the ...... day of .... 20 .. [having made and duly executed his last Will and Testament dated the ...... day of .... 20 .. wherein he appointed the partners in the firm of .... to be the executors of his Will.

Now we [252] being two of the partners in the said firm of .... at the date of death do hereby on our own behalf and that of all the other partners in the said firm and with their authority renounce all our right and title to probate and execution of the said Will [and to letters of administration (with Will annexed) as residuary legatees and devisees in trust] and we declare that we and the other partners have not intermeddled in

---

[246] Insert the full name and address of the deceased.

[247] Insert the name of the renunciant.

[248] Or as may be.

[249] Insert the name and relationship to the deceased, reciting the title to the grant and any clearings.

[250] To be signed by a witness who has no interest in the estate.

[251] Insert the full name and address of the deceased.

[252] Insert the names of the renunciants.

the deceased's estate and will not hereinafter intermeddle therein with the intent of defrauding creditors.

Signed *etc, as in Form 77.*

79. Retraction of Renunciation

In the High Court of Justice, *etc., as in Form 1.*

[253] deceased died on the ...... day of .... 20 .. [having made and duly executed his last Will and Testament dated the ...... day of .... 20 .. and therein appointed me [254] [his sole executor [255]] [leaving me [254]] [the residuary legatee and devisee in trust [255]].
[intestate leaving me [254]].

And whereas I renounced [probate and execution] [letters of administration [(with Will annexed)]] of the estate of the said deceased and whereas a grant of [probate] [letters of administration [(with Will annexed)]] was made at the .... Registry to [256] and whereas the said [256] died on the ...... day of .... 20 .. leaving part of the said estate unadministered.

Now I the said [254] do hereby declare that I retract my said renunciation of [probate] [letters of administration [(with Will annexed)]] of the estate of the said deceased.

Signed *etc, as in Form 77.*

80. Subpoena to Bring in Testamentary Document

In the High Court of Justice, *etc., as in Form 1.*

ELIZABETH THE SECOND by the Grace of God, of the United Kingdom of Great Britain and Northern Ireland and of the Other Realms and Territories, Queen, Head of the Commonwealth, Defender of the Faith. To [257]

TAKE NOTICE that [258] has stated in an affidavit sworn on the ...... day of .... 20.. and filed in [the Principal Registry of the Family Division of the High Court of Justice] [the .... District Probate Registry] that a certain document, being or purporting to be testamentary, namely a [Will]

---

[253] Insert the full name and address of the deceased.
[254] Insert the name of the renunciant.
[255] Or as may be.
[256] Insert the name of the grantee.
[257] Insert the name of the person alleged to hold the Will.
[258] Insert the name of the applicant.

[codicil [255]] dated the ...... day of .... 20 .. of [259] deceased late of .... who died on the ...... day of .... 20.. is now in your possession, custody or power.

NOW THIS IS TO COMMAND YOU the said [257] that within eight days after service hereof on you, inclusive of the day of such service, you do bring into and leave with the proper officer of the [Principal Registry of the Family Division, First Avenue House, 42–49 High Holborn, London WC1V 6NP] [the .... District Probate Registry at ....] aforesaid the said ....

Witness the Right Honourable Andrew Alexander Mackay Baron Irvine of Lairg, Lord High Chancellor of Great Britain.

Signed .... District Judge/Registrar

Subpoena issued by .... of ....

[*To be endorsed prominently on the front of the copy to be served:*]

You the within-named .... are warned that disobedience to this subpoena by the time therein limited would be a contempt of court punishable by imprisonment.

[The Principal Registry of the Family Division of the High Court of Justice is at First Avenue House, 42–49 High Holborn, London WC1V 6NP] [The District Probate Registry is at ....] and the proper officer is the Probate Manager.

81. Application for a Standing Search

In the High Court of Justice, *etc., as in Form 1.*

In the estate of .... deceased

I apply for the entry of a standing search so that there shall be sent to me an office copy of every grant of representation in England and Wales in the estate of:

Full name of the deceased:

Full address:

Alternative or alias name:

Exact date of death:

which either has issued not more than twelve months before the entry of this application or issues within six months thereafter.

Signed:

Name in block letters:

Address:

Reference (if any):

---

[259] Insert the name of the deceased.

Index